WORKFORCE EDUCATION

Issues for the New Century

Edited by Albert J. Pautler, Jr.

Tech Directions Books
Prakken Publications, Inc.

P.O. Box 8623, Ann Arbor, MI 48107-8623

Library of Congress Catalog Card Number: 99-070241
ISBN 0-911168-95-8

Printed in the United States of America

my best friend and wife
Marilyn S. Pautler
ink you very much—Al

CONTENTS

Introduction ix

Part I: Background

1 Vocational Education: Past, Present, and Future / *Cheryl L. Hogg* 3
2 A Philosophic View for Seeing the Past of Vocational Education and Envisioning the Future of Workforce Education: Pragmatism Revisited / *Melvin D. Miller and James A. Gregson* 21
3 Legislative Review of Workforce Education / *Michelle Sarkees-Wircenski and Jerry L. Wircenski* 35
4 Career Education: Basic Concepts and Current Status / *Kenneth B. Hoyt and Pat Nellor Wickwire* 49
5 Career Education: The Foundation for School to Work / *J. D. Hoye and Harry Drier* 65

Part II: Career Development

6 Overview of Career Development Theory / *Stanley H. Cramer* 77
7 Elementary- and Middle-Level Career-Development Issues / *Conrad F. Toepfer, Jr.* 87
8 High School Career Development Issues / *Cheryl L. Hogg* 101
9 Career Development for All / *Rich Feller and Timothy Gray Davies* 115

Part III: Program Areas

10 The Tech Prep Associate Degree Program / *John D. Craig* 129
11 Issues in Technology Education Related to the Evolution of the Field / *Karen F. Zuga and Phillip L. Cardon* 145
12 High School Vocational Education: Facing an Uncertain Future / *Kenneth Gray* 159
13 Postsecondary Workforce Education / *Richard A. Walter and Edgar I. Farmer* 171
14 Reclaiming a Lost Legacy: Integration of Academic and Vocational Education / *Debra D. Bragg* 181

Part IV: Special Topics

15 Vocational Teacher Education / *Curtis R. Finch* 199
16 Curriculum Issues / *David J. Pucel* 211
17 Gender Equity in Workforce Education / *Susan J. Olson* 223
18 A Canadian Perspective on Vocational Education and Training / *John Gradwell* 241
19 Trends and Issues in Workforce Education for Special Populations / *Lynda L. West and Arden Boyer-Stephens* 253

Part V: Future Perspectives

20 Research Priorities and Needs in Vocational Education / *Martin B. Parks and Ross E. Moreton* 267
21 Future Perspectives in Vocational Education / *William Blank* 281
22 The Transition from School to Careers / *Albert J. Pautler, Jr.* 291

INTRODUCTION

Gerald Leighbody's *Vocational Education in America's Schools: Major Issues for the 1970s* was published in 1972. Quotes from this book were frequently used by many writers during the past 20 years. It was my good fortune to have studied under Gerry's guidance during my graduate studies a the University of Buffalo. His ideas and scholarship have had a large impact on my own professional development and work over the past 30 years.

In 1990, I had the good fortune of editing a book with the good people at Prakken Publications that included chapters by many leaders in vocational education. This book, *Vocational Education in the 1990s: Major Issues*, included chapters by Melvin Barlow, Gerald Cheek, Charles Doty, Curtis Finch, John Hillison, Angelo and Lynne Gilli, David Pucel, Jane Ruff, Michelle Sarkees, Lynda West, and Merle Strong. My idea for this book was to follow up on Gerry Leighbody's book of the 1970s in some very small way. This book has remained in print and enjoyed reasonable sales during the years since it was published. It has been used in many college-level vocational teacher preparation programs.

Many changes in education and vocational education have taken place in the past decade. As a result, the people at Prakken Publications, now under the Tech Directions Books imprint, asked me to edit a new book to update the previous work and serve as a guide for the new century. I agreed to do this and asked many leaders in education to prepare chapters for this new book. Those familiar with my earlier book will recognize several authors' names. You will also note the names of some new people who have agreed to share their scholarship and ideas.

I want to note the passing of Dr. Melvin Barlow, who wrote the chapter on the field's history in the 1990s book. To many, Mel was a friend, scholar, and historian of vocational education. His many contributions to the field must be noted and remembered by all of us who labor in this field. For a number of years, at the American Vocational Association meeting a number of us would put together a seminar on the history and philosophy of vocational education. Melvin Barlow, Rupert Evans, Gordon Law, Melvin Miller, Gordon Swanson, and Merle Strong were key players in these programs. Let's not lose interest in our historical background.

A number of people suggested that the title of this book include the words "workforce preparation," which includes vocational education. A number of major university departments that used to carry the title of vocational education have changed titles to better describe their role and work. They use such terms as *workforce education; human resources education; workforce education and development; career, technical, and adult education; occupational studies;* and *technology and vocational education.* I selected *Workforce Education: Issues for the New Century* as the title of this book, and I hope that it meets with the approval and support of the members of the profession.

I take full responsibility for the selection of the scholars who were asked to prepare chapters for the book. I also take full responsibility for the themes of the various chapters.

My role as editor involved limited editing of the chapters provided me. The editors at Tech Directions Books provided the final editing necessary to produce a quality book. I give special thanks to Susanne Peckham, managing editor of Tech Directions Books. This the third book we have worked on together and it has always been a pleasure working with her and others at Tech Directions Books / Prakken Publications.

I have organized the chapters of this book in five parts, which I think will make sense to those using the book in college or university courses. Part I—Background includes chapters on historical, philosophical, and legislative foundations. Part II—Career Development covers topics related to career and vocational development theory and practice. Part III—Program Areas includes a number of selections on current issues of concern to the profession. Part IV—Special Topics includes material on teacher preparation, curriculum, gender, special populations, and Canadian VET. Part V—Future Perspectives addresses research concerns and a look at the future of our field.

This book is dedicated by my best friend and wife, Marilyn, who shared me with my professional employment and writing projects over the past almost 40 years. I love you very much and appreciate your support and encouragement.

To the end user of this book, I ask that you please share your thoughts and reactions with me and the other authors. We would all like to hear from you.

—*Albert J. Pautler, Jr.*
University at Buffalo

PART I: INTRODUCTION

I do not like work, even when someone else does it.
—Mark Twain

1

VOCATIONAL EDUCATION: PAST, PRESENT, AND FUTURE

By Cheryl L. Hogg

HISTORICAL BACKGROUND

Vocational education has deep roots, as humans have learned to work by imitation, trial and error, apprenticeship, and, more recently, by modern organized classrooms and laboratory instruction. "The evolution of vocational and applied technology can be traced from the Paleolithic period, through the Neolithic period, Agricultural Civilization, Bronze Age, Iron Age and Greek Civilization, Roman Civilization, Middle Ages, Renaissance and Reformation, Industrial Civilization and Power Age to our Post Industrial or Information Age of today" (Scott & Sarkees-Wircenski, 1996, p. 47).

Early America

At the time of the American Revolution, in 1776, school occupied a relatively minor place in American life. In school-conscious New England, Horace Mann estimated that perhaps 1 child in 10 attended school and then only sporadically. Some did manage to complete the basic instruction offered by the common school and the rigid classical curriculum of the grammar school. A select few graduated from the nine colonial colleges. Viewed as a prize, education would have to wait its turn behind more important things. The average American was far more concerned about making a living from the farm or trade than about schooling (Butts & Cremin, 1953).

Before the Civil War, well over 90 percent of Americans lived on farms. Education remained as it was in colonial times. Mainly through apprenticeship, children learned by imitating adults. From generation to generation, boys learned from working alongside their fathers and girls from their mothers. "The roots of social, religious, and political belief and behavior were inculcated in much the same way" (Butts & Cremin, 1953, p. 237).

While the education of the home, church, and community remained primary, the first century of the United States was marked by the growing role of schooling in children's education. In the colonial days, a system of voluntary and involuntary apprenticeship was a pathway to literacy for boys and girls who could not pay for an education. Apprenticeship flourished as a system that provided education that produced craftsmen for the colonies. Laws prevented orphans and children of the poor from becoming public charges and enabled them to become economically independent (Barlow, 1965). The city or town controlled the apprenticeship system and set what it provided: food, clothing, and shelter; religious instruction; reading and writing; skill training; and the "mysteries" of the trade.

Abundance of land, freedom and mobility of people, immigration of European-trained craftsmen and mechanics, and the factory system, with labor-saving machines, contributed to the declining importance of apprenticeship during colonial times and the industrial revolution. Charity schools and societies of mechanics originated to provide benefits and educational advantages of apprenticeship for factory workers and later provided regular schools and classes.

Lyceums, mechanics institutes, manual labor academies, agricultural societies, and commercial and business schools emerged. Many of these combined instruction with practical application to prepare people for work. The private role of the family and apprenticeship's role in vocational education, where the "mystery" of the trade, skill, or craft remained private, was being transferred into publicly available schools. Marking the end of a time of restrictive practices in the control of apprenticeship and education, this was an indication that the United States was going to be a more fluid and open society with a softening of the lines of social stratification. Schools would provide opportunities for careers (Barlow, 1976).

As the new constitution did not make provision for education, it became a role for the state governments. Over time "education was considered to be a *concern* of the federal government, a *function* of the state, and a *responsibility* of the local community" (Barlow, 1976, p. 24).

Public Education for All

During the first half of the nineteenth century, four important philanthropic movements—"the secular Sunday school, the semi-public city School Societies, the Lancasterian plan of instruction, and the Infant-School idea . . . supplemented one another and together accustomed a new generation to the idea of a common school for all" (cited in Barlow, 1976, pp. 24-25).

Schooling grew at different rates throughout the country. "In New England it became very much more the rule than the exception by 1840 for children to have some formal schooling" (Butts & Cremins, 1953, p. 237). Middle and western states made schooling the rule by the 1850s. While upper- and middle-class children enjoyed schooling, poorer children seldom attended and black children had little opportunity for formal education. There was a shift from earlier classical religious-based educational priorities to include more practical pursuits that embraced a wide range of social and economic goals as well as religious goals (Barlow, 1976).

A conviction developed to provide a general education for everyone. Compulsory education attendance legislation was passed in Massachusetts in 1852, and as early as 1847, "separate but equal" facilities for black children were considered legal. In 1886 the National Education Association considered the issue of "Race Education in the United States." As a result, the public school was pictured as the great "melting pot."

By 1860, America had made great strides in education. State school systems had taken form. More than 200 colleges and universities had been established, and more than a quarter of a million students enrolled in more than 6,000 private academies offering varied courses of instruction with various purposes and aims. Academies perceived as offering the most "functional" or practical application to life were popular with people seeking to improve their social or economic status.

"High schools, still in their infancy, were far less widely attended during these years. Only several hundred such institutions were reported by 1860 in the United States, and most were concentrated in New England, New York, and a few midwestern states" (Butt & Cremins, 1953, p. 239).

The first high schools were developed in the 1820s. By 1850, there were fewer than 60 U.S. public secondary schools—by 1870, about 500. But once the 1874 Kalamazoo decision of the Michigan Supreme Court clarified their legal basis, they began to be established as needed.

Before the 1890s, high schools were highly selective, mainly emphasizing preparation for higher education and the professions. But compulsory school laws significantly increased and diversified the high school population, which came "with different social and cultural backgrounds, with low to high abilities, and with a wide variety of future job interests . . . no longer a transition school for those planning to enter college, it became a terminal school for the masses" (Scott & Sarkees-Wircenski, 1996, p. 90). The industrial revolution changed the structure of society and created a large working-class population that desired an education for children to provide basic academic skills and include instruction in practical subjects for job preparation.

During and after the 1890s, there was an avalanche of high school legislation. At the end of World War I, there were 25,000 high schools with over 1,600,000 young people attending. Most high schools tended to offer at least two programs: a classical one for college-preparatory and a more practical one for "terminal" students. As communities generally could afford only one school, parallel programs were offered under the same roof of the "comprehensive" high school. This became the American standard, but larger communities moved toward differentiated special schools designed to focus on specialized purposes.

Aims of Education in the U.S.

By 1918, all states had compulsory education laws. Where did the development of the publicly supported common school and this revolutionary American ideal of "education for all" come from? Before 1918, education was dominated by "traditional" aims: Education was viewed as something that goes on for a period of time each day in school, and curriculum consisted largely of discovered facts and principles communicated to the young. Preparation for the real business of living would come later.

But more practical aims of education were becoming increasingly important and were expressed through vocational preparation for trades, industry, business, and the professions. This tended to affect all levels of schooling in the latter half of the nineteenth century.

Newer "progressive" aims of education were demonstrated in experimental schools that considered individual differences among students to cultivate potentialities and particular talents in students. Some of these schools expressed the philosophy of John Dewey and gave conscious attention to a curriculum that would inculcate skills of democratic living and equip young people to share power and responsibility as essential to democracy.

"Finally, the goal of individual success remained paramount in the minds of many." For European immigrants, school was seen as "an assimilating agency" and was the principal means for improving the quality of life for new generations. The school was a symbol of individual success and provided opportunities for social and political advancement (Butts & Cremins, 1953, pp. 433-4).

The Industrial Revolution and Beyond

While the history of vocational education existed separately from a more general education history during the first hundred years of the new republic, groundwork was being established for a "vocational education movement" that would gain importance as the nation approached the twentieth century.

The steam engine and industrial revolution that began in England in the 1750s greatly influenced the evolution of the United States. An expanded railway system, heavy industries, mining, and mechanized agriculture reflected qualities of rapid technological change and increases in geographic and occupational mobility. By 1890, the boundaries of frontier land had been reached.

Instruction such as training at home, apprenticeships, and on-the-job training that had taught people how to perform effectively in occupations were no longer sufficient in this rapidly changing society. A new industrial and urban America was forming. While industrialization created great wealth for a few, many lived and worked in deplorable conditions. A gap was widening between the wealthy and the working class. Education was looked on as a solution to economic and social problems.

With an increasingly recognized need to prepare students to earn a living as well as to study classical subjects, public schools were asked to take on a major role in occupational preparation. From 1826-76, independent schools reflected individual responses to meet the needs of the industrial revolution. The Kalamazoo court decision of 1874 determined the government's right to establish secondary schools supported through public taxation and later led to high school vocational education (Barlow, 1976).

Manual Labor Movement

In 1831, the Society for Promoting Manual Labor in Literary Institutions was formed and supported to make manual labor projects part of school work. While this movement ran its course by the Civil War, it was largely responsible for setting significant educational ventures in motion. There continued to be concern for agricultural, business, and women's education (Barlow, 1976).

Morrill Land Grant Act

In 1862, the Morrill Land Grant Act allowed public land grants to states to establish colleges for the benefit of agriculture and mechanical arts. Investment income from the sale of land into safe stocks was to constitute a perpetual endowment fund for the maintenance of colleges. The law addressed the "intense desire of the public for practical education" and provided that "the leading object shall be, without excluding other scientific and classical studies . . . to teach such branches of learning as are related to agriculture and the mechanical arts . . . to promote the liberal and practical education of the industrial classes" (cited in Barlow, 1967, p. 32). The Morrill Act and its amendments provided a foundation for present-day agricultural colleges and many of the state universities (Scott & Sarkees-Wircenski, 1996). It ushered in a period of increasing federal participation in, as well as aid to, education, and was followed by establishment of the Federal Department of Education in 1867.

The Trade School Movement

Following the Civil War, the Hampton Normal and Agricultural Institute was organized by General Samuel Chapman Armstrong. In 1868, assisted by the American Missionary Society, liberal education and trade skill labor training were provided for blacks. Aims of the institute included character development and improvement of social status. Graduate Booker T. Washington continued his education and returned to teach at Hampton. In 1881, he served as the first principal of the Tuskegee Institute, not only vastly expanding educational horizons for blacks but also furthering vocational education at the university level.

The Manual Training Movement

As early as 1870, industrial drawing had been introduced into the public school curriculum. Little progress had been made, however, in industrial training that required use of tools, perhaps reflecting lack of an adequate method of teaching tool skills. In 1876, the Russian exhibit at the Centennial Exposition in Philadelphia provided clues to an effective method based on the work of the Director of the Imperial Technical School at Moscow, Victor Della Vos. Instructional shops separated distinct types of work. "Each student had a set of tools and constructed models, in increasing order of difficulty, from his own drawings. The system presupposed a great amount of individual assistance and required that the instruction be given by a skilled craftsman" (Barlow, 1976, p. 46).

American educators including John D. Runkle, president of the Massachusetts Institute of Technology (MIT), expressed interest in Della Vos's exercises in wood and metal work instruction. Runkle realized the value of tool instruction in general education. Based on his recommendations, shops for tool instruction were introduced into the engineering and general education program at MIT the following year. It was believed the new methods would be more effective than apprenticeships (Barlow, 1976).

The "Pioneer Manual-Training School" in St. Louis was the next major step in tool instruction. Calvin M. Woodward had a background teaching university-level engineering students. Advocating a method of combining theory and practice, Woodward reasoned that, by teaching essential principles involved in all trades, it would not be necessary to teach any one specific trade. "He advanced the idea that all the manual arts, the mechanical processes, and the tools used in common should be arranged in a systematic course of instruction and incorporated into the general system of education" (Barlow, 1967, p. 35).

A school of general education based on a new plan for education was approved with the support of local industrialists and the trustees of Washington University. The prospectus was probably the earliest formation of ideas for manual training at the secondary level. On September 6, 1880, the first class of 50 boys selected by examination entered the first U.S. manual training school.

Woodward was interested in the general education of students and believed shop courses would help retain students in high school. The program was two hours of woodshop and one hour each of mathematics, science, Latin or English, and drawing. Although considered "tough," the school was, for many years, the most popular secondary school in St. Louis. By the time it closed, manual instruction needed by the university's preparatory students was being adequately supplied by the city's high school (Barlow, 1967).

"Manual training was not without its critics. Technical education was called a 'deceptive farce' by zealous guardians of liberal education who consider it a threat to the intellect and unacceptable in the public schools. In some ways these fundamental arguments are indicative of the problems faced by vocational education even today" (Barlow, 1976, p. 47).

The Trade School Movement

Recognizing that older modes of apprenticeship and "bookish" evening instruction did not meet the needs created by new factories, trade schools emerged, providing models that other schools followed. The first school to offer specific training with studies directed to each trade was the New York Trade School, founded in 1881 by Colonel Richard Tylden Auchtmuty. Although tuition was charged, much school financing was provided by its founder and through endowments. A board of trustees and a counsel of trade committees operated the school (Barlow, 1976).

The Hebrew Technical School, founded in New York City in 1883, offered a greater range of general area subjects. Considered more a technical school, it combined trade training with general education. The need for such a school grew in response to the number of Jewish immigrants coming to the country in the late nineteenth century. Many were poor. School founders believed the best way to help poorer classes of Hebrews was to give an education to the younger members to fit them for success in the mechanical trade (Barlow, 1976).

The Williamson Free School of Mechanical Trades, endowed by philanthropist Isaiah V. Williamson in Philadelphia in 1891, was to take the place of the old apprenticeship training. No charge was made for the school and only "the most worthy" applicants were accepted. "Boys from 16 to 18 years of age were bound as indentured apprentices for three years. After preliminary courses in manual training, general education, and specific trade training were completed, a student was assigned to a trade by the school trustees" (Barlow, 1967, p. 43). Regard was given to adaptability and inclination of the boy for the trade to which he was assigned. "Williamson was convinced that the abandonment of apprenticeship resulted in idleness, vice, and crime, and constituted a threat to society" (p. 43).

Corporation Schools

Employers supported forms of industrial education and those who could do so formed their own systems of education. In almost every case, school programs were developed to remedy employee deficiencies that hampered efficient production. Companies that began their own schools include General Electric, Westinghouse, and International Harvester. "In 1913, representatives from 37 manufacturers and railroads formed the National Association of Corporation Schools (NACS) to share information about factory-based educational programs and to promote an interest in corporation training" (Kantor, 1986, p. 408).

1900-1920: Growing Support for Vocational Education

In 1905, Massachusetts Governor William Douglas appointed a Commission on Industrial and Technical Education in response to a resolution of the state legislature to re-evaluate the educational system. Later known as the Douglas Commission, it investigated needs for education in the grades of skill and responsibility in the various trades in the commonwealth. To what degree needs are met and what new forms of education are needed were considered in accordance with similar educational work in other states, by the U.S. government and other governments throughout the world (Barlow, 1976).

"The Commission reached conclusions destined to have far-reaching effects on future vocational education" (Barlow, 1976, p. 52). In 1906, a bill made industrial education part of the Massachusetts school system. A second commission was appointed to develop a model program of interest to educators and industrial leaders throughout the nation.

National Society for Promotion of Industrial Education

"On June 9, 1906, three days after the second Massachusetts commission was appointed, a group of men met at the Engineer's Club in New York City to discuss the formation of a society in the interests of industrial education" (Barlow, 1976, p. 52), eventually leading to formation of the National Society for the Promotion of Industrial Education (NSPIE). "The aim of the society was to focus public attention on the value of an educational system which would prepare boys and girls to enter industrial pursuits" (p. 52). The central idea was to unify all forces of industrial education. Statewide organizational branches were formed to address local concerns.

With the factory system, corporate industrialism dominated economic life at the beginning of the twentieth century. While many large employers looked to corporation training and immediate job-specific training, they did not view private factory-based programs as sufficient to solve their labor problems. Business groups such as the National Association of Manufacturers (NAM) formed in 1895, began to explore how public schools could help American manufacturers in the growing international competitive market.

Imperial Germany emerged as a powerful competitor for worldwide markets, and NAM investigated and found the source of German achievement in highly differentiated vocational training programs geared to hierarchical skill needs of German industry. This "practical" system was separated from the general schools and administered by "practical men" from the Ministry of Commerce instead of by "fuzzy-minded educators." The dual system had classical gymnasia and universities for upper classes and ambitious middle classes and practical vocational training directed by industrial leaders. NAM wanted to set up a Committee on Industrial Education to secure an American version of German vocationalism. NAM originally believed American manufacturers could compete internationally only through separate vocational schools guided by men of industry and recommended "continuation" schools based on the German model (Kantor, 1986).

By 1912, it was concluded that separate trade schools were too costly to maintain and benefited only a small minority of youth. Larger-scale, more efficient training was needed. NAM proposed that public schools be geared more closely to industrial needs and recommended introducing manual and prevocational training in the grammar grades so children under age 14 might develop an "appreciation for the dignity of labor of all kinds and such moral qualities as diligence, concentration, perseverance, and respect" (Kantor, 1986, p. 407). High school curriculum should be differentiated into cultural, commercial, and industrial branches, and there should be a system of vocational guidance. Employers were anxious to have a "steady supply of labor equipped with general industrial-skills and habits" and "urged that public schools adapt their curricula to industrial needs" (Kantor, 1986, p. 408).

At first, labor leaders were reluctant to join a vocational education movement backed by businessmen, but in 1907, the American Federation of Labor (AFL) president, Samuel Gompers, joined the NSPIE to support vocational education. Union leaders agreed that apprenticeship was obsolete, new forms of vocational education were needed, and school curricula failed to hold the interest of youth. Unions wanted to influence the direction of vocational education. The AFL insisted on public rather than private control of vocational education and wanted a curriculum letting children learn the general principles of the trade but avoid specialization so as to protect the privileged position of the factory hierarchy.

Taylor Method of Management

"In earlier manufacturing enterprises, skilled workers had retained wide discretion in the direction of their own work, defining the timing and manner of production, determining the pace of work, ascertaining its cost and quality, and hiring and firing their own workers" (Kantor, 1982, pp. 17-18). After 1890, employers and managers increasingly sought ways to centralize and systematize control of factory operations in response to expanding production. The workplace was changing rapidly.

Using the "scientific method" of management advocated by Frederick W. Taylor, occupations became more specialized, and labor subdivision became more minute. As managers split work into smaller and smaller tasks, work could be done with fewer skills, and many skilled trades became obsolete. Tasks could be learned in a short period of time. As work became increasingly unskilled, the apprenticeship system eroded. While some semi-skilled labor was needed with a whole production overview, such as machine maintenance and repairmen, management and supervisory practices led to increased personnel separations in the work hierarchy based on status, wages, and authority.

The "Iron Man" and Social Concerns

By 1920, in many industries, "the muscle and cunning mind of the master craftsman" were replaced by the "batteries of the tireless iron man." (Kantor, 1982, p. 19). The transformation of industry challenged earlier beliefs about work as the "moral core" of life. Resistance to new work patterns showed in the rate of labor turnover. Increasingly, it was to education and particularly to vocational education that Americans turned for a response to industrial conflict and social alienation (Kantor, 1982, p. 26).

Several middle-class reformers and social scientists were attracted to vocational education as a reform movement. Jane Addams, founder of Hull House in Chicago, was concerned about the human consequences of changes in work. She spoke at the first conference and was active in the NSPIE.

Addams established a Labor Museum in Chicago to help people understand their role in the broader scope of work. She believed that an education was needed that unified practical and cultural training that would enable youth to understand the principles of industry. Addams advocated for a vocational education that would "not simply mirror the needs of an existing industrial system but must pervade it with a 'human spirit' and make it a 'kingdom of the mind'" (Kantor, 1986, p. 413). Others too thought vocational education might humanize factory work, including the National Education Association (NEA).

The idea that vocational training might

make industry more educational "clashed with the desires of employers who hoped that vocational education would impart skills and attitudes conducive to large-scale, hierarchical industrial production" (Kantor, 1986, p. 414). David Snedden, Massachusetts commissioner of education, and Charles Prosser, NSPIE executive secretary, accepted the imperatives from industrial expansion and division of labor. They stressed the need for efficiency and an education that would help workers fit into the industrial work world. They "scorned the idea that vocational education might transform the factory or even that this was desirable" (p.415). For Snedden and Prosser, efficiency meant adjusting workers to their "appropriate places in the division of labor." They seemed to ignore socio-political struggles.

Education Through Occupations—Integrated Curriculum

Addams, with friend and colleague John Dewey, was not convinced that industrial education and cultural education were separate matters. In 1915, a debate was published in which Dewey disagreed with Snedden's proposal for specific industrial skills and job training based on social and political grounds. Dewey argued that education was needed for "development of such initiative, ingenuity, and executive capacity as shall make workers, as far as they may be, masters of their own industrial fate." The aim of vocational education must not be to "'adapt' workers to existing industrial regime," but to "first alter the existing industrial system, and ultimately transform it" (as cited in Kantor, 1986, p. 417 & Copa & Bentley, 1992, p. 907).

Dewey believed that vocational education could help transform schools. While preparation for the work of the professions "has always been taken care of, it is, as we has seen, the future of the worker in industry which has been neglected" (Dewey, 1915, p. 308). He believed that a strong foundation of general education was necessary for "real success" on which to build technical skills. He was concerned that needed changes in general education would be overlooked by a narrow focus on industrial trade training.

High attrition rates from school and the condition of the youth labor market provided impetus for the hope of vocational education. Typically half of youth aged 13 to 15 dropped out of urban schools; only 40 percent of school children completed eighth grade. Children found work in unskilled, poorly paid, seasonal, and dead-end jobs. While economic necessity was cited for the high dropout rate, children's dislike for school seemed a more compelling factor.

High dropout rates were associated with inadequacies of schooling. Most jobs open to youth were unskilled and did not require extensive training. Concern about poverty, low wages, and enervating work was shifted from the economy to the school and intensified the drive to vocationalize education (Kantor, 1986).

Dewey recognized dangers in children leaving school for work too young. He wanted new approaches to education to preserve democracy by avoiding strict formation of fixed classes of people. People needed an appreciation of both the academic and occupationally oriented preparation, that would unite (rather than separate) "learning and social application, ideas and practice, and work and recognition of the meaning of what is done" (Dewey, 1915, p. 315).

Integrating Education and Industry

Prosser and Allen also believed in education for democracy but viewed vocational education as a special form of education. In 1925, they wrote that "Vocational training should follow, not accompany general education, and it should be built upon the largest foundation of general education which the youth is willing and able to lay before he undertakes training for an occupation or a pursuit" (p.94). Training should equip the person for the work he wants to do with preparation for success in meeting real demands of employment. Vocational education should conserve human resources and effort by providing efficient training.

There was a need for integration between education and industry. It was recognized early on that when industry or education "attempted to go its own way," the instructional product was inadequate.

NSPIE's original intent to promote national interest and value in industrial occupational training was later broadened. Early NSPIE bulletins say that the first task of vocational education is to develop citizenship and that this should be ever present in vocational instruction. All vocational programs should be open to all regardless of sex, creed, color, or nationality. "This was not a debatable issue—it was a social necessity and recognized as a foundation of vocational education" (Barlow, 1981, p. 23).

In 1917, federal support was provided for vocational education through the passage of the Smith-Hughes Act. Having achieved a major objective in securing federal funding for vocational education, the NSPIE changed its name to the National Society for Vocational Education, merging in the 1920s with the Vocational Education Association of the Middle West to form the American Vocational Association (Barlow, 1976).

Vocational Guidance

In 1907, Frank Parsons of Boston University addressed the graduating class of a Boston evening high school on choosing an occupation. In response to many asking personal appointments, Mrs. Quincy A. Shaw founded the Vocational Bureau of Boston the following January to provide vocational counseling based on Parsons' plans. The Boston public schools realized the need for services and in 1909 established the first school-based vocational guidance program (Copa & Bentley, 1992). *Choosing a Vocation* (Parsons, 1909) was the first textbook in vocational guidance.

Parsons believed that a balance of cultural and industrial education was needed for each child, that "society should guarantee to every child a thorough all-round development of body, mind, and character, and a careful planning of and adequate preparation for some occupation" (Parsons, 1909, p. 165). He emphasized good citizenship as being at least as important as being a good worker. He provided "A Plan for Life" and gave suggestions to develop habits of civic responsibility.

Compatibility of interest, attitudes, and abilities with occupational demands were considered partial requirements for successful occupational adjustment. "The vocational guidance movement developed almost simultaneously with the vocational education movement" (Barlow, 1976, p. 53). Early leaders in both vocational education and vocational guidance development recognized common objectives. "From the start of the vocational movement all programs were intended for those who could profit from the instruction. Mere acquisition of skills has never been the sole objective of the vocational education movement" (Barlow, 1976, p. 54). Over time, the scope of vocational guidance has been expanded into areas of school counseling and the broader concept of career education.

Commission on National Aid to Vocational Education

In 1914, to more fully study providing national aid for vocational education, the President appointed the Commission on National Aid to Vocational Education to study the views of more than 12,000,000 people. There was strong public sentiment indicating "an urgent social and educational need" for vocational education. National grants were necessary due to the national scope and character of the problem, and states varied widely in their resources to carry the costs of vocational education. Arguments for vocational education included: the need to ensure a competitive position in world markets; to eliminate dead-end jobs and increase economic returns to workers; to reduce social and industrial unrest; to democratize education, and to increase occupational mobility for working-class youth (Kantor, 1982). Recommendations were made for stimulating vocational education, teacher training, partial payment for educator's salaries, and for a federal board for continuous research and support of public schools of "less than college grade."

While it drew much criticism, the idea of separation of vocational and general education was a key point in the development of vocational education. The society wanted industrial education to be "unhampered by educational prejudice" in its early growth. "Industrial education was viewed as 'the missing link' connecting training with life." "The separation in the beginning did not mean that it must always be so," and it was believed that, over time, some phases of industrial education could be merged with general education (Barlow, 1967, p. 60).

The report of the Presidential Commission became a source book for future reference and may well be considered a classic in the literature of vocational education (Barlow, 1967).

The Smith-Hughes Act

With overwhelming bipartisan support, the Vocational Education Act, commonly known as the Smith-Hughes Act, was signed into law in February 1917. The Act was a plan of cooperation between the states and the federal government and provided funding for: salaries and training of teachers, supervisors, and directors of agricultural programs; teacher salaries and training in areas of home economics, trade, and industrial subjects. States and local school districts were required to provide dollar-for-dollar matching funds. Funds were to support public education in full-time day schools, part-time, and evening schools. Instruction designed for profitable employment in agriculture and the trades would be provided for those over 14 years of age at a less than college grade level. A Federal Board would be created to administer the new program and it was recommended that states develop plans for administering grants and vocational education programs (Copa & Bentley, 1992, p. 906; Scott & Sarkees-Wircenski, 1996, p. 108).

Four fundamental ideas were central to the Act: "First, that vocational education being essential to the national welfare, it is a function of the national government to stimulate the states to undertake this new and needed form of service; second, the federal funds are necessary in order to equalize the burden of carrying on the work among the states; third, that since the federal government is vitally interested in the success of vocational education, it should, so to speak, purchase a degree of participation in this work; and fourth, that only by creating such a relationship between the central and the local governments can proper standards of educational efficiency be set up" (Barlow, 1976, p. 58).

A Federal Board of Vocational Education

A Federal Board of Vocational Education (FBVE) was appointed to administer the new program, but the problem of control was touchy. The national board made efforts to "avoid a dictatorial attitude" with relations to the States and was successful in maintaining a basis of service and cooperation (Barlow, 1976, p. 75). The administrative powers of FBVE were transferred to the U.S. Office of Education in 1933. The transfer of knowledgeable staff members allowed for continued influence concerning vocational education. The functional role of the board became advisory and, to educators and labor leaders, represented a serious mistake and "steps backward in industrial education progress" (Barlow, 1967, p. 127-131). In 1946, the FBVE, the only national board concerning education, was abolished.

Vocational Education Development 1930-60

Manual arts and "industrial arts" continued to develop in the schools and by 1930, had achieved recognition as an important part of the curriculum. Pre-vocational instruction emerged for students in junior high grades 7-9. Conference focus was on teaching and instruction and the preparation of teachers. The Great Depression of the 1930s was an economic collapse which seemed to amplify the fears of industrial arts educators. Although they felt positive about the work, they articulated a need for research and continued improvement in teaching (Barlow, 1967).

Vocational education became more closely aligned with general education, but there was a cost: "The more vocational education came to share the goals of general education, the more it came to share the insularity of general education. . . . During the 1930s, in contrast, vocational education was falling under the control of educators who had little incentive to pay close attention to industry or to stay abreast of recent developments in the social sciences. Their niche within American education was narrow but comfortable. The American Vocational Association, founded in 1926, formed an increasingly strong lobby. . . . From time to time criticisms appeared, but these were quickly turned aside with calls for better implementation of existing programs" (Kett, 1982, p. 79).

The George-Reed Act of 1929 and George-Ellzey Act of 1934 authorized supplementary funds for vocational education, and enrollments increased. The George-Deen Act of 1936 authorized appropriations to agriculture, home economics, trade and industries, and to the new field of distributive education. By 1942, the silver anniversary of federal funding for vocational education, the total enrollment in all vocational education exceeded 2,600,000 persons.

Vocational Training: National Defense

The *Final Report of War Training Programs,* published by the U.S. Office of Education in 1946, carefully documented the vocational-education activities during World War II (Barlow, 1976). From 1940-46, the National Defense Training Program trained nearly 7,500,000 people for defense and war production employment, 20 percent of whom were women. The vast, rapid response of the successful war-time effort demonstrated a great deal about the nation's capacity for vocational education.

Among the national challenges following the war were: needed jobs and training for those returning from overseas; an increasingly diverse student population; educational opportunity inequities; and population increases created by the "baby boom." The George Barden Act, or Vocational Education Act of 1946, combined with the funding from the Smith-Hughes Act, provided more that $36 million for vocational-education contributions to the nation's post-war reconversion program. Amendments in 1956 and 1958 expanded vocational education to include health areas of nursing occupations and the fishing industry.

During the 1950s, federal administration for vocational education was moved to the Office of Education in the new cabinet-level Department of Health, Education, and Welfare (HEW). In response to the launching of the Russian satellite Sputnik 1, Congress passed the National Defense Education Act in 1958 to stress science, mathematics, foreign languages, and other technical occupations believed important to national defense and scientific progress. The Act encouraged postsecondary education. Title VIII authorized a $15 million annual appropriation over four years to establish area vocational-education programs of less than college level. Focus was to be preparation of skilled technicians important to national defense and scientific progress (Scott & Sarkees-Wircenski, 1996; Copa & Bentley, 1992).

1960s: Social Responsibility

The late 1950s and 1960s were a time of unrest, instability, and social revolution for the United States. Disruptive influences included the Vietnam War and concern for the disenfranchised and the unemployed. With technological advances, the nature of work was changing, and the population was becoming more mobile. Women were an established part of the workforce. Issues of equity and diversity were heightening. The civil rights movement challenged the nation to provide special efforts to enable minority groups to compete in a non-segregated society. Needs involving a variety of health, occupational, economic, and educational characteristics were translated into public laws in an attempt to find solutions to social and economic problems.

"Vocational education began to receive a

good share of criticism: It did not address the needs of the slow learner, the maladjusted, the handicapped, the disadvantaged (social, educational, and economic), and in certain circles vocational education was thought to be inefficient and unconcerned about its relation to social problems. It was true that vocational-education legislation previously had not dealt with these problems adequately, and the financial resources had not been provided to work in these areas. However, vocational education, because of its previous exemplary record for dealing with programs that prepared people for work, was beginning to receive attention" (Barlow, 1976, p. 77).

Vocational Education Act of 1963

In 1961 came President Kennedy's Panel of Consultants on Vocational Education. Its 1962 recommendations included: expansion of vocational and technical training consistent with national economic needs; provision of training opportunities for noncollege graduates; upgrading of skills for workers to retain employment; and making "educational opportunities available to all, regardless of race, sex, scholastic aptitude, or place of residence" (Barlow, 1976, p. 79).

The Vocational Education Act of 1963, with amendments in 1968, 1972, and 1976, "incorporated the permanent authority of the Smith-Hughes Act" and expanded the role of vocational education (Wolfe, 1978, p. 5). Funding authorization was substantially increased. Attention shifted from subject areas to "preparing all groups in the community regardless of their vocational emphasis or attachment to the labor force. The Act was also designed to assist those persons who had difficulty in succeeding in regular vocational education programs because of socioeconomic or academic reasons" (p. 4). Increased flexibility in using funds for postsecondary, adult, and junior high school levels led to enrollment increases from 12 million to 15 million from fiscal years 1973 and 1976. These increases, primarily at postsecondary and adult-education levels, were attributed to retraining, upgrading, or learning new skills for job market entry (p. 17). National, state, and local advisory councils were established to advise on direction, curriculum, and accountability. The first national council advised to consolidate all federal vocational education in one act to increase manageability and funding. "In 1976, the provisions brought attention to the need for increased external involvement in planning vocational education, reduction of sex stereotyping in programs, and increased efforts in vocational guidance and counseling" (Copa & Bentley, 1992, p. 909).

The 1970s: Career Education

The term "career education," so popular in the 1970s, was first coined in 1956. The foundations for career education are in the history of both vocational education and vocational guidance before the Smith-Hughes Act of 1917.

In 1971 Sidney Marland, Jr., U.S. Commissioner of Education, made career education his highest priority. In 1978, Kenneth Hoyt, named Director of the Office of Career Education, provided a concept of career education as the totality of experiences by which knowledge and attitudes about the self and work are acquired. Skills are developed to identify, choose, plan, and prepare for work and other life options potentially constituting a career. Career education is an effort to refocus American education and the actions of the broader community in ways to help individuals acquire and use the knowledge, skills, and attitudes necessary for each to make work a meaningful, productive, and satisfying part of his or her way of life (Herr & Cramer, 1996, p. 33).

Vocational education legislation through the 1960s and 1970s extended services to various groups. Guidance and counseling was expanded and provided indirect funding for career development. From 1974-81, legislation was enacted specific to the "hot topic" of career education (Scott & Sarkees-Wircenski, 1996, p. 138).

In a 1988 review of career education, Halasz states, "Much of the literature seems to take a defensive posture in attempting to prove that career education does exist, that it is successful, that it is a critical aspect of educational reform, that it was the precursor and definer of the reform movements of the 1980s, and that its value should be recognized. Perhaps it is time to accept its existence as a relevant construct or strategy and to move on to more useful pursuits, such as conducting research that can answer the many unanswered questions about career development in this complex and changing society" (cited in Copa & Bentley, 1992, p. 926).

Legislation for Vocational Education, Manpower, General Education, and Special Needs: 1960s-90s

While federal legislation for vocational education has provided about 10 percent of actual dollars for national efforts, the legislation has been significant in providing incentives and the framework for service delivery since the first Smith-Hughes Vocational Education Act of 1917. Here is a list of legislation indicating trends in vocational education development to guide further exploration.

The Vocational Education Act of 1963, amended in 1968, was revised and extended through the Perkins Vocational Education Act of 1984. The Perkins Act was amended in 1990 with the Carl D. Perkins Vocational and Applied Technology Education Act. In 1994, the School-to-Work Opportunities Act (STWOA) provided a framework to address "new" economic skill needs through education and business partnerships. Additional federal initiatives addressed training or retraining needs of underemployed or unemployed people. Major efforts included the Manpower Development and Training Act (MDTA) of 1962; and the Comprehensive Employment and Training Act (CETA) of 1973, with 1978 amendments, revised and extended through the Job Training Partnership Act (JTPA) of 1982 and amended in 1992.

Major general education legislation was enacted beginning with the Elementary and Secondary Education Act (ESEA) of 1965. The act was amended in 1966, 1967, 1972, 1974, 1976, and 1978; it was reauthorized in 1994 as Improving America's Schools Act and incorporates the Goals 2000: Educate America Act.

Major special-needs legislation included: The Rehabilitation Act of 1973, amended in 1983 and 1986, and extended in 1990; and the Education of All Handicapped Children Act of 1975 (PL 94-142), amended in 1983, 1986, and 1990 (Scott & Sarkees-Wircenski, 1996).

The legislation builds on previous acts in attempts to best meet current needs. Over time, extensions tend to reach out to more people in the hope of providing more equity and opportunity for all people. There are overlaps in service and attempts at coordination and aims for comprehensive service delivery within and between various legislation initiatives.

1980s Education Reform Movement: A Nation at Risk

The early 1980s witnessed economic recession and many large industrial plant closings. Many companies relocated to take advantage of lower tax and labor costs. There was a trend for industries in northeastern states to move south. Industrial changes resulted in dislocated workers, unemployment, and underemployment. The Job Training Partnership Act of 1982 was a response, extending previous manpower efforts and increasing the role of business and private industry in training and employment of unskilled adults and disadvantaged youth and adults. The main thrust of vocational training continued to be remedial in nature.

The federal government's National Commission on Excellence in Education 1983 report, *A Nation at Risk*, focused attention on ineffectiveness in public education and recommended corrections. But education researcher Gerald Bracey (1997) would later label this report a "masterpiece of propaganda" based on selective use of education data—a criticism to which many educators could relate. Vocational educators, noting that vocational education was not specifically included in the rhetoric or the commission's recommendations, believed that lack of substantial research data and a negative image hampered vocational education's position in national policy issues (Gilli, 1990).

Carl D. Perkins Vocational Education Act

In 1984, the Carl D. Perkins Vocational Education Act sought to assist states to expand, improve, modernize, and develop quality vocational-education programs to meet needs of the nation's future workforce and to improve productivity and promote economic growth. The act called for providing greater equity in access to quality vocational-education opportunities for women, minorities, and special-needs populations; greater cooperation between public service agencies and the private sector; improvement in academic foundations for students; and strengthening of the vocational-education research process. The act provided for use of state-certified counselors in programs designed to aid students in career planning, decision-making, and employability skills. The need to recognize and move students away from declining occupational fields and into emerging high-technology endeavors was supported, and a provision encouraged and funded industry-education partnership training programs in high-technology occupations.

Workforce 2000

In 1987, the U.S. Department of Labor commissioned research on work and workers in the last years of the twentieth century. The resulting Workforce 2000 report indicated: the American economy would grow; U.S. manufacturing would comprise a much smaller share of the economy by 2000; the workforce would grow slowly, characterized by older workers with an increase in women and the disadvantaged; and much higher-level skills would be needed in service industries. The report stated that 22 percent of jobs in 1987 required a college degree and that, for new jobs created from 1984-2000, 30 percent would require a college degree, and an additional 22 percent would require between one and three years of college. It was projected that the future high-skill service economy would require a high-skilled and productive workforce.

The Forgotten Half

In 1988, the Commission on Work, Family, and Citizenship (also known as the Commission on Youth and America's Future) released the reports *The Forgotten Half: Non-College Youth in America* and *The Forgotten Half: Pathways to Success for America's Youth and Young Families*. Central to the discussion was the indication that less than 30 percent of current school students will get a college degree. So what does the future hold for the majority?

The commission focused on school-to-work transition and the lack of linkage causing students to flounder as they move into the marketplace, with schools continuing to be isolated from the larger community. To construct an improved school-to-work system, the commission recommended community experimentation with a mix of "multiple elements, " which may include: monitored work experience (cooperative education, internship, apprenticeship, pre-employment training, youth-operated enterprises); community and neighborhood service (individual voluntary service, youth-guided services); redirected vocational education incentives (guaranteed postsecondary and continuing education, guaranteed jobs, guaranteed training); career information and counseling (career information centers, parents as career educators, improved counseling and career orientation, community mentors, and community-based organizations); and school volunteers.

The commission agreed "with John Dewey that the fundamental purpose of [vocational] education should not be to provide narrow occupational training but to link education with adult life. We recommend that the goal of vocational education be redirected away from specific job training and to the more realistic—and valuable—goal of motivating students to acquire the skills and knowledge they need for both work and active citizenship" (Commission on Work, Family, and Citizenship, 1988, p. 51). For students not going on to higher education, recommended "added chance" interventions included expansion of the Job Corps and the Job Training Partnership Act.

1990s: Rebirth of Vocational Education

The 1990s began with uncertainty in education, and themes related to the need for change and restructuring are constant. For general and vocational education, it is a time for redefinition and new directions. Different ways to think and behave based on rapid, seemingly unpredictable change will continue throughout the next decade.

America's Choice

In 1990, the National Center on Education and the Economy's Commission on the Skills of the American Workforce issued *America's Choice: High Skills or Low Wages!* It noted that, "Since 1969, real average weekly earnings in the United States have fallen by more than 12 percent" and "during the past two decades, our productivity has slowed to a crawl. It now takes nearly three years to achieve the same productivity improvement we used to achieve in one year" (p. 1). Concurrent with a slow-growth workforce is a need for higher productivity to maintain and perhaps improve our standard of living. "If productivity continues to falter, . . . [e]ither the top 30 percent of our population will grow wealthier while the bottom 70 percent becomes progressively poorer, or we all slide into relative poverty together" (p. 1).

A shift in production orientation, said the report, meant that the world's best companies are replacing the "Taylor" methods with high-performance teams. Bureaucracy is being reduced and front-line workers assume responsibilities using judgment and decision-making for more tasks. This shift will require companies to invest in training, and few companies have done it. Most are using past turn-of-the-century work organization. "If we want to compete more effectively in the global economy, we will have to move to a high productivity work organization" (p. 1). Companies did not report a skills shortage in the U.S. because "most American employers organize in a way that does not require high skills" (p. 1). It is believed these companies are making the choice for low wages.

Concerning skills, the report stated: "While businesses everywhere complained about the quality of their applicants, few talked about the kinds of skills acquired in school. The primary concern of more than 80 percent of employers was finding workers with a good work ethic and appropriate social behavior: 'reliable', 'a good attitude,' 'a pleasant appearance,' 'a good personality.' Most employers we interviewed do not expect their skill requirements to change. Despite the widespread presumption that advancing technology and the evolving service economy will create jobs demanding higher skills, only 5 percent of employers were concerned about a skills shortage. These were mainly large manufacturers, financial service organizations, and communications companies" (p. 1).

As for workforce preparation, "more than 70 percent of the jobs in America will not require a college education by the year 2000. These jobs are the backbone of our economy, and the productivity of workers in these jobs will make or break our economic future" (p. 3). If the choice is high skills, "we must fundamentally change our approach to work and education" (p. 5). Front-line workers will need new capabilities, and a technical workforce will be needed. Other nations were studied and compared with the U.S. in terms of economy, culture, approach to education, training, and high-productivity work organization. Recommendations were made and examples given for systemic improvements to include: national education standards and assessment; alternative learning environments; combined work and study programs; technical and professional certification; lifelong learning incentives; and a coordinating monitoring system.

Secretary's Commission on Achieving Necessary Skills (SCANS)

In 1990, the Secretary's Commission on

Achieving Necessary Skills (SCANS) was established to examine workplace demands and determine if the current and future workforce can meet them. It included 31 representatives from schools, businesses, unions, and government. Its reports include: *What Work Requires of Schools: A SCANS Report for America 2000* (1991); *Skills and Tasks for Jobs: A SCANS Report for America 2000* (1992); *Learning a Living: A Blueprint for High Performance: A SCANS Report for America 2000* (1992); and *SCANS in the Schools* (1992).

The SCANS report outlines what people need to know to succeed in the future economy. From interviewing employers and employees from widely varied work settings, results were stated in the Executive Summary of *What Work Requires of Schools*: "The message to us was universal: good jobs will increasingly depend on people who can put knowledge to work. What we found was disturbing: more than half our young people leave school without the knowledge or foundation required to find and hold a good job. These young people will pay a very high price. They face the bleak prospects of dead-end work interrupted only by periods of unemployment" (1991, p. 1).

SCANS identifies five competencies and a three-part foundation of skills and personal qualities essential to job performance and necessary preparation for all students. The five competencies are:

- **Resources**—allocating time, money, materials, space, and people;
- **Interpersonal Skills**—working on teams, teaching others, serving customers, negotiating, and working well with people from culturally diverse backgrounds;
- **Information**—acquiring and evaluating data, organizing and maintaining files, interpreting and communicating, and using computers to process information;
- **Systems**—understanding social, organizational, and technological systems, monitoring and correcting performance, and designing or improving systems;
- **Technology**—selecting equipment and tools, applying technology to specific tasks, and maintaining and troubleshooting technologies.

The foundation areas are:

- **Basic Skills**: reading, writing, arithmetic, mathematics, listening, and speaking;
- **Thinking Skills**: creative thinking, decision-making, problem-solving, seeing things in the mind's eye, knowing how to learn, and reasoning;
- **Personal Qualities**: individual responsibility, self-esteem, sociability, self-management, and integrity/honesty.

SCANS focuses on the role schools play in preparing young people for work. To succeed, educators must address changes taking place in the world of work. In discussing the SCANS report, Packer (1992) notes that some employers "have abandoned Frederick Taylor's 80-year-old assembly-line mentality; one that makes little use of employees' talents, relying on them only to perform repetitive, routine tasks. High-performance firms have replaced the Tayloristic approach with one advocated by Edwards Deming. . . . These businesses use all of their workers' skills to relentlessly pursue excellence, product quality, and customer satisfaction. They combine technology and people in new ways, moving decisions closer to the front lines, and drawing more fully on the abilities of all workers. The Deming approach means quality built in, not end-of-the-line quality control. And it means treating the workforce as an investment—not a cost" (pp. 29-39).

Packer explains that businesses cannot adopt the quality approach with ill-prepared workers: "The most disturbing finding of the initial SCANS report is that 'more than half our young people leave school without the knowledge or foundation required to find and hold a good job. These young people will pay a very high price. They face the bleak prospects of dead-end work interrupted only by periods of unemployment.' Simply put, low skills lead to low wages and low productivity" (pp. 29-30).

Schools and employers need to work together to close the skills gap. Otherwise, "we will consign millions of young people to a life of dead-end, low paying jobs. And we will weaken an American economy. . . . The twin worlds of school and of work both have to change" (Packer, p. 30).

SCANS is linked to America 2000: An Educational Strategy (1991), which was renamed Goals 2000: Educate America Act of 1994.

National Skills Standards Board

The Educate America Act of 1994 called for establishment of a National Skills Standards Board to help develop and implement a national system of voluntary industry skills standards to provide information on what industry requires of entry-level workers. How will an effective system be developed? Success requires four major tasks be accomplished: reaching some consensus on what constitutes an industry and the occupations within it; settling how specific and detailed our lists of skills will be and how we will determine them; determining how to set standards and who will decide; and figuring out how best to assess students and what certification signifies (Hoachlander & Rahn, 1994).

National Assessment of Vocational Education

In 1994, the National Assessment of Vocational Education (NAVE) issued the following recommendations for high-school-level preparation for work: Emphasize development of cognitive and broad technical skills through applied learning; stress competency-based education keyed to high standards; prepare students for some sort of postsecondary education; defer much, but not all, specific skill training to the postsecondary level; and support specific skill training for which there is growing demand (Goldberger & Kazis, 1996).

Our Responsibility to the Future

Education literature proliferates reflecting research, traditional and new viewpoints, examples of "best practice," and proposals for change. Legislation cannot do it. In their own settings, given a learning environment conducive and receptive to continuous improvement, people must make necessary changes.

Vocational education perspective allows continuous feedback on quality through placement follow-up data. Survey data of school leavers can also provide information on needed changes, in addition to school strengths. An awareness that we are preparing people for a world that appears to be changing more rapidly than at any time since the industrial revolution is an important component in the administration of vocational as well as general education.

Thinking about the future now and continuous adaptation are a responsibility that not only vocational but all educators must share and address. On what basis are changes being made? What are the underlying values and philosophic perspectives? What are the economic realities?

References

Barlow, M. L. (1965). A platform for vocational education in the future. In M. L. Barlow (Ed.), *Vocational education: The sixty-fourth yearbook of the national society for the study of education, Part I* (pp. 280-291). Chicago, IL: University of Chicago.

Barlow, M. L. (Ed.). (1965). *Vocational education: The sixty-fourth yearbook of the national society for the study of education, Part 1*. Chicago, IL: University of Chicago.

Barlow, M. L. (1967). *History of industrial education in the United States*. Peoria, IL: Charles A. Bennett Co.

Barlow, M. L. (1976). 200 Years of Vocational Education 1776 - 1976 [Special Bicentennial Issue]. *American Vocational Journal*, 57, (5).

Barlow, M. L. (1981). Our important past. In G. I. Swanson (Ed.), *The future of vocational education* (pp. 21-33). Arlington, VA: American Vocational Association.

Bracey, G. W. (1997). A nation of learners: Nostalgia and amnesia. *Educational Leadership*, 54 (5), 53-57.

Butts, R. F., & Cremin, L. A. (1953). *A history of education in American culture*. New York: Holt, Rinehart and Winston.

Copa, G. H., & Bentley, C. B. (1992). Vocational education. In P. W. Jackson (Ed.), *Handbook of research on curriculum: A project of the American Educational Research Association* (pp. 891-944).

Copple, C. E., Kane, M., Matheson, N. S., Meltzer, A. S., Packer, A., & White, T. G. (1992, June). *SCANS in the schools*. (Available from: Pelavin Associates Inc., 2030 M Street, N. W., Suite 800, Washington D. C. 20036).

Dewey, J., & Dewey, E. (1915). *Schools of tomorrow*. New York: E. P. Dutton & Co.

Gilli, L. (1990). The image of the profession of vocational education. In A. J. Pautler (Ed.), *Vocational education in the 1990s: Major issues* (pp. 239-254). Ann Arbor, MI: Prakken Publications.

Goldberger, S., & Kazis, R. (1996). Revitalizing high schools: What the school-to-career movement can contribute. *Phi Delta Kappan*, 77, 547-560.

Halasz, I. M. (1988). *Trends and issues in career education*. Columbus: Center on Education and Training for Employment, Ohio State University.

Herr, E. L., & Cramer, S. H. (1996). *Career guidance and counseling through the life span* (5th ed.). New York: Harper Collins.

Hoachlander, G., & Rahn, M. L. (1994). National skills standards. *Vocational Education Journal*, 69 (1), 20-22.

Johnston, W. B., & Packer, A. E. (1987). *Workforce 2000: Work and workers for the twenty-first century*. Indianapolis, IN: Hudson Institute.

Kantor, H. (1982). Vocationalism in American education: The economic and political context, 1800-1930. In H. Kantor & D. B. Tyack (Eds.), *Work, youth, and schooling: Historical perspectives on vocationalism in American education* (pp.110-141). Stanford, CA: Stanford University.

Kantor, H. (1986). Work, education, and vocational reform: The ideological origins of vocational education, 1890-1920. *American Journal of Education*, 94 (pp. 401-426).

Kett, J. F. (1982). The adolescents of vocational education. In H. Kantor & D. B. Tyack (Eds.), *Work, youth, and schooling: Historical perspectives on vocationalism in American education* (pp. 79-109). Stanford, CA: Stanford University.

National Center on Education and the Economy's Commission on the Skills of the American Workforce. (1990). *America's choice: High skills or low wages!* Rochester, NY: Author.

National Commission on Excellence in Education. (1984). *A nation at risk*. Cambridge, MA: USA Research.

Packer, A. H. (1992). Taking action on the SCANS report. *Educational Leadership*,49 (6), 27-31.

Parsons, F. (1909). *Choosing a vocation*. Boston: Houghton Mifflin.

Prosser, C. A., & Allen, C. R. (1925). *Vocational education in a democracy*. New York: The Century Co.

Scott, J. L., & Sarkees-Wircenski, M. (1996). *Overview of vocational and applied technology education*. Homewood, IL: American Technical Publishers, Inc.

Secretary's Commission on Achieving Necessary Skills. (1991). *What work requires of schools: A SCANS report for America 2000*. Washington DC: U.S. Department of Labor.

Secretary's Commission on Achieving Necessary Skills. (1992). *Learning a living: A blueprint for high performance: A SCANS report for America 2000*. Washington DC: U.S. Department of Labor.

Secretary's Commission on Achieving Necessary Skills. (1992). *Skills and tasks for jobs: A SCANS report for America 2000*. Washington DC: U.S. Department of Labor.

U.S. Department of Education. (1991). *America 2000: An education strategy* [Sourcebook]. Washington, DC: Author.

Wolfe, M. L. (1978). The Vocational Education Act of 1963, as amended: A background paper (LC 1043 U.S.). Congressional Research Service: Library of Congress.

Youth and America's Future: The William T. Grant Foundation Commission on Work, Family, and Citizenship. (1988). *The forgotten half: Non-college youth in America*. Washington, DC: Author.

***Cheryl L. Hogg**, candidate for the Ph.D. in Educational Administration at the State University of New York at Buffalo, currently serves as the graduate assistant for Leadership Initiative for Tomorrow's Schools (LIFTS). Her background includes more than 25 years as an educator with elementary-level through adult populations and includes such positions as principal/supervisor and assistant principal in the New York State Board of Cooperative Educational Services (BOCES); educational and vocational supervisor for the New York State Division for Youth residential and field services; school counselor with the Buffalo Public Schools; career education and placement for Buffalo Children's Hospital Adolescent Services. She has completed two master's degrees at Canisius College and was awarded a Rotary International scholarship from Manchester Polytechnic for postgraduate work in youth and community work.*

2

A PHILOSOPHIC VIEW FOR SEEING THE PAST OF VOCATIONAL EDUCATION AND ENVISIONING THE FUTURE OF WORKFORCE EDUCATION: PRAGMATISM REVISITED

By Melvin D. Miller and James A. Gregson

INTRODUCTION

Philosophy projects varied meanings and creates differing reactions among individuals—for educators and the general population. For both groups there is misunderstanding, if not confusion, about how the term philosophy should be used. Further, a variety of reactions, from anxiety to consternation to perplexity, is not uncommon in considering things that involve the abstract nature of philosophic thinking (Elias & Merriam, 1995).

The above paragraph depicts a confusing picture of philosophy as a field of activity. That is intended. In addition, philosophic thinking and the application of philosophy to practices in education are frequently absent in considering and shaping practice. For many educators, philosophy is to be left to philosophers questing for the intangible. For such educators, philosophy is not practical and is rightly given low priority in meeting demands and expectations to provide quality education. This is equally true for vocational educators.

Those who provide education for the workforce largely have shunned philosophy. Whether known as *vocational educators, vocational-technical educators, technical educators, workforce educators*, or one of a myriad of other terms, the tendency is to shun philosophy and its application to educational programs that lead to and further the ability of individuals to hold productive positions in the nation's workforce. In short, some vocational educators seem to declare that philosophy is not practical and therefore is of limited importance in a practice-oriented field.

That declaration is a disservice to vocational education and to philosophy, underestimating significant contributions that philosophic activity can make to vocational education and depriving the field of efforts to develop a coherent framework for thinking about, designing, implementing, and evaluating the field of practice. Through philosophy, vocational educators will find a consistent, coherent basis for continually seeking answers to persistent and recurring problems and also for thinking about alternative futures and creating strategies allowing the workforce educator to actively create the future of the field.

Philosophy, literally translated from the German, is a way of viewing the world. In formulating a philosophical view of the world, three questions guide that process. By asking, "What is the nature of reality?", "What is the nature of truth?", and "What is the nature of value?" the user of philosophic processes inquires into all that there is, with the exception of faith issues. These three philosophical questions provide individuals, as well as a field of practice, with a basis to formulate a consistent, coherent framework of how vocational education and vocational educators are viewed. The obverse process uses these same questions to view practice with the same consistency and coherence in attempting to understand the philosophic posture of past and present vocational educators and their programs—an inductive process.

The following section is an inductive examination of selected, significant activities, programs, and writings influential in furthering vocational education. At the same time, the fundamental questions of philosophy are held up as a template for examining the past. In addition, philosophy is stipulated to mean viewing the world in a consistent, coherent way.

VOCATIONAL EDUCATION: AN ELUSIVE FIELD OF PRACTICE

For present purposes, I ask you to accept a stipulated, broad definition for *vocational education* to encompass any planned and/or organized activity designed to prepare individuals for activity which produces a product or service not requiring a baccalaureate or higher degree. True, this definition is restrictive in that many baccalaureate or higher degrees have as a stated purpose the preparation for roles that fit within the broad definition stipulated. True too, this definition is not consistent with the concept of a seamless education and the new vocationalism. But it is broad enough to incorporate approximately 80 percent of those engaged in producing products and services and provides a view consistent with the Smith-Hughes Act. Later in this chapter, I will provide an alternative view as to vocational education's nature.

Using the definition stipulated, vocational education can be traced back to the earliest recorded history of mankind and it is logical to believe that vocational education precedes recorded history. Certainly, as our earliest ancestors undertook providing food, shelter, and safety for the various units of civilization, basic skills and service activities were passed on from generation to generation. It seems clear that vocational education has been an integral part of society from its earliest beginnings.

As civilization has developed, the form of vocational education has changed. Although oversimplified, the form has changed from one family member sharing his or her abilities with another family member, to a highly skilled person becoming the primary source of personal development for an unskilled person choosing to emulate the skilled person. In short, it has moved from the passing on from father/mother to son/daughter to early apprenticeship programs.

These same patterns endured through the first century of our nation. However, with the Morrill Act in 1862, a new form of vocational education began. Land-grant universities created after the Morrill Act had a primary mission to prepare individuals for roles in the agricultural and mechanical sciences (A&M) together with a number of occupational roles including some for which remuneration was not to be a goal. Too, many educational programs at these A&M colleges were not intended to result in a baccalaureate or higher degree. In fact, several A&M colleges continued to offer two-year diploma programs in a number of fields within our stipulated definition of vocational education well into the 1960's (e.g., Oklahoma State University).

The Smith-Hughes Act of 1917 signaled another change in the form of vocational education, which represented the grouping of less-skilled individuals under the direction of a number of individuals who collectively had the abilities to succeed in a field of endeavor. It was federal support that formalized vocational education as a part of America's public education system. Furthermore, this legislation provided that such education supported by federal funds would be under public supervision and control, that the controlling purpose would be to fit for useful (note not gainful) employment, and that it would be of less than college grade.

Thus a definition of vocational education began to emerge that had common acceptance among persons associated with public education systems. Given the long pre-Smith-Hughes history of vocational education, eventually some vocational educators divided vocational education into two types. Programs eligible for federal dollars provided by the Smith-Hughes Act and the several subsequent federal acts were described as "Vocational Education" ("big VE"). Other programs that might share common content and purpose but did not qualify for federal support were identified as "vocational education" ("little ve"). This latter categorization encompassed a significant range of activity designed to prepare people as producers of products and services. Private industry programs, educational activity offered under the local government, charitable organizations, state-wide organizations, and various military organizations are educational activity described under "little ve."

Technical education as a field of practice adds to the lack of clarity about how vocational education should be defined. Some individuals assign a different and often higher status to technical education (Evans & Herr, 1978). Others choose to think of it as a part of the total field of activity and frequently attempt to solve the definition problem by using the terms vocational-technical education. In the final analysis, the distinction may be in the eyes of the beholder. Regardless, technical education and technical educators have added another element to be dealt with in unraveling ideas about vocational education as a field of activity.

Another element to be dealt with involves those calling for all of education to be considered as contributing to the ability of individuals to assume roles as producers of products and services. Moreover, it is a commonly held position that education directly related to such roles has a high level of meaning for learners and thus should be the dominant type of education provided in our society. While it might be an overstatement, such education represents a homogenization and blending of much that is labeled basic skills or education with present day vocational education and would become the dominant theme around which public education is to be organized and delivered. Although a clear label has not emerged, proponents supporting this directional change in education claim it as different than the "career education" of recent times. This "new vocationalism," in addition to emphasizing preparation for productive roles in society (the homogenized and blended view of the purpose of schooling), requires an emphasis on acquiring lifelong learning skills and habits as preparation for the changing nature and demands placed on individuals living in a dynamic, world-wide culture (Grubb, 1995; Lewis, 1991).

DEVELOPMENT OF GUIDING IDEALS AND PRACTICES

Public vocational education emerged in America amidst controversy: Should vocational education be part of a comprehensive school system or designed as a separate but equal system—both offering complete and, in some instances, duplicate educational activity? The comprehensive design won. Yet, in the final decade of the twentieth century, public vocational programming is being offered in separate facilities, under separate administrative structures, and with separate funding different from K-12 education. Perhaps the single feature that distinguishes it from a dual system is the fact that such vocational schools combine their educational activity with that of nonvocational schools to allow students to complete requirements for a high-school diploma.

Out of this early milieu, vocational education's leaders established—by law in some cases—preferred practices for vocational education to follow. The Smith-Hughes Act provided specific requirements for activities for students beyond their classroom experience, established minimum qualifications for vocational teachers, directed states to create state-level administrative structures, and required that vocational teacher education programs be established.

In addition to helping formulate the early standards that became a part of the Smith-Hughes Act, Charles A. Prosser developed 16 theorems on vocational education. Some of these may have been limiting in their view; however, in their totality, they provided substantial guidance for establishing and conducting public vocational education programs. The leadership of Prosser and the many early supporters of vocational education gave rise to ideas that would establish the ideals and practices that would guide the development of vocational education in its first half-century as part of America's school systems.

PRINCIPLES AS A SOURCE OF ENLIGHTENMENT

Principles represented a further stage of development in conceptualizing vocational education. Principles, according to Miller (1985) "... are defined as generalizations that state a preferred practice and serve as guidelines for program and curriculum construction, evaluation, selection of instructional practices, and policy development" (p. 5). Barlow (1975) claims that, at the beginning of vocational education, "[t]he principles and practices had to be learned by each person" (p. 2). Yet, there is no published evidence, other than Prosser's theorems, of guiding principles being identified early in the development of vocational education. Regardless, it seems clear that Prosser's theorems provided a conceptual basis for thinking about vocational education. Later, Roberts (1957) and Miller (1985) furthered thinking on such principles.

Principles grow out of successful practice. According to Anthony (1965), they are valid when they "have strong support from practice, even though there is no known scientific explanation between cause and effect" (p. 162). Principles tend to be indicative of reflection, a thinking about what has transpired, considering what has worked, and an analysis of how such acts could be used to guide future behavior and practice. Putting it another way, it is an inductive process that considers the past in thinking about the future.

PHILOSOPHY: DOES IT HAVE A ROLE IN EDUCATION?

Questions about philosophy's role in our public education system are legitimate. Serious doubt can be raised about whether earnest philosophic thinking has had a significant influence in developing our educational programs. Most often, educational practice appears to have been implemented based on what previously existed rather than carefully developing a consistent and coherent philosophic system to design education. In short, what was will be.

Although change has occurred, it has tended to represent tinkering and fad rather than concerted effort to rethink practice based on a carefully articulated set of philosophic tenets—this, despite educators' declarations about their philosophy of education. What often was declared in the name of philosophy was best described as a collection of ideas about a variety of topics which lacked any underlying or unifying theory. Furthermore, such declarations did not consciously address in a consistent and coherent way the three fundamental philosophic questions about the nature of reality, truth and value. Nor did they tend to address the educational counter-questions about the nature of the learner, the role of the teacher, and the purpose of schooling.

Practice in American education has been largely influenced by two primary schools of philosophical thinking: idealism and realism. Although this may be oversimplified, it accurately depicts the origin and basis for much of our country's educational practice. Educational philosophy based on a blending of these two schools of philosophy is commonly labeled essentialism.

Educational practices supported by the essentialist's philosophic position include: the notion that ideas, concepts, and theory should hold a more dominant place than preparing for a life role as a worker and producer; learning theory reflecting a behavioralistic approach and memorization over building on the individual's personal experiences; and a subject-matter emphasis on the so-called basic skills and preparation for college as compared with any significant attempt to extend the range of options to be more inclusive of the needs and ultimate goals for all students. This list of educational practices of the essentialistic philosophy is not exhaustive, but it illustrates three major themes around which philosophy appropriately influences educational practice—the nature of the learner, the role of the teacher, and the purpose of schooling.

Current trends, as represented by home schooling and an expansion of private education in grades K-12, also reflect essentialistic philosophic leanings. Their views on the nature of the learner, the role of the teacher, and the purpose of schooling largely align with the essentialistic position. In fact, the behavioralistic tendency to prescribe and control is frequently more evident than in public schools. Too, both variations of K-12 education have a strong ecclesiastical bent that differentiates them from public schools. Regardless, much of what is practiced in the name of education in the venue of these expanding forms of education reflects the philosophic thinking of idealism and realism—essentialism, if you please.

Returning to a somewhat recent but historical point of view, John Dewey attempted to influence schools to hold a philosophic view that would influence practices to be different from the past. He wanted educators to give careful thought to educational programming and practice based on a unifying philosophic position.

In the same era, Snedden and Prosser also held to the need for schools to change. Both men worked long and hard to achieve educational opportunities for youth and thus to increase the public schools' range of influence. Despite debate on how the goals they held should be implemented, it was clear that change was called for.

The views of Snedden and Prosser have been assigned a philosophic descriptor, by some, as *instrumentalism* (Simon, Dippo, & Schenke, 1991). But we hold that Snedden and Prosser's views lack the inherent qualities to provide a basis for thinking of them as a philosophic system. Regardless, the ideas and efforts of Snedden and Prosser brought about change and the introduction of a system of vocational education as part of our public schools.

The interests of Dewey, Snedden, and Prosser had points of similarity as well as differences. Each wanted the schools to change, to be directed toward preparation for occupations, to become more democratic, and to play a more significant role in preparing a larger segment of the population for a democratic society (Wirth, 1980). Even with Dewey's socialistic emphasis evident in many of his statements and writings, there was agreement on the need for change. Regardless of the shared view that vocational education was important as a part of the change in America's schools, there was substantial argument between the Dewey and Snedden-Prosser camps (Gregson, 1994a, 1996; Simon, Dippo, & Schenke, 1991; Wirth, 1980, 1983).

On reflection and analysis, some of the inherent philosophical positions of these two factions are similar. Dewey's work is viewed as a significant part of the foundation of pragmatism. An understanding of the practices advocated by Snedden and Prosser and an analysis of those practices using inductive processes gives credence to pragmatism as the dominant theory implied by those practices. However, there is little evidence to suggest that either Snedden or Prosser were concerned about a philosophic label or making clear whether they had a specific philosophic position.

Articulation of a philosophic position was lacking during the first half-century of vocational education. According to Taylor in the forward to *Principles and a Philosophy for Vocational Education*, "For over 50 years, vocational education has relied on scattered, often unstated principles to guide its policies and practices, in the absence of a coherent philosophy" (Miller, 1985, p. xi). The consequence of this has been that "important assumptions about the nature of people, truth, and values have not been consistent and have encouraged opportunism, expediency, and a mindlessness in vocational education that has frequently replaced thoughtful analysis, synthesis, and reason-based decision making" (Miller, 1985, p. xi).

The last two decades of vocational education's existence have been different. After careful research to identify the principles of vocational education and through an inductive examination of those principles, Miller (1985) makes the declaration that "vocational education's philosophical position is pragmatism" (p. 222). Subsequently, others have supported pragmatism as the philosophic position representative of vocational education (Law, 1994; Wirth, 1980). The fundamental assumptions represented by the philosophy of pragmatism as it relates to questions about the nature of reality, truth, and value are highly evident in the practices of vocational education.

An identified philosophic position is a hallmark of a professional field; having one is critical to its future. It is a consistent and coherent philosophy that is a basis for thoughtful action. Not only does it provide parameters concerning judgments about present practices; but of even greater importance, it serves as a sound conceptual framework to guide implementation of the future it chooses to envision.

PHILOSOPHY GUIDING PRACTICE INTO THE FUTURE

It is instructive to observe how key elements representative of pragmatism continue to recur in vocational education.

Change is a significant feature of pragmatic philosophy. Concomitantly, evidence of change continues to exist in vocational education. Ongoing debate on the most fundamental of changes, the appropriate name for the area of practice, is highly evident. Ries (1997) indicates that a 1997 survey of state directors reveals that only 7 of the 40 states responding to this survey had the same program name it had 10 years ago. Furthermore, 15 states had undergone more than one name change in the past decade; and 26 do not have the word "vocational" as part of the title for the division or state level office administering vocational education.

The University Council for Vocational Education (UCVE) represents a significant force in preparing teachers and leadership personnel as well as scholars who help guide development of the knowledge base for the field. That organization is presently undergoing a delphi process that will result in a new name not including "vocational education." Further evidence of name changing exists in the title of this publication. *Workforce Education: Issues for the New Century* is an updated title for its preceding counterpart, *Vocational Education in the 1990s: Major Issues* (Pautler, 1990).

In keeping with pragmatism's processes, approval of a name change is also shared by a majority of the membership of the American Vocational Association (AVA) (Ries, 1997). Although there seems no single name representing the value system of a majority of members, there does seem to be an identification of a truth statement that vocational education no longer adequately describes the range of endeavors included under the auspices of AVA members.

The trend favoring a change of name is clear and appropriate. If practice does, in fact, embrace philosophic pragmatism, it has to be open to linking its practices with the processes of its philosophical framework. Vocational education's community of practitioners is moving toward a consensus that a new name facilitates an expanded understanding of the contributions of such educational activity.

Therefore, in keeping with philosophical pragmatism and its processes, a name change is imminent. "Vocational education" is going to be replaced with a term more accurately descriptive of the field. (While it would have been appropriate to reflect a name change throughout this chapter, the authors have used the term vocational education for clarity, but readers should expect to see the term *workforce education* as a dominant term in future writings.)

Changing the name of the field is at the very heart of the philosophic position of what we have heretofore called vocational education. In so doing, it underscores a significant, identifying characteristic of pragmatism and vocational education itself: change. Change, after all, is among the greatest of philosophic certainties for the pragmatist. To accept and even embrace change is necessary for recognition as a philosophic pragmatist, either as an individual or as a field of practice.

This extended discussion on change is to focus on examining the role of pragmatic philosophy in guiding change. Because of the importance change represents in pragmatic philosophy, it sounds repetitive to state that it should guide change. At the same time, the very nature of pragmatic reality, truth, and value are all under the influence of change.

Reality to the pragmatist is subject to change. It is defined and refined through the accumulating experience of individuals and community. As new experiences are acquired, there is a reconstruction of past experience and a changed sense of reality emerges. Individuals become through the process of experiencing and reconstructing experience—a process of change. For vocational educators, this notion of becoming is central to appropriate learning processes. Accordingly, learners are provided opportunities for new, active learning experiences which build on the learners' past experiences. A further role of the teacher is to then assist the learner in reconstructing these experiences as an act of becoming. Reality and change are interlocked.

Truth is like reality. It is subject to change, and it draws on the experiences of the individuals and community. Truth finds its basis through the validation of community. The totality of informed persons, according to the pragmatist, is a valid means whereby truth can be identified. As experience changes and reconstruction of experience occurs, the basis for verification of truth also changes. In short, truth is tentative.

For vocational educators, this understanding of truth is central to the nature of curriculum or what is taught. Vocational education curriculum is a representation of truth. Because curriculum is truth and because truth changes, vocational education curriculum must be in a state of nearly constant review for change to keep pace with changing truth. Since it is not possible to teach all that can be identified as truth in any area of vocational education, it is necessary to carefully select the most appropriate truth for final inclusion in the curriculum of vocational education—a value question.

Value is like reality and truth. They are subject to change and draw on the experiences of individuals and community for validation. Values then represent what it is that a community is willing to settle for. The curriculum of vocational education takes on the mantel of community values as decisions regarding specific goals and purposes for schooling and programs are determined through community-based processes.

Community-based processes are inherent in pragmatic philosophy. Reality is affirmed through a community of individuals sharing experiences and the reconstruction of those experiences. Reality is public and open to inspection and question by all community members. Truth, too, is verified in much the same manner. It is public in nature and validated through the collective experiences of individuals in the community. Because of this, it is generally held that no one individual has a grasp of truth that is greater than the collective truth of the larger community. Values are also a reflection of community and what it holds to be of highest priority. In the final analysis, there is a consistency and coherence among reality, truth, and value in the philosophic position of vocational education. It is pragmatism's framework, then, that provides a reliable and appropriate basis for guiding change and practice into the future for vocational education.

CHANGE, COMMUNITY, AND VOCATIONAL EDUCATION

Change and community are inextricably intertwined in philosophic pragmatism. To the pragmatist, community is essential in verifying reality, truth, and value. At the same time, as these three elements are being verified, the pragmatist accepts that all three are subject to change. However, a fundamental question on the nature of that change must be answered: Is vocational education going to be reactive or proactive?

It is the argument of the authors that the strand of pragmatism favoring proactive best reflects contemporary thinking in vocational education and the communities it serves. With the rate of change occurring in geometrical proportions, waiting to react to change will result in vocational education's products being ineffectively prepared. Clearly, the pragmatic nature of the enterprise mandates a posture reflective of proactive change.

Future vocational educators as proponents of philosophic pragmatism will be striving to produce agents of progressive change, not merely preparing worker-citizens equipped to cope with change in their communities and places of work. Thus, the notion of reconstruction means not just a conceptual rethinking of experiences but a commitment to make organizations, communities, and society-at-large more democratic (Campbell, 1995). And, while pragmatists concerned with reconstructionism may find the revolutionary focus of Marxism seriously flawed, they embrace the perspective in Marx's "comment in the Eighteenth Brumaire: Philosophers have tried to understand the world; the point, however, is to change it" (as cited in Grubb, 1997b, p. 133-134).

While several contemporary school-reform scholars have recognized vocational education as a powerful tool for promoting a more constructivist approach to learning/teaching (Bottoms & Sharpe, 1996; Grubb, 1997a; Raizen, 1989), they have neglected the role vocational education can play in social reconstruction. This is unfortunate because it is the reconstructionist possibilities of vocational education that are critical for contributing to democracy in communities as well as places of work (Bettis & Gregson, 1993; Gregson, 1996; Kincheloe, 1995; Lakes, 1994; Rehm, 1989; Shor, 1988; Simon & Dippo, 1987). Vocational education can provide students the opportunity to learn critically about work as well as how to do work. Through learning about work, students have the opportunity to examine collective struggles of unions, crafts people, and artisans (Herschbach, 1994). Dewey supported such an approach because he felt every generation of students must rediscover democracy through becoming involved in the struggle for freedom, social justice, and equality in places of work and in their respective communities.

RECONSTRUCTIONISM: A CRITICAL STRAND OF PRAGMATISM

In his text, *Understanding John Dewey*, Campbell (1995) stated that Dewey's philosophical view, pragmatism, includes: "(1) a metaphysics that emphasizes process and relations; (2) a naturalistic and evolutionary understanding of human existence; (3) an analysis of intellectual activity as problem-oriented and as benefiting from historically developed methods; and (4) an emphasis upon the democratic reconstruction of society through educational and other institutions" (p. 14).

Currently, numerous scholars concerned with reforming public schools advocate efforts that appear to draw heavily from the first three strands of a "Deweyan" pragmatism. Such reform efforts include but are not limited to: applied academics, experiential and/or contextualized learning, authentic assessment, project-based instruction, problem-based instruction, integrated curriculum, and service-learning. While these efforts may vary from having a strong or nonexistent vocational dimension, other efforts such as technology education, high-school career academies, tech prep programs, school-based enterprises, youth apprenticeship, and the integration of academic and vocational education have been conceptualized and operationalized to reflect these same three strands of Deweyan pragmatism and have been labeled as elements of a "new vocationalism" (Grubb, 1995; Lewis, 1991; Wirth, 1992).

It is exciting that strands of pragmatism, and thus the constructivist and experiential aspects of Dewey's vocationalism, seem to have begun transformation into practice in public schools across the United States (Pauly, Kopp, & Haimson, 1994). Cognitive scientists and other education reformers outside the field of vocational education have contributed greatly to the new vocationalism movement (Berryman & Bailey, 1992; Raizen, 1989; Resnick & Wirt, 1996). Nevertheless, for a comprehensive philosophic position to emerge, the fourth or last strand of a Deweyan pragmatism, reconstructionism, needs to also be reflected in the vision and practices of the future.

THE SOCIAL CONTEXTS OF RECONSTRUCTIONISM: PAST TO PRESENT

Dewey, as well as other pragmatists such as George Herbert Mead (1932) and George Counts (1932), contributed significantly to the literature and our respective communities when they became concerned with problems of "common people" rather than those of philosophers and other intellectuals. They, along with "feminist" pragmatists such as Jane Addams and Ellen Flagg Young, felt a reconstructionist approach was critical to help the most needy. And while they advocated an "education through occupations" for all students rather than just for those entering the world of work directly from school, they also recognized the potential that learning about work, as well as how to do work, had for helping women, people of color, members of the working class, and other marginalized groups. Specifically, they felt vocational education could contribute solutions to problems such as: (a) women working long hours for low wages and still having to be the primary caregivers for young children; (b) youth who worked low-skill, low-wage jobs with little chance for a meaningful career; and (c) hard-laboring workers who regularly confronted physical, mental, and spiritual hardships but lacked any real sense of security or ethic of care from their places of work (Seigfried, 1996).

Though some credit these social pragmatists for a major contribution toward advancement in gender equity, youth labor laws, and worker rights in the United States (e. g., Seigfried, 1996; Wirth, 1980), others conclude such problems have social, political, educational, and economic dimensions, and are pervasive in nature (Kincheloe, 1995; Simon, Dippo, & Schenke, 1991). For instance, current data suggest that, in what some have labeled the post-industrial era for the United States (e.g., Bell, 1973; Block, 1990; Smart, 1992): (a) a feminization of poverty has occurred (Aronowitz & DiFazio, 1994; Becker, 1993); (b) a high percentage of youth have considerable difficulty transitioning from school to meaningful, rewarding work (Bettis, 1996a; King & Peart, 1996; Mortimer, 1996); and (c) workers are experiencing a greater disparity in earnings and income, more frequent displacement and downward mobility, and a de-skilling of work due to new technologies, and have also become more dependent on contingent and part-time work (Aronowitz & DiFazio, 1994; Harrison & Bluestone, 1988; Moore, 1996).

U.S. citizens are arguably currently experiencing both positive and negative consequences in the shift from an industrial to a post-industrial society (e.g., Bettis, 1996b). For instance, while data supports Braverman's (1974) argument that technology and automation de-skill work, data also support the notion that technological innovation "upskills" work (Berryman & Bailey, 1992; Zuboff, 1988). There is evidence to suggest that future workers, in upskilled environments, will work in less defined environments and thus will need broader skills such as creative thinking, decision making, and cooperative problem solving (Berryman & Bailey, 1992; Carnevale, Gainer, & Meltzer, 1988; Commission on the Skills of the American Workforce, 1990; Samper & Lakes, 1994; Wirth, 1992).

Though much has appeared in the literature on how the nature of work is rapidly changing, it appears that deskilling and upskilling are occurring simultaneously. Further, though many social reconstructionists have supported upskilling work because they feel it can make a contribution toward making work more meaningful, they have now begun to recognize that upskilled jobs can also overwork employees to the extent that they lose leisure time, self-direction, and ultimately quality of work life (e.g., Aronowitz & DiFazio, 1994; Kincheloe, 1995).

Several contemporary pragmatists support the Deweyan notion that vocational education should contribute to making places of work and society more democratic and humane as well as productive. In addition, some of these scholars, who have recently tried to make meaning of post-industrial places of work, have concluded that places of work have probably become neither more nor less democratic. While numerous places of work are becoming organized as democratic enterprises where workers solve meaningful problems and have a real voice in the making of decisions (e.g., Krimerman & Lindenfeld, 1992; Noble, 1990), the rhetoric of democracy in the workplace seems to far exceed the practice (Kincheloe, 1995; Lakes, 1994; Murray, 1992).

RECONSTRUCTIONIST ROLE OF VOCATIONAL EDUCATION IN A DEMOCRACY

Though Dewey (as cited by Archambault, 1964) recognized that "'education' even in its widest sense cannot do everything" (p. 308), he did maintain that education plays a critical role in breaking free from unthinking social and institutional reproduction. Dewey (1916) envisioned a reconstructionist role for vocational education in a democracy: "It must be the aim of vocational education to take part in correcting unfair privilege and unfair deprivation, not to perpetuate them" (pp. 119-120). Contemporary social reconstructionists have expanded upon Dewey's concept of democratic education by maintaining that vocational educators should "educate in ways that go against the grain of hierarchical, oppressive workplaces and produce agents of progressive change" (Carnoy & Levin, 1985, p.16).

Reconstructionists, then, have conceptualized vocational education as potentially a powerful tool for the "humanization of work, workplace democracy, and in general, the more equitable distribution of knowledge" (Rubenson & Schutze, 1995, p. 114). The reconstructionist strand of pragmatism is explicit in that one of the purposes of vocational education should be to transform places of work into more democratic, learning organizations rather than perpetuating existing workplace practices.

However, some contemporary pragmatists, who embrace the philosophical position of reconstructionism, have also recognized that the instrumental contribution that can be made by vocational education does not inherently prevent the reconstructionist contribution. These reconstructionists adopt Dewey's position by rejecting the historical dualism of either a liberal (i.e., liberating) or a narrow, solely technocratic education (e.g., Wirth, 1992). They conceptualize instrumentalism considerably broader than did Snedden and Prosser and, like Dewey, feel that instrumentalism can and should have potentially liberating qualities. Lewis (1997), for example, argues for combating this historical dualism by suggesting that vocational education in the context of public schools should be both liberal and vocational. When thoughtfully conceptualized and enacted, the borders of liberalism and vocationalism can be crossed and sometimes blurred.

While Lewis's (1997) position is reasonable because it differentiates between the role of secondary and postsecondary education in a democracy, reconstructionists feel that the subject matter of vocational education must include rights and responsibilities, and relationships, as well as technical skill—whether it is experienced in public schools or in a postsecondary context. Admittedly, the nature of the post-industrial era is such that there is, and will continue to be, an increased need for the technical training and retraining of adults (Gordon, Morgan, & Ponticell, 1995; Hirsch & Wagner, 1995).

Nevertheless, it is the reconstructionist position that vocational educators, as opposed to technical trainers, have a moral obligation to help adults as well as youth to reach their capacity to change the material and social conditions of their lives. Some research also suggests that while vocational education students want to find and keep a decent job, "they also want an education beyond technical and vocational training . . . an education that would help them better control their lives, that would give them the tools to understand who they are and how they relate to the wider social structure" (Raissiguier, 1994, p. 166).

Thus, at least some reconstructionists contend that experiences in vocational education should provide opportunities for spiritual, physical, social, and political, as well as occupational, growth for all learners (Auerbach, 1990; Shor, 1988). To accomplish this, pragmatists who recognize the critical role of reconstructionism have advocated that vocational educators (a) encourage student voice; (b) help students to relate to work from a critical rather than solely a technical stance; (c) emphasize active student participation through liberatory dialogue; (d) seek to develop the same skills that are required to become an active citizen in a democratic society; and (e) combat social reproduction through teaching skills, knowledge, and values essential in the preparation of students for higher-status and greater-income employment (Bettis & Gregson, 1993; Gregson, 1994b; Kinchloe, 1995; Lakes, 1994; Rehm, 1989; Simon, Dippo, & Schenke, 1991).

CONCLUSION: A PRAGMATIC NEW VOCATIONALISM OR WORKFORCE EDUCATION FOR THE TWENTY-FIRST CENTURY

While pragmatists with a reconstructionist orientation are concerned with the content or subject matter of vocational education, they are also interested in how vocational education is learned/taught. Such concern and interest demonstrates the strong interrelationship among all the strands or dimensions of pragmatism.

Contemporary pragmatists reject Counts's (1932) contention that democratic content should be taught through an indoctrinational approach. They contend that Counts's advocacy of indoctrination violates basic democratic principles essential to the freedom desired in educational experiences (Elias & Merriam, 1995). As Dewey (1938) explained in addressing critiques of his vision for democratizing education, an indoctrinational approach to teaching contributes to a social docility and passiveness that makes learning experiences miseducative.

Dewey (1938) also spoke to the misconception that the principles of pragmatism supported a laissez-faire approach to learning. It was his position that teachers committed to transforming the philosophy of pragmatism into practice would not allow their students to do as they wished. Rather the pragmatist position would be that teachers have an intellectual as well as a moral obligation to provide a directive role with a general destination for their classes. However, they would not act as authoritarian figures in seeking that destination and would, in fact, encourage alternative perspectives—thus avoiding indoctrination.

While the reconstructionist strand of pragmatism legitimizes social action as a possibility for philosophers, it is also compatible with the other strands or dimensions of pragmatism discussed in this chapter. Pragmatists value human experience far more than authoritarian ways for gaining knowledge and understanding. Consequently, other dimensions of pragmatism such as student-centeredness and experimentation complement the notion that vocational education can and should contribute to social and industrial change.

Many contemporary scholars have embraced some of Dewey's democratic positions (e.g., Grubb, 1995; Wirth, 1992). However, they have also drawn and benefitted from the cognitive science literature. The following framework for facilitating learning then is based on sound pedagogical reasons as well as on pragmatic principles.

The overarching purposes of vocational education should be to help facilitate the growth of learners who are competent as: problem solvers, collaborators, makers of meaning, lifelong learners, worker-citizens adaptable to change and active as change agents, and practitioners of democratic processes. This is not to say that specific outcomes or purposes of vocational education developed through public processes shouldn't be determined. That would be contrary to the pragmatist's philosophy. Rather, these are the values against which all educational activity should be measured.

When the above framework and all the strands of pragmatism are considered, it becomes easier to understand why Dewey (1916) considered issues of democracy at both the "macro" (or societal) level and the "micro" (or classroom) level. Moving from the micro to the macro was important to Dewey because he believed that the skills students learn from being active participants in the classroom are the same skills needed for persons to become active worker-citizens in society.

Currently there seems an abundance of evidence that new opportunities have emerged for reconceiving the purpose and scope of vocational education (Grubb, 1995; Howard & Scheffler, 1995; Wirth, 1992). Further, current social conditions, the state of working America, and the state of schooling dictate that past practices be questioned and differing philosophical schools of thought be given serious consideration.

Nevertheless, it is the position of the authors of this paper that for vocational educators to have a greater impact on places of work and on society, they must first give serious thought to what they believe should be the purpose(s) of vocational education. This is not to suggest that all vocational educators should agree to a single set of aims, purposes, and beliefs. Such uniformity is unlikely and probably undesirable since it could discourage critical thinking about and reflection on important issues.

However, as evidenced by the references cited in this chapter, pragmatism has various strands or dimensions and allows for considerable diversity. Further, pragmatism continues to evolve. Critiques from contemporary perspectives, such as feminism, phenomenology, analytic philosophy, existentialism, critical theory, action theory, hermeneutics, and postmodernism, have promoted reflection and action among some pragmatists and, consequently, have helped to expand the breadth and depth of pragmatism (Campbell, 1995; Seigfried, 1996). For example, Richard Rorty (1980), a self-identified pragmatist, has critiqued and reworked pragmatism to the extent that it has been enriched and rediscovered. These contributions have not only expanded pragmatism but they have also added further support to the purposes of education identified earlier.

Our position is that the purposes of schooling (i.e., to help facilitate the growth of learners who are competent as: problem solvers, collaborators, makers of meaning, lifelong learners, worker-citizens adaptable to change and active as change agents, and practitioners of democratic processes) are appropriate for all of public education, not just vocational education. Transforming this position into practice is tantamount to implementing the philosophic position presented in this chapter.

In the final analysis, however, the task of making vocational education more sound philosophically does not fall to academicians but to vocational-technical teachers and administrators working daily with students. This chapter has aimed to contribute to a rethinking of practice for the future, promote reflection about what vocational educators should do, and bring some clarity to the philosophical issues currently confronting vocational education.

References

Anthony, R. N. (1965). *Planning and control systems, a framework for analysis*. Boston, MA: Harvard University.

Archambault, R. D. (1974) (Ed.). *John Dewey on education*. Chicago & London: The University of Chicago Press.

Aronowitz, S., & DiFazio, W. (1994). *The jobless future*. Minneapolis: University of Minnesota Press.

Auerbach, E. (1990). Toward a transformative model of worker education: A Freirean perspective. In S. H. London, E. R. Tarr, & J. F. Wilson (Eds.), *The reeducation of the American working class* (pp. 225-238). New York: Greenwood Press.

Barlow, M.L. (1975). *Policymaking for vocational education*. Los Angeles: University of California.

Becker, G. S. (1993). (3rd. Ed). *Human capital: A theoretical and empirical analysis, with special reference to education*. Chicago & London: The University of Chicago Press.

Bell, D. (1973). *The coming of post-industrial society*. New York: Basic Books, Inc.

Berryman, S. E., & Bailey, T. R. (1992). *The double helix of education and the economy*. New York: The Institute on Education and the Economy.

Bettis, P. J. (1996a). Urban students, liminality, and the post-industrial context. *Sociology of Education, 69* (2), 105-125.

Bettis, P. J. (1996b). Urban abstraction in a central city high school. *The Urban Review, 28* (4), 309-335.

Bettis, P. J., & Gregson, J. A. (1993). Democratizing secondary vocational education: Examples of critical pedagogy. *Journal of Vocational and Technical Education, 10* (1), 4-14.

Block, F. (1990). *Postindustrial possibilities: A critique of economic discourse*. Berkeley: University of California.

Bottoms, G., & Sharpe, D. (1996). *Teaching for understanding through integration of academic and technical education*. Atlanta, GA: Southern Regional Education Board.

Braverman, H. (1974). *Labor and monopoly capital: The degradation of work in the twentieth century*. New York: Monthly Review Press.

Campbell, J. (1995). *Understanding John Dewey*. Chicago & LaSalle, IL: Open Court Publishing Company.

Carnoy, M., & Levin, H. M. (1985). *Schooling and work in the democratic state*. Stanford, CA: Stanford University Press.

Counts, G. S. (1932). *Dare the school build a new social order?* New York: John Day.

Dewey, J. (1916). *Democracy and education*. New York: The Free Press.

Dewey, J. (1938). *Experience and education*. New York: Collier Books.

Elias, J. L., & Merriam, S. B. (2nd ed.). (1995). *Philosophical foundations of adult education*. Malabar, FL: Krieger Publishing Company.

Evans, R.N., & Herr, E. L. (2nd ed.). (1978). *Foundations of vocational education*. Columbus, OH: Charles E. Merrill Publishing Company.

Gregson, J. A. (1994a). From critical theory to critical practice: Transformative vocational classrooms. In R. D. Lakes (Ed.), *Critical education for work: Multidisciplinary approaches* (pp. 161-182). Norwood, NJ: Ablex Publishing Corporation.

Gregson, J. A. (1994b). Posing problems to raise student consciousness about values, attitudes and worker responsibilities: A democratic possibility. *Journal of Vocational Education Research, 19* (4), 13-35.

Gregson, J. A. (1996). Continuing the discourse: Problems, politics, and possibilities of vocational curriculum. *Journal of Vocational Education Research, 21* (1), 35-64.

Grubb, W. N. (1995). *Education through occupations in American high schools: Vol. I. Approaches to integrating academic and vocational education. Vol. II. The challenges of implementing curriculum integration.* New York: Teachers College Press.

Grubb, W. N. (1997). Not there yet: Prospects and problems for "education through occupations." *Journal of Vocational Education Research, 22* (2), 77-94.

Grubb, W. N. (1997). Finding common ground: A brief response. *Journal of Vocational Education Research, 22* (2), 133-139.

Harrison, B., & Bluestone, B. (1988). *The great U turn*. New York: Basic Books, Inc.

Herschbach, D. R. (1994). The right to organize: Implications for preparing students for work. In R. D. Lakes (Ed.), *Critical education for work: Multidisciplinary approaches* (pp. 83-94). Norwood, NJ: Ablex Publishing Corporation.

Howard, V. A., & Scheffler, I. (1995). *Work, education, and leadership: Essays in the philosophy of education*. New York: Peter Lang Publishing, Inc.

Kincheloe, J. L. (1995). *Toil and trouble: Good work, smart workers, and the integration of academic and vocational education*. New York: Peter Lang Publishing, Inc.

King, A. J., & Peart, M.J. (1996). Factors inhibiting the transition of youth to work and to adulthood (pp. 162-177). In B. Galaway and J. Hudson (Eds.), *Youth in transition: Perspectives on research and policy*. Toronto, Ontario: Thompson Educational Publishing, Inc.

Krimerman, L., & Lindenfeld, F. (1992). *When workers decide: Workplace democracy takes root in North America*. Philadelphia, PA: New Society Publishers.

Lakes, R. D. (1994). Education for democratic community and work: An interview with Len Krimerman. In R. D. Lakes (Ed.), *Critical education for work: Multidisciplinary approaches* (pp. 181-190). Norwood, NJ: Ablex Publishing Corporation.

Law, C. (1994). *Tech prep education: A total quality approach*. Lancaster, PA: Technomic Publications.

Lewis, T. (1997). Towards a liberal vocational education. *Journal of Philosophy of Education, 31* (3), 489-501.

Lewis, T. (1991). Difficulties attending the new vocationalism in the USA. *Journal of Philosophy of Education, 25* (1), 95-108.

Mead, G. H. (1932). *The philosophy of the present.* Chicago, IL: University of Chicago Press.

Miller, M. D. (1985). *Principles and a philosophy for vocational education.* Columbus, OH: National Center for Research in Vocational Education.

Moore, T. S. (1996). *The disposable workforce.* New York: Walter de Gruter, Inc.

Mortimer, J. T. (1996). U.S. research on the school-to-work transition. (pp. 32-45). In B. Galaway and J. Hudson (Eds.), *Youth in transition: Perspectives on research and policy.* Toronto, Ontario: Thompson Educational Publishing, Inc.

Murray, R. (1992). Fordism and post-fordism. In C. Jencks (Ed.), *The post-modern reader.* New York: St. Martin's Press.

Noble, D. D. (1990). High-tech skills: The latest corporate assault on workers. In S. H. London, E. R. Tarr, & J. F. Wilson (Eds.), *The re-education of the American working class* (pp. 131-144). New York: Greenwood Press.

Pautler, A. J. Jr. (Ed.). (1990). *Vocational education in the 1990s: Major issues.* Ann Arbor, MI: Prakken Publications, Inc.

Pauly, E., Kopp, H., & Haimson, J. (1994). *Home-grown lessons: Innovative programs linking work and high school.* New York and San Francisco: Manpower Demonstration Research Corporation.

Raissiguier, C. (1994). *Becoming women becoming workers: Identity formation in a French vocational school.* Albany, NY: State University New York Press.

Raizen, S. A. (1989). *Reforming education for work: A cognitive science perspective.* Berkeley, CA: National Center for Research in Vocational Education.

Rehm, M. (1989). Emancipatory vocational education: Pedagogy for the work of individuals and society. *Journal of Education, 171* (3), 109-123.

Resnick, L. B., & Wirt, J. G. (Eds.). (1996). *Linking school and work: Roles for standards and assessment.* San Francisco,CA: Jossey-Bass Inc.

Ries, E. (1997). To "V" or Not to "V." *Techniques, 72* (8), 32-37.

Roberts, R.W. (1957). *Vocational and practical arts education: History, development, and principles.* New York: Harper & Row Publishers.

Rorty, R. (1980). Pragmatism, relativism, and irrationalism. In *Consequences of Pragmatism* (pp. 160-175). Minneapolis: University of Minnesota Press.

Rubenson, K., & Schutze, H. G. (1995). Learning at and through the workplace: A review of participation and adult learning theory. In D. Hirsch & D. A. Wagner (Eds.), *What makes workers learn: The role of incentives in workplace education and training.* Cresskill, NJ: Hampton Press, Inc.

Samper, M. D., & Lakes, R. D. (1994). Work education for the next century: Beyond skills training. In R. D. Lakes (Ed.), *Critical education for work: Multidisciplinary approaches* (pp. 95-108). Norwood, NJ: Ablex Publishing Corporation.

Shor, I. (1988). Working hands and critical minds: A Paulo Freire model for job training. *Journal of Education, 170* (2), 103-121.

Seigfried, C. H. (1996). *Pragmatism and feminism: Reweaving the social fabric.* Chicago & London: The University of Chicago Press.

Simon, R. I., & Dippo, D. (1987). What schools can do: Designing programs for work education that challenge the wisdom of experience. *Journal of Education, 169* (3), 101-116.

Simon, R. I., Dippo, D., & Schenke, A. (1991). *Learning work: A critical pedagogy of work education.* New York: Bergin & Garvey.

Smart, B. (1992). *Modern conditions, postmodern controversies.* New York: Routledge.

Wirth, A. G. (1992). *Education and work for the year 2000.* San Francisco, CA: Jossey-Bass Publishers.

Wirth, A. G. (1983). *Productive work—in industry and schools: Becoming persons again.* Lanham, MD: University Press of America, Inc.

Wirth, A. G. (1980). *Education in the technological society.* Washington: University Press of America.

Zuboff, S. (1988). *In the age of the smart machine.* New York: Basic Books, Inc.

***Melvin D. Miller** is professor and director, school of occupational and Adult Education, emeritus, Oklahoma State University, Stillwater. **James A. Gregson** is associate professor, Oklahoma State University, Stillwater.*

LEGISLATIVE REVIEW OF WORKFORCE EDUCATION

By Michelle Sarkees-Wircenski and Jerry L. Wircenski

The development of a formal, organized, comprehensive system of vocational education in the United States has been a gradual one beginning in the late 1800s. Since that time, Congress has actively been involved in passing federal legislation in support of vocational education with the passage of the Morrill Act of 1862. Early federal legislation began as an attempt to address the urgent need in the United States for individuals with skills in agriculture and the mechanic arts around the 1900s. The following brief overview of federal vocational education legislation is synthesized from historical research conducted over the past two decades (Evans, 1971; Nystrom & Bayne, 1979; Calhoun & Finch, 1982; Scott & Sarkees-Wircenski, 1996).

FEDERAL ACTS AND AMENDMENTS

Morrill Act of 1862—Known as the Land Grant Act, this legislation gave states land that could be sold or leased to raise money to establish at least one college for the purpose of offering a combination of liberal and practical education preparation. The intent of Congress was to institute this new vocational curriculum to emphasize agriculture and mechanical arts as an acceptable means of encouraging economic growth to ensure the national welfare. Land grant colleges and universities were structured to provide an education to a wider range of individuals, which set the stage for the acceptance of vocational education in this country.

Hatch Act of 1887—This legislation, known as the Experimental Stations Act, provided funds for each state to sponsor agricultural experiment stations where research could be conducted. The pertinent and practical information from this research was to be used to assist people in applying new agricultural information and skills in agricultural science.

Morrill Act of 1890—The Morrill Act, also known as the Maintenance Act, authorized the sale or lease of public lands to be used to provide additional support for the agriculture and mechanical arts programs established under the Morrill Act of 1862.

Adams Act of 1906 (Public Law 47)—This legislation increased the appropriations of funds provided to states for the operation of the agricultural research stations established under the Hatch Act of 1887.

Nelson Amendments to Morrill Act of 1907 (PL 242)—The Nelson Amendments increased funding for support of land grant colleges established under the Morrill Act of 1862. A portion of the funds were to be spent to prepare instructors to teach agriculture and mechanical arts.

Smith-Lever Act of 1914 (PL 95)—Also known as the Agriculture Extension Act, it established a program of cooperative extension work in agriculture and home economics. It provided American homemakers and farmers not attending college with needed instruction, practical demonstrations, and project work in the home and on the farms. The states were required to finance half the cost of these extension programs, thus establishing the first practice of "50-50 matching" of federal and state dollars.

Smith-Hughes Act of 1917 (PL 64-347)—This landmark legislation, also known as the Vocational Act of 1917, established the pattern of federal/state/local collaboration in initiating and implementing public vocational education programs of less than baccalaureate level. It represented a national endorsement of vocational education in an attempt to cope with twentieth-century problems of industrialization, automation, urbanization, and the drastic need for skilled labor. It provided funding for agriculture, trade and industry, and home economics at the secondary level. Under this legislation, vocational education was designed to be an experience of less than college level for individuals over age 14 who wanted training during the day and for individuals over age 16 who wanted training in the evening.

In addition to establishing funds for appropriated provisions enacted, the Smith-Hughes Act also established controls over use and administration of these funds. To share in the funding, every state had to designate a state board with power and responsibility to administer the monies in collaboration with the Federal Board of Vocational Education. Key components of the Smith-Hughes Act were:

- creation of a Federal Board of Vocational Education;
- creation of state boards of vocational education to govern programs cooperatively with the Federal Board of Vocational Education;
- a mandate to develop state plans containing the type of vocational education to be delivered in the state;
- requirement of an annual report to the Federal Board of Vocational Education from each state vocational education system;
- provisions for annual state funding to a maximum of $7,000,000 for promotion of agriculture, home economics, and trade and industrial programs;
- provisions for annual appropriations for (a) a 50-50 federal/state responsibility for payment of salaries of teachers, supervisors, and directors of vocational education; (b) preparation of teachers in agriculture, home economics, and trade and industrial areas; and (c) support for the activities of the Federal Board of Vocational Education;
- a mandate that states cooperate with local school districts to fund high-quality vocational education instruction;
- a mandate that federal vocational funds be placed under public control and supervision;
- granting the Federal Board of Vocational Education control over state programs through categorical assistance with narrowly defined limitations; and
- a mandate that vocational education be provided to individuals who sought training in a selected vocational area, were employed, and wanted to develop greater skill proficiency, and/or were employed and wished to advance in their chosen occupational area.

Smith-Sears Act of 1918 (PL 178)—Looking for a realistic choice for returning service men and women, Congress authorized funds to establish retraining programs for disabled service personnel returning from duty after World War I.

Smith-Bankhead Act of 1920 (PL 236)—This legislation, also known as the Federal Rehabilitation Act, established rehabilitation programs for nonmilitary disabled individuals moving into civilian employment.

Smith-Fess Act of 1920 (PL 236)—This legislation, also known as the Industrial Rehabilitation Act, provided federal assistance for vocational rehabilitation to individuals who were industry-disabled and established a precedent that would result in additional vocational rehabilitation legislation during later years.

George-Reed Act of 1929 (PL 70-702)—This was a supplemental authorization of funds for home economics and agricultural education, to be divided equally between the two for five years. The authorizations ranged from $500,000 in 1930 to $2,500,000 in 1934. Allocation of funds in this act differed from the way funds were provided previously. Farm population, rather than rural population, was used as a basis for allocating agricultural education funds whereas funds for home economics education were allocated on the basis of rural population as opposed to urban population. No additional funds were authorized for trade and industrial education.

George-Ellzey Act of 1934 (PL 73-245)—Replacing the earlier George-Reed Act, it increased supplemental funding for home economics and agricultural programs. It also reestablished support for trade and industrial education programs terminated as a result of the George-Reed Act of 1929. Authorized funds were divided equally among the three program areas. Funds authorized in this legislation were in addition to the continuing funds appropriated under the Smith-Hughes Act.

George-Deen Act of 1936 (PL 673)—This legislation significantly increased the role of the federal government in vocational education. It was a supplemental authorization which increased funds for home economics, agricultural, and trade and industrial education. Annual appropriations authorized for vocational education were to be equally distributed among the three program areas. This act broadened the scope of vocational education program areas eligible for annual appropriations to include distributive education. This was the first act where federal vocational education funds were provided for individuals residing in territories held by the United States. In addition, money above that provided in the Smith-Hughes Act was authorized for teacher education programs.

Vocational Education for National Defense (1940-1946)—This series of 10 legislative acts, passed from 1940-1946, represented a vehicle for utilizing vocational education to prepare individuals for the war effort and identified vocational education as a strong framework for national defense training. Total funding by the federal government was provided to vocational programs that transferred over to national defense purposes.

Servicemen's Readjustment Act of 1944 (PL 78-346)—This GI Bill of Rights assisted veterans of World War II to readjust to civilian life. The cost of education and subsistence was provided for many World War II veterans. To be eligible for these funds, veterans selected the type of education and/or training they wanted to pursue and then applied for admission to a recognized program. Later, similar legislation was passed to provide benefits to veterans of the Korean War and the Vietnam War.

George-Barden Act of 1946 (PL 79-586)—Known as the Vocational Act of 1946, this was a supplemental authorization that increased funding for existing vocational education and further expanded the role of the federal government in vocational education. With this act, annual appropriations increased from $1.5 million under the Smith-Hughes Act to over $28 million. Contributing to passage of this act was the fact that thousands of returning World War II veterans needed to develop appropriate skills for the rapidly expanding economy. The act also extended eligible funds to the Office of Vocational Education in Washington and to vocational education for the fishery trades. More decision-making control was given to state and local education agencies regarding how monies provided by this act could be used, thus relaxing tight federal control over expenditures. This trend continues even today. In 1956, amendments were added to this act to include practical nursing, which thereafter received an annual authorization of funds. In 1962, an annual authorization was added for area vocational programs.

Health Amendments Act of 1956 (PL 84-911)—The Health Amendments Act of 1956 authorized funds to provide more nurses for the expanding health care system. Practical nursing was also added as an area which could be supported with federal vocational funds.

Fishery Amendment, George-Barden Act of 1956 (PL 84-911)—This legislation further promoted the fishing industry, with an emphasis on its distribution processes. Funding to support vocational education for fishery trades was allocated according to the size of the fishing industry in each state.

National Defense Education Act of 1958 (PL 85-864)—This was a response to the launching of Russian satellite Sputnik I and to the subsequent review of our country's development (or lack of) in the technical and scientific areas. This was the first act which stressed the importance of science, mathematics, foreign language, and technical competencies in preparing individuals for the workforce. The primary population served by this act was at the postsecondary level. Key components of the act were: creation of and funding for operation of postsecondary area schools in each state; provision of funds to establish and maintain vocational schools, geographic regions, and occupations not being adequately served by existing vocational programs; provision of vocational education and related training for youth, adults, and older persons; and provision of related instruction for apprentices, designed to prepare them for employment as skilled workers or technicians in technical or scientific areas.

Area Redevelopment Act of 1961 (PL 87-27)—This provided opportunities for retraining to individuals in economically depressed regions of the United States. Trainees were encouraged to enroll and stay in training programs through subsistence payments. Monies were allocated to support existing vocational education programs and vocational training programs which provided training for individuals residing in economically depressed areas.

Manpower Development and Training Act (MDTA) of 1962 (PL 87-415)—This was designed to provide training opportunities for underemployed and unemployed individuals based on specific training needs identified by the Department of Labor. Monies were authorized to be spent over three years on training programs that would be administered through existing state agencies for vocational education.

Vocational Education Act of 1963 (PL 88-210)—Also known as the Perkins-Morse Bill, this act signaled the initial total commitment of federal government to vocational education in this nation. It was designed to provide all individuals with access to vocational education or retraining in areas where employment opportunities exist. The act was intended to maintain, extend, and improve existing vocational education programs, to develop and initiate new vocational programs, and to provide part-time employment for youths so they could continue vocational training full-time. Key components of the act were:

• 90 percent of funds were allocated based on the population of each state;

• funds were to be spent for (a) vocational education for high school students, (b) vocational education for individuals who have completed or discontinued high school but are available to prepare for employment on a full-time basis, (c) vocational education for individuals already employed but in need of training or retraining to reach employment stability or advancement, (d) vocational education for individuals who have academic, socioeconomic, or other handicaps that prevent them from succeeding in regular vocational programs, (e) 10 percent of the funds to be spent on research and development of programs to serve handicapped individuals who could not succeed in regular vocational education programs, (f) construction of area vocational schools, and (g) teacher training, vocational guidance, job placement, curriculum development, and state leadership to assure the quality of vocational programs;

• a definition of "vocational education" as

well as the different types of area vocational schools;

• establishment of an Advisory Committee on Vocational Education in the Office of Education;

• ending strict specific categorical funding to vocational programs by allowing states the flexibility to transfer or combine categorical training allotments to meet their specific needs;

• establishment of an Advisory Council on Vocational Education to periodically prepare reports on progress of vocational programs in the country; and

• creation of work-study to allow vocational students, especially those with financial need, to work so that they could begin or continue their participation in vocational education.

Vocational Education Amendments of 1968 (PL 90-576)—This legislation canceled all previous vocational legislation with the exception of the Smith-Hughes Act. The primary purpose of this act was to provide access to appropriate training and retraining for all citizens in the country. Millions of federal dollars were appropriated for vocational education to be used for high school and postsecondary students, including those who completed or left high school, those in the labor market in need of retraining, and those with academic, socio-economic, or other handicaps.

Key components of the amendments were: creation of a 21-member National Advisory Council; creation of state and local advisory councils; funding for research to be conducted within states; funding for exemplary programs and projects focused on transitioning from school to work; funding for design or improvement of vocational education curricula; establishment of funds for vocational education leadership and professional development; funding for work-study programs for financially disadvantaged vocational students; funding for consumer and homemaking education; funding to support a teacher/industry exchange program for vocational instructors to increase their occupational competencies; and a requirement for state plans to provide more detail as a control over local plans.

Education Amendments of 1972 (PL 92-318)—These amendments continued support of programs identified in the Vocational Education Act of 1963 and introduced several new provisions, such as a new definition of vocational education that allowed federal dollars to be spent for industrial arts programs and for training volunteer firefighters. Special programs for serving disadvantaged individuals were also initiated. Separate titles of this act established the National Institute of Education and provided funds for expanded occupational education course offerings at the postsecondary level. This act required states to complete a comprehensive plan for delivery of postsec-ondary vocational programs. A Bureau of Occupational and Adult Education was instituted in the U.S. Office of Education to help with the expansion of postsecondary programs.

Comprehensive Employment and Training Act of 1973 (PL 93-203)—This was a consolidation of earlier manpower legislation dating back to the 1960s. Its purpose was to decentralize manpower programs and make them more efficient and responsive to local employment needs. The concept of prime sponsors was introduced as a vehicle to receive block grants to be used to operate training programs to meet labor market needs in the local geographic area. Established vocational education programs often received funds from this piece of legislation to provide these training programs.

Education Amendments of 1976 (PL 94-482)—This legislation extended and further revised the Vocational Education Act of 1963 to (a) extend, improve, and maintain existing programs of vocational education, (b) develop new programs of vocational education, (c) overcome sex discrimination and sex stereotyping, and (d) provide part-time employment to youths who need earnings to continue their vocational training full-time. Key components of these amendments were:

• mandate for each state to name a state board/agency to assume responsibility for administering all vocational education programs;

- mandate development of a five-year state plan for vocational education;
- mandate an annual program plan and accountability report for each fiscal year;
- mandate each state to develop an evaluation system to determine vocational programs' effectiveness in the state;
- continue funding for innovative programs, especially those (a) in urban settings with a high concentration of economically disadvantaged individuals, (b) for training unemployed and unskilled workers, (c) for training limited-English-speaking individuals, and (d) for occupational discovery programs for youth with academic or socioeconomic problems;
- emphasize providing professional development opportunities for (a) experienced vocational education personnel to become involved full-time in advanced study, (b) certified teachers of other subjects to become vocational teachers if their background includes experience in a vocational field, and (c) individuals from business and industry to become vocational teachers to share their experience with students;
- emphasize improving bilingual vocational education opportunities for students who have limited English-speaking ability;
- continue funding for consumer and homemaking education;
- mandate establishment of a national vocational education data reporting system;
- establish the National Occupational Information Coordinating Committee (NOICC) and a system of State Occupational Information Coordinating Committees (SOICCs);
- mandate each state to establish a state board/agency to be responsible for administering all public vocational programs in the state;
- facilitate improvement of vocational guidance and counseling programs;
- establish set-aside funding for programs to assist individuals from special populations enrolled in vocational education programs, including handicapped learners, disadvantaged individuals, and persons of limited English proficiency.

Comprehensive Employment and Training Act (CETA) Amendments of 1978 (PL 95-524)—This revised previous manpower legislation. Greater emphasis was on using existing services and facilities, including existing vocational education facilities, to provide training programs to prepare people for the labor force. Vocational boards and prime sponsors were required to consult with other agencies when developing the five-year plan for vocational education and training.

Job Training Partnership Act of 1982 (PL 97-300)—This major revision of the Comprehensive Employment and Training Act was intended to increase the role of the private sector in the training and employment of disadvantaged youth and unskilled adults. Special provisions were also made for training programs for summer youth employment, dislocated workers, older workers, native Americans, migrant and seasonal farm workers, and veterans. This act emphasized more local planning and involvement in vocational education, more active involvement from the private sector in vocational education programs, funds for outreach to disadvantaged individuals, and additional services to be provided to disadvantaged individuals (e.g., vocational exploration, basic skills training, on-the-job training, bilingual training, job search assistance, job counseling, and follow-up training).

Carl D. Perkins Vocational Education Act of 1984 (PL 98-524)—This legislation, also known as the Perkins Act, had these purposes:

- Assist the states to expand, improve, modernize, and develop quality vocational education programs to meet needs of the nation's existing and future workforce for marketable skills, and to improve productivity and promote economic growth.
- Assure that individuals inadequately served under vocational education programs are assured access to quality vocational education programs, especially individuals who are disadvantaged, who are handicapped, men and women entering nontraditional occupations, adults in need of training and retraining, individuals who are single parents or

homemakers, individuals with limited English proficiency, and those incarcerated in correctional institutions.

• Promote greater cooperation between public agencies and the private sector in preparing individuals for employment, in promoting the quality of vocational education in the states, and in making the system more responsive to the United States labor market.

• Improve the academic foundation of vocational students and aid in application of newer technologies, including use of computers, in relationship to occupational goals and employment.

• Provide vocational education services to train, upgrade, and retrain employed and unemployed workers in new skills in demand.

• Assist each state to use a full range of supportive services, guidance and placement services, and special programs to achieve the act's basic purposes.

• Assist the most economically depressed areas of a state to raise occupational and employment competencies of its citizens.

• Improve the effectiveness of consumer and homemaking education, and reduce the limiting effects of sex-role stereotyping on job skills, careers, occupations, and levels of competency.

• Authorize national programs designed to meet designated vocational education needs, and to strengthen the vocational education research process.

The philosophy reflected in this act was that the local community is the best entity to administer vocational education programs. This legislation encouraged implementation of vehicles at the local level to make decisions regarding vocational education in general as well as those which promote collaboration between public-school and private-sector needs through vocational education and training programs.

Key components of the act were:

• a change in the time-frame of state plans from an annual plan and five-year plan format to a plan covering two years;

• a requirement for states to submit an annual progress report based on stated objectives rather than a separate accountability report to be used as a tool in planning and improving vocational programs;

• a mandate for a national assessment of vocational education to be conducted by the National Institute of Education, the results of which were to be reported to Congress by January 1, 1989;

• a mandate that the following services be provided for each handicapped or disadvantaged individual enrolled in vocational education programs: (a) information about local vocational education opportunities, (b) assessment of each individual's interests, abilities, and special needs, (c) guidance, counseling, and career development activities, (d) counseling services to facilitate transition from school to employment, and (e) adaptation of curriculum, instruction, equipment, and facilities to meet specific needs of each learner;

• a mandate that equal access in recruitment, enrollment, and placement activities will be provided to handicapped and disadvantaged individuals to the full range of vocational programs available to all students, including occupationally specific courses of study, cooperative education, and apprenticeship programs;

• specification that vocational education programs and activities for handicapped individuals are provided in the least restrictive environment and, when appropriate, will be included as a component of the Individualized Education Plan (IEP) developed jointly between vocational education and special education personnel;

• creation of a State Council on Vocational Education with members from business and industry, labor organizations, and secondary and postsecondary vocational institutions;

• creation of state technical committees from the private sector to advise the state board on issues such as curricula which meet the labor-market needs of the state;

• permission for states to use funds to strengthen the academic foundations of vocational education by identifying and designing strategies to teach fundamental principles of science and math as an integral part of students enrolled in vocational programs by providing them with practical applications of academics; and

• a mandate for a full-time sex-equity coordinator in each state to assist in eliminating sex bias and stereotyping in vocational education and to administer funds to implement sex-equity activities through single-parent and homemaker programs.

Carl D. Perkins Vocational and Applied Technology Education Act of 1990 (PL 101-392)—This amended and extended the Carl D. Perkins Vocational Education Act of 1984, authorizing the largest amount of money ever funded for vocational education. There was strong emphasis on providing greater vocational opportunities to individuals from special populations, including basic state grants exclusively devoted to these groups. Major components of the act were that it:

• required each state to create a set of core standards and performance measures that would serve as a benchmark for evaluations of Perkins mandates;

• required each state to conduct an initial assessment of vocational programs, submit a three-year state plan detailing how Perkins funds would be administered, and make regular statewide assessments of vocational education programs as a form of accountability;

• extended support for state councils for vocational education;

• authorized funds for tech-prep programs which were to integrate vocational and academic education;

• emphasized career guidance and counseling to help students make the transition from school to other opportunities such as high-tech careers, job training programs, and higher education opportunities;

• authorized funds for programs to provide bilingual vocational education and English-language instruction to individuals with limited English proficiency;

• provided funds for states to develop or improve instruction in consumer and homemaking education programs;

• placed strong emphasis on improving vocational program opportunities for disadvantaged individuals;

• provided funding for local nonprofit groups to deliver vocational education programs and services to disadvantaged individuals;

• authorized supplementary grants for facilities and equipment to states and local districts with the highest concentration of disadvantaged learners;

• eliminated targeted funds, or set-asides, for support services for special populations;

• continued all the assurances for individuals from special populations, including due process, equal access, least restrictive environment, and supplementary services; and

• added the mandate to provide appropriate information about vocational program opportunities to individuals from special populations prior to entry into eighth grade.

Job Training Reform Amendments of 1992 (PL 101-367)—This legislation revised the Job Training Partnership Act of 1982. The new direction of programs focused on improving services to individuals faced with serious barriers to employment, enhancing the quality of all services administered, linking services to real labor-market needs, and improving the accountability of funds.

School-to-Work Opportunities Act (STWOA) of 1994 (PL 103-239)—This was enacted to provide a framework to build a high-skilled U.S. workforce. A collaborative effort between educators and individuals from business and industry is essential for this educational reform to succeed. Funds were provided to states and local agencies that met the basic program requirements in three major components:

• School-based learning components: career counseling; selection of a career major; program of study (Goals 2000); integration of academic and vocational education; evaluation; secondary/postsecondary articulation.

• Work-based learning components: paid or unpaid work experience; job training; mentoring; instruction in workplace competencies; instruction in all aspects of the industry.

• Connecting activities components: matching students with employers; establishing liaisons between education and work; technical assistance to schools, students, and employers; assistance to integrate school-based and work-based learning; encouragement of participation of employers; job placement, continuing education, or further training; collection and analysis of post-program outcomes of participants; linkages with youth development activities and industry.

THE FLOW OF VOCATIONAL EDUCATION FUNDS

National Level

At the national level, the U.S. Department of Education, in the Executive Branch of the federal government, provides leadership and direction for the field of vocational education. In addition, the United States Department of Labor has some input regarding the use of federal vocational education dollars. Within the Department of Education, vocational and technical education is the responsibility of the Office of Vocational and Adult Education, Division of Vocational and Technical Education.

The Office of Vocational and Adult Education helps fund vocational education through the Carl D. Perkins Vocational and Applied Technology Education Act. Under the Perkins Act, federal funds are made available to provide vocational-technical education programs and services to youth and adults. The vast majority of funds appropriated each year under the Perkins Act are awarded as grants to state education agencies, usually identified as state basic grants. Funds for these basic state grants are allotted to states using a formula based on the state's population in certain age groups and the per capita income. Only state boards for vocational education are eligible to apply for state basic grants.

State Level

The distribution of funds within a state is directed to priority items established by the state in accordance with an approved state plan for vocational-technical education. Eligible recipients for subgrants under the state basic grants are local educational agencies and postsecondary institutions. For example, at the federal level, the vocational education allotment for program year 1997-98 for the state of Texas was $79,034,344 in the state basic grant. These funds would be used to administer and implement the goals for vocational education as outlined in the state plan. (See Appendix A.)

The Texas State Plan for Career and Technology Education 1997-98, required under Texas Education Code §29.182, was developed as a guide to assist school districts in their efforts to offer effective career and technology education programs that prepare students for further education and eventual employment. The plan is based on the premise that a rigorous academic foundation contributes to success in school and in life, that all students should be provided equal opportunities to succeed, and that career and technology education should complement and enhance academic preparation by enabling students to apply academic principles to a variety of community and career situations. The plan strongly supports local control of Texas public schools by offering strategies that school districts may choose to implement based on their local needs and decisions.

The plan is based on the two goals for Texas career and technology education established by the Seventy-fourth Texas Legislature. Each public school student shall master the basic skills and knowledge necessary for: (1) managing the dual roles of family member and wage earner; and (2) gaining entry-level employment in a high-skill, high-wage job or continuing the student's education at the postsecondary level.

Individuals throughout the state provided input on the first draft of the document. The objectives are based on elements that contribute to effective career and technology education programs: academic excellence, quality guidance and counseling, partnerships that benefit students and schools, strong curriculum, professional development for educators, and ongoing evaluation.

The organization of vocational education at the state level is very diversified, with each state establishing its own organizational structure. Yet each state must have a state plan which establishes statewide direction for the implementation of vocational education directives and funds. Each state has some type of administrative unit to plan, organize, and administer education, including vocational education. Although each state may have significantly different philosophies and approaches for administration and implementation of vocational education, primary emphasis is on providing the academic and technical skills needed for an ever-changing workforce.

Local Level

Vocational education at the local level is significantly influenced by its counterparts at the state, and to a lesser degree, at the national level. The influence at the federal and state levels is primarily through legislation that affects state funding for vocational education. Eligible recipients for subgrants under the state basic grants are local educational agencies, such as a district-wide system, city-wide system, county-wide system, or any combination of systems which provide vocational education and services to youth and adults.

The local education agency must submit a local plan for use of basic vocational education monies to support the delivery of vocational education programs and services to its constituents according to the guidelines set forth in the state plan. Generally these local plans are submitted annually. State and local tax dollars are also used to support vocational education programs and services according to the local plan.

References

Calhoun, C., & Finch, A. (1982). *Vocational education: Concepts and operations*. Belmont, CA: Wadsworth Publishing Co.

Evans, R. (1971). *Foundations of vocational education*. Columbus, OH: Charles E. Merrill Publishing Co.

Nystrom, D., & Bayne, G. (1979). *Occupational and career education legislation* (2nd ed.). Indianapolis, IN: Bobbs-Merrill.

Scott, J., & Sarkees-Wircenski, M. (1996). *Overview of vocational and applied technology education*. Homewood, IL: American Technical Publishers, Inc.

APPENDIX A—TEXAS EDUCATION AGENCY STATE PLAN FOR CAREER AND TECHNOLOGY EDUCATION 1997-99

Goals for Career and Technology Education

Goal 1: Each public school student shall master the basic skills and knowledge necessary for managing the dual roles of family member and wage earner.

Goal 2: Each public school student shall master the basic skills and knowledge necessary for gaining entry-level employment in a high-skill, high-wage job or continuing the student's education at the postsecondary level.

Two-Year Objectives for Career and Technology Education

Objective 1: Academic Excellence. Provide additional opportunities for all students to develop and demonstrate the knowledge and skills necessary to read, write, compute, problem solve, think critically, apply technology, and communicate across all subject areas, through a career and technology education program.

Possible Strategies:

1. Expect all students to achieve high standards.

2. Enhance foundation skills by providing a rigorous career and technology education.

3. Recruit and retain adequate numbers of appropriately certified and qualified personnel.

4. Provide coherent sequences of engaging, rigorous, and relevant courses.

5. Encourage all students to enroll in advanced foundation and enrichment courses that will give them strong academic and career preparation.

6. Improve coordination between foundation and enrichment content areas.

7. Develop and make available career concentration areas for all students.

8. Encourage academic excellence and provide recognition for student achievement, through options such as various career and technology education student organizations and honor societies, the Distinguished Achievement Program, Texas Scholars, Tech-Prep, dual enrollment, and articulated credit.

Objective 2: Guidance and Counseling. Provide a quality guidance and counseling program for all students in pre-kindergarten through Grade 12.

Possible Strategies:

1. Plan, develop, and implement a comprehensive guidance program that contains a strong career development component designed to meet the needs of all students

2. Eliminate barriers to educational success for all students by facilitating access to assessments, information, recruitment, placement, resources, and support services appropriate to each student's needs.

3. Provide all parents and all students the opportunity to identify and develop broad career options through flexible individual graduation plans, and develop transferable employability skills and knowledge leading to entry-level employment and continuing education. Students should have the opportunity to re-evaluate and revise graduation plans based on their developing interests, talents, and aptitudes.

4. Provide students and parents with information about current and emerging careers.

5. Inform students and parents of opportunities for financial assistance for postsecondary education and training.

6. Provide opportunities for interested students to explore careers that are nontraditional for their gender.

Objective 3: Partnerships. Plan, develop, and implement partnerships that support efforts to help students develop the basic knowledge and skills necessary for managing the dual roles of family member and wage-earner, gaining entry-level employment, and continuing the student's education or training at the postsecondary level.

Possible Strategies:

1. Develop partnerships among teachers, counselors, administrators, parents, postsecondary education, the community, business and industry, and other entities to assist students in mastering the knowledge ands skills needed to succeed.

2. Encourage all school personnel to actively participate in partnership efforts.

3. Utilize partnerships with community organizations, business/industry, parents, and other individuals and groups to implement support programs and services for students.

4. Involve partnerships in developing work-based career development experience for all students.

5. Partner with two- and four-year colleges to provide students with seamless links to postsecondary education through articulated credit, dual enrollment, coordinated curriculum, tech-prep, or other programs and practices appropriate to local needs.

6. Utilize partnerships to promote community support for career and technology education programs.

7. Involve partnerships in identifying and securing resources.

8. Make career and technology education opportunities available to all students through partnerships with other school districts, public or private postsecondary institutions, and/or state-regulated trade or technical schools.

Objective 4: Curriculum. Provide all students with opportunities to participate in an academically rigorous curriculum that enables them to achieve their potential and participate fully in the economic and educational opportunities of Texas and the nation.

Possible Strategies:

1. Provide a curriculum that facilitates op-

portunities for all students to participate in career and technology education.

2. Ensure that the career and technology curriculum is provided through programs of sufficient size, scope, and quality as to be effective in improving academic and occupational skill competencies of all students, while providing strong experience in and understanding of all aspects of the industries students are preparing to enter.

3. Identify, develop, and implement curriculum using the State Board of Education-approved essential knowledge and skills as a framework.

4. Provide a dynamic curriculum that is engaging, rigorous, and relevant.

5. Provide all students with opportunities for a variety of learning experiences that address diverse learning styles.

6. With parental approval, offer all students opportunities to participate in programs that include work-based learning components.

7. Acquire and utilize information about current and emerging careers.

8. Provide opportunities for all students to participate in student leadership organizations.

9. Provide opportunities for all students to understand employer expectations and citizenship skills.

10. Develop career concentration areas to assist participating students in achieving academic career skills that apply to continued education and employment.

Objective 5: Professional Development. Plan, develop, and implement professional opportunities for all teachers, administrators, counselors, and other education partners that enable participants to provide a quality education for all students.

Possible Strategies:

1. Conduct ongoing assessments of professional development needs.

2. Provide orientation and ongoing professional development opportunities for all administrators, counselors, and teachers, emphasizing current research findings and effective practices.

3. Provide all teachers with staff development in coordinating academic foundation and career and technology education.

4. Provide counselors with professional development activities that emphasize the career development component of the comprehensive guidance program.

5. Develop professional development opportunities for administrators, counselors, and career and technology teachers in business/industry settings.

6. Form partnerships with teacher preparatory institutions to enhance preparation for all teachers, consistent with career and technology education needs.

Objective 6: Evaluation. Evaluate career and technology education programs in terms of (a) the program's effectiveness in enabling each public school student to master the basic skills and knowledge necessary for managing the dual roles of family member and wage earner; (b) the program's effectiveness in enabling each public school student to master the basic skills and knowledge necessary for gaining entry-level employment or continuing the student's education at the postsecondary level; and (c) if the district receives supplemental federal funding for career and technology education, whether the program meets requirements for receiving supplemental federal funding.

Possible Strategies:

1. Assess the career and technology education program and its individual components to determine strengths and weaknesses.

2. Evaluate career and technology education program facilities, equipment, and instructional resources.

3. Utilize business and industry partnerships in career and technology education evaluations: (a) At the school district's discretion, use information about graduates' participation in postsecondary education, the workforce, military, or other post-high-school opportunities as a measure when evaluating the local education system's success. (b) Develop and implement a plan to improve career and technology programs based on evaluation results.

Michelle Sarkees-Wircenski *is a professor in the Department of Technology and Cognition at the University of North Texas in Denton. This program area focuses on preparing Career and Technology Education teachers at the secondary level, preparing technology instructors at the postsecondary level, and preparing individuals for training and development positions in corporations. Her primary research areas include vocational preparation for individuals from special populations, school-to-work programs for all students, learning styles and teaching styles, and curriculum modification.* ***Jerry L. Wircenski*** *is a professor in the Department of Technology and Cognition at the University of North Texas in Denton. He is the program coordinator for Applied Technology, Training, and Development. This program area focuses on preparing career and technology education teachers at the secondary level, preparing technology instructors at the postsecondary level, and preparing individuals for training and development positions in corporations. His research interests include design, delivery, and evaluation in training and development programs.*

CAREER EDUCATION: BASIC CONCEPTS AND CURRENT STATUS

By Kenneth B. Hoyt and Pat Nellor Wickwire

Most federally funded education activities remain active only as long as federal funds needed to pay for them continue to exist. When federal funding ceases, these activities usually disappear very quickly. As a federal program, the concept of career education was abandoned in 1981. Had past custom been followed, it would have disappeared no later than 1983. But it didn't! As a national effort, it remains both viable and active today.

Reasons behind the continuing existence of career education activities can best be explained by thinking carefully and critically about the basic concepts inherent in the career education movement. These concepts have often been stated one at a time as special calls for change. The goal of this chapter is to put these concepts together in what will, we hope, be a logical and easy-to-understand manner.

To best explain the career education movement to those who today are involved in use of federal funds for other education/work efforts such as school-to-career and tech-prep programs, career education concepts are formulated here in terms that will make career education appear to be related to, but not synonymous with, such programs. A rationale for insertion of these concepts in new federal education/work efforts is provided.

BASIC CONCEPTS OF CAREER EDUCATION

Concept #1: The meaning and importance of the word "work"—The basic nature of and rationale behind any school-to-work program is dependent on the way the word *work* is defined. Thus, it is essential that those conceptualizing school-to-work programs make clear their definition of work. Unfortunately, this does not appear to have yet been done in terms of the bedrock definition of *school to work*. Instead, the word is usually either ignored or defined as meaning paid employment. Neither of these practices is defensible. The career education movement offers one way of defining work that deserves consideration.

When the first official United States Office of Education policy on career education was written in 1974 (Hoyt, 1975), the two key words that had to be defined were work and career. *Work* was defined as "conscious effort, other than that involved in activities whose primary purpose is either coping or relaxation, aimed at producing benefits for oneself and/or for oneself and others" (p. 3). *Career* was defined as "the totality of work one does in his or her lifetime" (p. 3).

As defined by career education, the key components in the meaning of work include (a) *conscious*, meaning the person chose to do it; (b) *effort*, meaning there is some difficulty involved; (c) *producing*, meaning some output is sought; and (d) *benefits*, meaning the output is aimed at helping the individual or the individual and others. There is no requirement here that the meaning of work be limited to paid employment or even to occupations.

These definitions of work and career have since been adopted by the National Career Development Association. Those who disagree with these definitions have a responsibility to offer and defend some other definition of work. This is not a topic that can continue to be ignored or criticized by conceptual leaders of today's school-to-work movement.

Concept #2: The classroom as a workplace—Since the concept of work presented earlier is in no way limited to paid employment, it is not difficult to conceptualize the classroom as a workplace and both pupils and teachers as workers. If the classroom is a kind of workplace, it seems reasonable to assume the same basic procedures found to improve productivity in workplaces in the occupational society can be expected to be useful in improving educational productivity—and so in helping pupils learn more of what teachers are trying to teach.

There should be no absolute need for the pupil to leave the classroom in order to experience work. This is the most basic assumption made by career education as a proposal for educational reform. To illustrate this, a number of basic procedures known to improve productivity in the broader occupational society will be presented along with examples of how each procedure can be used to improve educational productivity.

Procedure 1: *Show the worker the importance of her/his work.* Business and industry have, for years, made this procedure a high priority. Conscious efforts are made to show each worker the importance of what he or she is asked to do on the job. By making each worker feel what he or she is doing is important to the organization, it is hoped each worker will be better motivated to be productive on the job.

From an educational point of view, by showing pupils how what they are being asked to learn relates to success in various occupations found in the broader society, it is hoped pupils will be better motivated to learn the subject matter being taught. Note that often, but not always, teachers will find good examples of why it is important to learn the subject matter from the occupational society. When no good occupational examples appear to be present, the teacher is asked to think of some other kind of activity that can serve as an example to pupils of why it is important to learn what the teacher is trying to teach. Career education is a way—but not the only way—of helping pupils answer the traditional "Why should I learn this?" questions they have.

Procedure 2: *Reward work when it occurs.* Many business/industry organizations have elaborate schemes for recognizing and rewarding workers who are doing their work especially well. This approach seems to be a success.

Unfortunately, this has not been a popular procedure to use in K-12 American education. Instead of turning back student assignments showing pupils the questions they passed, it seems more common to turn them back by marking the answers they missed. Furthermore, the mediocre pupil who just "gets by" is rewarded fully as much as other students who, while scoring no higher, did their very best. Pupils who really try need and deserve some credit for their efforts. Teachers can find ways of providing such credit in a wide variety of ways.

Procedure 3: *Insert variety in the workplace.* It seems to be increasingly popular for business/industry leaders to train and use many of their workers for multiple purposes. Cross training of assembly line workers so they can operate at a number of different work stations has become commonplace. Industry has discovered that, if a worker is given only one work assignment with no variation in how it is carried out, productivity often diminishes. On the other hand, introduction of a variety of kinds of work assignments often increases productivity.

Instead of doing things in essentially the same way every day, many teachers find it helpful to interject field trips, classroom resource persons, and various kinds of activity assignments into the teaching/learning process. This is easy to do in teacher attempts to infuse a career education emphasis in any given course.

Procedure 4: *Emphasize and reward the practice of productive work habits.* Workers usually develop work habits primarily through their work activities. If ignored by their supervisors, sometimes these turn out to be good work habits—and sometimes they are bad work habits. Some kinds of work habits are almost certain to be acquired. As long as this is so, it seems sensible to concentrate on helping people develop good work habits. This can best be done by rewarding the practice of good work habits and emphasizing the price to be paid when poor work habits are utilized.

The basic good work habits most supervisors seem to value include: Come to work on time, maintain a goal of trying to do better each day, finish each assignment before moving on to the next, schedule work activities so they fit a prearranged time frame, follow the rules and directions of your supervisor, maintain a goal of excellence in every work assignment, and learn to cooperate and work with other people in a team effort.

Every classroom teacher has multiple opportunities daily to emphasize and reward good work habits used by pupils. Teachers do students a serious disservice if they fail to emphasize and develop pupils with good work habits. If these are the behaviors routinely rewarded throughout the entire K-12 system, there is every reason to believe these same work habits have a good chance of being practiced once the school-leaver is placed in a paid job.

If all four of these procedures are followed by the classroom teacher, there is every reason to believe pupils will learn more of the academic subject matter the teacher is trying to teach. When people talk about the need for education reform, they typically talk about the need for pupils to learn more in school.

Career education has, since its introduction in 1970, concentrated on approaches to education reform designed to lead to increases in pupil achievement. The "careers" emphasis found in career education is viewed by many K-12 classroom teachers as a means to the end of increased pupil learning—not as an end in itself.

In taking this point of view, teachers are simply recognizing that the K-12 education system's primary goals center around efforts to increase pupil academic achievement. Career education will be most strongly advocated by those teachers who are convinced career education can make positive contributions toward meeting this goal. To ask K-12 teachers to support and participate in career education solely because of its career development goals will, in the long run, not work. Relating career education to increases in pupil achievement will work.

Concept #3: Teachers and pupils as workers—The career education movement has been conceptualized based, in part, on the concept of the classroom being viewed as a form of unpaid work with both teachers and pupils being considered as workers. The four components of work identified above can certainly be identified as parts of the teaching/learning process in terms both of pupil behavior and teacher behavior.

When pupils operate in the classroom as workers, they have chosen to work because they understand the importance of the subject matter to be learned and so are motivated to learn it. Moreover, they are willing to engage in the variety of behaviors necessary for learning the subject and are convinced they will benefit if they learn what it is the teacher is trying to teach. When all of these things happen, the concept of pupils as workers becomes easy to demonstrate. Similarly, when teachers are convinced the subject matter is important and that, if they relate with pupils in ways that help pupils become workers, more learning is likely to occur, the teachers are also more likely to become workers.

In the absence of efforts to help both pupils and teachers become workers, many of them will fail to recognize the importance of their actions and, as a result, the total teaching/learning process will become less productive, resulting in minimal learning taking place. It has been the potential of career education as a vehicle for helping both pupils and teachers become workers that has caused so many teachers to become supporters and advocates of career education. To ignore the ways in which any school-to-work program benefits classroom teachers is to almost certainly ensure the program will die very shortly after federal funding is withdrawn.

Concept #4: The importance of work values—The first published definition of "career education" called it "the total effort of public education and the community aimed at helping all individuals to become familiar with the values of a work-oriented society, to integrate these values into their personal value systems, and to implement these values into their lives in such a way that work becomes possible, meaningful, and satisfying to each individual" (Hoyt, Evans, Mackin, & Mangum, 1972, p. 1).

Thus, from the beginning, career education was conceived as an attempt to help all individuals discover a set of reasons for working that will make work a meaningful and satisfying part of total lifestyle. If someone is asked if career education really wants people to want to work, the answer is "Yes."

The reasons for taking this position reflect what appears to be developing with respect to the nature of the emerging information society. That emerging society recognizes that chances are slim that most people will find it possible to select only one set of occupational values and stay with the same occupation during their key years of paid employment. At the same time, it recognizes that the work values developed by any individual can and should be useful in various positions the individual holds no matter how many occupational changes are involved.

Operationally, the work values of any individual are best conceptualized as the set of reasons that that individual has for wanting to work, that is, those elements involved in one's work that motivate the person to do his or her best and receive maximum personal meaningfulness and satisfaction from whatever work is experienced. What would lead various people to want to work?

For any given person to answer this question will demand that he or she choose some combination of several kinds of possible benefits to be derived from work, that is, things the individual values in his or her work. Examples of such possible perceived benefits from working include the concepts that work is: a way of earning money needed for a variety of things, a way in which one can be of help to other people, a way the individual can honestly say he or she did something, a way the individual can know better who she or he is through what she or he does, a way in which the individual can excel in something, a way the individual can understand why she or he is needed and what she or he is needed for, and a way of using one's time constructively.

The value of emphasizing work values as well as occupational values includes recognizing that one's work values can be applied in some ways and to some degree no matter what occupation the individual finds himself or herself in. In these times, the concept of career development as something that takes place over almost the entire life span applies far better to work values than it does to occupational values.

Concept #5: The importance of general employability/adaptability/promotability skills—The career education concept has, from the beginning, operated under an assumption that, for most people, the days of choosing, preparing for, entering, and progressing in a single occupation are past. Instead, most people will, because of changes taking place in the occupational society, be forced to change their occupational choices several times during their years of paid employment. As they do so, the continuing importance of a set of general employability skills will become more and more important. Such skills include (a) the basic academic skills, (b) a set of productive work habits, (c) a set of personally meaningful work values, (d) a set of specific career decision-making skills, and (e) a set of well-developed job seeking/finding/getting/holding skills that will enable them to change occupations relatively easily during their paid employment years.

The development of these skills should begin in the earliest elementary school years and extend throughout the educational system. To wait until the secondary school years to begin is almost sure to be counterproductive. If we ignore this fact, many elementary school pupils will develop (a) a dislike for learning the basic academic skills, (b) a set of bad work habits, (c) negative work values leading them not to want to work, (d) no systematic career decision-making skills, and (e) no set of general employability skills.

In this sense, the elementary school teacher is the key person to be involved in career education. Furthermore, the teaching/learning process becomes fully as important as the career counseling process in implementing career education. Together, they represent the career development process.

Concept #6: Collaboration in career education—From the beginning, career education has been advocated as a community effort, not something the K-12 educational system can do by itself. The assumption being made is that the best way to help pupils relate academic efforts to the broader occupational society will be to provide ways in which they can be learned together. Attempts to help pupils learn about the occupational society by locking them in a school system that keeps them away from that society won't work.

Both K-12 educators and members of the business/industry/labor community have the expertise required to help K-12 pupils learn such things as (a) how workers need and use basic academic skills in their jobs, (b) why workers need and use productive work habits, (c) how workers can operate in their jobs in ways that allow them to practice and further develop their own constructive work values, (d) the growing importance of general employability/adaptability/promotability skills on the part of most workers, and (e) the growing importance of specific occupational skills to be acquired at the postsecondary sub-baccalaureate level. Pupils will learn these kinds of things best if K-12 educators and members of the broader community work together in providing them.

Career education efforts work best if carried out in a collaborative rather than a cooperative manner. When the business/industry/labor community is officially asked only to *cooperate* with K-12 educators, there is usually an understanding that cooperation is sought so the education system can better meet its goals. As such, when these efforts succeed, the education system gets the major credit. When they fail, the education system gets the blame. Such systems ignore and/or play down both the expertise and the facilities of the business/industry/labor community and assume the prime experts to be educators.

The concept of *collaboration* differs from *cooperation* in that it is defined and operates as a joint effort of the business/industry/labor community and the education system operating in ways that call for partnership efforts aimed at sharing authority, responsibility, and accountability. When career education works, both partners receive some credit. Where it doesn't work, both partners must share some of the blame. The amount of both authority and accountability assigned each partner is directly related to the amount of responsibility each partner assumes.

While the concept of collaboration in career education has been advocated for at least 20 years (Hoyt, 1978a, 1978b), it has still not been widely implemented in K-12 career education efforts. The importance of this concept and the need for its application continue to grow.

Concept #7: Career education as education reform—Sidney P. Marland, Jr., is widely recognized as the "father" of the career education movement, which he launched in a speech to the National Association of Secondary School Principals on January 21, 1971 (Marland, 1971). His book on career education was *Career Education: A Proposal for Reform* (Marland, 1974). There was never any doubt that Marland's prime mission was to make a contribution to education reform and that he viewed career education as one of several possible ways of reforming education.

The first U.S. Office of Education policy paper on career education (Hoyt, 1975) listed 14 other basic policy education reform changes endorsed by career education. Examples include: an increase in occupational education offerings at the postsecondary level; a decrease in differentiating secondary schools by "general education," "college prep education," and "vocational education" curriculum types; installation of performance evaluation; increased use of learning in community as well as school settings; creation of open entry-open exit educational systems; substantial increases in adult and recurrent education; and creation of the year-round K-12 education system. These examples make it clear that the official U.S. Office of Education policies championed career education as one among a wide variety of education reform efforts—not as the only one needed.

During the decade of the 1970s, career education was the prime approach to education reform being advocated. The decade of the 1980s was recognized as the decade of education reform with a wide variety of reform proposals being advocated, none of which centered around or endorsed career education. It is interesting to note that, during the decade of the 1990s, most education reform proposals advocated during the 1980s were no longer being widely promoted. Instead, the prime change proposals appear to center around the broad school-to-career movement. It is even more interesting to note that the school-to-career movement is not currently being championed under the banner of education reform.

Career education remains a movement deeply committed to the concept of education reform sought under two broad approaches: (a) increasing the emphasis on career development in the entire K-12 level, and (b) increasing the emphasis on using the concept of work as a means of redirecting the teaching/learning process. With both approaches, changes in the entire K-12 system are called for. Further, both approaches call for implementation of such changes to be carried out primarily by classroom teachers. Career education advocates contend that, unless classroom teachers change their attitudes, knowledge, and actions, no real education reform can take place.

In the career development approach, teachers are asked to join with pupils and community-resource persons at each grade level in efforts to discover and illustrate the utility of what teachers are teaching in the broader occupational society. Beginning with career awareness activities in the early elementary school grades, this emphasis is designed to continue at least through the twelfth grade as career exploration. The purposes of this emphasis on career development are (a) to motivate pupils to learn the academic subject matter being taught by showing them it can be useful in future occupational experiences and (b) to provide multiple opportunities for every pupil in every grade to help further his or her career development through learning more about education/work relationships in the occupational society.

The major way that career education seeks to function as an education reform movement is through emphasizing the classroom as a workplace with both pupils and teachers being workers in that workplace. It is this concept that has met with the greatest resistance by many of those currently serving as national leaders in the school-to-career movement. Only if this resistance is overcome can career education function effectively as a component of education reform.

THE STATUS OF CAREER EDUCATION

Career Education and Federal Leadership

Career education was formally introduced as education reform in 1971 by the U.S. Commissioner of Education (Marland, 1971). Identified as the top priority by the commissioner, the career education movement was initially directed toward increased understandings by students of the connections of curricular content and workplace competencies. Although four models (school-based, employer-based, home-based, and residential-based) were developed, precise definition of career education occurred through field input, consensus conferences, local implementation, and state and national leadership.

Career education demonstration projects, primarily using discretionary funds, were conducted during the first several years of the 1970s. The Office of Career Education officially opened in 1974. Through a section of the Elementary and Secondary Education Act Amendments of 1974, Congress authorized and appropriated funds for career education demonstration projects for fiscal years 1975-1978 (Hoyt, 1981). In 1978, Congress authorized and appropriated funds for the Career Education Incentive Act. Federal government sponsorship concluded in 1981.

During the decade, mainly because of needs to target limited funds for optimal results, prime emphasis was placed on demonstrating school-based career education. Support and action from a wide variety and diversity of publics were strong. Thousands of career education programs, projects, and activities were implemented throughout the states. Funds were passed through to local school districts, which carried major responsibility for demonstration. Definition and program development were continuous, and program evaluation and research were significantly highlighted.

Infusion in curricula and classroom instruction was the primary approach, although career guidance and counseling, staff development, partnerships with business and industry, management modeling, liaisons with community organizations, and collaboration with parents and home were companion components. Career education was chosen for inclusion in specific fields, such as the education of exceptional children. Goals were variously stated, according to local needs. Generally, seven major goals were applied (Hoyt, 1987): to help people in career awareness/exploration/decision making, to equip people with general employability/adaptability/promotability skills, to promote and implement private sector/education system partnerships, to relate education and work so that better choices of both can be made, to reform education by infusing a "careers" emphasis in classrooms, to make work a meaningful part of total lifestyle, and to reduce bias and stereotyping and thus protect freedom of choice. The model for K-12 student career development included career awareness, career exploration, career decision making, and career planning and preparation (Woal, 1994), generally to follow grade groupings, but to be reviewed and recycled according to individual needs.

Quantitative and qualitative data on the efficacy of career education processes and products were amassed. Enderlein (1976) reviewed evaluation studies and found positive results for students in work knowledge and attitudes, occupational information, career decision making and planning, and career maturity. In a review of evaluation data for 45 demonstration projects, Bonnet (1978) found student growth in career awareness, desire to work, and career decision-making skills.

Hamilton and Mitchell (1978), in appraising evaluation studies which included comparison groups or standards, reported evidence of increased student career and economic awareness; awareness of nontraditional jobs; knowledge of self, environment, work, economics, decision making, employment and work adjustment, career clusters, and education and training opportunities; attitudes toward work; and basic, employability, and career decision-making skills.

Hoyt and High (1982), in a comprehensive review of 984 studies conducted between 1970 and 1980, identified positive results for career education in basic skills, oral communication, self-understanding, understanding of available educational and occupational opportunities, understanding and appreciation of private enterprise, personal work values, nonstereotyping of career choice, career decision-making skills, and job-seeking/finding/getting/holding skills.

The Far West Laboratory for Educational Research and Development (1984) summarized 23 proven career education programs approved by the U.S. Department of Education Joint Dissemination Review Panel for their effectiveness in positive educational change, and summarized 27 career programs selected as promising practices because of positive results. In reviewing 1985-1988 literature, Halasz (1988) typified career education as a lifelong need and as a viable construct for functioning in the changing workplace, and further attributed the success of career education to "common sense precepts supported by research" (p. 2).

CAREER EDUCATION AND NATIONAL LEADERSHIP

Grass roots support existed before, during, and after federal leadership in career education. Today, nationwide efforts continue, with programs and services in many public and private national, regional, state, and local agencies and organizations. Schools and school districts, departments of education and employment, businesses and industries, individual entrepreneurs, and professional and community organizations and agencies show commitment through their offerings (Wickwire, 1993, 1996).

To some extent, the precepts and practices of career education have been adopted by the larger society. That there are connections among careers, education, and work seems patently obvious; that there are reasons to make these connections the highest quality possible seems equally obvious. The infusion of the philosophy and practices of career education into the larger society makes good sense.

Many careers, education, and work challenges exist today (Wickwire, 1997a). Business, economic, cultural, and social trends and events in a globally interdependent world are changing the paradigms of work, education, family, and other institutions (Wickwire, 1997b). Work has evolved from agricultural and industrial to service and information periods, and is on the way to an experiential-existential age. Core competencies, transferable employability skills, adaptability, teamwork, value-added products and services, quality of performance, lifelong learning, education-work transitions, interagency linkages, and community-wide co-responsibility, among other items, are priorities on the current national agenda. These are career education.

Forward-looking career education is comprehensive, with an awareness-to-action sequence of learning that connects careers, education, and work (Wickwire, 1993, 1994). Preventive and developmental, and recycled as needed, career education begins at home and extends throughout schooling and lifelong learning.

During the school years, all staff and programs—management, instruction, pupil personnel, and classified—are appropriately concerned with supporting these connections. Furthermore, the education system as a whole is appropriately concerned with collaboration, cooperation, and partnerships with the larger community, in the interests of shared responsibility, authority, and accountability for the education of the populace.

The American Association For Career Education, the Ohio Career Development Program, Michigan Career and Employability Skills, and California Career Preparation Education exemplify current national efforts in career education. Each is discussed separately here.

American Association For Career Education. In 1981, the American Association For Career Education (AACE) was established as a nonprofit organization to serve as a vehicle for supporting nationwide leadership in career education. AACE functions primarily as a conduit of information, a builder of concepts and applications, and a broker of relationships for those interested in careers, education, and work. Members represent all segments of society, including business, education, government, industry, labor, commerce, the professions, human services, parents, citizens, students, and the community; more than half are involved in the planning and delivery of direct or indirect programs, services, and products.

The mission of AACE is to advance careers, education, and work for all throughout the life span. It offers the quarterly newsletter *AACE Careers Update*, a registry of member products and services, access to *Career Opportunities News* and other member products, a resource responder network, and a variety of publications and linkages.

The *AACE Distinguished Member Series, AACE Bonus Briefs, AACE CareerGram*, and *AACE Forum* address current topics of practice and theory, as well as trends, futures, challenges, issues, solutions, and opportunities. Voluntary interest networks are offered for career education and elementary schools, junior high and high schools, community colleges, colleges and universities, and adult schools; private practice, business and industry, government, and prisons; partnerships, parents and community, occupational/educational/job placement, and career resource centers; life-career development for seniors and for women; health/clinical/medical/physical sciences, and business and computer science; and retirement career planning.

Members are strongly supported in their individual efforts to enhance and to advance career education. AACE offers annual awards for excellence and innovation in categories which include: management, counseling, assessment, and evaluation programs; curriculum design and delivery; career resource centers; research; public information and inservice education programs; community coalitions, partnerships, and collaborative programs; books, in-house newsletters, and other publications; and other categories as applicable.

Annually since 1992, the association has offered AACE Citations for Career Education Initiatives—Programs, Practices, and Publications That Work (Wickwire, 1995). Awards to recognize excellence and innovation have been granted to the projects listed here. Their areas of study—and success—may be of interest to present readers:

American Careers Magazine, Career Communications, Overland Park, Kansas. Designed to help high school students explore careers, relate careers to their interests, and plan appropriate career and educational options.

Applied Technology Career Centers, Boulder Valley School District Middle Schools, Boulder, Colorado. Designed to prepare middle school students for the changing demands and career opportunities of the 21st century.

ASVAB Career Exploration Program, Defense Manpower Data Center, Seaside, California. Designed to assist high school students in military and civilian career exploration.

Beyond High School Magazine, Eugene, Oregon. Designed to help teenagers, their parents, and educators to explore career and educational opportunities of the 21st century.

Career Awareness Program, Boy Scouts of America, Columbus, Ohio. Designed to present information to high school students about specific expressed career interests.

Career Awareness Program, Byng Junior High School, Ada, Oklahoma. Designed to provide daily exploratory experiences and insights into technology and career opportunities.

Career Development Course, St. Helens High School, St. Helens, Oregon. Designed to assist students with self-assessment and occupational and educational program research.

Career Education Awareness Program, Louis M. Klein Middle School, Harrison, New York. Designed to introduce students to careers early in their education.

Career Education Program, South Orangetown Central School District, Orangeburg, New York. Designed to offer career exploration through career internships and career shadowing at community work sites.

Career Encounters Videos: Advanced Practice Nursing, Davis Gray, Inc., Narberth, Pennsylvania. Designed to inform a broad audience about the potential of careers in advanced practice nursing.

Career Encounters Videos: Architecture, Davis Gray, Inc., Narberth, Pennsylvania. Designed to inform a broad audience about the potential of careers in architecture.

Career Encounters Videos: Automotive Technician, Davis Gray, Inc., Narberth, Pennsylvania. Designed to inform a broad audience about the potential of careers in automotive repair.

Career Encounters Videos: Early Childhood Education, Davis Gray, Inc., Narberth, Pennsylvania. Designed to inform a broad audience about the potential of careers in early childhood education.

Career Encounters Videos: Optics and Photonics, Davis Gray, Inc., Narberth, Pennsylvania. Designed to inform a broad audience about the potential of careers in optics and photonics.

Career Encounters Videos: Radiology, Davis Gray, Inc., Narberth, Pennsylvania. Designed to inform a broad audience about the potential of careers in radiology.

Career Encounters Videos: Veterinary Medicine, Davis Gray, Inc., Narberth, Pennsylvania. Designed to inform a broad audience about the potential of careers in veterinary medicine.

Career Encounters Videos: Women in Engineering, Davis Gray, Inc., Narberth, Pennsylvania. Designed to inform a broad audience about the potential for women in careers in engineering.

Career Exploration Program, Saint Joseph's High School, South Bend, Indiana. Designed to assist students with career identification and educational planning skills.

Career Literacy Program, Tonasket School District, Tonasket, Washington. Designed to facilitate student cross-age mentoring, community service, and portfolio development.

Career Panels '91, University of South Carolina, Aiken, South Carolina. Designed to inform students about career, employment, university, and community connections.

Career Passport Program, Cincinnati Public Schools, Cincinnati, Ohio. Designed to assist students with job seeking, career planning, and making the transition from school to work.

Career Resource Center, Sunset High School, Portland, Oregon. Designed to provide high school students with comprehensive, well-organized, current career resource information and assistance.

Connecting to the Community, Kenmare Alternative High School, Jersey City, New Jersey. Designed to orient and educate young disadvantaged women about the specific aspects of careers as practiced in the work site.

Design Your Own Life—From High School to Career, Telesis Corporation, San Diego, California. Designed to help youth develop a positive approach to the search for meaningful and realistic career goals.

Educators for Tomorrow Program, Ector County Independent School District, Odessa, Texas. Designed to assist students who wish to pursue a career in teaching.

Four-Year Plan of Study, Oklahoma Department of Vocational and Technical Education, Stillwater, Oklahoma. Designed to assist students in coherent, sequential career planning and decision making.

Household Careers: Nannies, Butlers, Maids & More, Five Star Publications, Chandler, Arizona. Designed to provide information about new career opportunities.

Integration 2000, Malow Junior High School, Shelby Township, Michigan. Designed to integrate educational disciplines with industry to form a new delivery system to provide relevant learning experiences in which the learner has an active role.

Learning for Life Career Awareness Program, Central Ohio Council, Boy Scouts of America, Columbus, Ohio. Designed to provide students with information about careers and about skills of job search.

Mentoring: A Career Development Activity for Junior High School Students, United Technical Center, Clarksburg, West Virginia. Designed to proffer role models to support informed career decision making.

National Vocational-Technical Honor Society, NV-THS, Gramling, South Carolina. Designed to offer recognition for workbound high school students who reach high academic standards.

New Traditions Program, Tulare County, Visalia, California. Designed to train low-income women for employment in nontraditional occupations.

Nontraditional Career Conference, Ascension Parish School Board, Donaldsonville, Louisiana. Designed to provide eighth-graders with nonstereotyped business/industry and school information about vocational programs and organizations.

Peer Intervention Program, New York City Public Schools, New York, New York. Designed to assist participating teachers to evaluate unrewarding circumstances and to explore current openings in the job market.

Trouble in Mother Goose Land, Princeton Junction, New Jersey. Designed to educate children about conflict resolution, law, and careers.

Vocational Guidance Course, Pine View Middle School, St. George, Utah. Designed to assist students with organizational skills, career possibilities, self-appraisal, and long-range plans.

Work Force 2000: Drafting and Design Work-Based Learning, Ascension Parish School Board, Donaldsonville, Louisiana. Designed to offer high school students employment experience and articulation to postsecondary institutions.

AACE members are strongly encouraged to write for purposes of communicating information, conceptualization, progress in delivery, and expansion of career education theory and practice. Recent topics have included service learning; school-to-work; the Internet; industry-education cooperation; content, performance, and skill standards; career decision making; employment trends; and materials for career education delivery.

AACE implements a public information program to connect with local, regional, state, national, and international media. It engages in partnership and representation with the Educational Resources Information Center Clearinghouse on Career, Adult, and Vocational Education, and liaison with related groups such as the Youth Policy Institute, Coalition for Goals 2000, Women's American Organization for Rehabilitation and Training, National Center for the Study of History, National Association for Industry-Education Cooperation, and the National Consortium for State Career Guidance Supervisors.

Ohio Career Development Program. State-funded since the 1970s, it currently has 89 career development programs that serve 611 school districts (C. R. Gahris, personal communication, July 15, 1997). Each program is administered by a career development coordinator who provides core functions in career assessment, curriculum, career-related instructional materials, coordination of staff and activities, staff development, career information, and community involvement.

Each coordinator participates in one of four regional councils which operate autonomously, meet regularly, and provide professional development for coordinators. Three officers from each regional council, along with state department representatives, comprise a statewide task force that meets four times a year.

The Ohio program includes a focus on lifelong learning needs and the provision of career-focused education for all students (Ohio Department of Education, n.d.b). Twelve key topics are included in curricular offerings:

1. *Self-awareness:* structured means by which students gain knowledge of, understand, and express themselves.

2. *Self-assessment:* formal and informal methods that enable students to measure and interpret achievements, aptitudes, interests, and personality.

3. *Career information:* current and specific data concerning the world of work.

4. *Exploration:* experiential opportunities to explore career options related to one's choice.

5. *Academic planning:* the process by which one uses all information to relate educational choices to future career goals.

6. *Reduction of bias:* an expansion of individual career choices, based on personal inter-

ests and abilities and not limited by sex, race, ethnicity, age, or handicap.

7. *Future trends:* information related to social, economic, and technological changes and to the individual's need to adapt to those changes.

8. *Employability skills:* those work behaviors, abilities, and attitudes necessary to obtain, maintain, and advance in employment.

9. *Decision making and goal setting:* the process of developing plans specific to a determined outcome.

10. *Community involvement:* school-based activities that encourage responsibility to and citizenship within the community.

11. *Economics:* information relating income, work, and economic concepts to individual career choice and money management.

12. *Vocational orientation:* assuring that vocational career options receive equal emphasis in an individual's educational planning.

Each key topic includes one to three learner goals for K-5, middle school, and high school; numerous learning indicators; and numerous suggested learning activities. Career development liaisons and career development teams support implementation through career events and through instructional infusion. Parental involvement, community linkages, and staff development are primary components. Program development, monitoring, and evaluation are ongoing.

A significant element in the Ohio program is the student's individual career plan, a learning process initiated in kindergarten, formulated in writing in the eighth grade, and reviewed and revised annually throughout the high school years (Ohio Department of Education, n.d.a). The individual career plan includes the career pathway (career planner, educational planner), career skills builder (school-based learning, work-based learning, career passport activities), assessment record (career interest and aptitude, proficiency, and other assessment results), and other applicable information.

The Career Passport (Ohio Department of Education, 1996-97) offers students a process to assist in preparing for transition from school to work and/or additional education, and offers employers and admissions officers a process to assist in identifying clearer information about students. Established by legislative action in Ohio, the Career Passport is completed by high school juniors, and revised as appropriate in the senior year. The document includes, for example, a letter of verification of student status, a student resume, validation of student performance (career narrative, evidence of student skills, verification of employability skills), and additional contents, such as the school profile of educational environment, list of student accomplishments, documentation of community service, and letters of recommendation.

Michigan Career and Employability Skills. Michigan includes career and employability skills as one of nine essential curriculum content areas. School districts may use them as guidance in developing local curricula (K. Crooks, personal communication, June 16, 1997). The 10 content standards (Michigan Department of Education, 1996, p.2) are:

1. *Applied academic skills:* Apply basic communication skills (e.g., reading, writing, speaking, and listening) and perform mathematical operations in work-related situations.

2. *Career planning:* Acquire, organize, interpret, and evaluate information from career awareness and exploration activities, career assessment, and work-based experiences to make a career decision and to pursue a career direction.

3. *Developing and presenting information:* Demonstrate the ability to combine ideas or information in new ways, make connections between seemingly unrelated ideas, and organize and present information in formats such as symbols, pictures, schematics, charts, and graphs.

4. *Problem solving:* Make decisions and solve problems by specifying goals, identifying resources and constraints, generating alternatives, considering impacts, choosing appropriate alternatives, and evaluating results.

5. *Personal management:* Display personal

qualities such as responsibility, self-management, ethical behavior, and respect for self and others.

6. *Organizational skills:* Identify, organize, plan, and allocate resources (such as time, money, materials, and human resources) efficiently and effectively.

7. *Teamwork:* Work cooperatively with people of diverse backgrounds and abilities and contribute to a group process with ideas, suggestions, and efforts.

8. *Negotiation skills:* Communicate ideas to support a position and negotiate to resolve divergent interests.

9. *Understanding systems:* Understand complex systems, including social and technical systems, and work with a variety of technologies.

10. *Using employability skills:* Integrate employability skills into behaviors which result in obtaining, maintaining, advancing, and changing employment.

The content standards, along with benchmarks for elementary school, middle school, and high school, represent knowledge, skills, and behaviors to assist student progress into work and/or continuing education and toward career goals. They are designed to be integrated into all curricula, counseling programs, the school, and the community. Cross-disciplinary strategies are encouraged.

One of the important elements in the Michigan program is the Education/Employability Development Plan, developed by students during the middle-school years and reviewed annually throughout high school. Michigan, through the Employability Skills Assessment Project, offers leadership to schools for the development of student portfolios which include evidence of personal progress in employability skills.

California Career Preparation Education. California provides a kindergarten-through-university continuum of career preparation education programs to enable students to make rational decisions about their lives and to make positive contributions to the workplace (Dahl, 1996). Various programs with linkages of schoolplace learning and workplace learning are offered to prepare students for successful transition; worthwhile home, community, and workplace participation; and progressive lifelong learning. Career preparation education programs in California include:

1. Magnet schools, with college preparation and workforce preparation curricula, career path clusters, and linkages with related business and industry.

2. Academies, with school-within-a-school structure, collaborative team instruction, mentoring, and workplace learning experience.

3. Apprenticeships, with workplace-learning structure, employer-union sponsorship, on-the-job training, and technical instruction.

4. Youth apprenticeships, with secondary-postsecondary-business-industry collaboration, job learning, classroom training, and progress toward certification.

5. Tech-prep, with high school-community college coordination and articulation, occupational education, academic-occupational integration, and competency base.

6. Work experience education, with student-parent-community-school cooperation, classroom learning, community training, and cocurricular activity.

7. Business and industry partnerships, with business-industry-school collaboration, business-industry performance standards, career performance standards, and contextual experience.

California also offers school-to-career programs, an extensive network of regional occupational programs, school and community career resource centers, sequential comprehensive career education programs, and other programs and practices designed to support successful and satisfying careers, education, and work.

CONCLUDING REMARKS

The concepts inherent in the career education movement have been based on a number of societal changes forecast in the late 1960s and 1970s. They included (a) rapid change in occupations and so in occupational change, (b) the need for development of work values in career development, (c) the great and growing need for general employability/adaptability/promotability skills, (d) the continuing crucial importance of basic academic skills in kindergarten through grade 12 and specific occupational skills at the postsecondary sub-baccalaureate level, and (e) the need for all people to discover and utilize ways of making work a part of total lifestyle.

The career education movement was initiated, in part, as a means of increasing the nature and usefulness of education/work relationships. In part, it was initiated as one low-cost "people change" approach to education reform that concentrates on changing the attitudes of both classroom teachers and their pupils in ways that result in more pupil learning.

Career education has not in the past and does not now claim to be the only solution for use in education reform. Career education does claim to be a proven component of reform that deserves to be included in any comprehensive K-12 education reform effort. The need for career education existed long before the career education movement formally came into existence. That need continues today. It is a need that can and should be met under circumstances that call for a minimum expenditure of money and a maximum expenditure of effort on the part of both educators and members of the broader community.

References

Bonnet, D. G. (1978). *A synthesis of results and programmatic recommendations emerging from career education evaluation in 1975-76.* Washington, DC: U.S. Government Printing Office.

Dahl, R. (1996). *Career preparation in California* (AACE Bonus Brief). Hermosa Beach, CA: American Association For Career Education.

Enderlein, T. D. (1976). *A review of career education evaluation studies.* Washington, DC: U.S. Government Printing Office.

Far West Laboratory for Educational Research and Development. (1984). *Career education: Proven programs and promising practices.* Washington, DC: U.S. Department of Education.

Halasz, I. (1988). *Trends and issues in career education 1988.* Columbus, OH: ERIC Clearinghouse on Adult, Career, and Vocational Education.

Hamilton, J., & Mitchell, A. (1978). *Final technical report: Identification of evaluated exemplary activities in career education: K-12.* Palo Alto, CA: American Institutes for Research.

Hoyt, K. B. (1975). *An introduction to career education: A policy paper of the U.S. Office of Education.* Washington, DC: U.S. Government Printing Office.

Hoyt, K. B. (1978a). *The concept of collaboration in career education.* Washington, DC: U.S. Government Printing Office.

Hoyt, K. B. (1978b). *Refining the concept of collaboration in career education.* Washington, DC: U.S. Government Printing Office.

Hoyt, K. B. (1981). *Career education: Where it is and where it is going.* Salt Lake City: Olympus.

Hoyt, K. B. (1987). Trends in career education: Implications for the future. In Hoyt, K. B., & Shylo, K. R., *Career education in transition: Trends and implications for the future* (pp. 5-35). Columbus, OH: ERIC Clearinghouse on Adult, Career, and Vocational Education.

Hoyt, K. B., Evans, R. N., Mackin, E. F., & Mangum, G. L. (1972). *Career education: What it is and how to do it.* Salt Lake City: Olympus.

Hoyt, K. B., & High, S. (1982). Career education. In H. Mitzel (Ed.), *Encyclopedia of Educational Research.* Vol. 1 (pp. 231-241). New York: Free Press.

Marland, S. L., Jr. (1971). *Career education now.* Paper presented at the Annual Convention of the National Association of Secondary School Principals, Houston, Texas.

Marland, S. L., Jr. (1974). *Career education: A proposal for reform.* New York: McGraw-Hill.

Michigan Department of Education. (1996). *Career and employability skills content standards and benchmarks: Working draft.* Lansing, MI: Author.

Ohio Department of Education. (1996-97). *Career passport guidelines.* Columbus, OH: Author.

Ohio Department of Education. (n.d.a). *ICP: Individual career plan.* Columbus, OH: Author.

Ohio Department of Education. (n.d.b). *Ohio's career development blueprint: Individual career plan: K-5, middle school, and high school.* Columbus, OH: Author.

Wickwire, P. N. (1993). America at school and work in the 1990s: Career education—an opportunity. *Youth Policy, 15* (6-7), 16-23.

Wickwire, P. N. (1994). The school-to-work opportunity act and career education: Blending legislation with existing programs. *Youth Policy, 15-16* (12-1), 50-51.

Wickwire, P. N. (1995). *Career education that works.* Hermosa Beach, CA: American Association For Career Education.

Wickwire, P. N. (Ed.). (1996). *The school-to-work opportunities act* (AACE Forum: Solutions). Hermosa Beach, CA: American Association For Career Education.

Wickwire, P. N. (Ed.). (1997a). *Careers, education. and work* (AACE Forum: Trend Watch). Hermosa Beach, CA: American Association For Career Education.

Wickwire, P. N. (1997b). *The changing character of the workplace: Reframing work, the workplace, and the workforce.* Paper presented at the Annual Convention of the California Association for Counseling and Development.

Woal, S. T. (1994). *Career development model* (AACE Distinguished Member Series). Hermosa Beach, CA: American Association For Career Education.

***Kenneth B. Hoyt, Ph.D.**, is University Distinguished Professor of Education and Director, Counseling For High Skills Project, at Kansas State University. Since receiving his Ph.D. degree in Educational Psychology at the University of Minnesota in 1954, Hoyt has devoted most of his career to serving as counselor educator at the University of Iowa (1954-1969), University of Maryland (1969-1974), and Kansas State University (1984-present). From 1974-1983, he served as director or the Office of Career Education, U.S. Department of Education. His major academic discipline is career development. He has published 10 books and more than 150 articles/monographs, mostly on some aspect of education/work relationships. His major research interest, since 1962, has been career development of people seeking some form of postsecondary career-oriented education at the sub-baccalaureate level. In this connection he served as director of the Specialty Oriented Student Research Program, from 1962 until 1974 and of the Counseling for High Skills Project, since 1992. Hoyt has also served as president of the American Counseling Association (1966-67) and the National Career Development Association (1992-93). He was the founding editor of Counselor Education and Supervision from 1961 until 1965. The 23 special national honors awarded him include Distinguished Professional Service Award, American Counseling Association (1994); Outstanding Career Achievement Award, Association for Counselor Education and Supervision (1990); Outstanding Leadership Award, National Association for Industry-Education Cooperation (1989); Eminent Career Award, National Vocational Guidance Association (1981); National Vocational Educator of the Year (SHIP) Award, Education Exhibitors, American Vocational Association (1979); and Outstanding Service Award for Vocational Counseling, American Vocational Association (1972). **Pat Nellor Wickwire**, Ph.D., NCC, LEP, MFCC, is president of the American Association For Career Education and principal of The Nellor Wickwire Group, Hermosa Beach, California. She is past president of the California Association for Counseling and Development, California Women's Caucus, California Association for Measurement and Evaluation, and CACD Education Foundation. She has served as a member of the ERIC Adult, Career, and Vocational Education Advisory Council and the President's Committee on Employment of People with Disabilities. She is former consortium administrator for special education, district administrator for student services and special education, school psychologist, evaluator, counselor, teacher, lecturer, and trainer-supervisor. She is a member of the Women's Inner Circle of Achievement, recipient of the Clarion Modell Award, and recipient of a citation for contributions to education in California. She is a frequent presenter, consultant, trainer, and author on careers, education, work, futures, leadership, and management.*

5

CAREER EDUCATION: THE FOUNDATION FOR SCHOOL-TO-WORK

By J. D. Hoye and Harry Drier

In this chapter, we want to clarify how career education lessons of the past have been and should continue to be the foundation for construction of school-to-work transition attempts in this country. Career education professionals have always been involved in preparing youth for the "real world," and have always known that our nation's youth—with their uniqueness, needs, dreams, education, and career goals—must be the drivetrain that runs any learning-to-earning educational system.

Career educators have a unique understanding of the power of demonstrated relevance in motivating students to learn. Career education is a linchpin between the traditional segmented grade levels in our educational system and postsecondary goals; it ties the K-16 continuum together with life after high school through the addition of important elements such as career awareness, exploration, and experience.

Older educators—we like to refer to ourselves as "mature"—across the country are often skeptical about what we perceive to be new programs, particularly those launched at the federal level that are aimed at enhancing career education and training in our schools. Over several decades, hundreds of thousands of teachers and administrators have already been personally involved in designing and implementing career education efforts, with or without federal assistance. Business coalitions and partnerships with schools that have been quietly successful for 20 or more years exist in every state.

It shouldn't be surprising, then, to hear from many that current school-to-work activities are a mere reinvention of the wheel and unfortunately result in a huge loss of talent from those who fear involvement as just another lesson in frustration, or the rebirth of programs they have seen come and go many times in the past.

We believe that school-to-work is about *using* those lessons from the past, broadening them, and infusing them into comprehensive system-wide change to assure that, in the future, *all* students have access to effective career education experiences. School-to-work is about teaching *all* educators the value of relevant educational practices, and how to motivate students with instruction more closely aligned with the real world as practiced by vocational educators for decades. It is about partnering with business, industry, and services to bring the real world into the classroom, and taking the classroom to the real world. And, it is about seeing parents as a largely untapped but invaluable resource.

The school-to-work movement is actually the synthesis of all that has gone before: not a new "program," but a guide to system-wide change based on lessons learned from the past. It is not in competition with traditional educational practices; rather, it can be seen as the *framework* for schools wanting to increase academic achievement for *all* students.

A BRIEF HISTORY OF THE CAREER EDUCATION UNIVERSE

As early as 1909, U.S. education and labor leaders were searching for ways to more clearly connect schools with the workplace. In that year, Frank Parsons established a vocational bureau in Boston and began raising issues that continue to cause lively discussion among educators: What roles do individual choice, employability, and work satisfaction play in the education of students?

With close similarities to today's movement, nine decades ago Parsons outlined factors that he believed necessary for individual self-sufficiency and work satisfaction: a clear understanding of one's aptitudes, abilities, interests, ambitions, resources, and limitations; an understanding of the requirements and conditions of success within various career pathways, including the disadvantages, compensation, and opportunities; and clarity between the relationships of the first two factors.

These principles of work readiness have been institutionalized over the past 85 years through education and career research and development, career education, and guidance literature. In the United States, Don Super, John Holland, Edwin Herr, Norman Gysbers (Drier & Gysbers, 1993), and others improved and modernized Parson's theories over the years, reinforcing his basic premises and improving on delivery methods.

During this time, other countries were also analyzing the connections between learning and earning a living with a satisfying occupation. In Japan, during the World War II reconstruction period, Shigekazu Fukuyama, a vocational psychologist with the Japanese government, studied early career education-related theory, and in 1949 wrote:

> Unless work satisfaction is derived, an individual's self-fulfillment in life cannot be achieved, and consequently his or her true life happiness is not secured. Vocational development is a dynamic process, and an occupational choice should be the result of understanding and following a vocational guidance (career education) process. Work satisfaction is procured when an individual has acquired the ability to make the most effective occupational choice. Work satisfaction depends on an individual's ability to determine an occupation consistent with the needs of his or her personality, interests, aspirations, and his or her physical resources applicable in the world of work. To develop such ability, an individual has to acquire a sufficient understanding of self or his or her innate interests, abilities, and aptitudes, and thus be able to recognize the relationship to needs, values, capacities, and aspirations. By experimenting with various kinds of jobs, the individual should be able to identify the occupation in which he or she may be able to utilize his or her abilities and aptitudes most effectively, and develop potential to the fullest extent possible. (Fukuyama, 1991, p. i)

By the 1970s, career education was seen as a "top priority" by Sidney P. Marland, Jr., the Commissioner of Education in the U.S. Department of Education; Marland is regarded as the "father" of career education in this country. In 1974, career education was finally receiving its first official federal dollars, as part of the Elementary and Secondary Education Act Amendments. Although the allocations were not earmarked for program implementation, $40 million was spent to support career education demonstration projects at 425 sites.

As a U.S. Office of Education priority, career education concepts had an excellent opportunity to succeed at that point in time. Like the current School-to-Work Opportunities Act, it focused on a broad community approach, using known best practices and connecting teaching and learning with the workplace.

In 1976 Ken Hoyt, then associate commissioner for career education as the U.S. Office of Education, issued a statement that still resonates with relevance to today's transitional laws and policies: "Career education is defined as an effort aimed at refocusing American education and actions of the broader community in ways that will help individuals acquire and utilize the knowledge, skills, and attitudes necessary for each to make work a meaningful, productive, and satisfying part of their way of living" (p.1).

Much of the research conducted in the early 1970s provides valuable insights into today's school-to-work planning. The research engineering design used allowed career education concepts to be developed and tested in four innovative and distinct environments:

1. The school-based model. It was assumed that there were many effective career education programs in existence throughout the country, and that the model developers could quickly "engineer" a comprehensive program by assembling a variety of high-quality components from selected school districts in the vanguard of the career education movement. It was further assumed that the model developers could fit these pieces together into a rational system of K-12 education, filling in a few undeveloped voids, and organizing it in such a manner that other districts around the nation could readily adapt and implement the model in their own schools.

2. The employer-based model. This was an attempt by the U.S. Office of Education to respond to the growing chorus of critics expressing disenchantment with current vocational programs. The 1973 Forward Plan for Career Education Research and Development, National Institute of Education, identified four underlying assumptions of this model: Secondary school systems fail to prepare students for self-sufficiency and adulthood, and schools are irrelevant for a significant number of youth; the public school system is inherently incapable of even helping to solve the problem; the most appropriate way to prepare many adolescents for careers is through the employment community; there are untapped natural incentives that will induce employers to become involved in work-centered education for adolescents. The program was to be developed, operated, and entirely supported by a consortium of industrial, commercial, and other employers and assisted by parents, unions, community agencies, and other organizations.

3. The residential-based model. This model was designed and established to rehabilitate whole families, not merely individual breadwinners. Disadvantaged families from six states were brought to a center where they were given a "prescription," drawn from individual interviews, personal data (interests, needs, aptitudes), and the availability of resources. This prescription included counseling, recreation, home services for the family, and vocational preparation. Employment on completion of the residency was guaranteed by the home state of each family, and assistance with the job search was provided.

The underlying assumptions of this model included: Formal education alone is not sufficient to help poor families; the problems of many poor families go beyond the lack of specific job skills, also including lack of household management skills, health and nutrition knowledge, and child-care skills, and extensive family counseling is important; the best way to help poor families is to move them away from their present environment into a controlled residential environment.

4. The home-based model. The inspiration for the home-based model was *Sesame Street*, a successful, long-running educational television series for children. An attempt to develop and coordinate learning systems to reach certain home-based populations caught between formal education and work, the home-based model was never fully operable.

There were three general approaches conceived for this model: a career-oriented television program to motivate home-based target groups to study for careers, to provide related information, and to provide some limited instruction for selected occupational competencies; development of home and community-centered educational systems using television, correspondence programs, radio, and other instructional aids; and career clinics in the community to provide career guidance and counseling, referral services, and information on relevant educational programs.

All four of these models were practical inventions rather than the products of rigorous research and development. It became apparent that the school-based model, as an example, did not have in place the necessary changes in curriculum, school environments, teacher and counselor training, and infrastructures. The employer-based model found that industry and business were not geared to provide high volumes of academic training and were not yet predisposed to do so. The residential model became a cumbersome and expensive model with few proven effects and questionable objectives. The home-based model did not produce its goals, primarily due to underfunding and lack of existing mediated instruction.

Of all previously mentioned models, only the school-based approach continues to be replicated in our schools, and has proven to be the most effective in some states. However, despite the short lives of the other three, all have contributed valuable information and experiences.

It's clear that, during these years, we were building an infrastructure rich with trained leaders, libraries of materials, and evidence of what works—and what doesn't work—from the past. Newer efforts such as the School-to-Work Opportunities Act certainly encourage creativity, flexibility, and locally designed strategies—as long as they are grounded in lessons from the past. Newer efforts also must have a strong outcomes evaluation process to assure that, long after current funding ends, practitioners will know and understand what works, and what is worth replication.

THE IMPACT OF CAREER EDUCATION IN THE UNITED STATES

Not a great deal of empirical data exists on the effects of career education, particularly as it relates to student outcomes, employer satisfaction, and impact within the educational system (academic achievement, school retention, etc.) The lessons learned here were that (a) the issue of measuring effects was not addressed until too late in the short-term legislative effort, and (b) evaluation efforts that were in place targeted individual activities, not the overall outcomes of involvement. Curriculum units were designed and measured individually, while project efforts like community involvement were measured only at the school level.

An example of one state that has continued to legislate and fund career education is Ohio. Over the past 27 years, a state law with a Special Career Education line-item has generated over 80 million dollars. Career Education Coordinators and staff are still in place, as evidenced by 980 persons attending the 1997 Ohio Career Education Conference. Career Education Councils are still operating in several of Ohio's educational regions. It is reported that over 1.7 million K-12 students have been served annually within Ohio's 612 school districts. The state legislature mandates individual career planning for all eighth-grade students, and this is occurring. Career development and comprehensive guidance programs are now institutionalized and expected in all elementary and secondary schools (Drier & Heath, 1996, pp. 44-49).

The advantages educators have seen with school-to-work change is the emphasis on student outcomes, not just project process evaluations. If addressed sufficiently, 10 years from now Congress and education and labor leaders will have the evidence they need to understand and advocate for school-to-work changes.

As an example, statistics published in 1996 by the Center for Labor Market Studies at Northeastern University (Summ & Hall, 1996) compare 1995 Boston graduates of the ProTech program with the same class from the Boston Public Schools. As of April, 1996, 51 percent of Boston Public Schools graduates were attending college, while 69 percent of ProTech's graduates were in college; 54 percent from the public schools were working, while 77 percent of ProTech's graduates were working.

In Philadelphia, school-to-career participants (work-based learning students) were compared with the rest of the student population in terms of academic achievement, dropout rates, and graduation rates. The school district total for dropouts (eleventh- and twelfth-graders) in 1996 was 9.9 percent, while school-to-career students had a 1.1 percent dropout rate; the overall district total graduation rate was 85.8 percent while the school-to-career rate was 97.6 percent; and, academic achievement (Grade Point Average scores) compared as follows:

G.P.A.:	0.0-.99	1.0-1.99	2.0-2.9	3.0 +
District Total.:	18.0%	29.5%	32.9%	19.7%
STC Students:	5.6%	22.6%	43.3%	28.7%

THE ADVENT OF SCHOOL-TO-WORK LEGISLATION

In May 1994, President Clinton signed into law the School-to-Work Opportunities Act, legislation that enjoyed strong bipartisan support from Congress. For the first time the U.S. Department of Education and the Department of Labor had joint responsibility for implementing legislation that would impact employers and educators throughout the nation.

The strategy inherent in school-to-work legislation was to use federal dollars to leverage other federal, state, and private investments that support the nation's emerging workforce. Grants were awarded competitively based on the readiness of states applying. Federal resources were intended to be seed or venture capital that would be used to encourage and support "system building" at the state level.

There were clear indicators, prior to the Act, that a lack of synergy between workforce development efforts, education reform, and economic development projects existed. Unlike historical pieces of legislation, the School-to-Work Opportunities Act specified no presumed deliverer; instead, each state was allowed to identify its own delivery system. Also, governors were required to sign off on state applications.

In 1994, eight states successfully competed for funding and were awarded grants. In 1995, an additional 19 states were awarded grants, followed by an additional 10 states in 1996.

BUILDING A SYSTEM FOR EVERYONE

The systemic approach encouraged in the School-to-Work Opportunities Act has challenged states and local partnerships to think outside the traditional "silos" of programs, and to build bridges to assure that *all* students have opportunities that reinforce academic preparation with real-life and work opportunities. School-to-work legislation is predicated on three of the four "old" models of career education, reframing and emphasizing the importance and interrelationships between learning at school, at the workplace, and the connecting activities that result in relevancy for learners.

Historically we have viewed the workplace as the end result for learning, rather than seeing it as a learning opportunity in itself. School-to-work legislation and activities challenge the old assumptions by changing our perceptions of the workplace: Now we understand it is a place where education can be reinforced while at the same time providing a framework for the choices our children make for their futures. Our currently robust economy, our large number of retirees from the workplace, and rapid workplace changes due to technology all contribute to the openness we are experiencing from employers who now understand and promote the concept of "learning" rather than "training."

Eight system-building perspectives were

reinforced during the first year of implementation of the School-to-Work Opportunities Act:

1. The concept of all students—States are challenged to assure that their designs provide high-quality, rigorous opportunities from which *all* can benefit, including, but not limited to, at-risk students, disabled students, talented and gifted students, and students no longer in the public school system or in alternative learning environments. States are asked to raise the bar of achievement within their educational systems, which necessitates the offering of multiple strategies for all to achieve the standards.

In the past, we have spent great sums of money on programs for "some," putting them into a hierarchy of importance; systems change promoted by school-to-work legislation expects improvements to provide access and benefits to all, rather than to some. The "easy" answer is to make attempts at improving academic achievement, but the real challenge is finding ways to get all students at higher levels of performance. Relevant and motivational school-to-work activities, school-based and work-based, level the playing field and allow standards to promote all successfully, rather than separate and promote within disparate groups.

2. Career education K-16—School-to-work legislation expects students to receive well-rounded exposures to career education, with quality connections between academic instruction and work opportunities through a building-block approach, not just single events or services that occur at planned points in time. Elementary schools are encouraged to stress career awareness, middle schools to focus on exploration, and high schools and secondary institutions to address work experience and to tie learning in the classroom in with experience in the workplace. Schools at every level are encouraged to develop partnerships between teachers, counselors, parents, and employers. Career education, in general, offers opportunities for students to understand their own interests and abilities, work options, and further education requirements, while at the same time helping to build self-confidence, clarify lifetime goals, and provide students with marketable credentials and portfolios for employment or further education.

3. Employer involvement—The key to achieving scale with school-to-work legislation was the broad expansion of involvement by the employer community at every level, ranging from seminars by employers in schools to paid internships for teachers and students in the workplace. This may, in fact, be the single most important element for achievement of the goals envisioned in the Act. The Department of Labor's Bureau of Labor Statistics suggests that over 80 percent of high school juniors and seniors in this country are presently working, yet the mathematical evaluation sets a baseline of 2 percent of the seniors actually engaged in significant, connected learning activities that include employment.

4. Staff development—Preparation of our teachers and counselors is central to connecting the classroom with the workplace, improving curriculum to provide relevance for students, and involving the community as a framework for learning and achieving academic standards. The challenge is for both inservice and preservice. Too often our teaching and counseling staffs have little opportunity for current experience with work outside of teaching. Given the dramatic changes in the workplace with both technology and expectations of workers, simply asking teachers to make instruction more relevant misses the mark.

Central to our expectation of rigorous academics and relevant curriculum is the inclusion of staff development strategies which place the teacher and counselor *in* the workplace in varying roles and in varying industries, to assure that the curriculum shifts are real, meaningful, and true to life. In addition, school administrators are not immune to the need for relevant experiences; principals and others are key to encouraging and allowing change to happen in schools, and should be afforded the same school-to-work opportunities as other staff members.

5. Career majors—The act specifically addresses the need to develop broad career areas that begin to frame secondary experiences around major clusters. It's not necessary to change quality and rigorous content, but giving the student a context within which to understand that instruction greatly increases interest and motivation. It is critical that this be seen as a framework and not as an alternative strategy for the non-collegebound. Framing curriculum broadly should not lower standards or expectations, but motivate the learner to meet or exceed academic standards by answering the most commonly asked question of students: "Why do I need to know this?"

6. All aspects of the industry—New in this legislation was the concept of "all aspects of the industry." Too often the industry context has been so job-specific that career information was confused with job training for those individuals not slated for college. The new language helped local implementers to see career information on a scale that could support both entry-level and management-level job information, reinforcing the notion of *all* students and lifelong learning. At the same time it encouraged teachers to learn and experience more about industries and the curriculum content connection.

7. Accountability—Central to any investment strategy that hopes to be sustained over time is the development of key accountability areas which reinforce that the concept works, it moves all stakeholders to new roles, it adds value to student learning, and it validates that the investment made a difference. Most education facilities lack data systems to accurately show student progress and gains based on new strategies; central to system building is data system development and identification of those performance areas which should improve, based on the investment (attendance, reduced dropout numbers, test scores, student satisfaction, GPA, etc.) and the documented progress of getting to scale. How to collect gross information and value-added information is critical for program improvement, if changes are intended to be for all, while at the same time individualized for each student. Early student information suggests that connecting school-based instruction to real-world application does make positive differences.

8. Roll-out strategy—The eighth system element promoted in the early years of the School-to-Work Opportunities Act was an investment "roll-out" strategy. Unique to this legislation was the empowerment of states to develop such strategies that moved resources to local areas in a design that made sense for their states and localities. With five years of resources and increasing percentages of money spent locally, thinking through an investment strategy that leverages and maximizes other investments becomes critical to the sustainability potential when federal dollars cease to flow.

Most states have many substate structures to serve education improvement and workforce development; unfortunately, the geographic boundaries for these rarely match. So we see local efforts competing for employers, leadership, and resources, with a confused public left in the wake. Given the emphasis in the School-to-Work Act to see the new revenue as venture capital, the design and alignment of local service delivery became a first step for many in the new system design.

LESSONS LEARNED

It's fairly easy to look back and analyze the programs that could have been better, the ideas that might have come sooner, and the approaches that might have been more successful. Yet it is because of the past career education experiences that we now see extraordinary gains being made to move all children to high academic standards and solid career choices. What we require is a greater emphasis on designing the learning experience to include real applications and the valuing of education that occurs outside the traditional classroom.

School-to-work legislation places great value on local design rather than federal mandate. And, key to many of the gains has been the requirement that local partnerships move responsibility from schools alone to community-wide efforts, with specific roles and responsibilities outlined for each stakeholder. This, coupled with a clear message that there was no presumed deliverer of services, forced the debate of who should take the lead, based on talent and not on history.

Capacity building that moves professionals from ideas to strategic plans, with timelines and performance measures, is an absolute requirement for any comprehensive effort; without this planning, efforts can appear so huge that no one knows where to start. We must assure that capacity building is not done in groups of like professionals, but instead in teams with multiple stakeholders that, as a result, promise to move beyond the rhetoric into action.

We must remember to keep the compelling reasons for comprehensive change in front of our proposed efforts. Motivating change is nearly impossible without a clear expression of "*why*" that leaves no other alternatives to the individual who cares about kids and the future of this nation. This information is real and available through the U.S. Department of Labor's Bureau of Labor Statistics and the U.S. Census Resource Center.

Too often, parents are stakeholders who are not actively recruited—yet they are central to the success of this type of initiative. Where involved, they provide a wonderful bridge to the community and force us to keep our ideas and plans plain and understandable. Parents are the primary reason and method for the provision of ongoing communication with the community about changes we propose and goals we plan to achieve.

CHALLENGES REMAINING

Right now, "staying the course" is important; change that is necessary and thoughtful takes time. We must realize that we are not just changing education but how we think *about* the entire educational process as it relates to the future, which includes these enormous tasks: changing how we see ourselves and understanding how our future is tied to the performance of the emerging workforce—today's students; developing new curriculum that reflects reality, is flexible, and can change with societal and technological advances; encouraging and allowing teachers to learn different instructional strategies that work; mobilizing whole communities to understand change and participate in the solutions.

As a nation, our track record is not admirable in staying focused on the finish line and continuing to build on what makes sense and what works. Too often, we abandon good ideas that have not had a chance to flower, only to run to the next new program, making no connections to past ideas. It shouldn't come as a surprise to us that so many look to the new with eyes that say "this too shall pass." Leaders must promote and repeatedly demonstrate the connections between initiatives, helping practitioners to keep the momentum going and build on successes over time. In addition, we must resist the tendency to start anew with each new leader or idea, and instead add value to our past work.

The inclusion of communities in our thinking and the broader use of communities in our design and implementation strategies is central to achieving much that has been proposed over the past 10 years in education reform and workforce development. Too many citizens feel disconnected from public policies and actions; they see no roles for themselves and no direct benefits. Infusing real life into the education process adds value to communities, and designing learning experiences with the community in mind can begin to bridge the disconnect between our schools and our citizens.

Policies that reinforce the value of careers in relation to high academic performance—to sustain the lessons learned and counteract the historic belief system that "this too shall pass"—will require our traditional policies to be amended in ways that reinforce the principles of school-to-work, including credit for teacher internships, hiring practices that value contextual learning, college admissions that expect more than just classroom preparation, student assessments that seek demonstrated knowledge and the ability to apply that knowledge, employers who readily allow time off for employees to volunteer in school, and a concerted effort in preparing educational leadership for the role of community advocate.

Our future is tied to our willingness to change, and to listen to those we intend to serve—our children.

References

Drier, H. D., & Gysbers, N. C. (1993). *Guidance and counseling programs for the year 2000 and beyond: Strengthening work-related education and training.* (SP58N). Columbus, OH: Center on Education and Training for Employment.

Drier, H., & Heath, K. (1996). Build on lessons learned. *Youth Policy, 15 & 16* (1 & 2). Washington, DC: Youth Policy Institute.

Fukuyama, S. (1991). *A philosophical foundation of vocational guidance.* (2nd Ed.). Columbus, OH: Career, Education and Training Associates.

Hoyt, K. (1976). *Career education and the teaching/learning process*. Washington, DC: U.S. Department of Health, Education, and Welfare; Office of Education.

Parsons, F. (1909). Choosing a vocation (Reprinted in C. McDaniels (1994), *Journal of Career Development, 20* (4).

School District of Philadelphia. (1996, October). Philadelphia, PA.

Summ, A., & Hall, G. (1996, July). *Executive summary—Study for Boston Private Industry Council: Class of 1995 follow-up study.* Boston: MA: Center for Labor Market Studies, Northeastern University.

J. D. Hoye** is former director of the National School-to-Work Office in Washington, D.C. Prior to that she was associate superintendent for Professional/Technical Education for the Oregon Department of Education and Office of Community College Services. Hoye is president of Keep the Change, Inc., and lives in Silver Spring, Maryland. She speaks across the U.S. about education reform, workforce development, and systems change.* ***Harry Drier *is currently research scientist emeritus at Ohio State University, Columbus. He serves as president of two corporations: Career, Education and Training Associates, Inc., and the International Network of Education and Training Specialists, Inc.*

PART II:
CAREER DEVELOPMENT

The world is filled with willing people; some willing to work, the rest willing to let them.—Robert Frost

OVERVIEW OF CAREER DEVELOPMENT THEORY

By Stanley H. Cramer

Bona fide career-development theories have existed for approximately five decades. Each attempts to explain—beyond the phenomena of chance or accidental factors—how and why people choose careers and engage in the career behaviors that characterize their work lives. Fanciful theories have existed throughout history, ranging from clairvoyance (e.g., Edgar Cayce advising persons on what they should do for their life's work, based on his divining what they did in their previous lives) to hormone levels (e.g., classifying occupations according to the average amount of testosterone of those in the occupation: ministers low, used-car salesmen high) to physical characteristics (e.g., average brain weight of those in various occupations).

Of the legitimate theories, about a dozen have received serious attention and have added to our knowledge of how people choose and advance in their careers. Several volumes describe these theories (Brown et al., 1990; Herr & Cramer, 1996; Osipow, 1983; Sharf, 1992). Because of space limitations, this chapter will describe only two primary theories. Other theories are simply listed below. The so-called *trait-and factor* (*actuarial* or *matching*) *theory* more describes differences among occupations than it explains how people choose occupations. It assigns a purely cognitive conscious process to career development (in fact, it is more emotional than logical). According to this theory, one need only measure a person's traits (e.g., aptitudes, interests, values, etc.), determine how much of each trait an occupation requires, and get a match. Other less accepted, partial, or narrow theories include those of expectancy (Raynor & Entin, 1982), self-efficacy (Lent, Brown, & Hackett, 1994), decision (Gelatt, 1989), psychoanalysis (Bordin, Nachmann, & Segal, 1963), social learning (Krumboltz, 1994), child-rearing (Roe, 1956), early development (Ginzberg, Ginsburg, Axelrad, & Hemia (1951), ego-identity differentiation (Tiedeman & Miller-Tiedeman, 1984), subject-time (Savickas, 1994), aspiration (Gottfredson, 1981), life-stage adult development (Schlossberg, 1986), and the moderating influences of sociological factors (Bronfenbrenner, 1979).

Two theories, however, dominate the field of career development guidance: the developmental/self-concept/trait theory of Donald Super (1953, 1969, 1980, 1992) and the person-situation congruence theory (person-environment fit) of John Holland (1963, 1966, 1973, 1985, 1992).

Note that neither of these theories—nor any

theory in the social and behavioral sciences—possesses all of the characteristics that we ask of a good theory, although they do contain substantial elements of the following eight characteristics. We want a theory to be parsimonious (explains phenomena in the simplest possible form), consistent with extant data (agrees with facts already gathered from research), useful (helps people choose good careers), research stimulating (makes new discoveries as it tests a theory), comprehensive (pertains to males and females, majority and minority populations, etc.), clearly stated (uses obvious terms, constructs, and interrelationships among propositions), heuristic (defines operations well for research), and predictive (charts career paths to predict both job satisfaction and worker satisfactoriness). The rest of this chapter answers the most commonly posed questions about career-development theory.

DONALD E. SUPER

Donald E. Super, a magnificent synthesizer, applied constructs and concepts from various elements of psychology, sociology, and anthropology to the study of careers. Drawing from ego psychology (the self-concept), differential psychology (measuring individual differences relevant to careers), and developmental psychology (lifespan stages of career development), he fashioned the most comprehensive theory of career development and behavior. By 1990, Super had evolved 14 empirically testable propositions of career development (summarized from Super, 1990, pp. 206-208):

1. People differ in their abilities and personalities, needs, values, interests, traits, and self-concepts.

2. People qualify, by virtue of these characteristics, for a number of occupations.

3. Each occupation requires a characteristic pattern of abilities and personality traits, with tolerance wide enough to allow both variety of occupations for each individual and variety of individuals in each occupation.

4. Vocational preferences and competencies, the situations in which people live and work, and, hence, their self-concepts change with time and experience, although self-concepts, as products of social learning, increasingly stablize from late adolescence until late maturity, providing some continuity in choice and adjustment.

5. A series of life stages (a "maxi-cycle")—characterized as a sequence of growth, exploration, establishment, maintenance, and decline—sums up the process of change, which may in turn subdivide into (a) the fantasy, tentative, and realistic phases of the exploratory stage and (b) the trial and stable phases of the establishment stage. A small (mini) cycle occurs in transitions from one stage to the next or each time a force reduction, change in manpower needs, illness or injury, or other socioeconomic or personal event destabilizes an individual. Such unstable or multiple-trial careers involve new growth, re-explorations, and re-establishment (recycling).

6. A person's parental socioeconomic level, mental abilities, education, skills, personality characteristics (needs, values, interests, and self-concepts), career maturity, and opportunities to which he or she is exposed determine the nature of the career pattern—that is, the occupation level attained and the sequence, frequency, and duration of trial and stable jobs.

7. Success in coping with the demands of the environment and of the organism in that context at any given life-career stage depends on the readiness of the individual to cope with these demands (that is, on his or her career maturity). Career *maturity* comprises physical, psychological, and social characteristics; psychologically, it is cognitive and affective and includes the degree of success in coping with the demands of earlier stages and substages of career development, especially with the most recent.

8. Career maturity—a hypothetical construct perhaps as difficult to formulate as intelligence but possessing a much briefer history and vaguer achievements—does not increase monotonically and it is not a unitary trait.

9. Development through life stages may be

guided by facilitating the maturation of abilities and interests and by aiding in reality testing and developing self-concepts.

10. Career development essentially involves developing and implementing occupational self-concepts. A synthesizing and compromising process, the self-concept results from interactions among inherited aptitudes, physical makeup, opportunity to observe and play various roles, and evaluations of the extent to which superiors and fellows approve the results of role playing (interactive learning).

11. The synthesis of or compromise between individual and social factors, between self-concepts and reality, depends on role playing and on learning from feedback, whether the role is played in fantasy, in the counseling interview, or in such real-life activities as classes, clubs, part-time work, and entry-level jobs.

12. Work satisfactions and life satisfactions depend on the extent to which the individual finds adequate outlets for abilities, needs, values, interests, personality traits, and self-concepts. They depend on establishing a type of work, work situation, and a way of life in which a person can play the kind of role that growth and exploratory experiences have led him or her to consider congenial and appropriate.

13. The degree of satisfaction people obtain from work is proportional to the degree to which they can implement self-concepts.

14. Work and occupation organize personality for most men and women, although for some this focus is peripheral, incidental, or even nonexistent. In those cases, other foci, such as leisure activities and homemaking, may be central. (Such social traditions as sex-role stereotyping and modeling, racial and ethnic biases, and the opportunity structure, as well as individual differences, determine preferences for such roles as worker, student, leisurite, homemaker, and citizen.)

Super theorizes that people, as socialized organizers of their experiences, will choose occupations that allow them to function in roles consistent with their self-concepts (formed as a result of their developmental history). Most people, according to Super, are multipotentialed and can, consequently, find satisfaction and be satisfactory workers in a wide array of occupations. His emphasis on career rather than the narrower *occupation* arose from his concept of lifespan stages in career development (see item 5 above). Progress through career development incurs an expectation that people will master increasingly complex tasks. Super and others' (1992) C-DAC Model specifies and operationalizes these, and their mastery leads to *career adaptability* (originally termed *career maturity*).

To depict how various roles emerge and interact across the lifespan, Super invented the Life Career Rainbow. He argues that people play nine major roles in their lives: (1) child (son or daughter), (2) student, (3) leisurite, (4) citizen, (5) worker (including unemployed worker and nonworker, as ways of playing the role), (6) spouse, (7) homemaker, (8) parent, and (9) pensioner. The interaction of the various roles constitutes a career. People enact these roles in various theaters, principally (1) the home, (2) community, (3) school (including college and university), and (4) workplace. That people play several roles simultaneously in several theaters means that occupation, family, community, and leisure roles affect each other in symbiotic ways.

In Super's words, "The simultaneous combination of life roles constitutes the *life style;* their sequential combination structures the *life space* and constitutes the *life cycle*. The total structure is the *career pattern*" (1980, p. 288). These roles increase and decrease in importance with the life stage and in consonance with the developmental tasks encountered with advancing age.

The Life Career Rainbow gradually evolved into the Archway Model of Career Determinants, which basically places the same concepts in a different package: "The archway is important in illustrating the ways in which the qualities of the individual and his or her society contribute in systematic rather than chaotic ways to career development. It emphasizes, too, that it is the individual who in his or her own way, synthesizes the effects of these determinants: it is the person, the self—the keystone of the arch—who is the decision-maker" (Super, 1994, p. 67).

Super operationalizes many of his constructs in terms of instruments that contribute to the C-DAC model, including the Career Development Inventory, the Adult Career Concerns Inventory, the Values Inventory, and the Salience Inventory.

JOHN HOLLAND

The second major career development theorist is John Holland (1966, 1973, 1982, 1985, 1992), whose structural-interactive approach views personality type as the major influence on career choice and development, combining it with differential psychology (primarily, interest measurement). Specifically, he makes the following assertions:

1. The choice of an occupation expresses personality and not random events, although chance plays a role.
2. The members of an occupational group have similar personalities and similar histories of personal development.
3. Because people in an occupational group have similar personalities, they respond to many situations and problems in similar ways.
4. Occupational achievement, stability, and satisfaction depend on congruence between one's personality and the job environment. (Holland, 1982, p. 2)

Four assumptions undergird Holland's theory:

1. In our culture, most individuals fall into one of six types: realistic, investigative, artistic, social, enterprising, or conventional.
2. There are six kinds of environments: realistic, investigative, artistic, social enterprising, and conventional.
3. People search for environments that let them exercise their skills and abilities, express their attitudes and values, and take on agreeable problems and roles.
4. Interaction between one's personality and the characteristics of one's environment determine a person's behavior. (Holland, 1973, pp. 2-4; 1985)

Later, Holland added five new secondary assumptions:

Consistency: Some types of people or environments relate to each other more than do others. Thus, "degrees of consistency or relatedness are assumed to affect vocational preference."

Differentiation: "The degree to which a person or an environment is well-defined is its degree of differentiation. . . . Personal identity is defined as the possession of a clear and stable picture of one's goals, interests, and talents. Environmental identity is present when an environment or organization has clear, integrated goals, tasks, and rewards that are stable over long time intervals."

Congruence: Different personality types require different environments. "Incongruence occurs when a type lives in an environment that provides opportunities and rewards foreign to the person's preferences and abilities—for instance, a realistic type in a social environment."

Calculus: "The relationships within and between types of environments can be ordered according to a hexagonal model in which the distances between the types of environments are inversely proportional to the theoretical relationship between them."

Identity: The possession of a clear and stable picture of one's goals, interests, and talents. (1985, pp. 4-5)

The list below describes the six types of personalities, as designated by the first letter of their descriptors (RIASEC):

1. The r*ealistic* (R) type prefers activities requiring explicit, ordered, or systematic manipulation of objects, tools, machines, or animals. This type avoids educational or therapeutic activities. Examples of occupations that meet the needs of realistic types include surveyor and mechanic.
2. The i*nvestigative* (I) type prefers activities that entail observational, symbolic, systematic, and creative investigations of physical, biological, and cultural phenomena to understand and control such phenomena. This type avoids persuasive, social, and repetitive activi-

ties. Examples of occupations that meet the needs of investigative types include chemist and physicist.

3. The *artistic* (A) type prefers ambiguous, free, unsystematized activities that entail manipulating physical, verbal, or human materials to create art forms or products. This type avoids explicit, systematic, and ordered activities. Examples of occupations that meet the needs of artistic types include artist and writer.

4. The *social* (S) type prefers activities that entail manipulating others to inform, train, develop, cure, or enlighten. This type avoids explicit, ordered, systematic activities involving materials, tools, or machines. Examples of occupations that meet the needs of social types include social science teacher and vocational counselor.

5. The *enterprising* (E) type prefers activities that require manipulating others to attain organizational goals or economic gain. This type avoids observational, symbolic, and systematic activities. Examples of occupations that meet the needs of enterprising types include political scientist, salesman, and executive.

6. The *conventional* (C) type prefers activities that entail the explicit, ordered, systematic manipulation of data, such as keeping records, filing materials, reproducing materials, organizing written and numerical data according to a prescribed plan, operating business machines and data processing machines to attain organizational or economic goals. This type avoids ambiguous, free, exploratory, or unsystematized activities. Examples of occupations that meet the needs of conventional types include accountant and clerk. (Holland, 1973, pp. 14-18.)

Holland's theory contends that individual behavior results from interaction between one's personality and environment, and that choice behavior expresses personality. Thus, people seek educational and occupational settings that permit expression of their personality styles. Since persons inhabiting particular environments, occupational or educational, have similar personality characteristics, their responses to problems and interpersonal situations will likely be similar. For these reasons, interest inventories are personality inventories, and vocational stereotypes have important psychological and sociological implications. If people's preferences are clear and their information about self or occupations accurate, they will likely make effective choices. If their understanding of their personality type or appropriate occupations is unclear, they will likely be indecisive and vacillate among possible choices. In Holland's view, the adequacy of information about the self and various occupational possibilities is crucial.

The six personality types array themselves in a hexagon, according to Holland, with proximate types more likely to combine than distal types (see Figure 6.1). Hence, R types most likely include in their personality elements of I and C and least likely include elements of S, since it lies furthest from R in the hexagon.

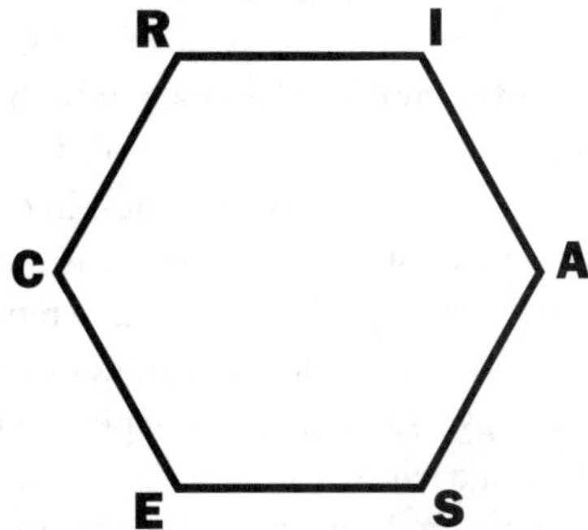

Figure 6.1—The Holland Hexagonal Arrangement of Personality Types

Like Super, Holland operationalizes his theory in a series of instruments widely used in career guidance and counseling and in research, including the Vocational Preference Inventory, the Self-Directed Search, My Vocational Situation, and the Vocational Identity Scale, among others. Holland's work has received much research attention, and hundreds of studies point to the strengths and gaps in his theory. Holland himself (1994) identifies its major weakness: "In general, the strengths of typologies lie in their ability to provide information. In contrast, the weaknesses of typologies lie in their neglect of the processes entailed in change and development" (p. 50).

ISSUES RELATED TO CAREER DEVELOPMENT THEORY

Is there a reputable and useful theory of career development?

Yes, several theories, including the "big two" just described, are reputable and useful. No theory, however, represents the ultimate theory. By choosing a theory or parts of several theories, those who intervene to enhance the career development of individuals will have a sound basis for practice.

Do we require separate theories of career development for males and females? People of color? People with disabilities? Gays and lesbians?

Differences in career development probably vary more in degree than in kind (Herr & Cramer, 1996). Males and females, for example, need to consider the same factors, but each gender, in aggregate, likely places different emphasis on many of the factors. For both men and women, for instance, the importance of family forms a major consideration in career development, choice, and behavior. Is it more important for females? Probably. But it remains important for both. The great bulk of career needs are universal, whether the person lives in a ghetto or a suburb, on a reservation or in a village. Few total career needs (perhaps 3 to 5 percent) are to a given group. Attempts to devise separate theories for females (Zytowski, 1969; Astin, 1984), immigrants (Krau, 1982), and people with disabilities (McDaniels, 1963) underscored, in general, that these populations resemble each other more than they differ, in terms of self-knowledge, education, training, and work, and decision-making skills that they must develop. Hence, career development theory—with certain obvious modifications—is basically a one-size-fits-all concept.

How significant are chance or accidental factors in career development?

Obviously, chance or happenstance plays some part in everyone's career development, an influence ranging from accidents of birth and geography to various fortuitous events. Bandura (1982), however, demonstrates that chance does not form the be-all and end-all of career development and that, in fact, while social and economic contexts produce unforeseen events that may disrupt or change career trajectories, the choices we make increases the likelihood of some types of chance encounters over others: "Fortuitous influences may be unforeseen, but having occurred, they enter as evident factors in causal chains in the same way as prearranged ones do" (p. 749).

Do all people, in fact, have a career choice or are careers chosen?

Some people believe that only those who select higher-level careers have a choice and that those who remain are chosen. The idea of self-agency in careers—of being "master of one's fate and captain of one's soul" —largely owes to self-efficacy. If individuals feel that they have a choice, they will take the necessary steps to exercise that choice. If they feel that they lack choice, they will be passive and more subject to the whims of accident or chance. Thus, establishing early a sense of responsibility for one's personal direction in life seems crucial.

How does early environment influence career development? To what extent do parents influence, and how?

Although some theories assert the all-importance of a person's early environment (cf. Roe, 1956; Bordin, Nachmann, & Segal, 1963), newer developmental perspectives suggest that just as many profound influences occur across the lifespan as in the early years. It makes sense that family of origin and early nurturing (or lack of it) influence career development, but at this point research results remain insufficiently clear to tell us to what extent and precisely how such influence occurs. The family is clearly a pot in which all sorts of melting occurs, manufacturing attitudes and values, aspirations, and skills; yet we lack hard data that demonstrate exactly how this process occurs.

Which psycho-social processes dominate the career choice-making process?

The parts of decision-making that intrapsychic, situational, and interactive factors influence is moot. Career indecision and indecisiveness form aspects of career choice requiring further research. Currently, we simply do not know how career-deciding individuals choose a process, how and why they weigh different factors, and what motivates mini-choices over time. No current theory offers definitive answers. Newer research by Peterson, Sampson, and Reardon (1991) and by Neimeyer (1988, 1989), Neimeyer, Nevilli, Probert, and Fukuyama (1985), and Parr and Neimeyer (1994) offers promising data on how people process information in making career choices.

What is the nature of the decision-making process?

Most career development theories and subsequent interventions based on the theories assume that choice-making is logical. As we have previously noted, it may be more emotional than logical. Usual procedures involve a by-the-numbers problem-solving approach: define the problem, generate alternatives, weigh the alternatives according to some defined criteria, choose the best alternative, and implement it. This approach typically ignores the person's internal frame of reference. But all career interventions assume that people learn decision making.

Do within-group differences exceed or equal between-group differences?

Thorndike and Hagen's (1959) pioneering work on aptitudes demonstrates clearly that group differences certainly exist in expected ways (e.g., accountants as a group have higher average numerical ability test scores than, say, truck drivers as a group, but some truck drivers score higher than many accountants). Similarly, differences *within* minority groups (e.g., African American, Hispanic, Native American, etc.) vary—on many career-related dimensions—as much as the differences *between* minority groups and majority groups. This finding certainly argues against stereotyping and for the need to recognize individual differences.

Do external or internal factors matter more in influencing career development?

To this hoary question of nature-versus-nurture we can say only that both nature and nurture contribute to career development in proportions largely unknown. Those who purport to have mathematical accounts for the variance caused by each generally provide voodoo statistics. Perhaps internal psychological factors dominate, and external factors moderate. Perhaps the obverse. Certainly, we cannot ignore such factors as access to education and occupation opportunities, availability of compensatory programs, status of the economy, and so on, or such cultural forces factors as peer influences, family aspirations and experiences, social class expectancies, and so on. Similarly, we cannot downplay such internal factors as a person's aptitudes, personality characteristics, self-esteem, physical characteristics, and so forth. Which predominates? We do not know.

How active a role does the individual possess in career choice and development?

Both major theories assume that people actively participant in their career development. Each rejects the notion that career decisions simply come into being at a single point in time as though sprung from the head of Zeus. Free and informed choice is a given.

How much emphasis should be placed on the process of career development and how much on its structural content?

Here, Super focuses on the developmental process of careers, while Holland focuses on the result. Most scholars of career development believe that the more we know about the process, the easier intervening to enhance that process becomes. On the other hand, taking people in the here and now, without concern for how they got here, results in exciting, descriptive, and immediately useful assessment devices.

What are criteria of a good career choice?

Obvious criteria for a good career choice include the satisfaction and satisfactoriness of the worker. Even with these criteria, however, questions arise regarding whether we should address initial career choice or a lifelong career. Since the goodness of many career choices cannot be gauged for years, we tend to accept appraisals arguing that a person who followed all of the rational steps in decision making made a good choice.

How great a role does biology play, and how does it function?

For many obvious occupations, physiological and neurological reactions are crucial (e.g., professional athletes and musicians). To what extent these characteristics pertain in other occupations is less clear.

When and how should theories be used in interventions? Differently with different groups across the lifespan?

Because Super's theory focuses on development and speaks to tasks that people must accomplish to attain career maturity, practitioners may develop with relative ease a curriculum of interventions throughout elementary, middle, and secondary schools that take people from career awareness to exploration to choice. Because Holland's theory takes people as they are, it assumes that some development has occurred and that a resulting type needs simply to be identified. Therefore, it offers little guidance on how to use his theory with youngsters but much more guidance for its use with adults.

When should career choices be made?

Some maintain that forcing youngsters to choose an occupation at too young an age harms them and asks them make choices not realistically within their ability to do so. Many curriculum choices come relatively early in life and act, in effect, as career choices, in that they limit future degrees of freedom. The facile answer is that people should choose when they have the readiness to choose. Given individual differences, this time will vary, although systematic interventions in the educational system can homogenize these differences to some extent. Some people make good early decisions (i.e., they have a "passion") while others make poor early decisions that prematurely foreclose other options.

Beyond initial choice, how may career development theories be useful?

A lifespan perspective such as Super's suggests stages in adult work lives that one may predict and address. Foci emerge—such as mid-career shifts, a renewal stage, dual-career couples, job dissatisfaction, and occupational stress—that Super discusses in terms of adult career maturity. One example: Even the pre-retirement and retirement sub-stages of the decline stage require mastering development to produce a good retirement adjustment. Knowing these tasks helps us design appropriate interventions.

Can any single theory define and predict the various influences on career development throughout the lifespan?

The message should already be clear that no single theory can effect this end. Super perhaps comes closest. Holland's theory is more descriptive and has been so since Spranger (1928) described six types of men, later adapted by Allport, Vernon, and Lindsey (1970) in their *Manual for the Study of Values* instrument. The quest for an all-encompassing theory continues.

Can we rely on descriptive research accomplished with restricted size and composition samples?

Patently, we cannot rely solely on such research. Super developed his initial theory in the Career Pattern Study using an all-male sample. Many other studies omit people of color, individuals with disabilities, or other non-male, non-majority groups. As we improve at wider inclusion in such studies, we also improve in large-scale research. Computers have made large research much easier than when Super and Holland developed their theories.

What contributions can lifespan psychology make to career development theory?

As indicated earlier, predictable lifespan stages occur throughout one's career development. Work by such theorists as Levinson (1986), Gould (1978), Vaillant (1977), Vondracek (1990), and Neugarten (1982), among others, has spurred greater attention to defining and elucidating these stages. The formation of career-related behaviors and their expression in work personalities, the description of work motivation, and other behaviors manifested throughout the lifespan have become a primary focus of career development theory.

What methodological deficiencies characterize career development research?

Until relatively recently, career development research has been largely quantitative. Of late, greater attention to so-called qualitative methods has emerged. The present task seeks to determine when to use which method to best advantage. Meantime, career development research requires greater sophistication of quantitative methodologies, in terms of longitudinal studies with enhanced composition and size of samples and treatment of data. Such techniques as path analysis, causal modeling, and structural equation modeling show promise.

AFTERWORD

In such a limited space, the field of career development theory can be given but a lick and a promise. This complex, profound focus gainsays simplified and easy explanations. Consequently, the caveat warns anyone devising any sort of career intervention to have a thorough grounding in career-development theory and to integrate, articulate, sequence, and developmentalize any interventions.

References

Alport, G. W., Vernon, P. E., & Lindsey, G. (1970). *Manual for the study of values*. Boston: Houghton Mifflin.

Astin, H. (1984). The meaning of work in women's lives: A sociopsychological model of career choice and work behavior. *The Counseling Psychologist, 12*(4), 117-126.

Bandura, A. (1982). The psychology of chance encounters and life paths. *American Psychologist, 37*(7), 747-755.

Bordin, E. S., Nachmann, B., & Segal, S. J. (1963). An articulated framework for vocational development. *Journal of Counseling Psychology, 10*, 107-116.

Bronfenbrenner, V. (1979). *The ecology of human development.* Cambridge, MA: Harvard University Press.

Brown, D., Brooks, L., & associates. (1990). *Career choice and development: Applying contemporary theories to practice* (2nd Ed.). San Francisco: Jossey-Bass.

Gelatt, H. B. (1989). Positive uncertainty: A new decision-making framework for counseling. *Journal of Counseling Psychology, 36*(2), 252-256.

Ginzberg, E., Ginsburg, S. W., Axelrad, S., & Herma, J. (1951). *Occupational choice: An approach to a general theory.* New York: Columbia University Press.

Gottfredson, L. S. (1981). Circumscription and compromise: A developmental theory of occupational aspirations. *Journal of Counseling Psychology, 28*(6), 545-579.

Gould, R. (1978). *Transformations: Growth and change in adult life.* New York: Simon and Schuster.

Herr, E. L., & Cramer, S. H. (1996). *Career guidance and counseling through the lifespan: Systematic approaches* (5th Ed.). New York: HarperCollins.

Holland, J. L. (1963). Explanation of a theory of vocational choice: Vocational images and choices. *Vocational Guidance Quarterly, 11*, 232-239.

Holland, J. L. (1966). The psychology of vocational choice. Waltham, MA: Blaisdell.

Holland, J. L. (1973). *Making vocational choices: A theory of careers.* Englewood Cliffs, NJ: Prentice-Hall.

Holland, J. L. (1982). *Some implications of career theory for adult development and aging.* Paper presented at the American Psychological Association, Washington, DC.

Holland, J. L. (1985). *Making vocational choices: A theory of vocational personalities and work environments* (2nd Ed.). Englewood Cliffs, NJ: Prentice-Hall.

Holland, J. L. (1992). Making vocational choices (2nd Ed.). Odessa, FL: Psychological Assessment-Responses.

Holland, J. L. (1994). Separate but unequal is better. In M. L. Savickas & R. W. Lent (Eds.), *Convergence in career development theories: Implications for science and practice* (pp. 45-51). Palo Alto, CA: CPP Books.

Krau, E. (1982). The vocational side of a new start in life: A career model of immigrants. *Journal of Vocational Behavior, 20*, 313-330.

Krumboltz, J. D. (1994). Improving career development theory from a social learning perspective. In M. L. Savickas & R. W. Lent (Eds.), *Convergence in career development theories: Implications for science and practice* (pp. 9-31). Palo Alto, CA: CPP Books.

Lent, R. W., Brown, S. D., & Hackett, G. (1994). Toward a unifying social cognitive theory of career and academic interests, choice, and performance. *Journal of Vocational Behavior, 45*, 79-122.

Levinson, D. J. (1986). A conception of adult development. *American Psychologist, 41*, 3-13.

McDaniels, J. W. (1963). Disability and vocational development. *Journal of Rehabilitation, 29*(4), 16-18.

Neimeyer, G. J. (1988). Cognitive interaction and differentiation in vocational behavior. *The Counseling Psychologist, 16*, 440-475.

Neimeyer, G. J. (1989). Personal construct systems in vocational development and information processing. *Journal of Career Development, 16*, 83-96.

Neimeyer, G. J., Nevilli, D. D., Probert, B., & Fukuyama, M. (1985). Cognitive structures in vocational development. *Journal of Vocational Behavior, 27*, 191-201.

Neugarten, B. L. (August, 1982). *Successful aging.* Paper presented to the annual meeting of the American Psychological Association.

Osipow, S. H. (1983). *Theories of career development* (3rd Ed.). Englewood Cliffs, NJ: Prentice-Hall.

Parr, J., & Neimeyer, G. J. (1994). Effects of gender, construct type, occupational information, and career relevance on vocational differentiation. *Journal of Counseling Psychology, 41*(1), 27-33.

Peterson, C. W., Sampson, J. P., & Reardon, R. C. (1991). *Career development and services: A cognitive approach.* Pacific Grove, CA: Brooks/Cole.

Raynor, J. O., & Entin, E. E. (1982). *Motivation, career striving, and aging.* New York: Hemisphere.

Roe, A. (1956). *The psychology of occupations.* New York: Wiley.

Savickas, M. (1994). Convergence prompts theory renovation, research unification, and practice coherence. In M. Savickas & R. Lent (Eds.), *Convergence in career development theories: Implications for science and practice* (pp. 235-257). Palo Alto, CA: CPP Books.

Schlossberg, N. K. (1986). Adult career development theories: Ways to illuminate the adult experience. In Z. Leibowitz & H. D. Lea (Eds.). *Adult career development: Concepts, issues, and practices* (Chapter 1). Alexandria, VA: National Career Development Association.

Sharf, R. S. (1992). *Applying career development theory to counseling.* Pacific Grove, CA: Brooks/Cole.

Spranger, E. (1928). *Types of men: The psychology and ethics of personality* (Paul Pogors, Trans.). Halle, Germany: Max Niemeyer Verlag.

Super, D. E. (1953). A theory of vocational development. *American Psychologist, 8*, 185-190.

Super, D. E. (1969). Vocational development theory: Persons, positions, and processes. *The Counseling Psychologist, 1*, 2-9.

Super, D. E. (1980). A life-span, life space approach to career development. *Journal of Vocational Behavior, 16*(3), 229-298.

Super, D. E. (1990). A life-span, life-space approach to career development. In D. Brown & L. Brooks Eds.), *Career choice and development: Applying contemporary theories to practice* (pp. 197-261). San Francisco: Jossey-Bass.

Super, D. E. (1992). Toward a comprehensive theory of career development. In D. Montross & C. Shinkman (Eds.), *Career development. Theory and Practice* (pp. 35-64). Springfield, IL: Charles C. Thomas.

Super, D. E. (1994). A life-span, life-space perspective on convergence. In M. L. Savickas & R. W. Lent (Eds.), *Convergence in career development theories: Implications for science and practice* (pp. 63-74). Palo Alto, CA: CPP Books.

Super, D. E., Osborne, W. L., Walsh, D. J., Brown, S. D., & Niles, S. G. (1992). Developmental assessment and counseling: The C-DAC model. *Journal of Counseling and development, 71*, 74-80.

Thorndike, R. L., & Hagen, E. (1959). *10,000 careers.* New York: Wiley.

Tiedeman, D. V., & Miller-Tiedeman, A. (1984). Career decision-making: An individualistic perspective. In D. Brown & L. Brooks (Eds.), *Career choice and development: Applying contemporary theories to practice* (Chapter 10). San Francisco: Jossey-Bass.

Vaillant, G. E. (1977). *Adaptation to life.* Boston: Little Brown.

Vondracek, F. W. (1990). A developmental-contextual approach to career development research. In R. A. Young & W. A. Borgen (Eds.), *Methodological approaches to the study of careers* (pp. 37-56). New York: Praeger.

Zytowski, D. G. (1969). Toward a theory of career development for women. *Personnel and Guidance Journal, 47*, 660-664.

__Stanley H. Cramer__ is a professor in the Department of Counseling and Educational Psychology, State University of New York at Buffalo. He received his B.A. in English (1955) from the University of Massachusetts, an M.A. in English (1957) from the State University of New York at Albany, and his Ed.D. in counseling (1963) from Teachers College, Columbia University. He has been a counselor in several settings, ranging from schools to agencies. Before his appointment at SUNY-Buffalo, he taught part time at Hostra, St. John's, and Columbia Universities.

The author and co-author of 20 books and approximately 50 articles, he has served as consultant to over 150 schools, colleges, agencies, and organizations. A member of the American Psychological Association and the American Counseling Association, Dr. Cramer is a former president of the New York State Association for Counselor Education and Supervision, and he has held a variety of other offices in professional associations. He has served in a number of administrative positions in higher education, including dean of the faculty of Educational Studies and associate vice-president for Academic Affairs.

7

ELEMENTARY- AND MIDDLE-LEVEL CAREER-DEVELOPMENT ISSUES

By Conrad F. Toepfer, Jr.

INTRODUCTION: A WATERSHED CHALLENGE

Conservative estimates project that increasingly larger numbers of Americans will be employed in jobs and careers that will be discovered and/or created between now and the year 2010 (Hodgkinson, 1990). This poses cataclysmic challenges to our educational system, including developing an educational paradigm that responds to the rapidly occurring changes in social, economic, and political life underway in our society. The advancing Information Age requires that schools move beyond massaging their current Industrial Age model to identifying the skills and information today's youth will need to qualify for evolving work and career opportunities, and articulating them into effective pre-K through twelfth grade programs of learning experiences.

Our schools must respond to the changes that will increasingly determine the quality of life in the next millennium. To deal with those changes, students must prepare for employability and be able to achieve personal and economic self-sufficiency. In light of shifting local, regional, and national realities, school communities must design educational approaches that provide students with that readiness. Our education paradigm needs to accommodate evolving differences of kind—not just of degree—from educational demands of the recent past.

New problems require new solutions. Tomorrow's education cannot be more or less what we now do. New, effective educational approaches require support to develop. Fashioning programs targeted toward agreed-upon goals requires adequate funding. For example, the American Space Project landed a man on the moon in a short time only because its planners had been given a blank check. American education should not expect a blank check to meet the challenges sketched here. However, meeting those challenges requires our nation to prioritize education substantially higher than ever before.

More cost-effective versions of existing practices will not meet the changing needs students already bring to school. The United States must recognize the difference between education cost effectiveness and the cost of effective education. The latter is now absolutely necessary. As we define the goals of those new challenges, we must develop educational programs that effectively achieve those goals. Only then may we determine the cost of effective education. Americans, living in the world's second-richest nation, can still have much of they want. The question is, do they want effective education more than they want other things?

The issue of employment has risen to center stage during the past decade. Some of Hodgkinson's data (1989) pointed to an unemployment problem: Increasing numbers of college graduates and advanced-degree holders now take jobs that do not require a college degree, and many graduates also work in fields other than those in which they earned degrees. Clearly, unless we generate more than minimum wage jobs, improving the educational achievement and skills of students will not jump-start our economy.

Some predictions by the National Alliance of Business (1987) have proven painfully accurate. That organization projected that

- youth unemployment will be triple the overall unemployment rate;
- young workers will drop from 30 percent to 16 percent of the workforce between 1985 and 2000;
- 75 percent of those who will work in the year 2000 are already in the workforce; and
- by the year 2000, an estimated 5 to 15 million service jobs will be obsolete.

Those predictions have already materialized, with less than one year remaining before the new millennium. This presents a major challenge to America's schools. Past school programs cannot provide today's youth with improved potential for continued employability. Shifts in the economy and the work world heighten our need to prepare today's youth with skills for continued learning in the future. School-to-career (STC) programs must provide students with skills that better enable them to maintain personal and economic self-sufficiency in adulthood.

SYSTEMIC CONCERNS

School completion is both a journey and a destination, and improving student journeys to school completion requires school professionals to gain a better big-picture perspective. Teachers must better understand the nature and needs of students before and after the school level they teach. Improving and developing effective pre-K-12 programs requires interactive planning and development among professionals from each school level.

School districts serve youth at three psychodevelopmental levels: as young children, young adolescents, and maturing adolescents/young adults. Too often, district-wide curricula merely sequence casually interfaced, largely free-standing programs within each school level. In addition to addressing pre-K-12 learning needs, schools should respond to learners' developmental needs at each level. District-wide curricular effectiveness resides in (1) how well programs at schools attend to the developmental needs of students at each level and (2) how well elementary, middle-level, and high school programs articulate as an educational continuum.

Middle-level education refers to school programs involving any combination of grades 5-9 for youth 10-14 years of age. The developmental changes experienced as students approach and achieve beginning adolescence during their middle-level school years require differentiated educational responses. It is important to separate and focus the needs of young adolescent students from those of elementary and high school students. Middle-level educational effectiveness centers on the degree to which those working with young adolescents understand the developmental and learning needs of that age group (Toepfer, 1992b). The wide readiness span during early adolescence recommends that middle-level school programs provide the widest range of program options locally possible.

STC programs that begin at the high school level will be too little, too late to equip the mass of students for the evolving demands of the world of work. The initial task is to develop elementary-level school programs that better help children develop career awareness. Middle-level school experiences must help young adolescents explore employment in our changing world toward defining their career interests. Such a platform will broaden the chances for high school programs to help more students develop and hone their employability skills.

Planning STC programs at any one school level out of context with pre-K-12 needs will have diminishing returns. Better results accrue when those efforts form part of changes designed to improve success at each level of the school system. Turf concerns also reduce interactive participation among school levels. To become more than the sum of their parts, school district STC programs must reach unanimity.

The pace and rate at which individuals learn varies during their school years. Alternative voyages planned at each school level should accommodate the changing needs of learners as they move through their local schools. District-wide curricular effectiveness resides in (1) how well school programs attend to the developmental needs of students at each level, (2) how well elementary, middle-level, and high school programs articulate and blend together, and (3) how well the programs overcome district-wide structural isolation.

Regardless of local program and housing arrangements, links that vertically articulate pre-K-12 programs benefit districts. Elementary/middle-level and middle-level/high school transition panels can facilitate that effort (Johnston et al., 1985). The first panel convenes a representative group of teachers from the last elementary and first middle-level program grades; the second convenes a representative group of teachers from the last middle-level and first high school program grades. Both panels work on program-curriculum-learning articulation issues with the principals and representative parent groups. To strengthen vertical program continuity, curriculum changes made at one school level should not create gaps or overlaps in program articulation from one school level to the next. Transition panels also increase the awareness of those needs among all three levels in the local district. Such links enhance the articulation of pre-K-12 programs in school districts (Toepfer, 1986).

Roderick's study (1991) highlighted the importance of successful transition from one school level to the next. Students who experience difficulties in transiting from one school level to the next face a greater risk of dropping out of school than those who perform poorly in elementary school.

> The results of this study challenge the conventional belief that dropouts are youth who can be distinguished early on in their school careers by their poor grades and lack of attendance. Late-grade dropouts, on average, did recover from losses incurred during the first year of middle school or high school. (p. 18)

This underscores the need for elementary, middle-level, and high school staff to plan local STC program voyages at each school level to accommodate the changing needs of learners as they move through the local district.

THE THEORY-PRACTICE CONTINUUM

It is important that districts recognize and respect the theory-practice continuum as they grapple with STC program needs and issues. Effective practice develops from good theory. Sound practice that allowed astronaut Neil Armstrong to become the first human to walk on the moon evolved from good theory. In like manner, developing effective school teaching/learning practice requires study of educational theory. STC programs must prepare today's students to land successfully in the adult-life environment they will face in the coming decades.

Herr and Cramer (1996) detailed the history and development of four career educational models in the nation:

> 1. The School-Based or Comprehensive Career Model was originally intended to revitalize education by infusing the curriculum from kindergarten through grade 12 and beyond with career education themes.
>
> 2. The Employer-Based or Experience-Based Model was designed to meet the individual needs of a cross-section of young people, ages 13-18, who need a significant alternative to their current educational environments. In contrast to the school-based model, which at-

tempts to redirect the formal educational model, this model assumes that some students are turned off by the formal educational structure and need a different way to acquire basic academic skills, self-understanding, and career awareness as career preparation.

3. The Home/Community-Based Model was the first of the national career education models that expressly dealt with adult populations, including those who are homebound and women considering entering the workforce after raising their children.

4. The Rural/Residential-Based Model was basically an attempt to test the hypothesis that entire disadvantaged rural families could be helped to improve their economic and social conditions through an intensive program of milieu therapy in a residential center. (pp. 37-38)

Current practice with school-aged youth now uses the first two of these models. Herr and Cramer (1996) identified the need for schools to match career education with career counseling services, characterizing the latter as follows:

- Career counseling is future-oriented and requires some reasonably accurate ideas about the occupational contours that are likely to exist when an individual is ready to enter the labor market.
- The occupational structure is in constant flux, as are the characteristics of the labor force. (p. 138)

In seeking to develop programs that better prepare youth for employability, schools must deal with a number of concepts as they relate to career education. Super (1976) defined *career* as

> the course of events which constitutes a life; the sequence of occupations and other life roles which combine to express one's commitment to work in his or her total pattern of self-development; the series of remunerated and nonremunerated positions occupied by a person from adolescence through retirement, of which occupation is only one; includes work-related roles such as those of student, employee, and pensioner, together with complementary avocational, familial, and civic roles. Careers exist only as people pursue them; they are person-centered. It is this last notion of careers, "they exist only as people pursue them," which summarizes much of this rationale for career guidance. (p. 4)

Raynor and Entin (1982) elaborated that definition as follows:

> A career is both a phenomenological concept and a behavioral concept. It is the link between what a person does and how that person sees himself or herself. A career consists of time-linked senses of self that are defined by action and its outcomes. A career defines how one sees oneself in the context of one's social environment—in terms of one's future plans, one's past accomplishments or failures, and one's present competencies and attributes. (p. 262)

Within that general frame, the concept of work requires specification as it relates to career. Super (1976) made the following distinction:

> The systematic pursuit of an objective valued by oneself (even if only for survival) and desired by others; directed and consecutive, it requires the expenditure of effort. It may be compensated (paid work) or uncompensated (volunteer work or an avocation). The objective of work may be intrinsic enjoyment of the work itself, the structure given to life by the work role, the economic support which work makes possible, or the type of leisure which it facilitates. (p. 20)

As schools agree on the distinctions of such terms, they can work to identify the skills students will need for employability. STC programs must help students recognize, understand, and identify the criteria required for particular jobs, work, and careers in which they develop interest to achieve personal and economic self-sufficiency.

STC programs must identify the factors that inhibit and prevent youth from becoming more employable. Borow (1989) identified several things that keep youth from making successful transitions to work and careers:

- negative self-image and feelings of inadequacy as workers-to-be,

- fatalistic attitude and distrust in the efficacy of rational planning,
- unrealistic picture of the world of work, and
- poor understanding of the sequence of preparatory steps leading to a stated vocational goal. (p. 10)

Schools must also identify attributes necessary for students to improve their employability. Again, that must be fashioned into sequences of developmentally appropriate experiences at each school level.

In studying the adaptation of youth to work, Ashley et al. (1980) identified five aspects of adjustment their subjects had to make for successful employability: performance aspects, organizational aspects, interpersonal aspects, responsibility aspects, and effective aspects. Seltz, Jones, and Ashley (1980) specified six functional competencies for adapting to the world of work, their findings drawn from national response samples from the general adult population, high school seniors, public school teachers, and employers. More than half of the responses from each group concurred that successful transition to employability requires the following abilities:

- Use reading, writing, and math skills the job calls for.
- Use tools and equipment the job calls for.
- Get along with others.
- Deal with pressures to get the job done.
- Follow rules and policies.
- Have a good work attitude.

It is essential to identify the skills and characteristics youth should develop to become personally and economically self-sufficient. *The Purposes of Education in American Democracy* (Education Policies Commission, 1938) spelled out the objectives of economic efficiency as follows (modified by this writer to eliminate gender-biased language): The educated producer

- knows the satisfaction of good workmanship;
- understands the requirements and opportunities of various jobs;
- has selected his or her occupation;
- succeeds in his or her chosen profession;
- maintains and improves his or her efficiency;
- appreciates the social value of his or her work;
- plans the economics of his or her own life;
- develops standards for guiding his or her experiences;
- develops standards for guiding his or her expenditures; and
- is an informed and skillful buyer.

Educators must examine present and past expectations for school programs in light of today's evolving needs and what they suggest for developing STC school experiences that prepare students to succeed in their adult futures. Students' employability centers on the degree to which they develop the skills to become and remain lifelong learners in their work and careers.

ISSUES OF CONTEXT: CONFRONTING REALITY

Today's youth face life in a society where upwardly mobile employment opportunities continue to shrink. STC programs must help students understand the changing circumstances they face in trying to achieve work success. As lifelong learning becomes a basic educational outcome, students must understand their need to develop that capacity. The twenty-first century may well become known as the *learning century*. As new occupations replace old ones, workers will need capacities for further learning for continued employability. Although always desired, a love of learning was unnecessary in earlier times when factual recall even more largely dominated our teaching and what students had to learn.

In the past, a world of work in need of non- and semi-skilled labor welcomed students completing or dropping out of school. Neither a person's capacity for retraining nor intellectual development nor academic achievement formed critical qualifications for hiring as they do now. Nonskilled workers in the blue-collar era benefited from job security, paid medical and hospital care, vacations, and retirement plans. Then, entering workers could maintain and increase their standards of living to levels that allowed them to marry, raise children, and send them to postsecondary schools. However, today, youth face life in a society that sees rapidly disappearing non- and semi-skilled job opportunities. The relationships young adolescents form with family, friends, educators, and citizens in the community at large can help them focus on the kinds of leadership, teamwork skills, and behaviors they will need for personal and economic self-sufficiency.

Effective STC programs deal with the major contextual issues for curriculum and program improvement efforts that Cornbleth (1996) raised. Curriculum-out-of-context issues included conceptual separation, structural and socio-cultural isolation. Curriculum-in-context issues included conceptual integration and structural and socio-cultural contextualization. Planning effective STC programs requires answering the following contextual questions:

- What are the demographic, social, political, and economic conditions and trends that seem to shape the existing curriculum and seem likely to affect the desired changes? How is the desired curriculum change compatible with cultural traditions and prevailing ideologies? What influential groups are affected? (What are the potential sources of support and opposition?) What historical, recent, or continuing events are apt to influence the curriculum change effort?
- Which education system components or subsystems could mediate (supporting of oppositional) socio-cultural influences? How are past experiences with curriculum change likely to influence the present effort?
- What system components are affected? (What roles, relationships, and patterns of activity?) At what levels? How is the desired curriculum change compatible or at odds with the prevailing culture of education systems? What are the bureaucratic operating procedures and challenges of formal and informal control of the affected system components? (Who controls what, to what extent, and how?) What and where are the tensions or contradictions within the system that might become loci for curriculum change? (p.160)

STC programs must identify and deal with local contextual concerns as they relate to regional and national realities, aiming to help youth understand their need for personal and economic self-sufficiency. Families in both urban and rural circumstances who have received welfare for several generations produce students whose siblings, parents, guardians, and neighbors seldom work. Those students must learn the work ethic, the requirements of employability, and the lifestyle of regular employment. Middle-level school career exploratory experiences can shadow and study work. Observing and later interviewing people who work in different jobs and careers can help students understand economic self-sufficiency and discover how employability relates to upward mobility and increased quality of life (Toepfer, 1994).

Shadowing, volunteerism, and participating in service-learning projects organized around local community needs can provide experiences to address those needs. It appears that welfare reform will continue to move in that direction as well. Regardless of how conditions may change, middle-level schools must consider the needs those changes pose for service learning in STC exploratory experiences. Because of the possibilities in the coming technocracy, it may be that, regardless of the skills they gain, increasing numbers of people will not be employed, in our Industrial Age sense of the term. The passing of that industrial society work ethic poses serious challenges to schools. In any circumstance, people's psychological wellness requires that they feel they have worth, dignity, and are useful citizens.

Again, schools must define changes in high school exit-outcomes and behaviors as they relate to developmentally appropriate tasks and expectations at each level. We must identify and match realistic expectations for young children in early childhood/elementary school programs with those developed for young adolescents in middle-level school programs. Local districts must recognize what is necessary to provide an effective foundation for high school programs and expectations.

ELEMENTARY SCHOOL STC CONCERNS

M. J. Miller (1989) maintained that the self-awareness children develop during their elementary school years is essential for their subsequent career development. Other stages of career development, including decision-making, can become meaningless unless career awareness is developed during those early years. Earlier, a different researcher, M. F. Miller (1978), examined childhood antecedents of career in relationship to maturity attitudes later found during early adulthood. He found attitudes and behaviors initiated during children's elementary school years associated with their career maturity attitudes as postsecondary school students. Earlier Miller (1974) identified that vocational maturity correlates with work values in adulthood.

Bailey and Stadt (1973) suggested that two stages occur during the elementary school years—awareness (kindergarten through grade three) and accommodation (grades four through six)—the goals for each subdivided as follows.

> Awareness (K-3)
>
> 1. Awareness of self
> 2. Awareness of different types of occupational roles
> 3. Awareness of individual responsibility for own actions
> 4. Development of individual responsibility for own actions
> 5. Learning cooperative social behavior
> 6. Development of respect for others and the work that they do
>
> Accommodation (Grades 4-6)
>
> 1. Development of concepts related to self
> 2. Development of concepts related to the world of work
> 3. Assuming increased responsibility for planning own time
> 4. Application of decision-making and classification skills
> 5. Development of desirable social relationships
> 6. Development of work attitudes and values (p. 351-359)

Elementary school awareness and accommodation learning experiences should provide the base for students to continue to learn and begin career-occupational-work exploration during middle-level school. At this level, STC programs must deal with specific career guidance needs (Herr & Cramer, 1996).

> • Career guidance in the elementary school involves systematic provision of knowledge and skills through the curriculum and extensive cooperation of teachers and counselors.
>
> • Career guidance in the elementary school is not intended to force children to make premature choices but to avoid closure of future options.
>
> • Major emphases of career guidance in the elementary school are on positive attitudes toward self and opportunities, feelings of competence, and ways in which school experiences can be used to explore and prepare for the future.
>
> • There are relationships between work habits and attitudes developed in the elementary school and work habits in adulthood.
>
> • Parental influence on children's career development is a major variable in the provision of career guidance in the elementary school.
>
> • Career guidance programs in the elementary school can be planned and sequenced to respond to the changing developmental characteristics of elementary school children. (p. 349)

Children's developmental characteristics and learning needs must frame elementary-level STC programs. In turn, middle-level STC programs must accommodate the changes students experience in approaching and entering adolescence. Young adolescents are neither children nor miniatures of what they will become in their high school years (Ames, Ilg, & Baker, 1988). Elementary and middle-level teachers must cooperate to develop middle-level STC experiences that effectively shift to exploring career interests in the middle-level school.

MIDDLE-LEVEL SCHOOL STC CONCERNS

Herr and Cramer (1996) identified the reality of wide ranges of learners found in the middle-level of the school system.

> Of the entire educational span, the junior high school years have the widest range of maturity levels in the student population. The effects of pubertal changes, differences in the rates of male and female growth, and the general unevenness of physical, emotional, and intellectual growth within and between the population of girls and boys contribute to this spectrum of maturational differences. Differences in readiness, questions of general academic progress, preoccupation with bodily change, peer conflicts, boy-girl relationships, and rebellion against family restrictions—each coexists with and often confounds the continuing process of career development. (p. 390)

Building on their childhood experiences, most people largely fashion their attitudes about learning and work, as well as many enduring adult values, between the ages of 10 and 15. Relatively few people substantially change their beliefs in those attributes after reaching high school (Toepfer et al., 1993). The Carnegie Task Force on the Education of Young Adolescents (Hornbeck, 1989, p. 8) noted that "the middle-level school years are the last best chance for early adolescents to avoid a diminished future." The report further stated that,

> Unfortunately, by age 15, substantial numbers of American youth are at risk of reaching adulthood unable to meet adequately the requirements of the workplace, the commitments of relationships: in families and with friends, and the responsibilities of participation in a democratic society. These youth are among the estimated 7 million young people—one in four adolescents who are extremely vulnerable to multiple high-risk behaviors and school failure. Another 7 million may be at moderate risk but remain a cause for serious concern. (p. 8)

Middle-level school STC experiences should help young adolescents define and explore their evolving career-occupational-work interests. Those experiences should relate here-and-now realities of life in local communities and the broader society. Attention to socio-cultural contextualization issues help youth understand what they must learn for personally successful STC transition. That is particularly critical for students whose lives have provided limited personal contact with or knowledge of work lifestyles. Observing workplaces and shadowing jobs build understanding of the work ethic and its role in economic self-sufficiency (Toepfer, 1994).

- Identify teaching and learning approaches especially appropriate for providing middle-level exploratory career-learning experiences;
- Develop middle-level teaching and learning approaches particularly suited for career exploration; and,
- Identify how extra class activities and other experiences available in the middle-level school programs can provide additional career exploration opportunities.

Young adolescents need more awareness of the employability skills needed to achieve self-sufficiency. School should integrate this awareness with learning in other middle-level content areas (e.g., in social studies on contemporary America and world economic issues, and related to local conditions; in industrial arts/technology on the changing world of work, and related to local conditions). Teaching teams that combine staff from academic and exploratory areas develop those curriculum units best. This has great potential for integrating learning around students' evolving vocational-occupational-career interests. This also has implications for middle-level school career guidance activities. Herr and Cramer (1996) identified specific targets for those experiences:

- Plans for career guidance and counseling in junior high/middle school must acknowledge the transitional character of this period and the importance of exploration and planning.
- Career guidance and counseling in junior high must help students understand the con-

sequences of curricular choices made now, and to plan for senior high school so as not to prematurely close later options.

• Students cannot explore or choose educational or occupational goals they do not know about. Quality career guidance programs impart timely, relevant, and accurate information.

• Gender determines the information, models available, self-efficacy, and bias toward or away from particular choices become major factors in planning and delivering career guidance and counseling at the middle level.

Middle-level school may be viewed as the work of young adolescents that helps them develop and understand the work ethics they will need as adults. Young adolescents typically want to know why they must learn certain things. Effective middle-level career exploratory programs relate students' here-and-now concerns to possible employability concerns.

That requires developing meaningful hands-on, applied exploratory experiences. In addition to school-to-work transition experiences, schools may develop apprenticeship-explorations to help young adolescents identify and explore their evolving career interests as they build an understanding of the work world.

Since actual hardware and equipment in cutting-edge technologies has long been too costly for schools to purchase and update, career exploratory programs could use computer simulations that provide situations for students to explore and learn about evolving, state-of-the-art innovations. Well-defined middle-level school apprenticeships, community service projects, and computer simulations help students explore and develop understandings about the changing world of work and the employability skills they must develop to become lifelong learners.

Skills today's students must develop for self-sufficiency include the following (Toepfer, 1995):

1. Developing a vision. Students must develop the skills necessary to build a vision, communicate that vision, and make it a reality. As adults they must identify attributes that changing conditions will require for their continued employability.

Guiding questions for developing student learning experiences:

• What does/will the vision look like?

• Do I/we want to accomplish it?

• What must I/we do to complete or accomplish it?

• How will I/we determine whether it has been accomplished?

2. Building self-awareness. Students must develop skills to identify their strengths and weaknesses to improve areas of weakness. As adults they must know and be able to use their strengths to develop skills that changing conditions will require for continued employability.

Guiding questions for developing student learning experiences:

• What will this task require of me/us?

• How does this task relate to my/our responsibilities?

• What strengths do I/we bring to this task?

• What areas of weaknesses/deficiency must I/we improve to accomplish this task?

• What skills/information must I/we have to accomplish this task?

• What commitment am I/are we willing to make to succeed at this task?

3. Gathering, processing, and using information. Students must develop the skills to gather information and use it effectively. As adults they must identify the information they will need and know how to access and analyze it to maintain their employability.

Guiding questions for developing student learning experiences:

• What types of information must I/we know?

• How will I/we find and access that?

• What technological/manual skills will I/we use to process that information?

• Are there new processes I/we must learn?

• If so, how will I/we learn them?

4. Developing decision-making skills. Students must develop the skills and strategies necessary to make informed decisions. As adults they will use decision-making skills to determine the skills and attributes they must develop for continued employability.

Guiding questions for developing student learning experiences:

• What issue(s) must be decided?

• What decision(s) must be made?

• Who will plan and make the decision(s)?

• What additional decision-making procedures must be investigated and/or learned?

• Are there alternative solutions that must be considered?

5. Developing communications skills. Students must develop and improve their written and oral communication skills. As adults they must communicate and interact effectively with colleagues in the work place to determine what they must learn to remain employable.

Guiding questions for developing student learning experiences:

• What must they know?

• Who (what individuals or groups) must know about this?

• How do I/we communicate that information (written, oral formats)?

• Have I/we received all of the necessary information to move ahead?

• If not, what additional information is needed to do so?

STC programs require developing the longitudinal elementary and middle-level school approaches discussed here. Although children grow up not down, bureaucratic and lay expectations continue to view school improvement as a top-down process. But a horizontal view of the district school continuum identifies and rectifies problems that trickle-down expectations create. Interactive staff planning and interaction at all three levels should formulate exit- and school-level STC goals.

TOP-DOWN DIFFICULTIES

The Secretary's Commission on Achieving Necessary Skills (SCANS) Report has bold targets (Packer, 1991). It maintains that by 2000, high school graduates will require the following specific competencies for entry-level jobs in business and industry.

1. Resources: Identifies, organizes, plans, and allocates resources.

• Time: Selects goal-relevant activities, ranks them, allocates time, and prepares and follows schedules.

• Money: Uses or prepares budgets, makes forecasts, keeps records, and makes adjustments to meet objectives, uses materials or space efficiently.

2. Interpersonal: Works well with others.

• Participates as member of a team; contributes to group effort.

• Teaches others new skills.

• Serves clients and customers: Communicates ideas to justify position, persuades and convinces others, responsibly challenges existing procedures and policies.

• Negotiates: Works toward agreements involving exchange of resources, resolves divergent interests.

3. Systems: Understands complex interrelationships.

• Understands systems: Knows how social, organizational, and technological systems work and operates effectively with them.

• Monitors and corrects performance: Distinguishes trends, predicts impacts on system operations, diagnoses deviations in system performance, and corrects malfunctions.

• Improves or designs systems: Suggests modifications to existing systems and develops new or alternate systems to improve performance.

4. Technology: Works with a variety of technologies.

• Selects technology: Chooses procedures, tools or equipment, including computers and related technologies.

• Applies technology to task: Understands overall intent and proper procedures for setup and operation of equipment.

• Maintains and troubleshoots equipment: Prevents, identifies, or solves problems with equipment, including computers or other technologies.

Little progress has been made toward developing these skills in high school graduates since the report came out in 1991. SCANS exemplifies the shortcomings of STC initiatives that begin in high school. Failing to develop the longitudinal background of learners before they reach high school makes the SCANS high school goals unrealistic. Lacking career awareness and exploration experiences in their elementary and middle-level school years, relatively few students will develop the SCANS skills in high school.

Schools and communities must either reallocate finances or seek additional funding to develop STC programs that improve students' employability skills. As does the business sector, schools must recognize that "the pursuit of quality may cause profits to fail in the short term, but quality pays off in the end" (Holt, 1993, p. 393). The need for the population at-large to develop technology literacy has led to re-thinking of the belief that high tech skills hold the key to employability. Instead, the technology background of all of our students must improve. Beane, Toepfer, and Alessi (1986) observed that

> [a]ll students need some technology education and to develop an awareness of how technology will increasingly impact on our culture and lives. This low-technology education needs to become a general education concern. (p. 368)

General education programs also must improve students' basic skills in communication, interpersonal relations, and in identifying and processing information. STC elementary and middle-level programs must provide career awareness, accommodation, and exploratory experiences needed to develop and refine employability skills in high school. Stemmer, Brown, and Smith (1992) identified general skill areas that middle-school level, career-exploratory programs could provide students, categorized as follows:

> **Academic Skills:** Provide the basic foundation necessary for a person to get, keep, and progress on a job.
>
> **Personal Skills:** Develop the attitudes and behaviors required to get, keep, and progress on a job.
>
> **Teamwork Skills:** Those needed to work with others on a job. (p. 33)

I modified and increased those skills as middle-level school STC exploratory outcomes (Toepfer, 1994, p. 63) (see Chapter 6). Combining elementary and middle STC experiences provides students with a better foundation to develop entry-level work skills in high school.

CONCLUSION: SEARCHING FOR A NEW PARADIGM

The notion of school restructuring continues in popularity. By definition, *restructuring* means re-arranging existing elements in a new order. However, school restructuring frequently fails to surpass such cut-and-paste efforts. Toepfer (1990) recommended that schools first revise or reconceptualize their current curriculum and program goals. In most cases, *all* elements in an existing school program are ineffective. One must identify program elements that (1) are sufficiently strong to be retained, (2) must be improved, and (3) must be discarded. Effective school restructuring occurs when weak program elements either strengthen and/or new ones develop to replace them.

Our changing post-industrial society requires a new school paradigm capable of accommodating today's educational needs. Old wine in new bottles will not provide new vintages that successfully deal with the demands our changing society presents to America's schools. In the current graded-school paradigm, time is the constant and learning is the variable. The graded-school paradigm poorly serves students capable of learning more than the set amount of content and skills in each grade. It is equally ineffective for students unable to accomplish the minimal expectations in each grade. For learning to be the constant requires an educational paradigm where time becomes the enabling variable to ensure that students will either learn as quickly as they can or as slowly as they must.

The wisdom of the educational standards movement escapes me. What will raising learning standards for students who cannot meet current expectations accomplish? We must find ways that help more students achieve existing standards before raising them. Students require time flexibility to achieve existing as well as new standards. Some students will even require more time—perhaps several years over the public school spectrum—to achieve essential standards. Thirty years from now it will not matter if some students needed more time to complete and master particular standards. However, it would be tragic if their inability to do so in fixed, graded-school expectations precluded their achieving those standards.

To increase the numbers of students achieving learning standards requires that school programs better accommodate the range of student abilities. Forty-three years ago, Goodlad and Anderson (1956) saw that the graded school's subordination of learning to time could not meet the needs of students at-large. Yet, despite the failure of efforts to soup it up, the graded school persists. The evolution of personal computers offers a lesson schools should consider. Regardless of what was added to the Apple II workhorse, it could not match the capabilities of the Apple Macintosh that replaced it.

Learning what students must do to improve their employability likewise requires that time become the variable for students to learn as fast as they can or as slow as they must to enter the world-class workforce the United States must maintain. While it is certainly critical to improve our national economy, that concern should neither drive nor limit the development of school programs. Developing school programs appropriate to the learning abilities of elementary, middle-level, and high school students will better serve both the economy and quality of life in the United States.

Our schools face changes of kind and degree beyond the challenges of the past. This watershed time requires an educational paradigm that accommodates those concerns. That paradigm must accommodate developing STC programs that better meet student employability skill needs. That can best be done by (1) career awareness and accommodation learnings for elementary school children, (2) middle-level exploratory learning programs that help young adolescents define and explore their evolving career interests, and (3) high school experiences that initiate and hone employability skills of maturing adolescents and young adults.

References

Ames, L., Ilg, F., & Baker, S. (1988). *Your ten- to fourteen-year-old*. New Haven, CT: Gesell Institute of Human Development.

Ashley, W., Cellini, J., Faddis, C., Pearsol, J., Wiant, A., & Wright, B. (1980). *Adaptation to work: An exploration of processes and outcomes*. Columbus: National Center for Research in Vocational Education, Ohio State University.

Bailey, L., & Stadt, R. (1973). *Career education: New approaches to human development*. Bloomington, IL: McKnight.

Beane, J., Toepfer, C. F. Jr., & Alessi, S. Jr. (1986). *Curriculum planning and development*. Boston: Allyn and Bacon.

Borow, H. (1989). Youth in transition to work: Lingering problems. *Guidance and Counseling, 4*(4), 7-14.

Cornbleth, C. (1996). Curriculum in and out of context. In E. Hollins (Ed.), *Transforming curriculum for a culturally diverse society* (pp.149-161). Mahwah, NJ: Lawrence Erlbaum.

Educational Policies Commission. (1938). *The purposes of education in American democracy*. Washington, DC.: National Education Association.

Goodlad, J., & Anderson, R. (1956). *The nongraded elementary school*. New York: Harcourt, Brace, and World.

Herr, E., & Cramer, S. (1996). *Career guidance and counseling through the life span: Systematic approaches* (5th ed.). New York: Harper Collins.

Hodgkinson, H. (1989). The same client: Demographics of education and service delivery systems. Washington, DC: Institute for Educational Leadership.

Hodgkinson, H. (1990, March). The demographics of school reform: A look at the children. *Demographics of Education Newsletter*. Washington, DC: Institute for Educational Leadership. 1, 3.

Holt, M. (1993). The educational consequences of Edward Deming. *Kappan, 74*(5), 382-388.

Hornbeck, D. (1989). *Turning points: Preparing American youth for the twenty-first century*. Washington, DC: Carnegie Commission on Adolescent Development.

Johnston, J. H., et al. (1985). *An agenda for excellence at the middle level*. Reston, VA: National Association of Secondary School Principals.

Miller, M. F. (1974). Relationship of vocational maturity to work values. Journal of *Vocational Behavior,* 5, 367-371.

Miller, M. F. (1978). Childhood experiences as antecedents of career maturity attitudes. *Vocational Counseling Quarterly, 27*(2),137-143.

Miller, M. J. (1989). Career counseling in the elementary school child: Grades K-5. *Journal of Employment Counseling, 26*(4), 169-177.

National Alliance of Business. (September 20, 1987). Employment in the year 2000. *New York Times Magazine* supplement.

Packer, D. (1991). *What work requires of schools—A SCANS report for America 2000*. Washington, DC: U.S. Department of Labor.

Raynor, J., & Entin, E. (1982). *Motivation, career striving, and aging*. New York: Hemisphere.

Roderick, M. (1991). Unpublished paper reported in *Education Week* (March 25, 1992: 18).

Seltz, N., Jones, J., & Ashley, W. (1980). *Functional competencies for adapting to the world of work*. Columbus: National Center for Research in Vocational Education, Ohio State University.

Stemmer, P., Brown, B., & Smith, C. (1992). The employability skills portfolio. *Educational Leadership, 49*(6) 32-35.

Super, D. (1976). *Career education and the meaning of work*. Washington, DC: Office of Career Education.

Toepfer, C. F., Jr. (1986). Middle-level transition and articulation issues. *Middle School Journal, 18*(10), 9-11.

Toepfer, C. F., Jr. (1990). Revisioning middle-level education: A prelude to restructuring. *Educational Horizons, 68*(2), 95-99.

Toepfer, C. F., Jr. (January, 1994). Vocational/career/occupational education at the middle-level: What is appropriate for young adolescents? *Middle School Journal, 25*(3), 59-65.

Toepfer, C. F., Jr. (1995). Learning to lead by developing relationships. Module in *Experiencing leadership—Helping middle level students through change*. Reston, VA: Future Business Leaders of America. pp. 5-95.

Toepfer, C. F. Jr., et al. (1993). *Achieving excellence through the middle-level curriculum*. Reston, VA: National Association of Secondary School Principals.

***Conrad F. Toepfer, Jr.**, of the Department of Learning and Instruction, State University of New York at Buffalo, is a curriculum generalist with a special interest in early adolescent education. A past president of the National Middle School Association, Toepfer sits on the Advisory Council for the National Resource Center for Middle Grades Education. He has worked with middle schools throughout North America and Europe, and has addressed several European Middle School League Conferences. The author of 37 books and monographs, he has also published more than 150 articles in major curriculum and middle grades educational professional journals.*

HIGH SCHOOL CAREER DEVELOPMENT ISSUES

By Cheryl L. Hogg

If one advances confidently in the direction of his dreams, and endeavors to live that life which he has imagined, he will meet with a success unexpected in common hours. He will put some things behind, will pass an invisible boundary; new, universal, and more liberal laws will begin to establish themselves around and within him. If you have built castles in the air, your work need not be lost; that is where they should be. Now put foundations under them.

—Henry David Thoreau

INTRODUCTION

In recent years, career development has broadened in meaning to include various life roles interacting, constituting a lifestyle. Life satisfactions depend upon finding adequate life roles consistent with self-concept, values, interests, and needs fulfillment. Career planning, choice, and negotiation or entry into an occupation comprise some of the most important tasks for young people, marking transition into adulthood. Career development is complex.

Perennial questions fueling debates concern how to best help teenagers and young adults move into adult careers. How do educators, parents, and community members help students prepare for life and careers as an integral part of joining the adult world? How do students connect theoretical and applied knowledge? Education standards emphasize high expectations; critical and high-order thinking skills; the need to cooperate, communicate, and compete; citizenship and character formation; teamwork; and the importance of learning how to learn. Career and human resource development need teachers, parents, business representatives, community members, school counselors, and administrators to join forces to work with students.

While the public still believes that a baccalaureate degree is the best path to success, only 25 percent of high school graduates will complete a four-year degree. While 65 percent of the jobs in the year 2000 will require technical skills, perhaps only 20 percent will require a four-year degree. Many high school graduates flounder for a number of years before establishing adult roles.

This chapter explores high school career development issues. A review of literature and research will provide discuss the nature and needs of adolescents; present concepts of career development, focusing on Donald Super's adolescent exploratory stage; and touch upon education and business issues. The meaning of career, adolescent career development, and comprehensive career development will be considered. Implications for high school practice include a sequenced, developmental, and integrated curriculum approach grounded in research-based career development theory. Career-assessment and follow-up studies by schools will allow them to develop databases to continuously monitor and improve the quality of their programs. From this overview and appreciation of issues and resources the reader may derive a framework and application for high school career development.

REVIEW OF LITERATURE AND RESEARCH

Frank Parsons's *Choosing a Vocation* (1909) marked the formal beginning of vocational guidance and counseling. Parsons noted three broad factors in wise vocational choice:

> (1) a clear understanding of yourself, your aptitudes, abilities, interests, ambitions, resources, limitations, and their causes; (2) a knowledge of the requirements and conditions of success, advantages and disadvantages, compensation, opportunities, and prospects in different lines of work; (3) true reasoning on the relations of these two groups of facts. (p. 5)

"Every young person needs help on all three of these points" and "needs counsel" through "careful and systematic help by experienced minds in making this greatest decision of his life" (p. 5). The fundamental issue is that of adaptation, "the question of uniting, so far as possible, the best abilities and enthusiasms of the developed man with the daily work he has to do" (p. 13). Each individual should take responsibility for his or her career decision making.

Parsons, concerned about the vocational floundering of youth, saw their drift from one job to another as a waste of human resources. He recognized the "plasticity and rapid development" of youth and the importance of the formative and transitional period between ages 15 to 25 years as critical for foundation and guidance (p. 164). Using the motto "Light, Information, Inspiration, and Cooperation," the Vocation Bureau of Boston and a school for vocational counselors were founded in 1908 to model its practice. The field evolved to include a broad sense of career development.

Parsons believed that education exists to provide an adequate preparation for life, to train for character, and to test for ability through the "successful performance of things that have to be done in daily life, rather than answering a series of questions about a book or a lecture course" (p. 163). He wrote of the importance of education to develop the body, mind, and character, and "a careful planning of and adequate preparation for some occupation" for which the youth is "best adapted" (p. 165). He advocated for a balance between "book work" (academic) and "industrial" (vocational) education, believing that boys and girls must be educated in both mind and hand, and that knowledge must be applied.

Parsons's principle-based "Suggestions for a Plan of Life" applies to developing habits of good character, civic responsibility, and general living, along with developing self-knowledge, occupational knowledge, and critical thinking skills. These attributes continue to set foundations for successful career development. He strongly believed in the need for human development, expressing his hope in the following statement:

> Not until society wakes up to its responsibilities and its privileges in this relation shall we be able to harvest more than a fraction of our human resources, or develop and utilize the genius and ability that are latent in each new generation. When that time does come, education will become the leading industry, and a vocational bureau in effect will be a part of the public school system in every community . . . and with experts trained as carefully for the work as men are trained to-day for medicine and the law. (p. 165)

A number of theories for career development have been developed since then. This chapter references approximately a dozen; Stanley H. Cramer in Chapter 6 presents two primary theories of Donald Super and John Holland.

Of particular note is the work of Super that has evolved over the past 50 years. Building on Parsons's trait-and-factor theory, matching people to occupations, Super constructed theoretical perspectives to improve practitioner and researcher comprehension and intervention in occupational choice and career development. Based on *functionalism*, a system of psychology founded by Dewey (1896) and Angell (1903), Super's work addresses individuals' adaptations to their situations by posing two fundamental questions: "What do people do?" and "Why do they do it?" Super constructed three theory segments (career maturity, self-concept, and life-space) over four decades and hoped to integrate them into his life-span, life-space approach to career development (Herr, 1997; Savickas, 1997). Super's life-space model does not assume that work is central to a person's life but instead focuses on how work fits into the person's overall life. The idea of *career* broadens to include lifestyle planning, exploring, and decision making. "Thus in addition to fitting people to occupations, counselors help people to fit work into their lives" (Savickas, 1997, p. 251).

Savickas indicates that future approaches to Super's theory may emphasize career adaptability over career maturity. *Adaptability* has a root meaning of *quick to learn or understand and to fit*, and is a central construct in the trait-and-factor or person-environment theory. Career adaptability would shift focus from the individual to the individual within a context, or "person-in-a-situation." Savickas defines career adaptability as "the readiness to cope with the predictable tasks of preparing for and participating in the work role and with unpredictable adjustments prompted by changes in work and working conditions" (1997, p. 254).

Planning, exploring, and deciding constitute important process roles of adaptability and apply to *all* life roles. Exploring life roles requires information, reality orientation, and a consideration of cultural and individual values within the changing global context (Herr, 1997). A shift in practice includes transforming career counseling from an occupational orientation to a life-planning orientation. "Balancing and sequencing commitments to school, work, family, leisure, worship, and the community requires careful planning. In other words, designing a life structure may eventually subsume managing a career, like career management has subsumed occupational choice" (Savickas, 1997, p. 256). In this framework, career development would encompass looking ahead, exploring the environment, developing the self, and choosing suitable opportunities to become the person one desires. Cross-cultural research discusses Super's concepts of life roles, values, careers, the role and meaning of work and work values, applying many theoretical constructs and assessment tools (Super, Sverko, & Super 1995).

For Super, career development has become a process for developing human resources that "has come to mean helping youths and adults of both genders to develop as competent and adaptable people for changing combinations of life roles, to be useful not only in an organization but to changing organizations, changing social conditions, and changing selves" (Super, Sverko, & Super, 1995, p. xviii).

A growing appreciation of developmental education approaches to career development has increased understanding young childhood as important in its implications for development within one's life span, reflected in career awareness at the elementary school level. Super adapted Buehler's (1933) theory of development to formulate five vocational stages: growth, exploration, establishment, maintenance, and decline. The exploratory stage of adolescence subdivides into fantasy, tentative, and realistic phases. The establishment stage includes trial and stability phases.

In the United States, adolescence most often begins in middle level and continues through secondary and postsecondary education, beginning with the onset of puberty and ending when one assumes the responsibilities of an adult life. Physical changes, rapid growth spurts, and sexual maturation characterize adolescence. Cognitive development includes logical reasoning, the ability to formulate and test hypotheses (Piaget's theory), and sophisticated moral reasoning or judgment (Kohlberg's theory). Growing evidence shows that full cognitive maturity and reasoning ability, particularly when applied to scientific thought, may need educational intervention in metacognition—the ability to think about cognition itself (Baron, 1992; Kuhn, 1989). Emotional change in adolescents indicates frequent and large mood swings (Csikszentmihalyi & Larson, 1984). Evidence suggests that adolescents are more prone to depression than children or adults (Angold, 1988; Garrison, Shoenbach, & Kaplan, 1985), which may relate to increases in adolescent suicide (Frederick, 1985). Girls tend to experience depression more than boys, which may relate to low self-esteem and dissatisfaction with body image, given social emphases on such standards of feminine beauty as thinness that few can hope to attain (Cash, Winstead, & Janda, 1986; Allgood-Merten, Lewinsohn, & Hops, 1990; Baron, 1992). Overall, however, teens report feeling generally happy and self-confident (Baron, 1992), and tend to agree with their parents on basic values and future plans, including whether they should attend college. Peer opinion becomes increasingly important as adolescents develop a strong desire for social approval.

In Erikson's (1950) stage theory, the developmental task of identity versus role confusion becomes central as various roles integrate into a consistent self-identity. Understanding one's personal traits and preferences become increasingly significant. Such questions as "Who am I?" "What do I like?" "What am I good at?" help form self-identity and are important to career development. An inner sense of assurance characterizes identity—a feeling of self-acceptance and direction in life—a sense influenced by reinforcement from significant others.

Drastic changes in work and life roles, compounded by a rapidly changing job market and technology, have increased the difficulty of career decision-making for adolescents. Occupational choice and its pervasive effects on other areas of life make it one of life's most important decisions. Career readiness and maturity are individually determined factors. While some may be ready to decide upon, actively plan, and activate a career, others may postpone making decisions. "If the adolescent uses this time for exploration of possibilities, it may lead to good choice and positive results. If adolescents cannot resolve inner conflict, they may develop negative identity and become involved in defiant and destructive behavior" (Drummond & Ryan, 1995, p. 116).

Csikszentmihalyi and Larson (1984) studied adolescent socialization, consciousness, and transformation into adulthood. Such social factors as "a bewildering variety of potential life goals, life styles, and values," and increased years of schooling and training exacerbate the universal tensions of adolescence (p. 12). Maturation requires a young person to "learn habits of thought, action, and feeling that are often difficult and unnatural. This is a process which, not surprisingly, is cause for much tension and conflict" (p. 12). To face the challenges of increasing complexity, adolescents must learn from experience to adapt and to view obstacles as challenges that provide them with opportunities to develop their skills.

Csikszentmihalyi (1990) summarizes decades of research on the positive aspects of human living. Referring to his concept of *flow*, he provides examples of joyful experiences, the process of total involvement, and creativity. One creates a state of life-meaning or happiness through conscious attention to the complexities of differentiation and integration. The flow experience "provided a sense of discovery, a creative feeling of transporting the person into a new reality. It pushed the person to higher levels of performance, and led to previously undreamed-of-states of consciousness. In short, it transformed the self by making it more complex" (p. 74). Flow activities occur through an individuals growth of self, initiated by making use of opportunities and by "an individual's ability to control and restructure consciousness so as to make flow possible" (p. 83). Five conditions provide an ideal training for enjoying life. "Children who grow up in family situations that facilitate clarity of goals, feedback, feeling of control, concentration on the task at hand, intrinsic motivation, and challenge will generally have a better chance to order their lives so as to make flow possible" (p. 89). Csikszentmihalyi believes that "as the individual's purpose merges with the universal flow," the problem of life's meaning resolves through the realization "that the entire universe is a system related by laws and that it makes no sense to impose our dreams and desires on nature without taking them into account" and through accepting "a cooperative rather than a ruling role in the universe" (1990, p. 240).

An annual review of literature conducted by Stoltz-Loike (1996) indicates that changes in the workplace continue to transform the way people live and work. "Lifetime employment no longer exists, and organizations expect their employees to engage in more career self-management" (p. 100). Feller (1995) discusses the changing structure of the workplace that includes fewer managers at the top who act as coaches to more broadly skilled workers. "To be successful, workers need (a) broader skills; (b) educational credentials, which represent the beginning of a lifelong learning process; (c) flexibility; (d) adaptability; and (e) problem-solving skills" (Stoltz-Loike, 1997, p. 100). Employees must pave their own paths, building new skills through on-the-job training and effective networking. Skills, talents, and organizational demand will determine the jobs people hold (p. 109). Although discussed in business literature, career-development literature rarely discusses the new economy; however, educators and others must familiarize themselves with global changes and implications.

In 1992, *What Work Requires of Schools—A SCANS Report for America 2000* outlined what people must know to succeed in the future economy. In interviews with employers and employees from a wide variety of work settings, researchers found that "good jobs depend on people who can put knowledge to work" (Packer, 1992, p. 28).

Three essential qualities form the foundation that five broad competencies build upon, generic, universal skills that apply to most jobs:

- *Basic skills:* reading, writing, arithmetic, mathematics, speaking, listening;
- *Thinking skills:* creative thinking, decision making, problem solving, abstract visualizing of problems, knowing how to learn, and reasoning; and
- *Personal qualities:* individual responsibility, self-esteem, sociability, self-management, and integrity.

One possessed of the five major competencies

- can allocate resources (time, money, and people);
- has good interpersonal skills to work on teams, teach, negotiate, and serve customers;
- uses information to acquire, process, communicate, and evaluate data;
- selects, uses, and applies technology; and
- understands social, organizational, and technological systems.

While the report recognizes that schools "prepare people to live full lives—to participate in their communities, to raise families, and to enjoy the fruits of their labor," and that a solid education is important in itself, "SCANS is focusing on one important part of education: the role schools play in making sure that young people are ready for the world of work" (Packer, 1992, p. 28). In order for students to succeed, schools and businesses must link. "While most high school teachers are quite familiar with the entrance requirements for college, few know what is needed to succeed at work" (p. 28). Employers are beginning to understand the changes needed to strengthen the economy.

> They have abandoned Frederick Taylor's 80-year-old assembly-line mentality, one that makes little use of employees' talents, relying on them only to perform repetitive, routine tasks. High-performance firms have replaced the Tayloristic approach with one advocated by Edward Deming. . . . These businesses use all of their workers' skills to relentlessly pursue excellence, product quality, and customer

> satisfaction. They combine technology and people in new ways, moving decisions closer to the front lines, and drawing more fully on the abilities of all workers. The Deming approach means quality built in, not end-of-the-line quality control. And it means treating the workforce as an investment—not a cost. (p. 29)

To make changes, companies need a skilled workforce. The initial SCANS report disturbingly notes that "more than half of our young people leave school without the knowledge or foundation required to find and hold a good job. . . . They face the bleak prospects of dead-end work interrupted only by periods of unemployment" (Packer, 1992, p. 29). Simply put, low skills lead to low wages and low productivity. Schools and employers must work together. "The twin worlds of school and of work both have to change. Already, a strong back and a willingness to work are not enough to earn a decent living. Nor can firms that cling to the old Taylor-like process survive in the twenty-first century" (p. 30).

While the literature focuses on business needs and approaches that schools may take rather than on youth needs, Herr and Cramer (1996) reviewed student-articulated needs. Students express concern about their transition from high school: "In both sociological and psychological terms, many teenagers are apparently worried that for them the American dream is being jeopardized, and their visions of the future are restricted by problems of money, future, the complexity of choices, and health" (p. 412). A survey of American teens conducted by the American Home Economics Association in 1988 presented 32 topics to a sample of 510 junior and senior high school students. Approximately one third of the students expressed high levels of concern about their ability to pay for college, making wrong decisions about their future that they would be unable to change, a big depression in the U.S. economy, not earning enough money to enjoy the better things in life, and learning in the future that some of the food they eat cause cancer or heart attacks. "Although 8 in 10 teens say that they are basically happy with their lives, nearly 6 in 10 say they have a friend who has considered suicide, and 5 in 10 indicate that some of their friends are flirting with disaster by taking drugs" (p. 412). Nearly half of the students—47 percent—seek parental support, and 55 percent turn to friends for advice and help in overcoming problems. One in six reported that they have no one to turn to help them make important decisions. "More than half of these teens report feeling that they do not have a handle on life" (p. 412).

Hamburg and Takanisi (1989, p. 825) argue that recent historical events have drastically changed the adolescent experience, introducing high levels of anxiety and uncertainty into the lives of many young people. Lengthened duration of adolescence, confusion about adult roles, difficulty in foreseeing the future, erosion of family and social support networks, the disjunction between biological and social developments, and greater access to potentially life-threatening activities have possibly or actually affected their decision-making styles and career maturity (Herr & Cramer, 1996, p. 412).

U.S. society persistently separates home and the workplace, extends the period of adolescence, and makes difficult for young people the transition into the adult world of work. Mangum (1988) notes that many youth are cast into marginal roles in adolescence. A substantial minority from culturally and economically deprived backgrounds "are permanently scarred by their unsuccessful experiences" (p. 1).

Gray (1996) believes that many students who start on the path to a four-year baccalaureate degree will be seriously disappointed, and may be heavily in debt, if they cannot complete their college requirements or fail to obtain a high-paying job on graduation. He believes that students and parents must be given realistic information about other preparatory options for high-skilled occcupations.

The landmark, 21-year-long Career Pattern Study that Super and his colleagues initiated in 1951, when the boys were in ninth grade and about 15 years old, concerned the boys' vocational maturity, and continues to provide a framework for field research in career development.. Super considered the boys to be of "average ability . . . from average homes" (Jordaan & Hyde, 1979, p. 184). They were followed in studies of 1955, 1958, 1962, and 1973, when they were about 36 years old. Several published monographs summarized comparisons of boys' characteristics in ninth and twelfth grades, changes between ninth and twelfth grades, factors associated with change and stability in vocational maturity, the nature of vocational maturity in ninth and twelfth grades, and their theoretical and practical implications. A planning approach to life attested to the ninth graders' vocational maturity (p. 6). Maturity factors included awareness of choices and options, use of school and community resources to obtain information, occupational information regarding areas of interest, and educational and vocational planning. Early high school planning focused on the near future and later; twelfth grade orientation included both immediate and more remote future concerns. Twelfth grade factors included commitment to and acceptance of responsibility for vocational choices, weighing alternatives and contingencies, and implementing steps. Few twelfth graders (20 percent), and fewer ninth graders (10 percent), had decided on an occupation or specialty, although about 50 percent had a particular occupational field or career cluster in mind. About 25 percent could not identify with a preferred choice (p. 184). Vocational preferences continued to be unstable, uncertain, and unrealistic. Much change took place between ninth grade and twelfth grade preferences, and 66 percent of twelfth graders and "an even higher proportion of ninth graders, had little or no confidence in their goals" (p. 184). Uses of information sources were deficient, and most knew little about the occupation they thought they might like to enter. "Fewer than 5 percent [of twelfth graders] had well-thought-out plans for actually getting the needed training, education, or beginning job, or for entering the occupation once they had completed their training." Furthermore, they "showed little awareness of the fact that circumstances might compel them to change their goals or their plans for achieving them, and very few (only one in three) had done anything to implement or give substance to their preferences" (p. 184).

Super's theoretical framework represents high school and early adulthood years (14 to 25 years) as the exploratory stage, which has three substages: tentative, transitional, and trial. The developmental tasks of this period include crystallization, specification, implementation, stabilization, and consolidation. Crystallization—forming appropriate ideas about work—is the primary developmental task of the high school years. Adolescents work toward specification by seeking information, planning, and learning more about occupational choices. Implementation, stabilization, and consolidation tasks are generally accomplished after high school during early adulthood.

In the Career Planning Study, high school students tended to formulate a general and then a more specific preference towards greater crystallization. However, "contrary to theory, twelfth grade vocational preferences are not more appropriate or realistic than ninth grade preferences" (Jordaan & Hyde, 1979, p. 186). While most twelfth graders had part-time work experience, they rarely sought jobs in line with their occupational preferences.

This implies for theory that "data support the conclusion that awareness of concern with present and future decisions, awareness of the factors to consider in making decisions, occupational information, and planning are important aspects of vocational maturity in adolescence" (Jordaan & Hyde, 1979, p. 195). Fundamental questions for high school youth include: How ready are students to make required decision? What can be done to help them develop the necessary state of readiness? (p. 196).

Herr and Cramer (1996) review recent studies concerning career development maturity for high school students, the results of which indicate that while some students show crystallization in narrowing their career choices, they still experience uncertainty and instability and may have unrealistic expectations concerning those choices (p. 427). Research also indicates that curricula affect work values and career maturity (p. 426), and that a variety of trends exist concerning students' career decision-making: "it is clear that career development among senior high school students are wide-ranging" (p. 413). A 10-year national follow-up study of career development compared high school students from 1973 and 1983 regarding their desire for help in career planning, perception of receiving assistance, and certainty about occupational choice, among other related issues. In both years, while over 70 percent of the students expressed need for help, little more than 50 percent said they had received help, and about 25 percent of eleventh graders were "not sure at all" about their occupational preference. "In the final analysis, however, it continues to be evident that high school students vary in the status of their career development and that most of them profess major needs for help with their career planning" (p. 413-414).

Each year graduates move from high school to the next phase of their lives, transitions that generally take the following forms:

- Some graduates will make the transition to college or some form of postsecondary training;
- Some graduates will seek and find employment immediately after high school; and
- Some graduates may seek and not find employment and will remain unemployed. (Pautler, 1994)

Many young people flounder for several years before entering an adult lifestyle. Data indicate that "high schools vary widely in the status of their career planning services, including planning for postsecondary and collegiate education," and studies "echo" an unevenness of guidance services in high schools across the country (Herr & Cramer, 1996, p. 414).

"In the U.S. literature describing the process by which adolescents make the transition from school to work, it is almost an accepted truism that typical high school graduates mill around in the labor market moving from one dead-end job to another until the age of 23 or 24" (Herr & Cramer, 1996, p. 46; Commission on the Skills of the American Workforce, 1990). Japan and Germany plan transitions at earlier ages, making them smoother. Pautler (1994, 1997) recommends creating a "handover system" whereby school leavers would be "handed over" to the next agent or experience. The school would help students take the next step by coordinating services and career planning and providing feedback to the school regarding overall program effectiveness.

To develop quality and continuous school improvement, follow-up studies that determine what students do when they leave school should be conducted to better inform boards of education, school personnel, and community members about the needs and progress of all school leavers. Pautler (1994) reports on school districts that are "developing a database culled from the experiences of their graduates both in work and college settings. The districts can compare results between and among graduates. This should help provide a solid database upon which to make curriculum, program, and staffing decisions" (p. 35).

Costello (1995) and Haberi (1996) investigated suburban students' perception of high school preparation for college. Costello's study involved 110 graduates of 1991 who anticipated attending a community college. Forty-one (37 percent) completed and 69 (63 percent) did not complete community college. Haberi found that of the 52 available subjects accepted into four-year colleges from the 1989 graduating class, 38 (73 percent) completed. Both studies established a systematic means of data collection to survey high school graduates that can help develop and improve a school district's approach to realistic life planning and career development.

The public believe that children who go to college will better succeed in life, reports indicate higher earnings for those who hold a college degree, and local school boards emphasize transition into college, many calling for placement rates of 80 to 90 percent into higher education. The W. T. Grant Foundation report *The Forgotten Half: Non-College Youth in*

America (1988a) indicates that while approximately 75 percent enroll in colleges, only 25 percent complete a four-year degree. Furthermore, while many jobs require further postsecondary technical education, 75 percent of jobs do not require a college degree.

Today, perhaps more than ever before, students face more opportunities to make lifestyle decisions. On what basis do they make decisions? What are the outcomes? What interventions can improve the process's effectiveness?

Research must continuously assess student career development and transition. In their handbook on career counseling, Savickas and Walsh (1996) consider the relationship between career theory and practice; the rapid, turbulent changes in the workplace from an industrial society to an information-intensive one; and changes in relationships between researchers, theorists, and practitioners. Herr and Cramer (1996) summarize a broad spectrum of research issues and concerns. In addition to empirical concerns, they find that many questions about career theories and interventions concern philosophy and values (p. 724).

THE MEANING OF CAREER

Herr and Cramer (1996, pp. 31-32) provide various interpretations of *career*; McDaniels (1978) views it as a sequence of lifetime work and leisure activities; and Hansen and Keierleber (1978) see it as helping individuals make choices related to integrating interrelated roles involving work, education, and family. Gysbers and Moore (1981) use the term *life career development* to reflect self-development through integrating the roles, setting, and events over the course of one's life; while the National Career Development Association defines *career* as the totality of one's lifetime work and leisure (Sears, 1982). Raynor and Entin (1982) maintain that a career is both behavioral and phenomenological, forging the link between how one sees oneself and what a one does. Super (1976) broadly defines career as the course of life's events. Occupations and other life roles sequenced and combined express a commitment to work within one's total self-development pattern, embodying such remunerated and nonremunerated positions as student, employee, and retiree, as well as familial, complementary avocational, and civic roles. Existing only as people pursue them, careers are person-centered, providing the rationale for career guidance (Super, 1976, p. 4). Unique to each person, one's choices create one's careers. Careers are dynamic, unfold throughout life, and integrate life roles.

CAREER DEVELOPMENT FOR ADOLESCENTS

Adolescent career development may be thought of as teens negotiating the ground on which they run their race or travel on a road or pathway. Paths may be narrow or wide, rough or smooth, uphill or downhill, the pace fast or slow. Some students may opt for a more well-worn pathway as a smooth direction in life. Others may decide on more challenging routes. Careers often offer challenges and at times a fight. Career development teaches about available options, becoming a time of trial and error as teens develop awareness of the realities of adult life. In all likelihood, their road will change contours throughout life, predictable, familiar terrain followed by surprises.

One prepares for the obvious and for contingencies. Most important perhaps are the skills and the strength and resiliency of spirit, personality, and character that best serve each person in the long run. The mark that one leaves along the path characterizes oneself and one's life and is one's legacy. This is what adolescents live and prepare for during high school and beyond.

Occupational exploration is particularly important in forming self-identity. Who am I? What do I think about myself? Who and what kind of person do I want to become? How does one choose a lifestyle? What must a teen-ager know? How is the information provided? Exploring and crystallizing life choices comprise the developmental tasks of this time in life. Adolescents fantasize, make tentative decisions, and through trial and error begin to approach realistic choices. This period of rapid change, confusion, and anxiety for students as they leave behind childhood to take on more independence can also be a time of exhilarating growth, maturation, and development of good character and self-esteem. Concerns about physical and emotional intimacy often accompany different rates of physical and sexual maturation. Peer-group norms, models, and values stand as standards and expectations contrasted against family beliefs and ways of being. Parental empathy, acceptance, and support provide a crucial sense of security and continuity.

Adolescents manifest considerable growth in intellectual capacity and can reflect on their own and other's abilities, personalities, thoughts, and feelings. They develop the abilities needed to formulate sound future plans and moral and ethical thinking. Career lifestyle and occupational choice help adolescents develop self-identity (Seligman, 1994, p. 255). Research indicates that career maturity—an important construct in career development for adolescents—positively correlates with later career satisfaction, status, and success, stability, use of assets, education and occupation levels, and realistic occupation choices. Career-related knowledge and career-planning behaviors are two important, distinct ingredients of adolescent career maturity (p. 258).

Career adaptability extends the construct of career maturity. To adapt means "to learn," "to learn rapidly," "to fit," a life-long process beginning at birth. Developmentally, babies and children rapidly learn about their bodies, language, symbols, surroundings, culture, and expectations of them. Career development involves the idea of a person-in-a-situation or person-in-context, in which the fundamental need to successfully navigate career paths includes the skill of learning how to learn, creating one's own lifestyle within the multitude of changing options. Skills and dispositions needed for successful career development include critical thinking, empathy, self-discipline, creativity, planning, cooperating with others, continuous learning and improvement, and caring for oneself.

Economic, educational, and societal issues repeatedly influence attitudes toward career development and the methods of preparing children for adulthood. The past may appear to have offered easier, smoother roads for young people, with more road signs for success. In comparison with the United States's industrial past, today's information age requires a different approach to education and business. Currently there is a tremendous shift in the global economy and more complex challenges in developing human resources. As education and the business worlds respond to world-class standards, individuals must demonstrate new forms of career adaptability.

COMPREHENSIVE CAREER DEVELOPMENT

Hoyt's broad definition captures the modern view of career development as a complex, comprehensive process that differs for each person: "Career development is the total constellation of psychological, sociological, educational, physical, economic and chance factors that combine to shape the career of any given individual over the life span" (Hoyt, 1991, p. 23).

People are socialized organizers of their experiences who choose occupations that allow them to act in roles consistent with their self-concept. Most people possess multipotential and can find satisfaction in a variety of occupations. While each person makes decisions for his or her own life, facilitating the maturation of abilities and interests and assisting in testing reality and developing self-concept can guide career development throughout life. Life and work satisfactions depend upon finding adequate outlets for values, needs, interests, abilities, personality traits, and self-concepts. For some, work and occupation may focus personality organization; for others, alternative foci may be central through other life roles. Goals for career development include knowing oneself, preparing for life-choices; expanding awareness of the range of options available; exploring; emphasizing the relationship of life roles to work; balancing and integrating life roles and work life; developing life and employability skills; learning, adaptating, and planning continuously; and creating one's life process. Career development continues throughout life.

In an educational approach to comprehensive career development, the high school years (grades 9-12) form one segment of a system beginning in early childhood and continuing through postsecondary education and adulthood. Transition from secondary school represents a critical phase in adolescent development. What must each student know to excel? What can be done to make the transition smooth and seamless? Maximizing career development requires an active, collaborative partnership of educators-teachers, administrators, school board members, counselors, and support staff at the school level working with students, parents, businesses, community members, and government officials. Such a partnership assumes that all students have the innate ability to learn what is required to live successfully. Students take primary responsibility for their learning, but they need adult guidance, support, and direction.

High school approaches to career development must be articulated with middle and junior high school level as well as with postsecondary placement services. Career preparation and sequences of career developmental tasks—integrated as academic, occupational instruction—should weave through the entire curriculum of all students' school life in order to prepare them to successfully advance along postsecondary career paths, with options of further education, training and/ or employment.

A number of resources and state models for comprehensive guidance and systematic educational career planning exist. To encourage career development, goal setting, and life plans for all students, a national consortium of State Career Guidance Supervisors and the U.S. Recruiting Command have united to identify, share, and reward effective practices of systematic education and career planning. The fall 1996 *Journal of Career Development* features a thematic issue on planning for life, and provides a detailed, step-by-step process to develop comprehensive career planning and development. Survey research sponsored in 1993-94 by the National Career Development Association and in 1995 by the National Occupational Information Coordinating Committee (NOICC) indicates that while high schools may adequately preparing students for postsecondary education, deficits in overall career planning exist (Starr, 1996, p. 10). For high school students, the process must extend learning about occupational clusters, career paths, self-knowledge of interests and aptitudes, decision making, and planning specific steps to further one's education, training, employability, and life skills. Students need knowledge of family responsibilities, how to understand and get along with others, value preferences, the changing world, how to enhance life-coping skills, and citizenship. Integrated curricula may include competencies, standards, scope and sequence, and evaluation. NOICC's set of competencies—the National Career Development Guidelines, piloted and implemented in several states—encompass career exploration and planning, knowledge of self and others, and education and occupation development, all representing the knowledge, skills, and attitudes needed to live, learn, and work in society. Work-based and community-based learning also provide opportunities to develop skills (McCharen, 1996, p. 75).

Exploring specific career clusters and paths teach students about an important aspect of career development, with knowledge transferable to other interest areas—knowledge more important for many students than a specific career plan. The overall effort must be on par and integrated with core subject area curriculum. Counseling and referral must be available to support all students. Comprehensive system support must be formalized and involve members from all segments of the community.

NEEDS ASSESSMENT FOR CAREER DEVELOPMENT

An advisory committee can support comprehensive high school career development efforts. Committee membership should include building principal, faculty, staff, school counselors, parents, students, business representatives, higher education representatives, public and private employers, governmental representatives, college and university professors, and school administrators involved in curriculum and instruction. The committee will help refine and implement the school's philosophy and mission concerning comprehensive career development by developing and administering a needs assessment for students, developing or identifying competencies, coordinating and assisting implementation, and designing and administering assessment for continuous improvement. The student needs assessment would be based on a review of literature and research concerning the career development needs of high school students.

A needs assessment and process may also be implemented for the career needs of faculty and staff for professional development. Plans may also include assessing career development needs for parents and community members, expanding the learning environment of the school to the full community.

At minimum, an individualized career planning document would guide each student's career development. Students would learn how to plan, monitor, and integrate life roles within a career development framework, taking care to maintain their plans and document their progress, perhaps using portfolios. These plans would be reviewed annually, at minimum, with parents and students. Such activities as professional faculty and school counselor monitoring of career development planning, individual portfolios, and short-term action research studies would help continuously improve students' approaches.

To help coordinate school transition assistance for school leavers and monitor their progress, follow-up contact with students within their first year of leaving high school is highly recommended. Longitudinal follow-up studies can determine graduates' longer range future development while identifying the school's curriculum needs to continuously improve its quality. Schools that conduct continuous research will be knowledgeable of and able to assess needs for overall school improvement.

SUMMARY

The perennial challenges of youths' transition into adulthood may be broadly viewed as career development, as teenagers and young adults navigate and explore paths leading toward establishment and stability. Developmental tasks form self-identity and a place within one's world, while occupational choices and the selection of work-life roles greatly influence other aspects of life and become very important at this time. Self-knowledge and knowledge of one's life roles require gaining information and understanding. Planning leads to trial and error, more learning, and career adaptation as one seeks to fit into roles congruent with one's developing self-concept. Rapid growth, change, and chaos mark this critical stage of development. Every young person needs help with career development. High schools that focus on students' growth can foster conditions for career maturation and adaptability for a more productive transition.

References

Allgood-Merten, B., Lewisohn, P. M., & Hops, H. (1990). Sex differences and adolescent depression. *Journal of Abnormal Psychology, 99*, 55-63.

Angell, J. R. (1903). The relations of structural and functional psychology to philosophy. *Philosophical Review, 12*, 243-271.

Angold, A. (1988). Childhood and adolescent depression: Epidemiological and etiological aspects. *British Journal of Psychiatry, 152*, 601-617.

Baron, R. A. (1992). *Psychology* (2nd ed.). Needham Heights, MA: Allyn & Bacon.

Buehler, C. (1933). *Der menschliche Lebenslauf als psychologisches Problem.* Leipzig: Hirzel.

Cash, T. F., Winstead, B., & Janda, L. (1986). The age of the beholder. *Psychology Today, 20*(4), 30-37.

Commission on the Skills of the American Workforce. (1990). *America's choice: High skills or low wages.* Rochester, NY: Center on Education and the Economy.

Costello, M. A. H. (1995). *High school preparation quality: Students' perceptions and experiences in the transition process.* Unpublished doctoral dissertation. State University of New York: Buffalo.

Cramer, S. H. (1999). *Overview of career development*

theory. In A. Pautler, Jr. (Ed.) *Workforce Education: Issues for the New Century.* Ann Arbor, MI: Tech Directions Books.

Csikszentmihalyi, M. (1990). *Flow: The psychology of optimal experience.* New York: HarperCollins.

Csikszentmihalyi, M., & Larson, R. (1984). *Being adolescent: Conflict and growth in the teenage years.* New York: Basic Books.

Dedmond, R. M. (Ed.) (1996). A thematic issue on planning for life [Special Issue]. *Journal of Career Development, 23* (1).

Dewey, J. (1896). The reflex arc concept in psychology. *Psychological Review, 3,* 357-370.

Drummond, R. J., & Ryan, C. W. (1995). *Career counseling: A developmental approach.* Englewood Cliffs, NJ: Prentice Hall.

Erikson, E. H. (1950). *Childhood and society.* New York: Norton.

Feller, R. W. (1995). Action planning for personal competitiveness in the "broken workplace." *Journal of Employment Counseling, 52,* 154-163.

Frederick, C. J. (1985). An introduction and overview to youth suicide. In M. L. Peck, N. C. Faberow, & R. E. Litman (Eds.), *Youth suicide* (pp. 1-116). New York: Springer.

Garrison, C., Schoenbach, V., & Kaplan, B. (1985). Depression symptoms in early adolescence. In A. Deal (Ed.), *Depression in multidisciplinary perspective* (pp.60-82). New York: Bruner/Mozel.

Grant Foundation (1988a). *The forgotten half: Noncollege youth in America.* Washington, DC: The William T. Grant Foundation.

Grant Foundation. (1988b). *The forgotten half: Pathways to success for America's youth and young families.* Washington, DC: The William T. Grant Foundation.

Gray, K. (1996). The baccalaureate game: Is it right for teens? *Phi Delta Kappan, 77,* 528-534.

Gysbers, N. C., & Moore, E. J. (1981). *Improving guidance programs.* Englewood Cliffs, N. J.: Prentice-Hall.

Haberi, M. A. (1996). *The graduates of 1989: A study of intended and actual career paths and students' perceptions of their high school years.* Unpublished doctoral dissertation. State University of New York: Buffalo.

Hamburg, D. A., & Takaniski, R. (1989). Preparing for life: The critical transition of adolescence. *American Psychologist, 44*(5), 825-827.

Hansen, L. S., & Keierleber, D. L. (1978). Born free: A collaborative consultation model for career redevelopment and sex-role stereotyping. *Personnel and Guidance Journal 56*(17), 395-399.

Herr, E. L., (1997). Super's life-space approach and its outlook for refinement. *The Career Development Quarterly, 45,* 238-245.

Herr, E. L., & Cramer, S. H. (1996). *Career guidance and counseling through the lifespan: Systematic approaches* (5th ed.). New York: HarperCollins.

Hoyt, K. B. (1991). The concept of work: Bedrock for career development. *Future Choices, 2*(3), 23-30.

Jordaan, J. P., & Hyde, M. B. (1979). *Vocational maturity during the high school years.* New York: Columbia University.

Kuhn, D. (1989). Children and adults as intuitive scientists. *Psychological Review, 96,* 674-689.

Mangum, G. L. (1988). *Youth transition from adolescence to the world of work.* Paper prepared for Youth and America's Future: The William T. Grant Foundation Commission on Work, Family, and Citizenship. Washington, DC: The William T. Grant Foundation Commission.

McCharen, B. (1996). Measuring the effects of career planning: The seventh C—Competency. *Journal of Career Development, 23*(1), 73-82.

McDaniels, C. (1978). The practice of career guidance and counseling. *INFORM, 7,* 1-2, 7-8.

National Occupational Information Coordinating Committee. (1990). *National career development guidelines.* Washington, DC: Author.

National Occupational Information Coordinating Committee. (1994). *Gallup Poll, 1994.* Washington, DC: Author.

Packer, D. (1992). *What work requires of schools—A SCANS report for America 2000. The Secretary's Commission on Achieving Necessary Skills.* Washington, DC.: U.S. Department of Labor.

Parsons, F. (1909). *Choosing a vocation.* New York: Houghton Mifflin.

Pautler, A. (1997). 6...5...4...3...2...1... Countdown to graduation. *Tech Directions, 56*(7), 16-18.

Pautler, A. (1994). How do they exit your school? *Tech Directions, 53*(4), 34-35.

Raynor, J. O., & Entin, E. E. (1982). *Motivation, career striving, and aging.* New York: Hemisphere.

Savickas, M. L. (1997). Career adaptability: An integrative construct for life-span, life-space theory. *The Career Development Quarterly, 45,* 247-259.

Savickas, M. L., & Walsh, W. B. (Eds.) (1996). *Handbook of career counseling theory and practice.* Palo Alto, CA: Davies-Black.

Sears, S. (1982). A definition of career guidance terms: A national vocational guidance association perspective. *Vocational Guidance Quarterly, 31*(2), 137-143.

Seligman, L. (1994). *Developmental career counseling and assessment* (2nd ed.). Thousand Oaks, CA: Sage.

Starr, M. F. (1996). Comprehensive guidance and systematic education and career planning: Why a K-12 approach? *Journal of Career Development, 23*(1), 9-22.

Stoltz-Loike, M. (1996). Annual review: Practice and research in career development and counseling—1995. *The Career Development Quarterly, 45,* 99-139.

Super, D. E. (1976). *Career education and the meaning of work.* Monographs on career education. Washington, DC: Office of Career Education, U.S. Office of Education.

Super, D. E., Sverko, B. & Super, C. M. (1995). *Life roles, values, and careers: International findings of the work importance study.* San Francisco: Jossey-Bass.

Cheryl L. Hogg, *candidate for the Ph.D. in Educational Administration at the State University of New York at Buffalo, currently serves as the graduate assistant for Leadership Initiative for Tomorrow's Schools (LIFTS). Her background includes more than 25 years as an educator with elementary-level through adult populations and includes such positions as principal/supervisor and assistant principal in the New York State Board of Cooperative Educational Services (BOCES); educational and vocational supervisor for the New York State Division for Youth residential and field services; school counselor with the Buffalo Public Schools; career education and placement for Buffalo Children's Hospital Adolescent Services. She has completed two master's degrees at Canisius College and was awarded a Rotary International scholarship from Manchester Polytechnic for postgraduate work in youth and community work.*

9

CAREER DEVELOPMENT FOR ALL

By Rich Feller and Timothy Gray Davies

Communities support education that improves student achievement. However, innovations and new programs typically meet resistance and fail to sustain momentum, especially when change questions school cultures, functions, and incentives. Will school-to-career (STC), the latest innovation in school to include work-based learning, be able to mollify the resisters and build on-going local and national momentum? Perhaps as resisters and supporters recognize STC as a learning strategy to motivate *all* students to achieve more and prepare them for new forms of work, increased citizenship demands, and lifelong learning, it will hold great promise.

Having been called *school-to-work programs, school-to-career initiatives,* and *school-to-employment*, STC may be viewed as a systems-building effort to stimulate school improvement, reinvent how all youth prepare for careers, and expand partnerships with community colleges. Unfortunately, STC faces many challenges without much constituency understanding or support. While the task of equipping youth for employment, lifelong education, and career advancement receives national attention, it faces many local challenges.

As does any challenge to one of society's stabler institutions, STC efforts polarize those who resist educational change from those who point to the downside of "doing schooling the way it has always been done." Forty-three percent of community citizens give their local schools an "A" or "B," with 8 in 10 giving them a "C" or better. Two-thirds (66 percent) of parents assign a grade of "A" or "B" to the public school their oldest child attends ("The Twenty-Eighth Annual Gallup Poll," 1996). Few argue that education shouldn't adapt, and most agree that it can be more rigorous and relevant. Yet educational change remains slow and complex.

This chapter examines four critical issues shaping STC's future: (1) Changing schools is hard work with little prior success; (2) STC's guiding principles have not won approval from the college-bound or their parents; (3) high-performance, workforce-preparation systems are limited and rarely align with community colleges; and (4) leaders must step forward to maintain STC's challenge to the status quo. The chapter concludes with a brief look at career development as the organizer of hope within the STC effort.

CHANGING SCHOOLS IS ALL ABOUT HARD WORK

Schools have changed little in the last 50 years, with the exception of their response to students with special needs. Parental efforts to initiate a diagnostic system leading to individual education plans and federal oversight for "some types" of students has been revolutionary. Although a litany of programs remold the educational wheel, little has changed the structured, time-based, teacher-focused approach to learning. As Thomas Payzant, superintendent of Boston Public Schools says, "Questions of incentives, job design, methods of measuring progress, obtaining agreement on goals, while at the core of most discussions of improving the performance of firms, rarely are included in discussion of how to improve schools" (Murname & Levy, 1996, p. xi). Murname and Levy (1996) argue that the educational system has undergone incremental improvement in an environment of exponential change that leaves fewer students prepared for a global economy.

Because all school critics have attended schools, making schools museums of their past is a politically safe and expedient response to changing demographics and anticipated, but misunderstood, needs of future workers and citizens. Changing school cultures and adult/student relationships concerns the difficult tasks of changing values and beliefs and the time-consuming tasks of changing pedagogical methods, curriculum, and assessment strategies. Cuban (1993) suggests seven phases of reform that illustrate the difficulty in mobilizing communities to agree on why, how, and what students should learn:

> 1. Social, political, and economic changes in objective conditions of life or in ideologies create situations that opinion makers in society define as problems.
>
> 2. Policy makers, academics, and opinion makers, such as journalists and top corporate officials—outsiders to the educational enterprise . . . [develop consensus] about what the problems are and what solutions are feasible.
>
> 3. Groups and individuals outside the schools develop policy proposals and programs to solve the perceived problem.
>
> 4. Through various mechanisms (legislation, pilot projects, school board decisions) groups and individuals connected to the educational enterprise come to be known as reformers and press insiders to adopt and implement reforms.
>
> 5. Some policies do get adopted and superintendents, principals, and teachers attempt to implement these policies. Efforts to incorporate the deliberate reforms into routine practice get under way within districts, schools and classrooms.
>
> 6. Growing criticism of educators' seemingly slow or halfhearted efforts to implement reforms give way to shrinking attention to whether schools are solving the problem that had been defined earlier. Disappointment sets in.
>
> 7. Social, economic, or demographic conditions in society again shift and the cycle begins anew. (p. 244)

As history shows, sustaining change will be a major problem for STC advocates. However, the hardest work ahead lies in convincing go-to-college zealots that STC concerns more than preparing the noncollege-bound for work, maximizing the role of community colleges, and finding courageous leaders willing to listen to students not well served.

STC: FOR MORE THAN THOSE IN THE MIDDLE

Improving a community's quality of life demands more than high academic standards as measured by traditional assessment and attained by only the "top" students. High standards and effective teaching leading to competencies needed by all responsible, economically self-sufficient, and culturally rich citizens are imperative.

No less important, in order for a nation's standard of living to improve, all must share in the cost of its competitive advantage. As Thurow points out in *Head to Head: The Coming Economic Battle Among Japan, Europe, and America* (1992), natural resources, technology, capital, and workers shape strategic advantage. The market system prizes educated workers with ample natural resources and comparable production technology. Thurow argues,

> If the route to success is inventing new products, the education of the smartest 25 per-

> cent of the labor force is critical. If the route to success is being the cheapest and best producer of products, new or old, the education of the bottom 50 percent of the population moves to center stage. This part of the population must staff those new processes. If the bottom 50 percent cannot learn what must be learned, new high-tech processes cannot be employed. (p. 52)

Competitive, global, and technical advances pressure all workers. As the economy centers on the flow of information and knowledge creation, employers increasingly expect from blue-collar workers in the primary labor market more competency in communication, math, computer, and decision-making skills. Parents and students make up part of the 93 percent of Gallup poll respondents who interpreted this to mean that individual future success depends on attending college ("The Twenty-Sixth Annual Gallup Poll," 1994). Unfortunately, this perspective, when seen as the only way to win (Gray & Herr, 1995), ill-serves those who learn and perform in ways not valued by traditional transcripts and seat time—those who enter unprepared for four-year college, and baccalaureates who incur great college debts without translating their experience into added value.

Until recently, few questioned the college-prep curriculum. Many suggested it as the way to improve all student performances. Few advocated integrated curricula for all or different-but-equal learning strategies that prepare students for work, postsecondary education entry, *and* the competencies necessary for completing college. While STC targets this, many fear that work-based learning and career-focused education threaten the college-bound by dumbing down academics and stunting intellectual achievement. Others fear that career-development activities and career pathways force high school students to choose their future too early. Yet, evidence continues to mount that these concerns need not be realized.

Heebner (1996) found that graduates of New York City magnet schools completed more college courses two years after graduation than similar graduates from traditional comprehensive schools. Bailey and Merritt (1996) argue that steering students away from STC opportunities—because it harms the chances of getting into good colleges—actually limits choice. They conclude that the practical aspects of STC programs can help students develop a better sense of their goals. Students with some sense of their goals choose better postsecondary activities and use of time in college.

The Commissioner of Education Statistics, in the *Condition of Education 1995* (U.S. Department of Education [USDE], 1995), notes that high rates of incompletion may indicate that "students do not have enough information about the actual skills in demand in the labor market" before making education decisions. In 1992, 4 percent of those who held a bachelor's degree were unemployed and 23 percent held jobs that did not normally require a college degree ("Education and Work," 1996). Bard College economist Oren Leven-Waldman's study (as cited in "Smart Managing: Best Practices and Ideas," 1997, p. 133) reports that people with four-year college and postgraduate degrees face higher long-term unemployment than those with less education. He argues that they lack the technical and managerial skills needed in today's marketplace. Actions taken by such prestigious schools as the University of Wisconsin ("UW System Explores Use of Competency-Based Admission (CBA)," 1996) and MIT offer similar support. Hoye (1996) reports that 20 percent of students accepted in MIT's class of 1997 had to have work-based learning and portfolio work as part of their application.

While STC implies greater opportunities for the "middle students," it improves academic or basic skills and competencies needed by all students when taught in ways that students learn best. Howard Gardner (1985) concludes that the verbal/mathematical model of intelligence rewarded in the twentieth-century model of education and represented by standard IQ tests is much too narrow. School learning is so heavily symbol-based that connections to the objects symbolized are often lost when transfer to a context is not made (Resnick, 1986). As Parnell notes in *Why Do I Have to Learn This?* (1995), Gardner's, Sternberg's (1988), and others' work on intelligence points to a conclusion:

> Unless we enlarge our definition of intelligence we will continue to send the message that intelligence is a fixed capacity, that people either have it or don't, and that those who don't have it, don't have much hope of any real success in school or life. (p. 88)

Parents of college-prep students know political pressure can preserve the status quo. As a result, they must be convinced that changes brought forward by STC's expanded-learning strategy will not remove their child's option to go to college. Removing the fear that colleges will not recognize the competencies learned in STC programs and reducing the conflict between STC activities and admission to selective colleges requires three groups of strategies (Bailey & Merritt, 1996):

1. accommodation of the STC program within the existing college admissions system;
2. communication between individual schools and colleges; and
3. attempts at broad reform in assessment and college admissions procedures. (p. 13)

Cognitive science, advances in interactive learning technologies, and challenging traditional beliefs may increase the ability to teach the way all people learn. Yet, for STC to serve more than the middle students, the question "Will my students be able to go to college if they participate?" is the bottom line for most critics.

THE COMMUNITY COLLEGE ROLE IN WORKFORCE PREPARATION

Community colleges have been in the business of providing vocational/technical education and training since the 1920s. How effectively and efficiently they have done so is still being debated. More importantly, are today's community colleges willing and able to provide the high-performance workforce required by their STC partnerships? To play such a role, community colleges must counter the cooling out myth, address the career-counseling deficit, and re-energize their own curricula.

The Cooling Out Function of the Community College

Clark (1960), in his study of San Jose Junior College, first used the term *cooling out* to describe the systematic process that redirects students' aspirations from university transfer to vocational terminal program entrance, a more modest goal. Clark describes San Jose Junior College's societal role in the open admissions process as having "the junior college available to face the multitude with the open door, while the other public colleges select students. The junior college in effect is asked to 'cool out' the incompetent. . . ." (p.163). Brint and Karabel (1989), Dougherty (1994), Zwerling (1976), and Pincus (1980) extended Clark's work at San Jose to community colleges in general and describe their higher education role as gatekeepers. They were to systematically divert certain students from universities to allow the universities to remain elite. In addition, community colleges funneled more and more workers into the corporate workforce's lower strata.

Community colleges must address this mistaken notion held by its critics. W. Norton Grubb, in *Working in the Middle: Strengthening Education and Training for the Mid-Skilled Labor Force* (1996), refutes with three arguments the cooling out role alleged to community colleges. First, the concept of cooling out students assumes that they would have initially attended a four-year college if the community college had not been there to siphon them away. However, many of these students would have been unable to attend college, if they had not first studied at a community college.

Second, Grubb states that Clark puts too much importance on the role counselors play in cooling out. Based on student interviews, Grubb ascertains that, for the most part, students did not frequently or consistently use counselors, and the few who did found them of little help and not detrimental to their academic goals and progress. Davies and Dickmann (in press) support this finding through focus-group interviews with community college transfer students.

The third point Grubb declares to be normative:

> [T]he mechanisms associated with cooling out are probably more equitable and more supportive than any of the alternatives. As Clark (1980) himself has argued, any relatively inegalitarian society that promotes high aspirations among its young people must eventually reconcile the two. If it cannot create more places at the top—and this country has been notably resistant to reducing inequality directly—then it must either reduce aspirations in the "soft" ways associated with cooling out, providing second best alternatives to students that seem more attainable and realistic, or it must reduce them in the "hard" ways used in many other countries, for example by using high-stakes exams that deny individuals places in postsecondary programs once and for all. (p.66).

Community colleges must move beyond the critics' cooling-out arguments and address substantive systems problems within their organizations that have more far-reaching effects on their students and on their role as an STC partner.

Career Counseling Deficit

Virtually all community college students attend to begin or continue the process of entering society and its workforce. The university transfer student majoring in English, the displaced worker enrolled in the high-tech program, the high school drop-out struggling in the developmental studies program, and the future nurse all aspire to find employment that will provide internal satisfaction and material compensation.

One of the major tenants of the School-to-Work Opportunity Act (1994) is to serve *all* students. Thus in STC community colleges, career counseling must serve *all* students. The National Occupational Information Coordinating Committee's (NOICC) *National Career Development Guidelines* (1989) identifies three areas in which *all* students need assistance: (1) increasing self-knowledge, (2) educational and occupational exploration, and (3) lifelong career planning. These three areas are germane to *all* students, not just those in the vocational programs. Career counselors need to be as well-versed in exploring transfer programs leading to the world of work as technical programs leading more immediately to the world of work. Unfortunately, this is not the case, as Stern (1992) points out:

> [T]he major responsibility for finding jobs for vocational/technical graduates falls on the students themselves, with help from their instructors rather than from the placement services. Further, counseling and placement services have been more successful at helping students who want to move on to further education than those who want to move into the labor market. The NCRVE report recommends that two-year colleges give increased attention to counseling and placement for students who plan to move directly into the labor market.

Career counselors need the help of community college faculty to help students develop a career for now and the future. If community colleges cannot forge internal teams of career counselors and faculty to help students pursue work-based learning experiences, then the current dismal numbers of community college students involved in STC programs will not improve.

Community College Curriculum

Community colleges must integrate academic and technical content in their school- and work-based learning by connecting activities to the world of work. Externally, the community college must integrate its content and skill expectations with its feeder school districts. The most positive and far-reaching integration program in the last decade resulted from Parnell's push in *The Neglected Majority* (1985), which initiated the tech prep two-plus-two programs in many communities. Community colleges and their K-12 partners need to build on this concept and carry it beyond the technical curriculum, as Pauly, Kopp, and Haimson describe in *Homegrown Lessons* (1994).

Second, community college developmental programs do not carry equal status on campuses with transfer and technical programs. Community colleges must increase the status and importance of developmental programs by making some basic systemic changes: (1) Make placement in the developmental program mandatory, based on placement exam results. The "right to fail" philosophy of the late 1960s and early 1970s is unfair to students (who pay the ultimate penalty for declining developmental help and then cool out of college), tax payers (who rely on the community college's professional judgment in making best use of tax dollars), and professional faculty (who now have a wider range of heterogeneity in their classrooms than would be otherwise necessary). In addition, those who choose to exercise their "right to fail" penalize students who legitimately score well enough on the placement exam to enter the traditional classroom. (2) While over half the students in developmental programs are recent high school graduates, the other half are nontraditional students who have not recently been in the classroom. Community colleges need to show exemplary teaching practices through updated nontraditional pedagogy. Too often these courses, taught in a condescending and repetitive manner, are antithetical to the way adult students learn best. (3) Faculty teaching developmental students must concentrate on their own innovations and experiments to develop new approaches that help students who failed in previous traditional classrooms. Through requested assistance to evaluate these new techniques, some techniques will sort themselves as effective best practices that may be generalized to other developmental classrooms and the campus at large.

Third, the general education program must have a resurgence. Students often come to a community college and instructionally mill around, aimlessly taking classes with little direction toward the worlds of work or transfer. Many community colleges have drifted back to their smorgasbord or distributive-elective general education program rather than return to the common-core approach. Higginbottom and Romano (1995) present eight general education models for community colleges looking to upgrade their present general education program.

Fourth, community college technical faculty need to systematically keep current with the world of work. Traditionally, academic faculty have used sabbaticals to help them break new ground in their disciplines, but the sabbatical leave is too infrequent to be of much assistance to technical faculty members. Other mechanisms—such as paid leave, temporary assignment, or periodic exchange with someone in the field—must be implemented to maintain currency in the technical field. Technical instructors must move away from strict theory-based teaching models. Employers continually ask for more practical applications to accompany the theory, exactly what the School-to-Work Opportunity Act requires.

LEADERSHIP AVAILABILITY TO CHAMPION STC

The fourth critical issue centers on the concept of leadership champions. Important issues facing STC leaders include understanding key debates within STC, valuing career development, understanding the emerging workplace, and delivering basic skills to all.

Key STC Debates

The following debates challenge any STC leadership effort: Is STC the latest staff-development fad, repackaged vocational education, or a corporate effort to fortify economic productivity and social-class advantages? Is it an effort to embrace technology and business partnerships in the fight against educational and socioeconomic inequality? Does it challenge industrial models of education, deemed inappropriate for an information-rich, technologically enhanced global workplace? Can it provide access to the best educational strategies for *all* students without threatening those now receiving an elite advanced placement education? Is it a plot to cool off aspirations by slotting students into the sub-baccalaureate labor force? Does it beg for community colleges to meet the needs of the mid-skilled worker? Does it turn accountability to the business community's doorsteps by demanding sustained local partnerships? Does it demand career-development efforts connecting the school and workplace while supporting parents convinced that college acceptance offers the only way to win? Many of these questions need addressing, as local resolutions determine the size, shape, and sustainability of the STC response. These issues excite public reaction, demanding that leaders think carefully about using STC as a means to improve student achievement.

As was the career education movement, the School-to-Work Opportunities Act of 1994 is designed to *not* be a federal program. It competitively provides venture capital to implement school- and work-based learning and connecting activities sustainable through local public and private resources. With strong local autonomy in an age of accountability, can STC leverage workplace development and business dollars to build systems that won't turn STC into a program for only "those" students?

Understanding the Changing Workplace

The golden age of manufacturing and management peaked in the 1970s when personal computers redefined how work would be accomplished, managed, consolidated, and compensated, as illustrated in *Accidental Empires* (Cringley, 1992). Since then, the work world has changed dramatically. Transportation and satellite transmissions reduced location importance. The world labor force offers abundant cheap labor at the expense of job security, permanent workers, and step-ladder career paths. In the past, traditional workplaces filled very narrow job descriptions with stable skill requirements; thus, students leaving high school had ample entry-points. Beginning and low-skilled workers were welcomed and treated as robots in the assembly line. Work, designed for rote learners performing a few routine operations, didn't require many thinking, team work, or "soft" skills. With little interest in what noncollege-bound students knew or thought, most employers prized a worker's ability to conform, tolerate repetition, and respond to command-and-control hierarchical supervision. North America dominated the world economy, and its competitive advantages created jobs for relatively low-skilled, middle-wage workers who saw little value in postsecondary education. Through seniority, collective bargaining, and continuous economic growth, workers could obtain above-average wages in the traditional triangle-shaped workplace (Feller, 1995).

In the 1990s, the prohibitive cost of management's many layers and the computer's ability to disseminate information in real time shattered assumptions about traditional jobs, workplaces, school-to-work, and career transitions (Feller, 1996a; Feller & Splete, 1996; Feller & Walz, 1996). The new workplace rewards different skills, seeks broader responsibilities from more flexible workers, and employs far fewer supervisors. Supervisors coach an expanded number of broadly skilled workers seeking to be core workers. Rewarded more by adding value to a company's core mission than by degrees and titles, workers seek core competencies through self-directed learning, risking failure and seeking opportunities within new projects. The new workplace has fewer primary, entry-level, livable-wage jobs for students lacking basic skills. As a result, STC must promote ways to support all students as they prepare for, enter, and learn within the emerging workplace.

Leaders who champion STC's purpose, potential, and probability of success must be fully aware of education's responsibility to prepare students for the changing workplace. Parents, taxpayers, and STC advocates alike must hold schools accountable for making sure that all students acquire and demonstrate these needed basic skills.

Delivering No Less Than Basic Skills for All

Believing in the possibility of having a successful career is a "profound motivator for young people to work harder, achieve more, and modify their behavior to accommodate workplace expectations" (Packer & Pines, 1996, p. 262). However, workplace success is predicated on acquiring strong basic skills. As Payzant argues, communities are beginning to "recognize that all students must leave high school today with the knowledge and ability to apply what was once required of only the select few who continued their formal education in colleges and universities" (in Murname & Levy, 1996, p. vii). Murname and Levy (1996) argue that, for high school graduates who possess the new basic skills, college will not be a prerequisite for earning a middle-class income. If true, then what basic skills do students need to learn, since primary labor market employers have little demand for present high school graduates?

Murname and Levy describe what they call the New Basic Skills as those needed by all students to earn middle-class incomes, regardless of post-high school plans, namely,

• the "hard" skills: basic mathematics, problem-solving and reading abilities at levels much higher than many high school graduates now attain;

• the "soft" skills: the ability to work in groups and to make effective oral- and written-presentation skills many schools do not teach; and

• the ability to use personal computers to carry out simple tasks like word processing. (p. 9)

As high-wage employers search for new workers with these new basic skills, they bypass current high school graduates they deem lacking such skills. As a result, they hire persons with some college for jobs formerly held by high school graduates. Yet, if all students left high school with these new basic skills, and their diplomas verified these competencies, the demand for a four-year college degree as an entry-level credential would decrease. In this regard, STC's leadership must provide incentives that motivate students to master and teachers to focus on these new basic skills, and promote such performance measures as portfolios and demonstrations, and such self-report ability tools as the *Ability Explorer* (Harrington & Harrington, 1996).

Recognizing STC in Action

Earlier, the authors defined STC as a systems-building effort and a stimulus to reform how all youth prepare for careers. They argued that STC is a learning strategy that can motivate all students to achieve more. As does any stimulus with such all-encompassing abstract goals, STC must encompass enough to affect all students and not become a targeted program for "those" students. It must be concrete enough to face evaluation, simple enough for lay persons to understand, and popular enough to be taken seriously. As a result, STC from a national level must provide a vision while leaving implementation to local leadership. For educators, parents, and students to challenge school cultures, functions, policies, and incentives, successful leadership must necessarily identify exemplary efforts that create demand for STC's elements.

Murname and Levy (1996), drawing from best practices in schools and the private sector, identified five principles to elicit improved performances from teachers, students, and parents. Incorporating their insights into STC may change the culture of schools. (Murname and Levy's words (p. 77) are in quotation marks, followed by my remarks.)

1. "Ensure that all front line workers (teachers, parents and students) understand the problem." While skill requirements for livable-wage jobs have increased exponentially, schools have failed to keep up with the changes. Only when teachers, parents, and students identify this as a problem can they act upon it.

2. "Design jobs so that all front line workers have both incentives and opportunities to contribute to solutions." Most students see little connection between what they learn in school and their future career development; thus, they

have little reason to display focused efforts. Teachers have little contact with the evolving workplace and find few opportunities or rewards for learning how basic skills apply. Without insights from the workplace, most inputs to curriculum come from university admission requirements and commercial textbook companies. With career choice seen as a hard-to-measure event rather than a process, no accountability or incentive exists to help students demonstrate career-development and transition competencies (NOICC, 1989).

3. "Provide all front line workers with the training needed to pursue solutions effectively." Educators have little opportunity to see how workplaces use the new basic skills. They receive little or no school-transition data from employers or postsecondary institutions. As a result, professional development has little relationship to STC goals. Time committed to integrating curricula, designing alternative assessments and team-counseling efforts, developing partnerships and articulation agreements, and connecting to local labor-market information and work-based learning sites could pay great rewards. Developing meaningful roles for parents within STC can pay strong dividends to academic achievement (Bempechat, 1990; Epstein, 1987; and USDE, 1994).

4. "Measure progress on a regular basis." Many of the new basic skills required in the workplace go unmeasured. Such alternative assessment methods as portfolios can change the way teachers teach and cause college admissions offices to expend greater effort to obtain morereliable data on student performance.

5. "Persevere and learn from mistakes: there are no magic bullets." Most critics think there is one right and painless way to improve student performance. Reforms often promote simple, short-term solutions rather than comprehensive, continuous improvement across the entire system. Challenging belief systems, structures, and policies that fail to acknowledge individual differences takes time, resources, and political courage.

Provocative research in cognitive science, effective school practices, educational technologies, alternative delivery systems, accelerated learning, alternative assessment, and observations about the changing structure of careers get to classroom teachers and counselors much too slowly or in ways hard to implement. With frustration and mistrust common in many school cultures, comprehensive community efforts and continuous improvement across entire systems offer the only ways to gain support for confronting the status quo.

Career-Development Perspective Demands No Allegiance

Challenging a school's ability to prepare agile students for global and dynamic careers and responsible citizenship is unpopular, yet imperative. Primary labor-market jobs increasingly go to the most competent workers at world wages. Globalization makes it possible to use human and material resources from anywhere. Companies can produce, market, and sell items from virtual offices.

These companies tie compensation to how well one can solve problems, define new opportunities, embrace technology, motivate people, accept learning as part of work, and commit to lifelong career development (Feller & Splete, 1996). This requires new and flexible attitudes for those seeking livable wages or economic self-sufficiency. Yesterday's high-school-only graduates continue to lose earning power in jobs and total income over a lifetime (Phillips, 1996).

Career development takes an interdisciplinary perspective toward how people learn, transition, work, and find satisfying life roles; thus, it should theoretically hold no allegiance to school departments, programs, or courses. Egalitarians most often challenge programs or policies that marginalize students or reify the status quo or class stratification. Those best served resist changing policies or structures that sort educational winners from losers. Fortunately, quality career-development systems offer inclusive perspectives that help students better their sense of goals and help them think systematically about their interests and efforts related to educational and occupational options.

CAN STC SURVIVE? CAREER DEVELOPMENT ORCHESTRATES HOPE

Career-development activities that promote expanded learning options for all are advocated when strong leaders embrace STC. Accelerated career exploration motivates students to expend efforts in self-directed learning and placement. In global workplaces and communities seeking a high quality of life, learning time has become the variable, and learning has become the constant. Agile, accountable, and self-directed learners able to demonstrate the new basic skills are at a premium as workers and citizens. Schools where all students express hope about their future commonly expect school- and work-based learning and connecting activities.

Can STC overcome the critical issues and problems of building systems and reforming how all students prepare for careers? The verdict is still out but a growing consensus grows about the need to create agile students able to learn, work, and act responsibly. Clearly, as Grubb (1996, p. xviii) says in *Working in the Middle: Strengthening Education and Training for the Mid-Skilled Labor Force*, "While occupational preparation is important, I would never want to be interpreted as saying it is all important."

Today's increasingly bifurcated incomes, economically and technologically segregated groups of haves and have nots, remind us that democracy cannot embrace work, learning, and economic efficiency at the expense of preparing politically active, morally developed citizens. In most cases, only those able to apply expanded basic skills can critically assess their addiction to money, consumption, and job identity at the expense of finding balance, community, and fulfillment (Feller, 1996b).

With this perspective, lessons learned from earlier innovations, data-driven reform efforts, and rigorous, relevant professional development tied to comprehensive system change, STC will survive as a continuous-improvement effort. Can STC counter the present backlash and Cuban's seven phases of reform? Hopefully, leadership will emerge and Murname and Levy's five principles will motivate communities to challenge the status quo. STC leaders understand that students need to achieve more to be personally productive, active participants in democracy, culturally enriched and prepared for a smaller world with more frequent career changes.

STC advocates with a career-development orientation must provoke communities to demand instructional and policy changes that best serve *all* students. Such a perspective has led the authors to develop five litmus tests to measure a community's commitment to STC:

1. STC will succeed to the degree it can show any critic that it can tailor education to each student.

2. STC will succeed to the degree it can show students that what they learn in school will add value to (offer them greater control over) their future.

3. STC will succeed to the degree it can give teachers leverage to motivate students to display more focused efforts to improve their basic skills acquisitions and demonstrations.

4. STC will succeed to the degree it can demonstrate that each program, classroom, and course provided meets the standards for each educator's and schoolboard member's child.

5. STC will succeed to the degree that businesses will facilitate integrity and worth in each work-based learning experience it provides to the community's students.

These five tests, should communities use them, subject everything to negotiation.

Communities that expand quality learning options for *all* will drive these high expectations, not any federal program or short-term solution. Only then will youth receive educational experiences preparing them for lifetime learning rather than acquire knowledge through time-based classes within initial schooling. STC efforts demonstrate that communities can provide more learning options (American Youth Policy Forum—Jobs for the

Future, 1995; Pauly, Kopp, & Haimson, 1994; Rogers et al., 1995) to improve academic skills and prepare students for college (Bailey & Merritt, 1996). A community's quality of life and standard of living and STC's survival depend on reducing the number of students who choose *not* to learn.

STC must demand sustaining strategies that change the daily experiences of students and teachers into communities and workplaces as contexts for learning. While greatly affected by the economy, education cannot account for the economy. And yet, as schools teach so more students can learn more, STC will increase the probability that future workers will design and manipulate technology to produce world-class products and services in a global economy. As it does so, STC will become the systems-building effort many hope for.

References

American Youth Policy Forum—Jobs for the Future. (1995). *Promising practices: A study of ten school-to-work career programs. Congressional briefing overview*. Boston: Jobs for the Future.

Bailey, T., & Merritt, D. (1996). *School-to-work for the college bound*. New York: Institute on Education and the Economy.

Bempechat, J. (1990). *The role of parent involvement in children's academic achievement: A review of the literature*. New York: Institute for Urban and Minority Education, Columbia University. (ERIC Document Reproduction Service No. ED 322 285)

Brint, S., & Karabel, J. (1989). *The diverted dream: Community colleges and the promise of educational opportunity in America, 1900-1985*. New York: Oxford University Press.

Clark, B.R. (1960). *The open door college: A case study*. New York: McGraw-Hill.

Clark, B.R. (1980). The cooling out function revisited. *New Directions for Community Colleges, 8*. San Francisco: Jossey-Bass.

Cringley, R. (1992). *Accidental empires*. Reading, MA: Addison Wesley.

Cuban, L. (1993). *How teachers taught: Constancy and change in American classrooms* (2nd ed.). New York: Teachers College Press.

Davies, T.G., & Dickmann, E.M. (in press). Can we hear them? Do we listen? Student voices in the transfer process. *Community College Journal of Research and Practice*. Washington, DC.

Dougherty, K.J. (1994). *The contradictory college: The conflicting origins, impacts, and futures of the community college*. Albany: State University of New York Press.

Education and work. (December, 1996). *Career Opportunity News, 14*(3), 16.

Epstein, J.L. (1987). Parent involvement: What research says to administrators. *Education and Urban Society, 19*(2), 119-136.

Feller, R. (1995). Action planning for personal competitiveness in the "broken workplace." *Journal of Employment Counseling, 32*, 154-163.

Feller, R. (1996a). The future of work. *Vocational Education Journal, 71*(4), 24-27.

Feller, R. (1996b). Redefining "career" in the work revolution. In R. Feller & G. Walz (Eds.), *Career transitions in turbulent times: Exploring work, learning and careers*. Greensboro, NC: ERIC/CASS and NCDA.

Feller, R., & Splete, H. (1996). Career transitions to adulthood. In J. Rotter & W. Bailey (Eds.), *Transitions: Education and employment* (pp. 151-176). Dubugue, IA: Kendall/ Hunt.

Feller, R., & Walz, G. (1996). *Career transitions in turbulent times: Exploring work, learning and careers*. Greensboro, NC: ERIC/CASS and NCDA.

Gardner, H. (1985). *Frames of mind: The theory of multiple intelligence*. New York: Basic Books

Gray, K., & Herr, E. (1995). *Other ways to win: Creating alternatives for high school graduates*. Thousand Oaks, CA: Corwin Press.

Grubb, N. (1996). *Working in the middle: Strengthening education and training for the mid-skilled labor force*. San Francisco, CA: Jossey-Bass.

Harrington, T., & Harrington, J. (1996). *Ability explorer*. Chicago. IL: Riverside Publishing.

Heebner, A. (1996). *The impact of career magnet high schools: Experimental and qualitative evidence*. Berkeley, CA: NCRVE.

Higginbottom, G., & Romano, R. M. (Eds.). (1995). Curriculum Models for General Education, '92. San Francisco: Jossey-Bass.

Hoye, J.D. (Speaker). (1996). *Going to scale with school-to-work* (Cassette Recording No P 802). Portland, OR: NW Regional Educational Laboratory.

Murname, R., & Levy, F. (1996). *Teaching the new basic skills: Principles for educating children to thrive in a changing economy*. New York, NY: Free Press.

National Occupational Information Coordinating Committee. (1989). *National Career Development Guidelines*. Portland, OR: Northwest Regional Education Laboratory.

Packard, A., & Pines, M. (1996). *School-to-work*. Princeton, NJ: Eye on Education.

Parnell, D. (1985). *The neglected majority*. Washington, DC: Community College Press

Parnell, D. (1995). *Why do I have to learn this?* Waco, TX: Center for Occupational Research and Development.

Pauly, E., Kopp, H., & Haimson, J. (1994). *Homegrown lessons: Innovative programs linking work and high school*. New York: Manpower Demonstration Research Corporation. (ERIC Documentation Reproduction service No. Ed 369 939)

Phillips, M. (1996, December 23). Inequity may grow for lifetime earnings. *The Wall Street Journal*, 1.

Pincus, F.L. (1980). The false promises of community colleges: Class conflict and vocational education. *Harvard Educational Review, 50*(3), 332-361.

Resnick, L. (1986). Constructing knowledge in school. In L.S. Liben & D. H. Feldman (Eds.), *Development and learning: Conflict or congruence* (pp. 19-50). Hillsdale, NJ: Erlbaum.

Rogers, A., et al. (1995). *Learning from experience: A cross-case comparison of school-to-work transition reform initiatives*. Washington, DC: Academy for Educational Development.

School-to-Work Opportunities Act. (1994). U.S. Public Law 103-239. 103d Congress, May 4, 1994.

Smart managing: Best practices and ideas. (January 13,1997). *Fortune*.

Stern. D. (1992). *School-to-work programs and services in secondary schools and two-year public postsecondary institutions*. Paper prepared for the National Assessment of Vocational Education. Berkeley: University of California at Berkeley, School of Education.

Sternberg, R. (1988). *The triarchic mind: A new theory of human intelligence*. New York, NY: Viking.

Thurow, L. (1992). *Head to head: The coming economic battle among Japan, Europe, and America*. New York: William Morrow.

The twenty-sixth annual Gallup poll. (September, 1994). *Phi Delta Kappan, 76*(1),41-56.

The twenty-eighth annual Gallup poll. (September, 1996). *Phi Delta Kappan, 78*(1), 41-59.

U.S. Department of Education. (1994). *Strong families, strong schools: Building community partnerships in learning*. Washington, DC: Author.

U.S. Department of Education. (1995). *Condition of Education 1995*. Washington, DC: Author.

UW system explores use of competency-based admission (CBA). (Autumn, 1996). *Wisconsin Careers, 3*.

Zwerling, L.S. (1976). *Second best: The crisis of the community college*. New York: McGraw-Hill.

***Rich Feller** is a professor of counseling and career development at Colorado State University. He is a former school, admissions, and vocational school counselor and co-author of* Career Transitions in Turbulent Times, Exploring Work, Learning and Careers, *and* The CDM Career Video: Tour of Your Tomorrow, *used in over 3,000 schools. Dr. Feller speaks nationally about school-to-work and the changing workplace. At Colorado State University he directs the Career Development Institute, which places counselors in the workplace to shadow workers. He has served on the boards of the National Career Development Association, the Council on Accreditation of Counseling and Related Programs, and the American Vocational Association Guidance Division. **Timothy Gray Davies** is an associate professor at Colorado State University. Program chair of the Ph.D. program in Community College Leadership and a former community college president, Dr. Davies has served seven community colleges in five states over the past 32 years. Beginning his community college career as faculty member in English, he also served nine years as Dean of Faculty and nine years as president of two community colleges. In addition to developing the new Ph.D. program, he serves as a site evaluator for School-to-Career Partnerships in Colorado.*

PART III: PROGRAM AREAS

Labor disgraces no man, but occasionally men disgrace labor.
—Ulysses S. Grant

THE TECH PREP ASSOCIATE DEGREE PROGRAM

By John D. Craig

INTRODUCTION

The Neglected Majority (1985), by Dale Parnell, details the national issues and problems associated with high school completion rates, college degree attainment, employability trends, and the need for better secondary and postsecondary links, especially between high schools and community colleges. In his book, Parnell expresses the need for career education programs to better serve the two middle quartiles of high school students in completing an associate's degree. He argues that these students, to whom he attaches the phrase *neglected majority*, require more exposure to applying knowledge by doing, as opposed to knowing for knowledge's sake. Parnell stresses that the absence of a sound foundation in math, science, technology, and communication limits high school graduates' ability to succeed beyond secondary school. As a result, student success, in completing a college degree or in immediate employability after school, becomes increasingly difficult. Thus, the concept known today as the Tech Prep Associate Degree (TPAD) program was established.

Dr. Parnell, who in the 1980s served as president of the American Association of Junior and Community Colleges (AACJC), urged the government to allocate federal grants to enhance technical education programs and emphasize basic literacy, math competencies, critical thinking, and responsibility skills. The AACJC, through Parnell and federal legislators, lobbied for financial support of 2 + 2 programs for technical education and the completion of an associate's degree through the tech-prep model.

In 1990, Congress amended the Carl D. Perkins Vocational Education Act of 1984 to become the Perkins Vocational and Applied Technology Education Act to allocate funding for tech-prep program development (U.S. Congress, 1990, pp. 52-53). As a result of that legislative change, the federal government provided \$63.4 million for fiscal year (FY) '91, \$90 million for FY '92, and \$104.1 million for both FY '93 and FY '94 to states to plan and implement tech-prep programs through state education departments or designated agencies. Legislation requires that funded programs include the following seven elements: (1) articulation agreements—the effective link between secondary schools and community colleges; (2) a 2 + 2 design—with a common core of math, science, communication, and technology over a four-year program sequence; (3) a tech-prep curriculum—enriched applied instruction; (4) joint staff development for secondary and postsecondary faculty; (5) training to promote effective student recruiting, retention, and post-program placement; (6) measures to ensure access for special populations; and (7) preparatory services—to include counseling and assessment (U.S. Congress, 1990).

This chapter will explore the major themes surrounding the TPAD program, including program concepts and definitions, organizational and governance structures, contextual/applied learning, articulation and transfer, school-to-work, recent evaluation reports, future directions, and program recommendations. This chapter will focus on the major movements that founded the program and provide insight on future implications for the national tech-prep movement. I believe that tech-prep has helped local communities improve education through regional systems planning, reform, and articulation that provides seamless career-related success, but more work needs to be done to recognize and account for students' successful transition through the programs.

CONCEPTS AND DEFINITIONS OF TPAD

The idea for articulated programs of study in postsecondary institutions evolved during the latter half of this century (Knoell, 1990). Therefore, the founding of articulated programs in community and technical colleges has had a short history in terms of the national two-year college movement. While state and local consortia interpret many components of the federal legislation attached to the concept of TPAD programs, the following six core variables serve as overarching principles (Bragg, Kirby, Puckett, Trinkle, & Watkins, 1994): (1) program articulation, (2) curriculum integration, (3) school-to-work transition, (4) outcomes, (5) organizational and individual collaboration, and (6) accessibility for all students. These core components, when successfully planned, organized, and implemented, make up the essential ingredients of TPAD program development.

According to Bragg (1996), Silverberg (1996), and the U.S. Department of Education (1995), much of the confusion surrounding the national concept in developing and evaluating TPAD programs concerns definitions. Who and what constitutes tech-prep students and programs? The obscurity of tech-prep's conceptual foundation exacerbates its lack of consistent definition, apart from its parent legislation. Practitioners need such a foundation as they design strategies, connect tech prep to other education reform efforts, and evaluate its effectiveness in improving instruction for their students (Law, 1994). The task of defining tech-prep has been left up to local decision makers and consortia advisory boards.

In contrast, Mathematica Policy Research (MPR), an independent contractor hired to nationally evaluate TPAD, states the that following five core features describe the essence of TPAD students, who must take one or more of the following actions: (1) develop a plan of study; (2) choose a broad career cluster; (3) take or complete one or more applied academic courses; (4) take required or career-education courses related to a career cluster, or a minimum of elective courses related to a cluster; (5) participate in career awareness and development activities (Silverberg, 1996). This widely varying view—the result of a federal study of nation-wide consortia reporting—has led to both state and local interpretations and discussions of what a TPAD program should consist of.

Daniel Hull (1993) and the National Tech Prep Network believe that a TPAD program includes a sequence of study beginning in high school and continuing through at least two years of postsecondary occupational or technical education. The program parallels the college-prep course of study and presents an alternative to the minimum-requirement diploma. It prepares students for high-skill technical occupations and allows either direct entry into the workplace after high school graduation or continuation of study leading to an associate's degree in a two-year college.

These various interpretations infer a number of things: (1) that tech-prep students have taken one or more career-related courses of study; (2) they may have taken a sequence of core articulated subjects in math, science, and communication, and completed a technical career-related course component while in high school; (3) their district or consortium may have to identify them so that they may transfer to the local two-year college to complete an associate's degree in an articulated career field of interest. These differing interpretations of what constitutes a tech-prep student have blocked state-wide and national TPAD program development. The national view, from evaluations made by MPR, goes against the basic principles under which Parnell and Hull originally intended the TPAD program to operate. But MPR directly evaluated the TPAD coordinators to develop an idea of what each consortium considered to be key defining variables in their projects.

Nationally, tech-prep programs extend between secondary and postsecondary institutions and follow a variety of articulated program pathways, such as a 2 + 2 (grades 11-14), 4 + 2 (grades 9-14), or 2 + 2 + 2 (grades 11-16) framework (see Table 10.1).

This development, while flexible, has limited identifying, at state and national levels, tech-prep participants and completers, overall, as well as program concepts. As with the student identification issue, the nature of program development has experienced the same qualifying distinction. Is tech prep a 2 + 2, a 4 + 2, or a 2 + 2 + 2 program model? According to Silverberg (1996), consortia take one of two approaches to defining participation. Some argue that a TPAD program should not be labeled as distinct because it becomes identified as a program that tracks students in vocational coursework. While students may take a course or two relating to a particular career major or cluster, they may not know of their involvement in tech prep. On the other hand, identifying tech prep as a legitimate program in which students enroll, participate in activities, and complete sequences of related courses,

10.1—The Tech Prep Associate Degree Program Models Table

Grade 11-14 (2+2)	Grade 9-14 (4+2)	Grade 11-16 (2+2+2)	Grade 11-14 (2+2) Apprecticeship
Junior Year - Grade 11 - Tech Prep Course (s)	Freshman Year Grade 9 - math & science	Junior Year - Grade 11 - Tech Prep Course (s)	Junior Year - Grade 11 - Tech Prep Course (s)
Senior Year - Grade 12 - Articulated Course(s)	Sophomore Year Grade 10 - math & science	Senior Year - Grade 12 - Articulated Course(s)	Senior Year - Work-based experience & Work-based con't
College Year 1 Career Major courses (s)	Junior Year Tech Prep focus	College Year 1 Career Major courses (s)	Technical College Year 1 Work-based con't
College Year 2 Assoc. Degree	Senior Year Grade 12 Articulated courses (s)	College Year 2 Assoc. Degree	Technical College Year 2 Assoc. Degree Work-based
Employment	College Year 1	College Year 3	Employment
Options for BS/BA Degree	College Year 2 Assoc. Degree	College Year 4 BS/BA Degree	Options for BS/BA Degree
Advancement	Employment	Employment	Advancement

creates programs apart from other school programs. This trade-off of program definition and purpose results in programs labeled as either another "vo-tech repackaging scheme" or as a new way to look at career options for students. Any way one might look at it, a failure to make a common and distinct definition of TPAD programs in a consortium, state, or nationwide has weakened the overall image of TPAD.

From another viewpoint, one could argue that flexibility in tech-prep program development makes it adaptable to the local needs of each consortium. Regarding the local perspective, Law (1994) believes that the TPAD program forms a more effective systemic education movement when built on these six foundational components: (1) demographic changes, (2) changes in the workplace, (3) corporate and political pressures, (4) research findings about effective learning, (5) student experience in vocational education, and (6) pedagogy and educational philosophy inference. When taking this view, practitioners must come to terms with where their TPAD program fits into the needs of their consortium. They must question and research which program elements need to change for the process to fit into other education initiatives and have their local consortium schools and agencies value them. While states and communities change their policies and educational goals, whether on issues of raising academic standards or employability, TPAD coordinators must mind how their program fit into the overall picture of improving local education.

In many consortia, the definitions of or processes for identifying students have also formed weak links. According to the U.S. Department of Education's (1995) executive summary on tech prep, only one third of the states have adopted formal definitions for tech-prep programs and students, while another 27 states were still settling on a common meaning. Bragg (1997) states that only Delaware, Illinois, Rhode Island, and Ohio have attempted to flag TPAD student outcomes using evaluation designs of a longitudinal nature or that involve comparison groups. To identify programs as a success, TPAD coordinators must develop sustainable courses and program links between institutions. They must also account for student enrollment and completion results in a variety of ways. For evaluation purposes, coordinators must rely on participating school districts and colleges to report student course enrollment data and help define levels of year-to-year programming. Without formal reporting mechanisms in place, consortia may only speculate on how many students participate in their program. To date, this issue obstructs the effectiveness of programs in measuring outcomes on state and national platforms.

Most state agencies must report program delivery figures to the federal government in a variety of ways to justify their expenditures of grant resources. This potentially extensive data reporting and documentation includes, but is not limited to, the following areas: (1) number of students participating, by grade level (male/female); (2) number completing a high school diploma; (3) number entering two- and four-year colleges; (4) number entering the military; (5) number entering the workforce, in both career-related studies and unrelated studies; and (6) number of economically disadvantaged, educationally disadvantaged, and handicapped students. This type of information gathering requires extensive and accurate reporting and a consortium database, which may present difficulty in maintaining, in terms of reaching the required audience with any level of consistency from year to year.

However, many secondary and postsecondary institutions do not keep records of student transition beyond graduation because they do not have to do so, or they cannot justify spending time and resources on keeping such records. Tracking or flagging student success after graduation would help institutions better decide about program revision, student success, and employability (Pautler, 1994). Longitudinal studies would enable communities to make school districts and colleges more accountable for student success and would identify some possible reasons for failure. Do we, as educators, pass along students to college or work with no real insight of their personal and professional growth? Does education, as a body of institutions, have a responsibility to police itself to recognize both successes and failures to the public that supports it?

Cohen and Brawer (1996) state that community colleges, in the next century, must sort, test, guide, and matriculate students into programs having measurable entry and exit criteria. If this holds true, students will have difficulty finding institutions anywhere that will simply let them walk through the curriculum without accounting for them in some way. TPAD programs can help identify entry and exit criteria but only with help in reporting from participating schools and community agencies. It appears that, while state and local consortia try to define variables for programs, measuring program outcomes and progress could become problematic. While many high schools and colleges maintain that their graduates either go to college or work in a related field of study, where their graduates actually end up may surprise them. Do secondary and postsecondary institutional missions and goals value employability statistics and placements? Having to account for long- and short-term academic and career program effectiveness would enable institutions to make timely adjustments in programs to serve local business and industry employment needs. Realistically, education and institutional training always lag behind employability trends.

In many cases, the Family Privacy Act protects information about students under 18, and school districts and agencies may not disclose certain personal information about students. Although TPAD coordinators have been asked to maintain student data beyond high school and the associate degree level to determine overall program effectiveness, some high schools will not provide—or simply have no way to acquire—that data, so identifying student involvement remains sketchy.

Some states that do not develop a consistent tracking of tech-prep students find too much latitude in what it means to be a TPAD student, while others do not have a rationale to track. Other states have designated tech prep as an identifiable program because of group identification; it is easier to cluster students in groups and plan integrated curricular activities that set tech prep apart from other school programs. Some tech-prep models in the country do not necessarily extend between secondary and postsecondary institutions. These few examples raise the issue of a widely shared TPAD model, valued as either a program, process, or philosophy.

The willingness of consortia and partnerships to make decisions have determined the definitions and concepts of the TPAD program. Some states follow a strong 2 + 2 model, while others have developed a 4 + 2 framework to work under, which opens TPAD coursework to the general high school population in grades 9-10. More progressive models have expanded their programs to link the high school with a community/technical college as well as to a four-year college using a 2 + 2 + 2 format. Still others have developed comprehensive 2 + 2 apprenticeship models, such as Wisconsin's tech-prep programs. Loose interpretations have variously hurt and helped TPAD's success by letting interpretations evolve as local initiatives servicing local needs.

On national and state levels, TPAD programs' overall conceptual make-up is not of cloned partnerships with equal numbers of school districts and college partners, giving each consortium an individual identity. On the other hand, a defining framework may limit a consortium's flexibility when working in the environment, including the many different institutional philosophies organizing each consortium. Flexibility gives the TPAD program a "bend but don't break mentality"—one of the strongest components holding together the tech-prep philosophy. While consortia tailor their programs to fit local needs and workable processes, failure to define the nature of TPAD programs and their students limit national and state evaluation data and may limit the ability to determine the value of TPAD's effectiveness at many levels of accountability.

ORGANIZATIONAL STRUCTURE

One of the most interesting, yet challenging features of the TPAD program is the makeup of national, state, and local partnerships or consortia. Over 1,000 tech-prep consortia exist today and include over 50 percent of all U.S. school districts (5,700), representing 75 percent of all secondary students (Silverberg, 1996). These consortia establish themselves upon each state's vocational/occupational education system within their region.

According to the U.S. Department of Education (1995), states must designate a sole state agency to administer Perkins Act grants. Each consortium must have at least one postsecondary and secondary institution with which it can develop an articulated program. Thirty-three states designate their agency as the state education department (U.S. Deptartment of Education, 1995). Six states designate their agency as one responsible for postsecondary technical education or community college development. The remaining 13 states chose an individual agency, board, division, or commission to distribute the Perkins funds. Although individual agencies in each state took responsibility for the funding mechanism of TPAD programs through Perkins, the financial agent differed in each state. This situation arose because some states took advantage of a pre-existing structure that organized related programs, and some states' eligibility to receive Title IIIE funding depended on designating a new structure.

American federal education governance does not have a national ministry that oversees all aspects of education and policy-making. Although the U.S. Department of Education maintains a federal framework for delivering education, individual states decide most policies and practices. This feature of American education governance provides flexibility to states to regulate education policy to fit their own needs while limiting the federal government's role in dictating policy.

One of the most popular organizing bodies of the program is the National Tech Prep Network (NTPN), an association of TPAD supported under the guidance of the Center of Occupational Research and Development (CORD) in Waco, Texas. NTPN and CORD have helped develop and organize curricula, materials, and support media for consortia throughout the country. Many consider CORD president Daniel Hull one of the key leaders of the tech-prep movement along with Dale Parnell. CORD has developed a successful framework through which program coordinators may share information on best practices and new strategies. CORD also provides a variety of professional development training workshops in Texas and has established an extensive teleconference system that enables consortia to deliver technical support and staff development on site.

Federal funds allocated to each state agency have enabled each region to develop its own plan of program coordination. For example, in New York, 30 consortia, community/technical colleges fund 14 projects; vocational centers (Boards of Cooperative Education Services) fund another 14; and the State University of New York at Albany's Two-Year College Development Center and the City University of New York's Graduate School of Education each fund a campus technical assistance center. This network of consortia and technical assistance centers provides information on how services, programs, and partnerships function within the state. A number of school districts, along with a supporting community or technical college, comprise each consortium, at least in New York. Developing links with schools can take on an urban, suburban, and/or rural setting, and can establish a network of schools to initiate programming, forming the base of local consortium building.

School districts, of which over 700 individual schoolboard structures set policy, structure New York's K-12 education. Conversely, Florida structures its State Department of Education in K-12 around its 67 county districts. County boards organize school policies and procedures, as opposed to the New York's 700+ schoolboard structure. Organizationally, it would appear that working with 67 school districts as opposed to 700 would make setting state policy and adhering to it less problematic, arousing arguments of local versus state control over programming. If a school district has a strong preference for some, but not all, aspects of TPAD programs, are they considered members of the consortium and the local tech-prep model? How flexible should TPAD coordinators be when defining and setting local policy? What will the state policy-making body do or say in response to school-based management philosophies?

TPAD consortia take responsibility for organizing, developing, and maintaining school and college partnerships as well as establishing links to local business and community service agencies. Giving students and teachers an opportunity to develop with business and industry a seamless curriculum incorporating workplace readiness skills effectively links them to the community as part of a local workforce development system. Although the original legislation in 1991 did not mention developing business-education partnerships in tech-prep programs, new proposed guidelines and amendments in legislation for continued funding from the Senate Subcommittee on Vocational Education for TPAD and other programs do. The final consolidated package for continued support for TPAD programs could change dramatically from the guidelines used today. The Seattle, Washington, consortium developed a model of partnering with the Boeing Corporation to create a summer internship program that helps as many as 300 local high school juniors connect their high school tech-prep studies to the world of work (Gayton, 1994; Owens, 1994, 1995). As mentioned earlier, Parnell states that learning unconnected to work or career applications exemplifies one of the main problems in career education. Boeing's commitment to help its local schools also identifies future workers who possess the skills Boeing looks for. This connection, while a large-scale production in Seattle, shows how TPAD may help businesses locally develop future employees.

A major drawback is that most communities do not host corporations like Boeing that employ thousands of individuals. According to the U.S. Department of Labor (1991), small companies that employ fewer than 50 people comprise 80 percent of all American businesses. Developing local tech-prep programs that can cater to a variety of business needs is difficult. Career programs that address meeting the skills and abilities of the Secretary's Commission on Achieving Necessary Skills (SCANS) report of 1991 offer a starting point. The result of work done jointly by the Departments of Labor and Education, the SCANS report documents education's need to teach the essential skills required for employability. Each consortium has its own make-up of business and industry, into which TPAD programs need tailoring to fit. TPAD programs function under diverse organizational structures. Each state has its own delivery system to distribute and account for Perkins funds and its own school-district structure. Some states operate county-wide systems, while others use local district boards. These structures dictate the development, support, and deliverance of student programs and services. They also decide what their districts should deliver to the public while ensuring that the districts meet state policies and guidelines. Tech-prep coordinators must be sensitive to many issues in and around the region as well as the state-sponsoring agency for funding.

CONTEXTUAL AND APPLIED LEARNING

Applying knowledge through contextual or applied learning by developing articulated curricula forms one of the major building blocks of many TPAD programs. Parnell (1985) states that many secondary and postsecondary faculty do not understand the concept of contextual and applied learning. Knowledge for knowledge's sake accomplished through theory and lecture-based instruction serves as the platform for many teachers and educators, especially in the stand-alone sense of coursework.

Multidisciplinary teaching and applying

knowledge to skills and abilities shape the building blocks of TPAD program development (Parnell, 1985; Hull, 1993). Just knowing subject matter or content or relating the content to another principle(s) does not necessarily constitute the ability to apply that knowledge to accomplish a task or duty. TPAD applied academics weds vocational content to academic content by blending knowledge and application. Rosenstock (1991) argues that integrating academic content with vocational education requires that faculty adopt a different view. As using standardized tests to evaluate student success in applying knowledge becomes more difficult, working in a collaborative setting of secondary and postsecondary articulation, using the TPAD approach, best defines actual content and pedagogical processes (Pucel, 1994). In my opinion, two of the challenges in developing a seamless articulated tech-prep program include ensuring that participating school districts practice the agreed-upon curriculum in daily classroom sessions and that, to adequately articulate student success beyond high school, the districts meet the outcomes.

To ensure the currency of program content requires continual updates by committee in curriculum planning. Grant funding through TPAD increases the capacity of postsecondary and secondary faculty to work collaboratively in programs that have articulated programs. It also helps secondary faculty to regionally share program strategies and best practices in classroom planning. According to the New York state tech prep evaluation report (Brodsky, Newman, Arroyo, & Fabozzi, 1997), both secondary and postsecondary faculty agree that TPAD improves teaching relationships and provides opportunities to work with parents, community members, and business. Teachers agree that they become better educators and have more leeway to develop curriculum; they also have to keep more updated on teaching applications. TPAD allows educators to increase innovation and response in their classrooms and institutions.

The SCANS report provides the framework for developing a sound academic and career-related course of study for students to succeed and find work in the future America workplace. In many states throughout the country, the ability to meet the needs of the changing economy will increase a region's or state's productivity and global-market viability. The applied academics and higher standards that tech prep promote give students skills and abilities to affect our changing economy, although some argue that TPAD lowers academic standards by replacing vital academic content with work-based learning components.

Many TPAD programs establish applied academic courses with help from CORD. CORD focuses its efforts on creating supportive classroom materials in a variety of curricula in applied math, science, communication, and principles of technology—still the backbone of many programs. One danger in solely using CORD materials in classrooms as stand-alone curricula lies in the fact that their content may not meet examination requirements in states having multiple exit tests for graduation purposes. As a matter of practice, I believe that complying with local or state standards may require additional curricular content and activities. Walter and Turlington (1994) state that delivering appropriate TPAD materials and content requires additional staff development in cooperative and integrative learning.

Applied academics looks to blend the practical knowledge of vocational education with academic mindfulness. A rich applied-academics course helps students understand the nature of what they learn. In the majority of classrooms today, students frequently ask, "Will this be on the test?" Knolwedge unconnected to relevant applications is soon lost. Students and teachers need to make those connections in daily classroom experiences; without them students lose interest and value in their learning. John Dewey (1915), one of the first education pioneers to review academic and vocational integration, wanted a vocational education system that would first alter the existing industrial system and, ultimately, transform it. Initially, many in education and industry feared Dewey's comments, and separating vocational from academic education became a public issue. As a result of that fear, academic and vocational education separated, and public education developed a two-tier system. Not until the 1970s did the integration issue reemerge, reexamining the notion that the two practices reunite to institute educational change (Wirth, 1972).

Applied academics, or contextual learning, indeed shapes the essence of TPAD learning. TPAD funding and consortium building enable schools and colleges to jointly develop a seamless curriculum that ensures student success beyond high school. But TPAD needs continual support from business and industry to develop coursework relevant to the local marketplace. Effective TPAD programming continues to build on applied or contextual articulated curriculum development. Uniting partners who make coursework realistic and applicable to higher levels of learning makes TPAD possible. End users of the learning—students and employers—also need to verify applied academics. "What am I learning? Why am I learning it? How can it help me beyond the classroom?" Nothing is more tragic than failing to discover one's true business in life or finding that one has drifted or that circumstances have forced one into an uncongenial calling (Dewey, 1916).

ARTICULATION AND TRANSFER

Another major part of TPAD program development concerns the ability of consortia to articulate study sequences with a postsecondary institution. As mentioned earlier, Knoell (1990) states that the concept of community college articulation is a fairly recent trend, as early as the 1960s. Expanding a local college network—in essence, the community college—has provided many areas of the country with a postsecondary institution. According to Cohen and Brawer (1996), over 30 percent of all college students in the United States live near a community college system, a trend that will continue through 2005. Thus, articulated programs of study relating to a broad-based career major within TPAD consortia and a community or four-year college make sense. Alfred and Peterson (1990) argue that concentrating on transfer and articulated education will alter the community college's focus on maintaining community alliances and lessen its commitment to help the community it resides within. Well-thought-out and -supported tech-prep programs can increase student articulation and transfer.

Parnell designed TPAD mainly to ensure success beyond secondary school. Parnell (1985) reports that collaboration and program articulation pose difficulties: three of four community, technical, and junior college leaders perform little or no program articulation. He sights seven areas that restrict high schools and community colleges from working together: (1) turf, (2) state leadership, (3) resources, (4) scheduling, (5) community college image, (6) lack of communication, and (7) a focus on machinery rather than action. A well-supported tech-prep program produces well-thought-out, well-planned, and solid articulation agreements in a variety of student service areas.

For TPAD to maintain viable, functional programs that meet the needs of schools, communities, and business partners, they must maintain and ensure articulation and student services. This will happen only if all parties communicate—in a timely and accurate fashion—information about curricula, students, and employers to program coordinators and key personnel. From the practitioner's perspective, a supporting college can serve well-informed students only if its admissions counselor has information about program involvement and appropriate transcript information is notated and documented before students enroll in the articulated college program. Without proper sequences and information reporting by all consortium constituents, losing identified students will lead to a poor image of program servicing among students that the consortium serves, as well as its schools and community. Soon, college-level TPAD coordinators will have to maintain a reporting system that effectively measures articulated successes in their program. It would be even better if each state's TPAD programs could articulate so that students throughout each state could transfer outside of their servicing consortium and receive credit for participating in advanced placement or TPAD.

SCHOOL-TO-WORK AND TECH PREP: BUILDING UP OR TEARING DOWN?

In 1994, President Clinton signed into law the School-to-Work Opportunities Act (STWOA), which states that business, community agencies, and schools need partnerships to better prepare students for the changing nature of work and employability. The legislation provides a five-year cycle (1994-1999) of decreasing funds to help local communities connect school to work. State departments of education or related agencies receive the funds to begin community partnership-building.

School-to-work (STW) legislation builds on three foundations of development: (1) school-based activities (i.e., curriculum, programs, and services); (2) work-based activities (i.e., mentoring, shadowing, internships, co-ops, and apprenticeships); and (3) connecting activities (i.e., agency relationships, community organizations, business partnering, and links to parents, schools, and educators). These key components unite to develop a network of local partners who help students and communities build a competent, reliable workforce. One vital link to economic stability, especially in areas of the country that see high levels of underemployment, seeks to keep highly visible, trained workers local.

STW creates a rationale for systemic education reform, a philosophical way to deliver programs that help schools, businesses, and communities connect student learning to employment. Falcone and Mundhenk (1994) maintain that STWOA intends to strengthen TPAD and other initiatives that emphasize connecting school and careers. While many consider the relationship between STW and TPAD a natural fit to deliver career awareness to all students, the legislation does not require schools to align STW funds with already established TPAD projects that provide the same platform of services. This lack of vision and coordination in passing the STW legislation caused some initial confusion in local partnerships.

In some states and regional consortia across the country, support for TPAD and STW became an issue of turf (regarding funding for programs and services for school districts and colleges) and confused the business community (regarding support and delivery of student services in field trips, mentoring, internships, and curriculum revision activities). To many outside the education system (businesses, parents, and community agencies), the efforts of STW overlapped those of TPAD. How do STW and TPAD differ, if at all? Why do the same things and recruit the same services from the same schools, businesses, and community-based agencies? Does education know what it is doing here? In many instances, much of this confusion depended on the way each state organized its STW agency or advisory council or determined who received federal funding. Unfortunately, some states lost ground in developing a comprehensive STW system by separating the directors of tech prep and STW.

Both TPAD and STW initiatives vitally depend on business support. But the political climate and party agendas cause local community and collaboration problems for practitioners. TPAD is the Republicans' education reform platform, while STW is the Democrats' answer to better career education for all students. While people believe that government intervention in local affairs is daunting, the lack of a federal vision in establishing a sound policy for connecting TPAD and STW because of party politics brought failure for local collaboration and systemic change in secondary and postsecondary environments.

TPAD and STW must unite and share common strategies and goals on a regional level. Many communities host a variety of employment and training agencies, from private industry councils, to job training and partnership agencies, to county and city departments of labor. These groups jointly develop solid connections with employers and prospective employees through training or placement services. TPAD and STW coordinators must make inroads to help support these agencies through regional partnership building. Unfortunately without these connections, each consortium could find itself struggling to provide student services in work-based and connecting activities.

LEGISLATION AND FUNDING IMPLICATIONS

By eliminating funding, many initiatives, such as TPAD and STW, will fade, as did the career education movement in the 1970s. As of this writing, STW has just two more years of diminishing funding. Most STW projects in the 1998-1999 school year will receive at least 50 to 75 percent of their funding from the previous one, and the funds will be cut during the final year, 1999-2000. On the other hand, TPAD anticipates another VATEA cycle of funding to extend program development into 2003. Local consortia, provided that the mechanisms for funding consortia remain consistent with present policy, will undoubtedly welcome this support. For the last two years, 1995-96, continued funding to TPAD looked very bleak. Grassroots help from the National Tech Prep Network, CORD, the American Vocational Association, and local consortia partners, helped reinstate federal support for TPAD. This display of public support for the program reveals that TPAD was improving local education. Plain and simple, TPAD had gained support and people liked what it delivered.

One of the most interesting pieces of feedback received from the first Mathematica Policy study (Silverberg, 1996b) reveals that most consortia agree that without a local coordinator most programs would be lost or dropped within a year. Little national support exists for local consortia to continue without federal support. Today, many school districts and colleges feel a financial crunch, and any level of funding that supports local programming can keep links in tact. The author believes that if local two-year community/technical colleges realize an increase in full-time equivalents, based on local TPAD developments, they could establish hard money to continue support for TPAD in the absence of federal grants.

RESEARCH AND EVALUATION

Since 1991, TPAD programs have progressed, and many state and federal studies have been conducted. Mathematica Policy Research (MPR), which starting in 1993 reviewed questionnaires and conducted a formal accounting of TPAD national consortia, has begun the first in a series of national studies. From 1994-1996, MPR again reviewed coordinators, as more programs were established and expanded. Texas released a status report in 1996 that evaluated programs and baseline student data during their first four-and-one-half years of development through 1995. In a formal evaluation in 1996, New York outlined its progress from 1991-1996, including a pairs study with extensive student transcript information relating to certain program outcomes. Ohio is now conducting an extensive five-year review of its TPAD outcomes.

The MPR (1993) study reveals that TPAD nationally helped begin the discussion on articulated courses of study in math, science, communication, and technology. Silverberg (1996) states that, according to MPR findings, TPAD programs (1) may help facilitate career majors or cluster options for STW systems, (2) have helped introduce some forms of integrated curricula, (3) have strong articulation efforts with postsecondary institutions, (4) offer skills certificates rarely recognized by industry standards, (5) involve only small percentages of students in workplace activities, and (6) according to reporting consortia, received aligned STW funding 22 percent of the time. While some of this information is encouraging, note that many consortia were just beginning to develop programming and could establish only limited outcomes in such a short time. MPR, in 1998, planned to release a comprehensive five-year look at TPAD, but the results were not available in time to include in this publication.

In October 1997, the New York State Department of Education released a five-year evaluation of TPAD programs in its 30 consortia that outlined results in five areas of student performance (Brodsky, Newman, Arroyo, & Fabozzi, 1997): (1) The majority of participants (90 percent) believe that TPAD benefits students, faculty, and the community. (2) As the program raises standards, students who may have not normally considered college now do so. (3) Relationships between secondary and postsecondary institutions have improved. (4) Some consortia feared that certain state requirements would alter the progress of TPAD programs through changes in state graduation goals. (5) Loss of funding to support local efforts would eliminate any progress made to date. New York, as did many other states, phased in consortium expansion over three years, so developments and program perceptions varied.

New York's pairs study was designed to explore TPAD's contribution to student performance in high school and postsecondary institutions. The study reviewed 2,000 transcripts of TPAD and non-TPAD students for attendance, course selection, grade-point averages (GPAs), and college-level success. According to Brodsky (1997), in grades 11 and 12, TPAD students attained higher GPAs than their non-TPAD peers, missed less high school, and in their second year of postsecondary study achieved higher GPAs than non-TPAD students. Note, however, that few students in New York have completed a full sequence of TPAD coursework, and their exposure to high school classes may be limited to one to two years.

In April 1996, Texas released its state summary on TPAD and reported on (1) program development and implementation, (2) consortium organization and governance, and (3) federal funding (Brown, 1996). The study reveals that TPAD is employer-driven, universally available to students, and locally designed and implemented. Also, TPAD provides seamless, lifelong learning opportunities and measurable, accountable short- and long-term results. Texas has 24 regional consortia. Unlike in New York, community/technical colleges in Texas manage 84 percent of these consortia, and three different agency groupings manage the rest. Texas has developed a student identification code through its Education Agency, which also includes a transcript code and articulation catalog (Brown, 1996). These overarching coding systems should help with evaluation of student populations as the program expands and students progress through their course of study.

Ohio, in the third year of a five-year plan to evaluate the success of its tech-prep program, has hired MGT of America as an outside consultant to pull together information for the Ohio Board of Regents and the State Education Department. Ciesla (1997) reports the following findings regarding Ohio's progress: (1) High levels of support from stakeholders (educators, parents, students, business, and government agencies) are being recognized. (2) Tech-prep is looked upon as a process of positive educational change rather than as a program. (3) There are signs of immediate changes in both curricula and teaching methodologies in secondary and postsecondary institutions. (4) The state follows a strong 2 + 2 model and does not include grades 9 and 10 in its student numbers in terms of participation. Ohio, like many other states, is seeing just the tip of the iceberg in terms of tech-prep impact. In two years, at the completion of its five-year study, it may have interesting outcomes in meeting the goals of its tech-prep implementation plan.

National and state-wide evaluations of TPAD programs show promising results but have yet to show students becoming employed in high-skill, high-wage jobs. Spring 1998 marks the first placement, in many consortia, that most students who graduate from TPAD programs will be eligible for. To verify that TPAD works and is worthy of support necessitates tracking student success in and out of school, with or without federal and state support.

THE FUTURE OF THE TECH PREP ASSOCIATE DEGREE PROGRAM

The future of the TPAD program holds some

promise for and cautious assumptions about vocational education. As of this writing, it appears that the next cycle of Perkins VATEA funding will include TPAD programs to continue into the next century, although the House and Senate subcommittees on vocational education must agree on a final proposal for legislative action. Funding continues to drive local and state projects; without the support of federal funding, TPAD programs may slowly fade, leading a return to the general track of academic programs. When state and federal governments push for accountability in preparing all students, TPAD provides foundational networks to establish effective programs. Although the guidelines for future funding have yet to be established, they may alter how TPAD programs are implemented. Initially, tech prep was to be funded for five years, with local institutionalization strategies in place by 1996.

But with the funding issue somewhat secure, local practitioners critically need support for comprehensive student identification systems to evaluate information and articulate changes. Longitudinal data that support growth, placement, and employment success of TPAD students will ensure that the model for articulated systemic change produces a win-win process for education, business, and the community. But for the evaluation to proceed, schools and colleges must share information in reporting student transfers and graduates, as well as TPAD course listings in definable terms. Only then can long-range progress be measured and evaluated for the project's success.

TPAD's guidelines require each consortium to expand its services and include more schools districts and colleges. Based on my experience, tech-prep needs to establish quality, committed partnering. Adding institutions to a consortium is a delicate subject. Institutions should join a consortium only if the institutions will commit to established consortium policies and help create new ones. Institutions looking for services and funds to increase their involvement in community relations should note that doing so infringes on the ability of original consortium members to meet their goals. Many consortia must yet determine whether their system is delivering on its original intentions. Institutions also need commitments from their faculty (to develop applied curricula), administration, and policy board. Quality institution partnerships, with business and community support, can enhance TPAD's identity and help identify and correct its weaknesses.

TPAD programs must nationally deliver on their intended articulation agreements; in short, students must receive either advanced standing or credit, as outlined by the consortium. Processes for reporting student identification and course-outcome assessments need to reach a college's admissions department when students enroll. A formal state/TPAD master-articulation agreement catalog, as exists in Texas, would help to outline just what goes on inside state and local partnerships. Expanding articulation agreements to other two- and four-year colleges would also be a good strategy for state master plans over the next five years.

TPAD programs must continue to refine and qualify their programs and processes. State agencies and education departments must realize that successful change takes time and that most educational funding for programs is typically short-lived and does not deliver immediate results. TPAD's continued funding must show identifiable local and state-wide results. State agency guidelines for funding may change as the project moves forward. If they do, coordinators must ensure that their programs deliver to those ends and outcomes.

RECOMMENDATIONS

The Tech Prep Associate Degree program appears to progressively reach "the neglected majority" as well as increase student focus on career education. Establishing and building successful programs or philosophies takes commitment, money, and time, but, more important, it takes communication and articulation between education, business, and the community. The changing nature of organizations, public and private, increases the need for closer relationships. The notion of working in a vacuum, away from the daily fabric of society at any level, is gone or fading. TPAD has initiated conversation to articulate and collaborate for change and success for institutions and students.

TPAD has also initiated interesting communications between secondary and postsecondary programs, and it has established fine relationships with business and industry in flexible systems. Areas of the country that have linked TPAD programs into the supporting STW systems by using seamless processes will better handle local workforce development trends. Consortia with weak leadership and advisory boards and a fragmented school-to-work system may continue to create friction between local business needs and educational purposes.

The last two years of STW funding, 1998-2000, should establish long-term projections that regard local employment pictures and that include the local TPAD consortium to help build articulated courses of study that meet local needs, if the consortium does not already do so. Although no crystal ball can forecast future jobs, state departments of labor and county-based industrial development agencies offer good, timely business information. The real challenge lies in convincing parents, school districts, and children that high-paying jobs will require technical skills and broad-based knowledge with the ability to learn and adapt. Most growth in the American economy will occur in corporations of 60 or fewer employees, meaning that to contribute productively each person must know more than just one skill. TPAD programs that establish strong career majors may help local partnerships develop strong economic systems in their communities.

TPAD programs must also link with more four-year colleges and universities as well as graduate schools of education to help future teachers and administrators understand the natures of curriculum revision and applied and practical learning. Future teachers need better preparation to understand the nature of work and employability and how they affect teaching and student preparation. Program enhancements require ongoing developments in contextual learning in daily lessons and units. Students who continue to learn subject matter without understanding how to apply their learning in practical career-related ways will have great difficulty in the next century in terms of employability and future success.

TPAD is not another "vocational education repackaging scheme." TPAD does not dumb down the curriculum. TPAD raises educational standards for students through local educational and economic strategies for desperately needed change. With the variety of definitions and functions of TPAD programs nationwide, TPAD may be difficult to assess because of its local nature, philosophy, support, and development. People today sometimes quickly believe or disbelieve in something based on names, labels, and titles, but the education and employability of students—college-bound or not—continues. If consortia do not like the name *tech prep* because it conjures up notions of voc-ed, they should call it whatever they see fit; some may call it "education with excellence in mind." When we label things, we tend to organize them into boxes and store them in our memory, maybe never reexamining their worth for the overall good. TPAD tries to establish working relationships with secondary and postsecondary institutions, with local and regional planning strategies, to improve student choice. More quality work needs to be done nationally, statewide, and locally, well into the twenty-first century for the Tech Prep Associate Degree program to make its mark on America's plan for education excellence.

References

Alfred, R. L., & Peterson, R. O. (1990). Keeping transfer in perspective. *Community, Technical, and Junior College Journal, 60*(6), 27-30.

Bragg, D. (1996, December 6). *The status of tech prep in the United States*. Cincinnati, OH: American Vocational Association Convention.

Bragg, D. (1997). *Educator, student, and employer priorities for tech-prep student outcomes*. Berkeley: National Center for Research in Vocational

Education, University of California at Berkeley.

Bragg, D., Kirby, C., Puckett, P., Trinkle, K., & Watkins, L. (1994, October). *Building a preferred future for tech prep systems*. Berkeley: National Center for Research in Vocational Education, University of California at Berkeley.

Brodsky, S. M., Newman, D. L., Arroyo, C. G., & Fabozzi, J. M. (1997). *Evaluation of tech-prep in New York state: Final report*. Albany: New York State Department of Education.

Brown, C. H. (1996). *Tech prep in Texas: Status report state summary*. Beaumont, TX: Region V Education Service Center.

Ciesla, G. (1997). *Ohio tech-prep evaluation study*. Tallahassee, FL: MGT of America.

Cohen, A. M., & Brawer, F. B. (1996). *The American community college*. San Francisco, CA: Jossey-Bass.

Dewey, J. (1915, April 17). Spliting up the school system. *The New Republic, 2*, 10-25.

Dewey, J. (1916). *Democracy and education*. New York: MacMillian. p. 308.

Falcone, L., & Mundhenk, R.. (1994). *The tech prep associate's degree challenge*. Washington, DC: American Association of Community Colleges.

Hull, D. (1993). *Tech prep associate's degree: Every student wins!* Waco, TX: Center for Occupational Research and Development.

Knoell, D. (1990). *Transfer, articulation, and collaboration, twenty-five years later: The report of a research project funded by the Ford Foundation*. Washington, DC: American Association of Community and Junior Colleges.

Law, C. (1994). *Tech prep education: A total quality approach*. Lancaster, PA: Technomic Publishing.

Owens, T. R. (1994). *Seattle tech prep demonstration project—final evaluation report*. Portland, OR: Northwest Regional Educational Lab.

Owens, T. R. (1995). *The Boeing company's manufacturing technology student internship evaluation*. Portland, OR: Northwest Regional Educational Lab.

Parnell, D. (1985). *The neglected majority*. Washington, DC: Community College Press.

Pucel, D. J. (1994). Curriculum considerations to improve school-to-employment transitions. In *High School to Employment Transitions: Contemporary Issues*, Albert J. Pautler (Ed.). Ann Arbor, MI: Prakken Publishing.

Pautler, A. J. (1994). Improving the school-to-employment transition for the forgotten half. In *High school to employment transitions: Contemporary issues*, Albert J. Pautler (Ed.). Ann Arbor, MI: Prakken Publishing.

Rosenstock, L. (1991). The walls come down: The overdue reunification of vocational and academic education. *Phi Delta Kappan, 72*(6), 434-436.

Silverberg, M. K. (1996a). *Building school-to-work system on a tech-prep foundation*. Princeton, NJ: Mathematica Policy Research.

Silverberg, M. K. (1996b). *The continuing development of local tech-prep initiatives*. Princeton, NJ: Mathematica Policy Research & Washington, DC: U.S. Department of Education.

U.S. Congress. (1990). *Carl D. Perkins Vocational and Applied Technology Education Act Amendments of 1990*. Washington, DC: U.S. Government Printing Office.

U.S. Department of Education. (1995). *The emergence of tech-prep at the state and local levels—executive summary of findings*. Washington, DC: U.S. Government Printing Office.

U.S. Department of Labor. (1991). *Secretary's commission on achieving necessary skills: A SCANS report for America 2000*. Washington, DC: U.S. Government Printing Office.

Walter, D., & Turlington, A. (1994). Tech prep—A practitioner's perspective. In L. Falcone and R. Mundhenk (Eds.), *The tech prep associate's degree challenge*.Washington, DC: American Association of Community Colleges.

Wirth, A. G. (1972). *Education in the technological society*. Scranton, PA: International Textbook.

John D. Craig directs the Niagara County Tech Prep Consortium at Niagara County Community College in Sanborn, New York. A candidate for a Ph.D. in higher education administration from the State University of New York at Buffalo, Craig holds an M.S. in business education and a B.S. in commerce from Niagara University. He also received an A.A.S. from Niagara County Community College in business adminstration. He serves on the New York State Tech Prep Advisory and Strategic Planning Committees and has chaired their state conference for the past two years. Craig's dissertation focuses on the educational impact of tech-prep funding in New York, which Dale Parnell has supported. Craig has been a classroom teacher, counselor/advisor, and academic dean at a private business college, and he is a veteran of the U.S. Navy.

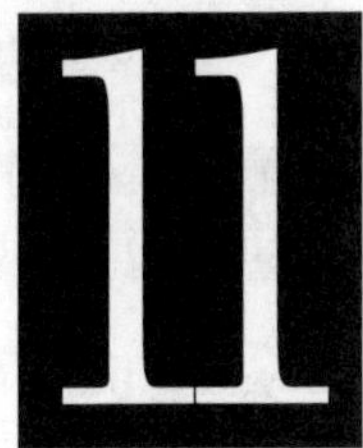

ISSUES IN TECHNOLOGY EDUCATION RELATED TO THE EVOLUTION OF THE FIELD

By Karen F. Zuga and Phillip L. Cardon

Over years of implementation in schools, technology education and vocational education have had a relationship that could be characterized as a continuum of beliefs and practices held by the practitioners of both fields. In this chapter, we will discuss the theory and historical growth of technology education as a form of general education. We will also consider the influence of vocational ideology and opportunity on the evolution of the technology education field.

By analyzing a variety of roles that technology education has played and continues to play in schools, we hope to address many of the historical and contemporary issues and problems that shaped the field's evolution from manual training to its present form of practice. We also hope to address the larger problem that arises from confusion about the field's role and purpose that exists both within the technology education community and in the broader education community and society.

While we will approach the discussion of technology education in a linear fashion, with a continuum running from general to vocational education purposes, our conceptualization of the schema takes the form of a Ven diagram (Figure 11.1), which has both distinct and overlapping circularly arranged roles and purposes. We will discuss several categories of education, including general, general-secondary, general elementary, vocational, vocational-secondary, and vocational-elementary, as they relate to the roles and purposes of technology education in schools.

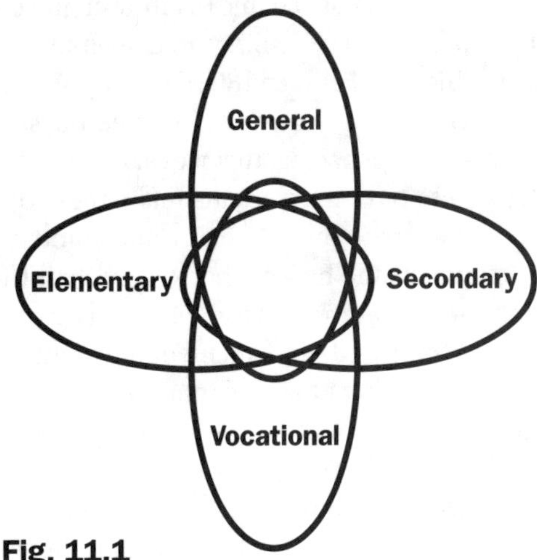

Fig. 11.1

TECHNOLOGY EDUCATION

For more than 100 years, a select group of educators has wanted to include all students in the study of technology. This has taken the form of manual training, industrial arts, and now technology education. In both secondary and elementary schools, these educators labored to create, nurture, and sustain what they considered a viable and necessary subject. Because they viewed technology education as a subject for all students, they considered it to be a general education subject rather than a vocational subject.

The roots of technology education began in two distinct environments: secondary and elementary schools. Its beginning and its evolution helped to shape the nature of the field today.

Secondary School Technology Education

The general education of all children has always been an important part of secondary schools. General education has an array of subjects, including technology education. A review of the evolution and history of the field should help readers understand how technology education fits into the pattern of general education in secondary schools.

Manual training. One of the earliest supporters of technology education as manual training was Calvin Milton Woodward, a professor in the O'Fallon Polytechnic Institute engineering department at Washington University, St. Louis, Missouri. Between 1868 and 1871, Woodward had difficulty teaching engineering students about abstract mathematical models. He decided to have his students make these objects in wood to further their understanding of geometry, and he was shocked by their inability to perform simple technical skills. Eventually, Woodward implemented a curriculum that included the most common and basic technical skills of the time—drafting, woodworking, and metalworking—to improve students' technical knowledge for general educational purposes. This model of teaching proved so successful that Woodward formed a manual training school in 1880 to prepare students for either college or technical careers. Essentially, Woodward viewed his new form of education as essential for all boys, regardless of their ultimate career goals (Woodward, 1887).

The method of teaching manual training followed in Woodward's manual training school may have come from Victor Della Vos's curriculum model (Bawden, 1950). Between 1868 and 1871, Woodward had engineering students construct models from wood. Having been to the Centennial Exhibition in 1876 (National Education Association, 1904) where the Imperial Technical School exhibition was prominently displayed (Post, 1976), Woodward, like many other technical educators of his day, was probably influenced by the use of a graded series of activities. This later became the primary method of manual training instruction.

In 1873, in an address given at Washington University, Woodward described manual training as "the best aid toward securing a wholesome intellectual culture, and . . . the only means for making that culture of practical use" (Woodward, 1887). It would appear from this quote and from much of his other writing that Woodward supported woodworking activities for boys primarily for general education purposes because it improved their education by combining theory and practice.

Industrial arts. After Woodward's time, there was a period when his version of manual training—influenced by the manual arts movement, the educational philosophy of the progressives, and manual arts practices in elementary schools—was renamed *industrial arts*. However, with this name change, little was done to alter what or who was taught in secondary schools, though significant recommendations for change were made regarding industrial arts teaching methods. These changes in method were heavily influenced by progressive education ideology and included Dewey's focus on the social purpose of technology and the study of industry as a societal institution (Dewey, 1916) and Kilpatrick's recommendation of the project as a method of instruction (Kilpatrick, Bagley, Bonser, Hosic, & Hatch, 1921). Warner continued to contribute to the subject's evolution by supporting efforts to select a common name (Warner, 1928); leading the political movement toward separating industrial arts from vocational education by creating organizations for the industrial arts community (Ray, 1979); favoring the "laboratory of industries" as a general laboratory over unit drafting, wood, and metal shops (Warner, 1931; Harrison, 1940); and promoting a view of technology as the content base for industrial arts (Warner, Gary, Gerbracht, Gilbert, Lisack, Klientjes, & Phillips, 1965)

Also during this time, industrial arts at the secondary level began to serve many societal needs, including that of keeping boys in school longer and giving them technical skills that could lead to employment when they left school (Van Duesen, 1940; Olson, 1974). During this time and throughout the middle of the twentieth century, the ideas on trade and job analysis of Allen, Selvidge, and Fryklund influenced vocational education. These ideas also eventually made their way into industrial arts practice (Lux, 1979; Zuga, 1991).

Due to the infusion of vocational education ideology and the role industrial arts instruction played in educating both school dropouts and those high school graduates who would not attend college, industrial arts seemed to lose its focus on general education. Often, industrial arts became indistinguishable from vocational education, with class period length considered the only important difference (Fryklund, 1956)!

From this confusion, a number of educators who were committed to industrial arts developed new secondary curriculum models. One resulted in the Industrial Arts Curriculum Project (IACP), completed at Ohio State University. This project focused on delineating a rationale and structure for the industrial arts secondary education curriculum (Towers, Lux, & Ray, 1966).

However, the IACP document follows a vocational education curriculum structure, focusing a comprehensive approach to organizing and teaching skills as processes (Ray, 1980). The similarities between the two curriculum designs of trade and job analysis and IACP's socioeconomic analysis (Ray, 1980) show vocational education's influence on industrial arts throughout the twentieth century. The IACP project had nationwide influence in middle- and secondary-level industrial arts courses throughout the country (LaPorte, 1980)

Two other influential curriculum projects were the Maryland Plan and the American Industries Project. The Maryland Plan was created by Maley (1972) at Maryland State University. Influenced by past progressive educators in industrial arts, Maley focused on developing students' abilities and self-perceptions. He stated that the industrial arts curriculum should not be defined by content areas but rather should emphasize (1) technology, its evolution, use, and significance; (2) industry, its organization, materials, occupations, processes, and products; and (3) problems for and benefits to society that result from technological and industrial activities. In the American Industries Project, Face and Flug (1965) discussed 13 industrial arts concepts: communication, transportation, finance, property, materials, processes, energy, research, procurement, relationships, marketing, management, and production. This project reflected the influence of the earlier curriculum work of Warner and others (1965) and Olson (1963).

As a result of increased educational funding and changes in vocational funding legislation to include industrial arts projects during the 1960s and 1970s, innovative curriculum plans for industrial arts continued to flourish (Cochran, 1970). Due to the differences in opinions expressed by the various curriculum plans, a general attitude of confusion arose within the field regarding its purpose and rationale. Many educators did not know which curriculum to follow.

Technology education. In an attempt to develop and implement a common ideology and curriculum for industrial arts, 21 industrial arts educators met at the Jackson's Mill Convention Center in West Virginia. The results of the Jackson's Mill project formed a rationale and a content structure for industrial arts (Snyder & Hales, 1981). Several key points emerged from the Jackson's Mill study. Conference participants determined that the field should involve the study of human adaptive systems of technology. The productive activities of communication, construction, manufacturing, and transportation serve as the focus. Using the core curriculum structure of the IACP, Jackson's Mill participants recommended viewing these activities as systems with inputs, processes, outputs, and feedback.

Although the Jackson's Mill "meeting of the minds" proved very productive, it did not cause all teachers in the field to abandon their teaching methods or content of drafting, woodworking, and metalworking. Many appeared to think that the curriculum changes were intended to make the field more technical, and they consequently changed their program names to reflect the concept of *industrial technology education*. A proliferation of "technology" classes—wood technology, metal technology, drafting technology, and so forth—appeared in schools. General education content in the industrial arts curriculum continued to diminish.

Ten years after the Jackson's Mill conference, technology education leaders felt that the curriculum's focus had once more grown vague. On the one hand, change did not occur rapidly enough in schools. On the other, some technology educators called for further curriculum revision. In 1990, a group of educators led by Savage and Sterry (1990) met to redefine technology education and build a new consensus on content. The meeting resulted in a publication titled *A Conceptual Framework for Technology Education*, which slightly modified content and adapted as its primary instructional method a British approach of design by problem solving. This report suggested that people satisfy their needs and wants by applying a problem-solving process to change resources into desired outcomes. The conceptual framework focused on four areas: bio-related processes, communication, production, and transportation. Yet, as we approach the millennium, this curriculum revision has yet to be widely adopted and implemented.

More recently, in another effort to promote technology education as a general education subject and to ensure its status in all schools, the field's leadership has turned to creating standards for technology education. Like subject specialists who have created new standards for the academic fields of mathematics, science, and social studies, technology educators want to create standards to help them bargain on behalf of what they view as every student's need for technology-related knowledge. William Dugger of the Virginia Polytechnic Institute and State University, in conjunction with the International Technology Education Association, is trying to establish national standards for technology education. These standards will include a definition, rationale, and yet another change in curriculum structure (*Technology for All Americans*, 1996).

Along with the curriculum efforts sponsored by professional associations, universities, and state departments, we have seen a growing presence of laboratory equipment vendors who serve as curriculum developers. Also concerned about dwindling enrollment in technology education and responding to a market niche, laboratory equipment vendors who sold primarily to technology educators now create modular technology education activities for schools nationwide (LaPorte & Sanders, 1995). The first modules appeared in the late 1980s and their number has grown as we near the end of the century.

The modules usually consist of a nice-looking workstation, curriculum and instruction materials—at first in a workbook or flip chart, and now generally on a computer—and the equipment needed to carry out a small activity, such as making a note-card holder, testing solar equipment, or doing a small drafting project. Teachers and school administrators find these modules an alternative to the traditional curriculum and methods of that often fits well in the reduced time allocated to technology education classes (Petrina, 1993). The modules have a number of other perceived benefits for teachers and administrators. Teachers who have six- or nine-week introductory classes can implement several modules and have all curriculum, instructional, equipment, and material needs met by one vendor—thereby simplifying their professional lives.

Administrators can point with pride at the impressive-looking equipment and laboratory their students use to learn about technology—especially when there is a computer in the midst of each module.

Another idea being implemented by some technology educators involves the integration of technology education with other subjects, especially mathematics and science (Zuga, 1988; LaPorte & Sanders, 1995). This concept is not new, but it has remained largely untested over the years. It has begun to gain advocates in all the professional communities served by the three subjects. At present, schools and universities are trying integrated educational programs, with additional recommendations coming from state supervisors of technology education. These programs are still in an experimental phase as each team of educators forges new relationships and works through years of ignorance about the others' disciplines.

Elementary School Technology Education

At about the same time that Woodward created the manual training school, elementary educators learned of educational *sloyd*, a system of manual training that arrived in the U.S. with Scandanavian immigrants. On the east coast, Grace Dodge and Emily Huntington emerged as proponents of industrial education for children. These two women believed that the "industrial" in *industrial education* refered to industriousness, as in keeping one's hands and mind actively engaged in making and doing (Bennett, 1937). They formed the short-lived Kitchen Garden Association in 1880 and helped to found the Industrial Education Association in 1884. Dodge, an education writer and philanthropist, later helped to found Teachers' College Columbia for the purpose of training industrial education teachers (Bennett, 1937). Huntington, an elementary school teacher, provided educational ideas about implementing handwork in the schools. These two women were the first in a long line of primarily female elementary-level educators who supported and helped to develop manual arts, industrial arts, and technology education in the elementary school.

Teachers' College Columbia became a prime location for the growth of elementary school industrial arts with an outstanding manual training faculty and vocational education faculty, as well as an outstanding general education faculty, which included John Dewey. The mix of faculty in the teacher education program, along with the teachers involved in the experimental school, allowed for experimentation in classrooms that integrated industrial arts into elementary school classrooms.

This work was reflected in an early industrial arts text, *Elementary School Industrial Arts* by Frederick Gordon Bonser and Lois Coffey Mossman (1923). Departing from the secondary school manual training and industrial arts tradition, Bonser and Mossman recommended a comprehensive curriculum for all elementary students that included the study of food, clothing, shelter, utensils, and records, along with tools and machines as industrial arts for children. Alongside the growing use of the project method in secondary school industrial arts, Bonser and Coffey also implemented a project approach through a thematic unit of study that integrated academic and industrial content.

There is evidence during the first half of the twentieth century of widespread practice of elementary school industrial arts, and a number of related books were written. In fact, practices recommended by industrial arts educators that focused on elementary school education probably influenced the ideology and practice of industrial arts educators in secondary schools.

With the end of World War II, the baby boom, and a distinct shift in educational philosophy from progressive ideology to social efficiency through the use of workbooks and basic academic instruction, the practice of elementary school industrial arts tapered off. It was slowly eliminated from mainstream practice. It remains now in some schools as an isolated subject of study supported by limited grant funds or the enthusiasm of a single individual or small group of local advocates.

Examples of such projects include Hunt's Technology for Children (T4C) project in New Jersey, Scobey's *Technology for Children* textbook, Heasley's Technological Exploratorium project in Northeastern Ohio, and Thode's elementary school technology education implementation in Ketchum, Idaho.

However scattered the efforts in the practice of elementary school technology education, though, threads of consistency remain. Women are more frequently involved in creating and implementing elementary school projects than secondary school projects. Perhaps, as a result of their influence in focusing on all children in elementary school, or distancing from the vocational aspects of secondary schools, the content of the elementary school technology education curriculum tends to be more comprehensive than that at the secondary level (Zuga, 1998). Another traditional trait of elementary school technology education is that, due to the nature of the elementary school curriculum, technology education is often integrated with academic subjects and it becomes method as well as content. Finally, several of these factors combine to create a fertile ground for innovation in the broader field of technology education through its practice at the elementary level. In fact, curriculum innovation in technology education often appears in elementary school practices and texts before it does in secondary school practices and texts (Zuga, 1998).

VOCATIONAL EDUCATION'S INFLUENCE

As early forms of technology education were taking hold during the late nineteenth century, forms of vocational education were also put into practice. Educators experimented with a variety of approaches to teaching about technology in the schools; they used a varity of terms to describe their educational experiments; and they claimed a variety of benefits to and purposes for these new forms of education. A main goal of the new technology-related curriculum involved the vocational goal of preparing children for the workforce. In the late nineteenth century, this was a very important goal for most children since less than 10 percent of students went on to high school. It made sense that educators in both secondary and elementary schools would have a vocational goal for their students. Throughout most of the twentieth century, this goal not only spawned specific vocational education programs, but it also greatly influenced the ideology and practice of the subjects that preceded technology education: manual training, manual arts, industrial arts, and industrial technology education.

In addition, vocational educators also promoted the classification of work by gender, separating technologies under the subjects of home economics and trade and industry education. In the late nineteenth century, the Industrial Education Association included both men and women interested in teaching about a wide range of technologies for industry and homes (Bennett, 1937). However, when the American Vocational Association formed, it set up separate subdivisions that included home economics and trade and industry education. Even though many women—especially poor women—worked in all types of industry during the early part of the century, girls were not typically included in secondary school industrial education.

Secondary Level Vocational Education

Several vocational education ideas have helped to shape the practice of technology education. They include curriculum ideology, life skills, school-to-work transition, and tech prep.

Curriculum ideology. Over the years, technology education curriculum grew out of industrial arts, which in turn came from the manual training concepts of the late nineteenth century. Technology educators have always viewed their field as part of the general education of all students. Its leaders have tried to focus technology education as closely as possible to the "general education" side of a curriculum continuum that moves from general knowledge to specific vocational knowledge and skills. The curriculum of vocational education has reflected the job-training ideas and goals shaped primarily by John D. Runkle, Charles A. Prosser, Charles R. Allen, R. W. Selvidge, and Verne C. Fryklund. Industrial arts educators have often used vocational education curriculum designs, which has led to their own and the public's confusion about the general nature and purpose of industrial arts as a subject for all students. Planning industrial arts curriculum with vocational education curriculum design led industrial arts practice to look like vocational education.

One of the first influences on vocational education came from Runkle, the president of the Massachusetts Institute of Technology. He incorporated technical manual training concepts heavily into his engineering courses, believing that they would help students to develop required mechanical skills needed to effectively perform their job responsibilities (Barlow, 1990). Vocational educators who followed took curriculum design ideas from Runkle and incorporated them into their programs.

Prosser, who served in many positions at the state and federal levels, also had great influence in shaping the curriculum for vocational education. His philosophies concentrated on teacher selection and training and promoted the ideology that academics should not take precedence over mechanical abilities and knowledge. Prosser's ideas, as embodied in his 16 theorems of vocational practice, were incorporated into the field of vocational education, with emphasis on teaching the job skills needed in industry (Barlow, 1967).

Three of the strongest educational philosophies to influence industrial arts were presented by Allen and others in *The Instructor, the Man, and the Job* (1945), Selvidge in *How to Teach a Trade* (1923), and Fryklund in *Trade and Job Analysis* (1942). These philosophies rested on improving teacher education and curriculum to improve the training of workers in the trades of industry. All these philosophies found wide acceptance in vocational education for training people for the industrial trades. They greatly influenced the industrial arts curriculum in many parts of the country. Because of the influence of these three men, many industrial arts educators incorrectly incorporated a vocationally oriented curriculum design into their programs, thinking it was a better way to teach elementary and secondary education students industrial arts (Lux, 1979; Zuga 1991).

Vocational influence is apparent in the Industrial Arts Curriculum Project (IACP), produced at Ohio State University through the efforts of Towers, Lux, and Ray (1968). They define industrial arts as the study of industry and the economy through two primary activities: manufacturing and construction. The structure and goals of the IACP document and curriculum materials focus on teaching middle and secondary education students about industry in a vocational manner. Commenting on the socioeconomic curriculum derivation in the IACP, Ray (1980) stated: "Looked upon in an objective way, one might propose that the 'economic emphasis' comes close to being a kind of progressive vocationalism" (p. 11).

School-to-work transition. One of the major vocational curriculum designs influenced by Runkle, Prosser, Allen, Selvidge, and Fryklund is that of *school to work*. Contemporary concerns for school-to-work transition continue a century-long trend in vocational education, industrial arts, and technology education. In recent years, education proponents have determined that secondary school students who do not plan to attend college should gain skills that will allow them to make the transition from school to employment (Fraser & Charner, 1993). Over the years, many industrial arts programs, seeking vocational funding, have been enticed to change their curriculum to reflect school-to-work objectives. Since many industrial arts educators already accepted the vocational aspects of manual training through curriculum, this transition was an easy one.

Life skills. Life skills in education began in the early 1950s with the idea that, in addition to a general education, students also need the skills to satisfy the basic needs of life (Whitesel, 1956). The *life skills* movement was closely associated with general education, with curriculum and instruction provided partly by industrial arts programs. According to Osburn (1963), "Industrial arts education provides constantly expanding and intensifying experiences in many important aspects of living." However, industrial arts curriculum as practiced in schools was influenced by the ideas of Selvidge and Fryklund (Ericson, 1946), resulting in life skills courses that focused on teaching students a trade.

Tech prep. The program of technical preparation, or *tech prep*, grew out of the school-to-work philosophies of previous decades. This program focuses on preparation of secondary students in their junior and senior years for postsecondary education and for a possible associate degree in a technical specialty (Parnell, 1994). Tech-prep programs often include arrangements that give students postsecondary educational credit at cooperating institutions for technical courses they take in high school. Tech-prep programs are usually highly technical in nature and guide students into very specific technical careers. Some technology educators have sought and secured vocational tech prep funding, demonstrating, once again, the ease with which technology educators can adopt vocational ideology and practice.

Contemporary programs such as school-to-work transition and tech prep have their roots in the history of secondary school vocational education and can influence the direction of technology education toward vocational ideology and practice. They represent one end of a continuum and have even influenced elementary school education.

Vocational-Elementary

Elementary school curriculum has traditionally focused on general educational goals such as literacy and numeracy. However, early in the twentieth century there was a trend to prepare children for work by informing them about adult work roles through study of the community. During the latter part of the century this tradition gave way to incorporating career education in the elementary school curriculum. The educational concept of community and adult work roles and career education programs have served a prevocational educational role in elementary schools. Federal funding for career education sustained the effort in schools during the 1970s.

The presence of vocationally inspired programs such as career education have provided funds for teaching industrial arts and technology education in many elementary schools. The T4C project in New Jersey is but one example of an elementary school technology education project that has benefited from career education funding. Such funding often introduces vocational goals at the elementary level.

ISSUES

Throughout this chapter, we have raised issues related to technology education. They include (1) the past relationship of technology education to vocational education and the current relationship of vocational and technology education through programs such as tech prep and school to work; (2) the manner in which vendors influence technology education curriculum toward modularized instruction; (3) the creation of national standards for technology education; (4) the integration of technology education with math, science, or other disciplines, and, perhaps the most important issue; (5) the unfulfilled general education promise of technology education for all students.

The Relationship between Technology and Vocational Education

In the past, industrial arts educators have clung tightly to industrial and vocational ideologies that directed their curricula away from general education and toward technical and skill-oriented curricula through the influences of Runkle, Prosser, Allen, Selvidge, and Fryklund. Shaped by this kind of ideology, technology education practices grew more vocational than general. They were vocational in the way in which curriculum was constructed with trade and job analysis methods. And, they were industrial in that the curriculum was perceived to be for boys, which eliminated half of all potential students at the outset (Zuga, 1998).

Many in the field still endorse more vocationally oriented curriculum theory and planning practices (Zuga, 1991). The issue of teaching technology education through vocational curriculum and instruction models should be addressed. Using vocational curriculum theory and practices leads technology educators to offer vocational education through technology education laboratories by default (Lux, 1979). To function as general educators, technology educators need to study, know, and use general education purposes and ideologies in teaching technology education. The problem-based curriculum and contemporary plans for instruction of technology education have much more to do with the situated learning and constructivism discussed by general educators in fields such as social studies, mathematics, and science education, than it has to do with the tradition of skill development in vocational education and training. Technology educators must learn to incorporate general education concepts and activities into their curricula (Zuga, 1989).

Due to the concerns we discuss above, participation in school-to-work transition and tech-prep programs becomes an issue for technology educators. As vocationally funded programs, school to work and tech prep offer the benefit of funding for technology education, but this funding comes at the expense of requiring the overshadowing of technology education's general educational goals by the skill development and preparation for work goals of vocational education. While the opposite ends of the continuum on this issue are clear—either maintain a separate identity from vocational education and give up vocational funding or ally with vocational education to gain available funding—local patterns of implementation are confusing. Embracing a prevocational role for technology education has created a muddy pattern of practice throughout the United States. This muddy pattern has resulted in confusing the role and meaning of technology education for other educators and the general public. The resulting confusion has often been promulgated by technology educators, themselves, as they have created a vocational-looking practice in schools and universities.

A more contemporary example of this kind of field and public confusion is the inclusion of technology education in the *Vocational Education Standards for National Board Certification* of the National Board for Professional Teaching Standards (1997). The general educators who designed this project perceived technology education to be a vocational education subject. The technology teachers who worked on the standards supported their conceptualization when they permitted teaching standards for technology education to be subsumed under 13 broad and vague vocational education standards for teaching. Once again, the focus of technology education is not toward vocational ideologies, but it is focused on providing students with the additional knowledge and skills students need to live in a technological society. We would hope that technology educators would carefully conceptualize their relationship and role with respect to tech prep and school-to-work programs, and related teaching standards, bearing in mind the long-term influence that these programs have on the field's image and curriculum.

The Influence of Vendor Curricula

The use of vendor curricula in technology education has become commonplace throughout the field. While attractive to many technology teachers and educational communities, this type of curriculum makes the teacher not a curriculum developer but a mere facilitator of activities. Petrina (1993, pp. 73-76) cites four major problems with the modular approach to technology education (MATE):

- It tends to make educational activities similar to those used in the past, using structured curricula with traditional industrial arts equipment.

• It represents outdated educational theories that specify knowledge to be acquired and activities to be performed.

• It takes authority from the teacher and gives it to product companies.

• It skirts curriculum theory by using equipment instead of laboratory instruction and takes the responsibility for curriculum development away from the instructor.

The concept of allowing primarily industrial arts laboratory supply corporations to dictate curriculum and instruction in technology education programs is not only incorrect but also very dangerous for the field (Zuga, 1992). The issues and underlying questions for technology educators regarding the corporate curricula should be: Who is creating and writing technology education curriculum and instructional material, and for what purpose? The responsibility for the development and progress of technology education rests squarely on the shoulders of its administrators and teachers. Technology education curriculum should be selected to fulfill the needs of local students and the community.

National Standards

Technology educators have a history of addressing issues regarding the existence and purpose of their field. Leaders such as Woodward, Warner, and others created a pattern of behavior that has led to thoughtful revisiting of curriculum. Technology educators continue to try to do the best job possible in presenting technology content in the schools. The Technology for All Americans project (1996), led by William Dugger of Virginia Tech, addresses the issue of establishing standards for technology education. It is the latest in a series of projects that have attempted to create a national consensus for technology education standards. This project may have greater credence than earlier ones because standards have evolved as an issue of great concern among contemporary educators. Most school subject matter professionals in fields such as mathematics, science, and social studies have recently created standards for guiding teachers and test developers toward basic knowledge and skills that all students should gain. In all fields, standards efforts are directed at promoting change in curriculum and teaching practice and taking a step closer to a national curriculum.

In collaboration with the International Technology Education Association (ITEA), Dugger and his staff are developing standards for technology education focused on establishing curriculum guidelines for the field. It is hoped that the new technology education standards will positively promote the field. However, standards have limited effect when it comes to reforming practice in a field. Based on the prevalent ideologies regarding national, state, and local control over education in the United States, and the evolving nature of those ideologies, the exact influence of standards is open to question. While accrediting agencies and professional organizations usually endorse current standards, teachers can often continue to operate with little regard to standards. The United States has a strong tradition of local control over curriculum.

The teaching standards being promoted by the National Board for Professional Teaching Standards (1997) are a related concern. These standards are also fraught with difficulties. They take an elitist position, in that the credential they offer is both time consuming and expensive to acquire. As a consequence, only a few teachers will ever earn the certification, and because it is temporary, it will be costly for teachers to maintain. Moreover, the board's technology education standards are folded into its vocational education standards, which means that technology teachers would have comply with vocational education teaching standards and would be designated master vocational education teachers.

Integration

Integration of subject matter is a growing grassroots educational trend. Recently, emphasis has generally gone toward the integration of subjects to create a more collaborative curriculum, and technology educators have followed suit (LaPorte & Sanders, 1995). The integration of science, mathematics, and technology education began in the late 1980s with Project 2061, designed to assist in the reformation of these fields (American Association for the Advancement of Science, 1989). As integration develops at various levels, we must ask if it is and will be of value for technology education teachers and students.

The promoters of integration say that technology educators will benefit from association with their math and science educators, and with contemporary curriculum analysts (Zuga, 1991; LaPorte & Sanders, 1995). Local school administrators and teachers often support the effort to integrate as a way to bring constructivist curriculum to the schools. On the other hand, some technology educators fear the loss of technology education's unique content and role through integration.

The integration of technology education with mathematics and science education is a recent phenomenon that has been tried in schools and universities throughout the country, with support from state departments of education and a number of educational projects. Only time will show the success and true value of integration.

TECHNOLOGY EDUCATION AS GENERAL EDUCATION

Throughout this chapter, we have analyzed a number of roles assigned to technology education. We have discussed several historical aspects related to technology education and the development of its curriculum ideologies as it relates to vocational education. It appears that, although the basis of technology education ideology is established firmly in general education, technology education's curricular content and structure reflect vocational education influence. We hope that technology education administrators, policy makers, faculty, and teachers will see the real focus of their field: the promotion of general education aspects of the subject.

At this point, technology education is not viewed as a subject worthy of study for all children in the United States. Here, unlike in Great Britain and many other countries, we have no national and few state mandates to require that all students learn about technology. In part, technology educators are responsible for this state of affairs. In addition to curriculum design confusion, the lack of diversity among technology educators and students has created a condition that has allowed women, who make up more than half the population of this country, to perceive technology education as irrelevant to them. In addition, though their numbers are growing, the small representation of minorities as professionals in technology education exacerbates problems with the perception of technology education's role and importance in every citizen's life. Technology educators need to concern themselves not only with their basic ideology with respect to curriculum, but also with the way they represent diversity in the culture to their constituency, the general public. Practice and image both contribute to the perceived value of technology education.

SUMMARY

Technology educators stand at an important crossroads in the history of their field. The field's historical traditions have led them to develop a dual view and purpose for technology education, including general and vocational education goals. Both ideologies actively influence the direction of the field, as we have noted, regarding standards, integration, vocational education funding, and the promise of general education.

How these issues are resolved and what happens to the future of technology education rests with the efforts of the professionals who practice in the field. They will define technology education for the public and the public will determine its value for all students. Beliefs will influence action, but action will make the future.

References

Allen, C. R., Hambrecht, G. P., & Welch, R. L. (1945). *The instructor, the man, and the job*. Chicago, IL: J. B. Lippincott.

American Association for the Advancement of Science. (1989). *Science for all Americans: A Project 2061 report on literacy goals in science, mathematics, and technology education*. Washington, DC: Author.

Barlow, M. L. (1967). *History of industrial education in the United States*. Peoria, IL: Chas. A. Bennett.

Barlow, M. L. (1990). Historical background of vocational education. In A. J. Pautler, Jr. (Ed.), *Vocational education in the 1990s: Major issues* (pp. 5-24). Ann Arbor, MI: Prakken Publications.

Bawden, W. T. (1950). *Leaders in industrial education*. Peoria, IL: Chas. A. Bennett.

Bennett, C. A. (1937). *History of manual and industrial education 1870 to 1917*. Peoria, IL: Chas. A. Bennett.

Bonser, F. G., & Mossman, L. C. (1923). *Industrial arts for elementary schools*. New York: Macmillan.

Cochran, L. H. (1970). *Innovative programs in industrial education*. Bloomington: McKnight.

Dewey, J. (1916). *Democracy and education*. New York: Free Press.

Dugger, W. E. (1995). Technology education: A global influence. In G. E. Martin (Ed.), *Foundations of technology education* (pp. 479-501). Peoria, IL: Glencoe/McGraw-Hill.

Ericson, E. E. (1946). *Teaching the industrial arts*. Peoria, IL: Chas. Bennett.

Face, W. L., Flug, E. R. F., & Swanson, R. S. (1965). Conceptual approaches to American industry. In G. S. Wall (Ed.), *Approaches and procedures in industrial arts*, (pp. 60-72). Bloomington, IL: American Council on Industrial Arts Teacher Education.

Fraser, B. S., & Charner, I. (1993). *Challenging our communities: Purposeful action for youth transition from school to work*. Washington, DC: Academy for Educational Development. (ERIC Document Reproduction Service No. ED 403 421)

Fryklund, V. C. (1956). *Analysis techniques for instructors*. Milwaukee, WI: Bruce Publishing Co.

Fryklund, V. C. (1942). Trade and job analysis. Milwaukee, WI: Bruce Publishing Co.

Harrison, P. E. (1940). A laboratory of industries. *Industrial Arts and Vocational Education*, *29*(7), 260-261.

Kilpatrick, W. H., Bagley, W. C., Bonser, F. G., Hosic, J. F., & Hatch, R. W. (1921). Dangers and difficulties of the project method and how to overcome them. *Teachers College Record, 22*(4), 283-321.

LaPorte, J. E. (1980). The degree of utilization of industrial arts curriculum project materials relative to their perceived attributes, teacher characteristics, and teacher concerns (Unpublished doctoral dissertation, Ohio State University, 1980).

LaPorte, J. E., & Sanders, M. E. (1995). Integrating technology, science, and mathematics education. In Eugene G. Martins (Ed.), *Foundations of technology education* (pp. 179-220). Peoria, IL: Glencoe/McGraw-Hill.

Lux, D. G. (1979). Trade and job analysis—The scourge of IA. *School Shop, 38*(7), 2.

Maley, D. (1972). The Maryland plan. *School Shop, 32*(8), 52-54.

National Education Association. (1904/June 27-July 1). *Journal of Proceedings and Addresses*, pp. 45-46.

Olson, D. W. (1963). *Industrial arts and technology*. Englewood-Cliffs, NJ: Prentice-Hall.

Olson, D. W. (1974). Interpreting a technological society: The function of industrial arts. *School Shop, 33*(7), 35-6.

Osburn, B. N. (1963). Industrial arts in modern education. In R. Miller & L. H. Smalley (Eds.), *Selected readings for industrial arts* (p. 173). Bloomington, IL: McKnight & McKnight.

National Board for Professional Teaching Standards. (1996). *Vocational education standards for national board certification*. Washington, DC: Department of Education. (ERIC Document Reproduction Service No. ED 398 429)

Parnell, D. (1994). *The tech prep associate degree program revisited*. Paper presented at the Annual Conference on Workforce Training of the League for Innovation in the Community College. (ERIC Document Reproduction Service No. ED 369 441)

Petrina, S. (1993). Under the corporate thumb: Troubles with our MATE (modular approach to technology education). *Journal of Technology Education, 5*(1), 72-80.

Post, R. C. (Ed.). *1876: A centennial exhibition*. Washington, DC: National Museum of History and Technology, Smithsonian Institution.

Ray, W. E. (1979). Councils and associations related to the industrial arts profession. In G. E. Martin (Ed.), *Industrial arts education: Retrospect, prospect* (pp. 392-412). Bloomington, IL: McKnight.

Ray, W. E. (1980). Toward consensus regarding an industrial arts curriculum base. *Journal of Epsilon Pi Tau, 6*(2), 8-12.

Savage, E., & Sterry, L. (1990). A conceptual framework for technology education. Reston, VA: International Technology Education Association.

Selvidge, R. W. (1923). *How to teach a trade*. Peoria, IL: Manual Arts Press.

Snyder, J. F., & Hales, J. F. (1981). Jackson's Mill industrial arts curriculum theory. Charleston, WV: West Virginia Department of Education.

Technology for all Americans. (1996). Reston, VA: International Technology Education Association.

Towers, E. R., Lux, D. G., & Ray, W. E. (1966). *A rationale and structure for industrial arts subject matter*. Columbus, OH: Ohio State University, Industrial Arts Department of Education. (ERIC Document Reproduction Service No. ED 013 955)

Van Duesen, C. S. (1940). Place, program, and function of industrial arts. *Industrial Arts and Vocational Education, 29*(7), 257-258.

Warner, W. E. (1928). *Contributions in industrial arts education, No. 1*. Columbus, OH: Ohio State University Press.

Warner, W. E. (1931). The laboratory of industries plan. In *Bruce's School Shop Annual* (pp. 261-266). Milwaukee, WI: Bruce Publishing Co.

Warner, W. E. (1934). Studies in school-shop planning. *Industrial Arts and Vocational Education, 23*(2), 31-38.

Warner, W. E., Gary, J. E., Gerbracht, C. J., Gilbert, H. G., Lisack, J. P., Klientjes, P. L., Phillips, K. (1965). *A curriculum to reflect technology*. Columbus, OH: Epsilon Pi Tau.

Whitesel, J. A. (1956). The derivation of goals and purposes of instruction. In C. R. Hutchcroft (Ed.), *Problems and issues in industrial arts teacher education* (pp. 72-3). Bloomington, IL: McKnight & McKnight.

Woodward, C. M. (1887). *The manual training school*. Boston: D.C. Heath, p. 256.

Zuga, K. F. (1998). Historical view of women's roles in technology education. In B. Rider (Ed.), *Diversity in technology education*, (pp. 13-35). Bloomington, IL: Glencoe.

Zuga, K. F. (1988). Interdisciplinary approach. In W. H. Kemp and A. E. Schwaller (Eds.), *Instructional strategies for technology education*. Mission Hills, CA: Glencoe, pp. 56-71.

Zuga, K. F. (1989). Relating technology education goals to curriculum planning. *Journal of Technology Education, 1* (1), 34-58.

Zuga, K. F. (1992). Social reconstruction curriculum and technology education. *Journal of Technology Education, 3* (2), 53

Zuga, K. F. (1991). Technology teacher education curriculum. *Journal of Technology Education, 2*(2), 60-70.

Karen F. Zuga *is an associate professor in the School of Teaching and Learning at Ohio State University, where she specializes in integrated mathematics, science, and technology education teacher education and graduate education for technology educators. She is the author of more than 30 publications that focus on history, philosophy, curriculum, integration, and diversity issues with regard to technology education. She has served as the president of the Technology Education for Children Council and as a board member of the International Technology Education Association. She will be the next editor of the* Journal of Industrial Teacher Education. ***Phillip L. Cardon*** *received his B.S. from Weber State University in 1992 and his M.S. from Brigham Young University in 1996. He is the author and co-author of several articles in technology education. He is currently a graduate student at Ohio State University, where he is pursuing a doctoral degree in technology education.*

12

HIGH SCHOOL VOCATIONAL EDUCATION: FACING AN UNCERTAIN FUTURE

By Kenneth Gray

Without a known port of call, no wind is favorable.—Socrates

During the 1980s and 1990s, high school vocational education in the U.S. became a curriculum under duress. Enrollment declined as most American youth hoped and dreamed for a college education. In a national sample of 1992 high school seniors, for example, only 11.7 percent identified themselves as having concentrated in vocational education in high school (National Center for Education Statistics, 1996, Indicator 26). While this figure underestimates the actual number of vocational education students, it also hints at the level of esteem, or lack thereof, in which the curriculum is now held.

This chapter will explore the present condition of high school vocational education in the U.S. and discuss various points of view about its possible future direction. For this discussion, the definition of vocational education is limited to programs with employment outcome goals, including: vocational agriculture, business education, health occupations, marketing education, and trade and industrial education. Not included are home economics (family and consumer science) and industrial arts (technology education).

THE PAST

Vocational education, as it exists today, developed at the start of the twentieth century in response to a complex set of social, economic, and political forces (Gray, 1991). Of these, the most central was the practical problem created for educators by the sudden increase in the high school enrollment of children from working-class families. Between 1890 and 1918, one new high school opened each day each year, as enrollment more than doubled nationally (Tyack, 1974). The motive for this enrollment growth was economic. With increases in manufacturing, a nonprofessional, nonagrarian middle-class developed. Families from this group sacrificed to keep their children in school, hoping that doing so would lead to a better job after graduation (Hogan, 1978).

The dilemma was that at that time preparation for employment was not generally the perceived mission of high school. In the later 1800s, for example, the National Education Committee issued an influential report indicating that high school was for children from professional families who planned to become a professional or marry one. Such a mission required only one curriculum: the classical curriculum. Educators who daily faced this new group of working class students quickly realized, however, that the classical curriculum was not a good fit. Industrialists argued that the existing high school curriculum offered nothing of value to the average American (Gray, 1989). Something different was needed. The curriculum had to be changed or differentiated to offer programs of study to students not pursuing either a profession or a life of leisure. The solution was vocational education.

This differentiation of the curriculum, or *vocationalizing*, of the U.S. high school to include preparation for employment (vocational education) was not without controversy. Such preparation was viewed by some, most notably John Dewey (1913), as "illiberal" and "mean spirited." Dewey suspected a plot to serve industry by providing a better grade of labor. Dewey wanted vocational education to teach academic content and empower graduates with knowledge needed to transform the economic system into a more democratic and egalitarian form of capitalism. On the other hand, industrialists, particularly middle-level manufacturers, believed that educators were biased against them and sought to break vocational education completely away from the public schools. They wanted to see the creation of a "dual" system like that in Germany. I describe this dispute here because later in this chapter I will point out that it lies at the heart of the present debate about the future direction of vocational education.

With the enactment of the 1916 Smith Hughes Act, the U.S. Congress dictated a compromise. Vocational education would not be separated into a dual system but would remain within the existing public education structure under the control of general educators. Its mission, however, was to deliver occupational skill training that would lead to job placement.

As in any compromise, neither side was very happy. Industry sensed that its involvement would in fact be minimal and mostly abandoned the effort. General educators accepted the responsibility but were never really comfortable with the mission. They particularly worried about forcing students to make premature, and thus perhaps limiting, occupational choices. As a consequence, what evolved was a high school vocational education system that lacked strong ties to either employers or educators. This separateness was accentuated by federal funding for vocational education which, while common today, was quite unique then.

One additional historical point is important. The high school vocational education programs that developed were typically in nonprofessional but skilled or semi-skilled occupations where prerequisite work skills would offer an advantage in competing for positions. This design was consistent with both the career expectations of youth and the economy's occupational structure. Relatively few people went to college, and those who did not usually sought skilled-craft occupations as an alternative to low-skill employment.

Enrollment in vocational education programs grew slowly at first but then rather dramatically in the 1960s and 1970s when federal funds dedicated to construction of vocational education facilities expanded availability. Beginning in the early 1980s, however, a period of "punctuated equilibrium" (Thurow, 1996) occurred in the economy, ending the post-World War II era of high-wage/low-skill work in the U.S. and thereby changing both the occupational structure and youth expectation. These winds of change blew strongly in the vocational education community.

THE PRESENT

Having established the historical prelude for high school vocational education today, this chapter now turns to the present state of the curriculum as evidenced by data collected by U.S. National Center for Educational Statistics (NCES) and the federally mandated 1994 National Assessment of Vocational Education (NAVE).

Vocational Education Course Taking

While figures for relative enrollments in

vocational education versus the academic or general high school curriculum are always suspect due to definition problems, the data are consistent in direction. Since the early 1980s, enrollment has declined in vocational education when measured in terms of concentrators (defined as students taking three or more units in a single occupational area) and of total vocational education courses taken by all students.

NCES data collected between 1982 and 1992 indicate that the percentage of high school seniors completing a vocational education program declined from 27 percent to 12 percent (NCES, 1996, Indicator 26). Those most likely to be concentrators were students from low socioeconomic level families in urban and rural regions. The majority of these concentrators pursued full-time employment after graduation (Li, 1996).

As vocational education enrollment declined, the proportion of students taking college preparatory programs of study grew from 38 percent to 43 percent. Yet the largest group of students are those who complete neither college preparatory nor vocational education programs—by 1992 the largest percentage of students (45 percent) were in the default or "general" program. Ten percent of the 15 percent decline in vocational completers between 1982 and 1992, for example, can be attributed to growth in the general program, not to increases in the number of college prep completers.

Data regarding the number of vocational education Carnegie units completed by high school students confirm the trend cited above (NCES, 1996, Table 134). These data are the best available to measure participation in vocational education because they result from transcript analysis. Between 1982 and 1992, total average vocational education credits declined from 4.6 to 3.7, or 19 percent. This decline cut across race/ethnicity. The most dramatic decline occurred among Hispanics, who now take fewer vocational education courses than any other group except Asians.

One notable exception to this decline is the participation rates of special populations: special needs, limited English proficient, disabled, and economically/educationally disadvantaged students. As highlighted in the NAVE 1994 study, the only group not experiencing a decline in vocational education participation were at-risk youth. Increasing enrollment by these special populations had been a national policy priority in the 1970s. By the early 1990s, however, the decline of majority students caused the opposite problem—special needs students were becoming the majority group engaged in vocational education. The impact on high school vocational education was dramatic. As an indication, by the early 1990s vocational teachers cited as their number one problem the placement of students in their program who could not benefit from it. In particular, they felt that this development contributed to the flight of majority students into general or academic programs (NAVE, 1994).

Declines in vocational education enrollments have meant the elimination of programs. For example, while the enrollment decline in trade and industrial programs was less than other program areas, even these program were being lost at a rate of 12 percent a year in the mid-1990s ("Where Is Vocational Education Headed?" 1996).

Changing Teen Aspirations

When enrollment in vocational education began to slide in the early 1980s, a variety of hypotheses was offered to explain the development. According to one hypothesis, increases in high school graduation requirements made it difficult for students to take vocational education and still meet the academic requirements for graduation. There was, however, little data to support this conclusion. The real reason was a rather sudden increase in the number of students who wanted to go on to four-year colleges.

NCES national data demonstrate the increased interest in higher education among high school graduates. The percentage of students planning to attend postsecondary education right after high school, for example, increased from 58 percent in 1982 to 77 percent in 1992 (NCES, 1996, Indicator 60). In 1982, 69 percent of high school graduates had a clear plan to attend higher education; by 1992, the percentage had risen to 91 percent.

It is interesting to note that while the percentage of all students who aspired to postsecondary education increased, the percentage of this group who planned to pursue a two-year degree or certificate declined. Not only were students' aspirations turning toward college, but they were also moving away from anything but a four-year degree that led to professional work. Among students participating in the NCES longitudinal study of the high school class of 1992, 50 percent of males and 69 percent of females hoped to have professional jobs by the time they were age 30 (Gray and Herr, 1995, p. 9).

High School Graduates Pursuing Full-Time Employment

Arguable even in the 1990s, full-time employment was still the central outcome objective of vocational education. Thus, it is useful to note how few young Americans share this goal and enter the labor force directly after high school. A perspective on this issue can be gained from comparing those who did not go to college and were employed in 1994 with similar youth in 1980 (NCES, 1996, Indicator 64). In 1980, 51 percent of high school graduates did not go on to college, and 69 percent of that group were employed directly after high school, for a total employment rate of approximately 35 percent. In 1994, only 38 percent of graduates did not go on to postsecondary education, and 64 percent of them were employed for a total employment rate of 24 percent. Thus, by the mid-1990s only about one-quarter of graduates went to work directly after high school. Even two years after graduation, fewer than half work full time. A 1994 follow-up of 1992 high school graduates found that only 34 percent were full-time employees (NCES, 1996, Indicator 61).

Academic Course-Taking Patterns of Vocational Students

Beginning in 1990 with the Perkins Act reauthorization, national priorities for vocational education expanded to include increases in the academic achievements of participants. Termed *academic integration*, the objective was to enable students to complete higher levels of academic courses. Data suggested that there was much to be done. NCES research (1994) found that while homework was required in 95 percent of academic classes, it was required in only 59 percent of vocational classrooms. The same study found that while math and science content was prevalent in the vocational education curriculum, few vocational educators reported spending more than 25 percent of classroom time on that content.

One indicator of the recognized need to the academic skills of vocational students was the success of the High Schools That Work program sponsored by the Southern Regional Education Board. The objective of this program was to bring academic rigor to the courses taken by vocational education students. By 1996, 17,000 students were participating in the program and exceeding the academic achievement levels of previous vocational education students (Bottoms, 1997).

NCES (1996, Indicator 28) data suggest that these and other efforts have been modestly successful. Between 1982 and 1994, the percentage of vocational education students completing an academic program that included four years of English and two years of math, science, and social studies had increased from 5 percent to 21 percent. In 1994, vocational education students' overall high school grade point average (GPA) was actually higher (2.4) than that of general students (2.0). And while vocational education students do score lower on most standardized tests, it is estimated that 80 percent of the difference is attributed to the fact that students who take vocational education have lower academic skills in the first place (NAVE, 1994).

Tech Prep and School-to-Work

Two other federal initiatives emerged in the

early 1990s: *tech prep*, and *school to work*. Both were federal responses to concerns that the schools were not aligned with new global economic and labor force realities. Tech prep's objective was to increase the numbers of vocational education concentrators who went on to postsecondary two-year technical education. While states were not required to set up tech prep programs, categorical funding was provided and most states began efforts to develop formal articulation agreements to link high schools with postsecondary technical education in a traditional two-plus-two arrangement.

In a similar way, the School-to-Work Act of 1994 was a congressional reaction to the perceived lack of an effective system to help students make the transition to full-time employment. While a well-financed and effective system enables students to make the transition to college, no such system existed for high school or college graduates who needed to make the transition to employment. Thus, the Act focused initially on school-based programs that arrange work-based learning to enable a better transition to full-time employment. By the late 1990s, however, the real impact of school to work seemed to come through raising educators' awareness of the need for school-sponsored activities to improve student career maturity. Thus, growing numbers of high schools began implementing systems of career majors, career pathways, individual career plans, job shadowing, and so forth, to promote an appropriate level of career focus and to facilitate more effective career planning.

Unfortunately, by the mid-1990s much of the activity related to tech-prep and school-to-work took place not in vocational education programs, but in comprehensive high schools and middle schools. In particular, states that had separate regional vocational schools and programs often were not involved in either tech prep or school to work. For example tech-prep articulation agreements sometimes failed to include a technical skills course. Thus, while these movements seem to have some impact on the comprehensive high school curriculum, their effect on the high school vocational education curriculum has been unclear.

Vocational Teacher Preparation

As enrollment declined and high school programs closed, the number of programs preparing vocational education teachers also declined. Apparently, as fewer students blessed with college-level academic ability took vocational education, fewer aspired to become vocational teachers, particularly in the areas of business education and vocational agriculture. Likewise, many states cut funding for vocational teacher preparation when Perkins Act regulations required allocation of a larger percentage of funds to local school districts .

The problem was significant enough for the September 1993 issue of *Vocational Education* to include an article by the editor titled "Who Will Teach the Teachers." It was reported that the number of higher education vocational teacher programs (432 in 1983), had declined by one-third by 1993. By the mid-1990s, many teacher training programs had reduced the number of program areas for teacher preparation. To rebuild, programs were added to prepare trainers and human resource development professionals for business and industry (Gray, 1997). Ironically, by the late 1990s the decline in vocational teacher preparation programs resulted in a shortage of vocational education teachers despite the overall enrollment declines.

Program Effectiveness

Throughout the post-World War II era, the effectiveness of high school vocational education has been major issue: first, because of the level of federal and state investment and, second, because of equity issues stemming from the fact that vocational education students tend to be kids from poorer families. While in the 1990s states were required to develop performance assessment methods, traditional outcome assessment—namely, job placement and college placement concerns—still dominated the criteria for evaluating program effectiveness.

Job placement. NCES data (1996, Table 30-

1) indicate labor market advantages for vocational education completers. Students completing either a vocational education curriculum, or both a vocational program and an academic program, were twice as likely to have been employed for 10 months following graduation than those from the default general curriculum. Of particular note, students who had taken two to four vocational credits had the highest annual earnings ($10,808) among those in the workforce. These data are consistent with Bishop's (1989) findings that vocational completers were more likely to graduate from high school, experience less unemployment, and earn higher earnings than a comparable group of graduates who were in the labor force but had not taken vocational education. It is important to note, however, that this result was only for those graduates who succeeded in finding work in the occupational area they studied in high school.

Postsecondary education. With the re-authorization of the Perkins Act in the late 1980s, increasing postsecondary higher education enrollment of vocational education students became a federal policy goal. Thus, of interest is the percentage of vocational education completers who go on to higher education. An analysis of the National Education Longitudinal Study of 1988 data set reveals that 31 percent of vocational education concentrators from the class of 1992 attended higher education directly after high school. Of these, 20 percent were attending four-year colleges; 63 percent, two-year institutions; and 17 percent, one-year certificate programs.

THE FUTURE

By the late 1990s, at least two schools of thought existed regarding the direction that high school vocational education would/should take in the future. The two differ in their assessment of the relative importance of the traditional goal of preparation for full-time employment. In the first model, termed here *education through occupation* (ETO), high school vocational education would/should be recognized as an educational/ instructional modality for teaching traditional academic content, not job skills. With this approach, job skills are considered less important because fewer students go directly to work after high school. In the second model—"traditional/tech prep" approach—the mission of teaching occupation-specific skills still has importance. Why? Because at least one-quarter of high school graduates still pursue full-time employment. Added to this task is the new mission of providing introductory technical skills for student who have an interest in pursuing a two-year postsecondary technical education (tech prep).

Education Through Occupation (ETO) Model

Education through employment was conceptualized by Grubb (1997) but best explained by Bragg (1997) as follows. When woven together, academic and vocational integration acts as the foundation for education through occupation when (1) broadened occupational content (clusters) is integrated with (2) traditional academic subjects (math, science etc.) using (3) new institutional structures (career pathways etc.) and (4) other types of school to work (work-based learning).

Unlike traditional vocational education where the intent is to teach skills identified as being related to occupational success and thus labor market advantage, the new vocational education follows John Dewey's vision. Skills training will become relatively less important (how much so is unclear), while teaching of academics and nonskill content (all aspects of an industry) takes its place. The philosophy is summarized by Rosenstock ("Where Is Vocational Education Headed?" 1996, p. 24), who argues that the real value of skill training lies not in labor market outcomes but in "accessing academic skills."

ETO is predicated on an assumption that in the future, little labor market advantage can be gained from skills training at the high school level because the entry-level credential for high-skill/high-wage work will be a two-year associate degree in the technologies. Therefore, moving away from skills training in high school to a more general occupational education will not hurt students who go to work. Implied, though not stated, is the belief that for those students who do go to work, on-the-job training (as prescribed in the School-to-Work legislation) would better facilitate their transition.

ETO proponents also argue that a more general type of high school occupational education (sometimes referred to as a *new vocationalism*) will be of value to all high school students. It is hoped that when occupational education becomes more general and more academic (and by so doing becomes viewed as complementary to the hope of higher education), then it will be more attractive to students from middle-class families (Grubb, 1997). Increased enrollments would result.

At the heart of the ETO movement is the old, yet still unresolved, issue of the common school versus differentiated curriculum approach to a high school education. Pennington ("Where Is Vocational Education Headed?" 1996) expresses a common ETO argument: Now that almost every adult engages in further education, they all need the same program of study. Social reconstruction advocates also endorse the ETO model. Larke ("Where Is Vocational Education Headed?" 1996) argues, for example, that "when we 're looking at who participates in college prep and tech prep this is a division by race, class, and gender. . . . Whether or not it is the intent of the education system the fact remains that it happens." The implied solution is a common curriculum for all. Proponents of the ETO approach also frequently voice conventional wisdom about the inappropriateness of high-school aged students making career choices; in light of this view, high school vocational education should not require such commitments

In summary, the ETO model is quite similar to the historical manual arts/industrial arts/technology education model of occupational education. The outcomes goals are only loosely related to employment, seeking instead to generalize the curriculum into a more academic and career exploration mode. To quote Parnell (*"Where Is Vocational Education Headed?"* 1996, p. 24) "A portion [of vocational education] will still be a laboratory experience, but it will be much broader approach . . . to prepare students for the next step at the postsecondary level or some kind of apprentice program."

The Traditional/Tech Prep Model

The traditional/tech prep model can be traced to the Perkins Re-authorization Act of 1990. By funding tech prep, the Act signaled a new federal mission for high school occupational education—namely preparation for postsecondary education. Based on the assumption or observation that an associate degree in the technologies would be the common credential for nonprofessional high-skill/high-wage work in the future and students growing preference for college, facilitating the transition from high school to two-year postsecondary technical education (tech prep) became a new outcome goal for vocational education.

The intent in the Re-authorization Act of 1990 was not, however, to necessarily de-emphasize skill training. Such instruction now has two outcome goals: (1) advantage in seeking full-time employment for students going to work after high school and (2) technical skills training that would serve as the basis for subsequent preparation in postsecondary technical education. While for some high school students vocational education would provide skills and experience needed to obtain career work on graduation, for other students it is a course or several courses that build technical skills related to their intended postsecondary two-year technical education major. Much like the way most college prep students now select typing, word-processing, and spreadsheet classes from the business education curriculum, students aspiring to pursue two-year technical education would select one or more one-credit education courses related to their technical interest.

ETO or Tech Prep?

Which of the two models for high school

vocational education will prevail in the future, ETO or tech prep? Will high school vocational education disappear altogether from the nations' high schools? As Grubb points out (1997), the practices of teachers and administrators will determine the future. One could add that it also will be the perceptions of the true decision makers in the high school curriculum process—parents and students who select courses (Gray, 1997)—that in the end determine the future. And just as "all politics is local," the future of vocational education will be decided in each local community across the nation. (Note that most money spent on vocational education is still raised by local school districts.) With this in mind, pragmatic considerations suggest that predictions of the demise of traditional high school vocational education are perhaps premature and that the tech prep model is the likelier of the two models to evolve into the next decade.

There are a number of reasons to believe in the future of traditional vocational education linked with tech-prep. First, many states have invested heavily in traditional occupational education facilities, programs, and staff. This type of education has tremendous face-validity; it has the support of the general public (even if not preferred for their own kids) ("What Do People Think of Us?" 1997). Historically, efforts by general educators to eliminate it or shift its mission in a more general direction have met stiff local resistance from both vocational educators and local employers. Reformers and traditionalists alike would do well to remember that high school vocational education has been the stepchild of the public schools for *75 years*, yet is still little changed.

Second, vocational education represents a significant amount of all high school course work in America. One wonders which curriculum will meet the needs of students who now take vocational education. Using NAVE data, I estimated that about 15 percent of all high school course work in the U.S. is in vocational education. It's important to note that vocational education concentrators tend to be at-risk students. Whether they would be best served in a work-based transition model is arguable, but many still need school-based skills training before they can be safely placed. In the absence of traditional occupational programs, what will the curriculum be for these adolescents: college prep? It also is useful to remember that keeping students from dropping out is still a very sensitive issue at the local level. In some communities, the effectiveness of traditional vocational education in reducing dropouts is reason enough to support it.

Thus, we can predict that traditional vocational education will survive but with a tech prep component. A close look at developments in the mid-1990s provides evidence for this prediction. By that point, many regional vocational schools had moved beyond the two-plus-two concept to a one-plus-one system. In such a system the first year of a technical education associate degree is actually offered in the senior year of high school vocational education. This development is particularly evident in states that have developed regional high school vocational education centers and postsecondary community or technical colleges. Promoting this development is the reality that in many states high school vocational education facilities have better instructional labs than most postsecondary providers. Thus, as states seek to increase the percentage of students pursuing two-year technical education, financial considerations alone will promote a closer union of the two systems.

Thus, I predict that traditional employment-oriented vocational education will persist. Averaging enrollment of all the states, however, will result in the percentage of all students who concentrate in this curriculum hovering around 12 percent nationally. The state of Connecticut provides a good indicator of this. It is a wealthy state where a large percentage of all high school graduates have traditionally gone on to higher education. Yet this Commonwealth also has an effective system of four-year technical high schools, though it serves only 9 percent of state's the high school population.

We can anticipate that of the predicted 12

percent of high school students who concentrate in high school vocational education nationally in the future, typical participants will come from special populations and low-income families. While this is logical because these students are the most likely to pursue full-time employment after graduation, the concentration of this population in vocational education will continue to result in charges of tracking, and so forth. The unknown variable in this enrollment prediction is the current huge number of "general" students who complete neither academic nor vocational programs of study, which has led many states to embark on efforts to eliminate this option. Many of these students are currently quasi-academic students who would benefit from a tech-prep type curriculum. Whether this will swell the ranks of vocational education remains to be seen.

CHALLENGES AHEAD

Regardless of the direction taken by high school vocational education—ETO or traditional/tech prep—it will face at least two persistent challenges: curriculum revision and assessment.

Curriculum. To some extent the mid-1980s to mid-1990s can be characterized as a time of debate regarding whether vocational education programs had the correct curriculum but the wrong students (special needs) or the wrong curriculum for the new population. The debate and resulting curriculum modifications will continue as vocational educators seek to market their programs to more academically able tech prep students while revising the curriculum in many programs to address different occupational objectives that are more in tune with the talents of those now enrolled.

A second curriculum challenge revolves around the question of whether programs should be occupation specific, stressing depth of preparation, or have a broad-based or occupational cluster orientation that stresses breadth of preparation. In this regard, both ETO and traditional/tech prep advocates agree that the objective should be breadth not depth. ETO advocates argue that a broad-based design is best for teaching academic subjects and all aspects of industry (Grubb, 1997). Traditional/tech-prep advocates also argue for broad-based programs because they believe that students' employment opportunities are maximized in today's labor market not by depth but by having entry-level skills in a variety of related occupations that permit them to compete for a greater number of different jobs. Finally, the type of high school technical education relevant to tech prep students is more general in scope (Gray, 1991).

Nevertheless, occupation-specific programs still dominate the structure in at least trade and industrial vocational education. Vocational education facilities were designed for this mission; in many states, teacher certification regulations for trade and industrial teachers are still occupation-specific. In many locales, employers continue to prefer this type of program, which serves them best when and if they need a new employee. Thus, while most agree that a broader approach is preferable, change has and will come slowly.

A final curriculum debate that will shape the future of high school vocational education is the relative importance of work-based learning. Of the three types defined by Hamilton & Hamilton (May 1997) visits to workplaces, work-like experiences, and employment, the last, "employment," is of relevance to this discussion. It is predicted that in the future an ever-growing number of high school vocational education programs will have a "capstone" work-based learning component such as an internship, clinical experience, or actual part-time employment. The rationale for a final work-based experience is based on the (1) documented effectiveness of on-the-job training and (2) rather low placement rates of high school vocational education graduates in the occupational cluster they were prepared for. It is hoped that a final work-based experience for those who will go on to work after graduation will lead to a more effective school-to-work transition system.

Demonstrating program effectiveness. Considering the $1.3 billion federal investment in 1998 alone ("Teachers on Vocational Education," November 13, 1997), we can expect to see pressure to provide evidence of the effectiveness of high school vocational education. Unlike in the past, however, effectiveness is less likely to be based solely on outcomes such as graduation rates, job placement, or annual earnings. In 1993, Congress passed the Government Performance and Results Act, which requires federally funded agencies and programs to conduct performance assessment (Gray & Herr, 1998, p. 273). Earlier Perkins Act requirements contained similar provisions. The objective of performance assessment is to determine students' level of actual skill on completion, regardless of their post-program pursuits. Thus, we can predict that the high school vocational education community will be pressured to develop more effective performance assessment models. While we can assess soft skills, such as math, relatively easily, the challenge will be to develop valid and cost-effective authentic assessment techniques for measuring performance of psychomotor work skills.

A MODERN PHOENIX?

In 1991, the *Phi Delta Kappan* included an article (Gray, 1991) containing the suggestion that high school vocational education has always been a "perplexing issue" for public educators, policy makers, and the public, alike. The article asked this question: Would high school vocational education regain the participation rates of the 1970s and 1980s and thus "rise again" like the mythical Phoenix or would it become a program for students with no hope of a college education. In 1991, the answer was unclear; seven years later the answer is still unclear. Without a doubt, the hopes and dreams of the nation's youth have turned to college, and credentialing for high-skill/high-wage nonprofessional occupations has moved in this direction as well. Ultimately, the direction taken by high school vocational education toward becoming part of this trend will determine its future. By the mid-1990s, successful vocational education programs were adjusting, but it seems appropriate to recall the "old saw" that "only time will tell."

References

Bishop, J. (1989). Occupation training in high school: When does it pay off? *Economics of Education Review, 8,* 1-15.

Bragg, D. (1997). Grubb's case for compromise: Can "education through occupation" be more. *Journal of Vocational Education Research,* 22(2), 115-122.

Bottoms, G. (1997, June). Keeping the future alive for youth in high school vocational studies. (Research Brief). Atlanta: Southern Regional Educational Board.

Dewey, J. (1913). An undemocratic proposal. *Vocational Education,* 374-377.

Fiscal 1998 spending for voc ed, adult ed, and job training. (1997, November 13). *Vocational Training News.* (Alexandria, VA: Capital Publications).

Gray, K. (1989). The role of business and industry in the transformation of the schools. *Journal of Vocational Education Research,* 1-15.

Gray, K. (1991, February). A modern phoenix. *Phi Delta Kappan,* 437-445.

Gray, K. (1997). Seeking a tie that binds: Integrating training and human resource development and teach preparation. *Journal of Industrial Teacher* (4), 81-86.

Gray, K., & Herr. E. (1995). *Other Ways to Win.* Thousand Oaks, CA: Corwin Press.

Gray, K., & Herr, E. (1998).*Workforce education: The basics.* (p. 273). Boston: Allyn & Bacon.

Grubb, N. (1997). Not there yet: Prospects and problems for "education through employment." *Journal of Vocational Education Research, 22*(2), 77-94.

Hamilton S., & Hamilton, M. (1997, May). When is learning work-based? *Phi Delta Kappan,* 677-681.

Hogan, D. (1978, Fall). Education and the making of the Chicago working class. *History of Education Quarterly,* 227-235

Li, J. (1996). *The relationship between demographic and achievement variables and preferences for work among U.S. high school graduates.* Unpublished dissertation, Pennsylvania State University, State College.

National Assessment of Vocational Education. (1994, July). *Final report to Congress: Volume II.* Washington, DC: Office of Research and Improvement, U.S. Department of Education.

National Education Longitudinal Study of 1988. *Second follow-up study.* Washington, DC: U.S. Department of Education, National Center for Education Statistics.

National Center for Educational Statistics (1994, January). *Public secondary school teacher survey on vocational education.* NCES 94-409.

National Center for Educational Statistics. (1996). *The Condition of Education.*

Teachers on vocational education. (1994, January). *Vocational Education Journal,* 26-27.

Thurow, L. (1996). *The future of capitalism.* New York:

Morrow.

Tyack, D. (1974). *The one best system.* Cambridge: Harvard University Press. p. 58.

What do people think of us? (1997, September). *Techniques*, 14-15.

Where is vocational education headed? (1996, November/December). *Techniques*, 24-29.

Kenneth C. Gray *is a professor in the Workforce Education and Development program at Pennsylvania State University, State College. He holds a B.A. in economics from Colby College, an M.A. in counseling psychology from Syracuse University, and a doctorate in vocational technical education from Virginia Tech. Before joining the faculty at Penn State, he was the superintendent of the vocational technical high school system in Connecticut and has been a high school English teacher, guidance counselor, and administrator. Gray has published widely and is frequently quoted in the national press. He is the principle author of* Other Ways to Win: Creating Alternatives for High School Graduates, *the* Phi Delta Kappan *article "The Baccalaureate Game: Is It Right for All Teens," and most recently the* Techniques *article "The Gatekeepers: Will Parents Hear the School-to-Career Message."*

POSTSECONDARY WORKFORCE EDUCATION

By Richard A. Walter and Edgar I. Farmer

EARLY INITIATIVES

Largely due to the USSR's 1957 launch of the satellite Sputnik, attention in the United States at that time quickly focused on a perceived weakness in the educational system's preparation of people for work in technical fields. This resulted in the passage of the National Defense Education Act of 1958. Targeted at addressing the slow rate of construction of vocational education facilities and the shortage of technical workers, the Act was incorporated into the George-Barden Act of 1946 as Title III. Venn (1964) points out that Congress's decision to make Title III an amendment to the existing legislation also subjected the funds to the existing restrictions placed on vocational education programs. This presented four specific challenges to postsecondary vocational education programs. It also is likely one of the reasons for the continuation of the debate regarding "transfer versus occupational" mission of community colleges.

First, as originally specified in the Smith-Hughes Act and as continued in the George-Barden Act, the funds distributed to each state were to foster less-than-college-grade programs. Although the regulations promulgated by the Office of Education permitted two-year colleges to also use the money, many viewed the decision to accept it as equivalent to declaring their programs to be at a lower level than those offered at "genuine" higher education institutions.

Second, since any institution adhering to the funding guidelines could secure Title III money, the distinction between secondary, post-high-school, and postsecondary educational programs grew even more blurred. This further discouraged many higher education institutions from engaging in technical or semiprofessional education.

Third, the technical education programs funded through the Act were administered through the Office of Education's Division of Vocational and Technical Education rather than through the Division of Higher Education. Following this lead, many states chose to administer the funds through their existing boards or agencies charged with supervising secondary-level vocational programs.

Fourth, the funding formula used to distribute federal funds for the states established under the George-Barden Act was not amended to reflect the geographical distribution of defense-related industries. As a consequence, states that reported large rural and farm populations were allocated more Title III funds than states with more industries that needed technical workers.

Nevertheless, Venn (1964) stresses that the National Defense Act resulted in a number of positive outcomes. Since the Act used existing administrative structures, results were produced more quickly than they could be through other new federal initiatives. Thus, many newly trained and retrained technicians were prepared for the workforce, many states completed surveys of occupational training needs that resulted in state plans, and interest in technical education grew and gained focus.

The renewed interest in the need for technical education quickly revealed that the current vocational-technical education system could not satisfy the demands of the workforce. To address this issue, President Kennedy, in his message to Congress on American Education on February 20, 1961, called on the Secretary of Health, Education, and Welfare to convene an advisory group to reappraise the existing federal legislation. The advisory group, known as the Panel of Consultants on Vocational Education, released its official report, *Education for a Changing World of Work*, in the spring of 1963. The report encouraged increased funding and the refocusing of vocational education's mission away from occupational categories to five specific service areas: high school youth; high-school-age youth with academic, socioeconomic, or other handicaps; post-high-school opportunities; the unemployed or underemployed; and services to assure quality.

The Higher Education Facilities Act of 1963 authorized $230 million for construction projects to provide access for the growing numbers of students seeking opportunities through postsecondary education and to address the economy's demands for a skilled workforce. Twenty-two percent of those funds were specifically targeted for community colleges, technical institutes, and two-year branch campuses to facilitate the delivery of occupational preparation programs.

THE ROLE OF POSTSECONDARY VOCATIONAL EDUCATION

The Mission of Community Colleges

On behalf of the American Association of Community Colleges, George Vaughn (1995) asserts that the mission of these institutions is simply to provide the educational opportunities that residents of their service regions want and need. Fulfilling that mission requires that community colleges commit to open-door admissions policies, offer comprehensive curricula, operate as community-based institutions, reward teaching performance, and abet lifelong learning. Vaughn cautions, however, that commitments are not effective unless they translate into actions. Thus, he advises that the mission must be enacted through college transfer programs, occupational-technical programs, developmental/remedial education, community/continuing education services, and student support services.

Brint and Karabel (1989) disagree with Vaughn's inclusion of occupational programs as part of the mission of community colleges. In their book, *The Diverted Dream: Community Colleges and the Promise of Educational Opportunity in America, 1900-1985*, they contend that by offering terminal degrees in occupational programs, community colleges have distorted their mission of transfer education and risk becoming vocational schools rather than institutions of higher education.

In a *Chronicle of Higher Education* article by Robert Jacobson (1993), former Community College of Philadelphia president Judith S. Eaton expresses a similar viewpoint. Eaton declares that by emphasizing training programs, community colleges provide postsecondary education that is not legitimately higher education.

Eaton's comments prompted a letter-to-the-editor response from Leland W. Myers(1993), executive director of the Pennsylvania Commission for Community Colleges. Myers emphasizes the importance of the word *community* and the implications of the terms "community-based" and "community-serving" in the institutions' responsibility to address the needs of the residents of their regions. Thus, according to Myers, both remedial and vocational education programs will continue to be major components of the mission of community colleges.

Apparently, the members of the communities served by Northern Virginia Community College agree with Myers rather than with Eaton. According to Ben Gose (1997), 62 percent of the Ph.D. holders present on that institution's five campuses are *students* rather than faculty or administrators. The president of Northern Virginia Community College, Richard J. Ernst, estimates that 15 percent of the college's students have earned at least a bachelor's degree. Personal circumstances vary, but the underlying motivation for all of those students is the desire to secure job-specific training as a result of continuing changes in the economy and the nature of jobs.

Beckman and Doucette (1992), associate directors of The League for Innovation in the Community College, conducted a study titled *Community College Workforce Training Programs: Expanding the Mission to Meet Critical Needs.* They undertook the study to determine what community-college-based training programs existed, the types of businesses served, how training was funded, and obstacles encountered. Responses from 763 of the 1,042 colleges contacted indicated that

• 96 percent provide customized training programs to meet the needs of local employers, with 20.2 percent being job-specific, and 18.6 percent computer-related.

• 66 percent of the training was provided for employers with less than 500 employees.

• 90 percent of training programs were conducted as part of the institutions' continuing education or community services.

• 35 percent of training was funded by contracts with businesses, 26.9 percent by college operating funds, 16 percent by tuition and fees, and 15.5 percent by state and federal funds.

• 35 percent described inadequate budgets as the largest obstacle to effective training, followed by business's lack of funds (25.3 percent), lack of recognition as a training provider (23 percent), shortage of experienced trainers (22.3 percent), and lack of funds for curriculum development (22.2 percent).

The authors conclude that the survey clearly demonstrates the role community colleges play in meeting the need for lifelong learning that will enhance the country's overall competitiveness in the global economy. However, they also point out that their potential will not be fulfilled without adequate investment in the effort. Community college leaders must incorporate training as part of their fundamental mission to increase opportunities to attract both public and private investments.

However, the best investment is that of human capital to increase the growth and development of stakeholders within their respective communities. For example, according to the National Center for Education Statistics, the percentage of the U.S. population with an associate degree as the highest degree attained has risen from 5.9 percent in 1992 to 7.2 percent in 1996. We know that an educated community leads to a more productive workforce.

Proprietary Schools

Lerner (1987) defines *proprietary institutions* as for-profit schools or colleges, which may be privately or publicly held, that offer occupational programs. The concept of proprietary or private career schools as part of vocational education in the United States has existed for nearly two centuries. However, the growth in both the number of schools and the scope of the curricula offered accelerated after World War II due to increases in the complex technology present in the workplace and to availability of tuition money through the Veterans Education Benefits program. The 1972 Amendments to the Higher Education Act provided an even greater stimulus. Lee and Merisotis (1990) refer to these amendments as a watershed event since they permitted students who enrolled in proprietary schools to participate in the same grant and loan programs as their counterparts at traditional higher education institutions. Likewise, the vocational education legislation permitted secondary-level schools to contract with proprietary institutions to give students access to programs not otherwise available to them.

Proprietary institutions are a major competitor for community colleges since they often provide similar programs of study and are typically not constrained by faculty senates or imposing bureaucracies. Therefore, proprietary schools can more quickly adapt programs and staffing to reflect changes in the local labor market. They also tend to be more flexible in the delivery of courses, offering them as either credit bearing or noncredit bearing, with many offered in a time frame shorter than a semester. Thus, proprietary schools are able to attract students from a broad spectrum of the population—in many cases, people who are not being served by more traditional higher education institutions that provide vocational education. For example, in Pennsylvania, proprietary schools represent a significant source of technical training for citizens and employers. During the 1992-93 school year, proprietary two-year institutions awarded a combined total of 65,052 associate in specialized technology degrees, associate in specialized business degrees, diplomas, and certificates (Pennsylvania Council on Vocational Education, 1995).

Exemplary Programs in Postsecondary Vocational Education

The use of technology has enabled educators in community colleges and proprietary institutions to make a paradigm shift in the way academic instruction is delivered to students in their respective service areas. One such shift is evident in the Colorado Electronic Community College, which was recently developed to deliver community college courses through telecommunications technology. This new development has an accredited curriculum that is student focused and available 24 hours a day, seven days a week. According to Mary Beth Susman, instructors are encouraged to think of themselves as random-access support systems for students who are linked to each other and to faculty through a voice-mail system. A classroom environment is simulated through the creation of a voice-mail network that allows students to complete an associate degree using just a telephone and VCR. Instructors in the Colorado Electronic Community College have real-time office hours over the telephone or through e-mail, at no cost to students (Lazarick, 1998).

Another exemplary program in postsecondary vocational education takes place at the Wytheville Community College (WCC), located in southwestern Virginia. WCC is meeting the educational needs of stakeholders in its rural Appalachian service region through the use of a mobile unit that delivers technological education to several rural high schools. The mobile unit is sponsored by five community colleges in Virginia under the auspices of the WCC Manufacturing Technology Center. WCC president, William Snyder is the visionary leader who is credited with creation of the educational mobile unit. The 34-year-old institution has a degree enrollment of more than 2,700 students.

Other noteworthy programs in postsecondary vocational education are Austin Community College (Texas), Midlands Technical College (South Carolina), Tidewater Community College (Virginia), and Oakland Community College (Michigan). These four exemplary programs are among the 14 model sites identified by the Center for Occupational Research and Development (CORD) under the auspices of the U.S. Department of Education. Austin Community College is member of the Capital Area Tech Prep Consortium which consists of 8 counties and more than 30 school districts (both urban and rural). It has a population of almost one million students. The tech prep curriculum has changed from a 2 + 2 to a 4 + 2 model which leads to an associate degree in a postsecondary technical program. The consortium has involvements with business, industry, and education, including IBM, 3M, Motorola, and Texas Instruments.

In Swansea, South Carolina, nine area

school systems and Midlands Technical College formed the Central Midlands Tech Prep Consortium. The consortium serves more than 2,300 students in the rural bedroom community of Columbia, South Carolina. The students participate in a 4 + 2 + 2 articulation plan that leads to a baccalaureate degree. The consortium has experienced tremendous success over the past two years. For example, the dropout rate has been reduced by 8 percent and the transfer rate to four-year colleges and universities has increased 22 percent.

In Norfolk, Virginia, Tidewater Community College and four urban school districts formed a tech prep consortium using a 4+2 +2 articulation plan with Old Dominion University, Norfolk State University, and Virginia Wesleyan College. The consortium serves a student population that is approximately 60 percent African American, 36 percent Caucasian, and 4 percent Hispanic, Asian, and Native-American. Since the start of the consortium in 1988, students' scores on state mandated TAP tests have increased annually.

The last noteworthy consortium was formed by the Oakland Community College with 27 of the 28 school districts in Oakland County, Michigan. This county ranks as the third wealthiest in the nation among counties with populations over one million. Its wealth comes from automotive manufacturing and other business in the Detroit metropolitan area. The program's success rests on the 4+2 articulation model, which has produced the positive result of approximately 50 percent of all tech prep students transferring to postsecondary programs at Oakland Community College.

Quantitative Data Regarding Postsecondary Vocational Education

Before discussing how many people participate in postsecondary vocational education programs, it is important to clarify terms. According to the 1990 Perkins Act, vocational education can be defined as:

> preparation of individuals in paid or unpaid employment in current or emerging occupations requiring other than a baccalaureate or advanced degree. Such programs shall include competency-based applied learning which contributes to an individual's academic knowledge, higher-order reasoning, and problem-solving skills, work attitudes, general employability skills, and the occupational-specific skills necessary for economic independence as a productive and contributing member of society. (Carl D. Perkins Vocational and Applied Technology Education Act Amendments of 1990, Public Law 101-392, Sec. 521 (41))

Postsecondary programs at the nonbaccalaureate level tend to emphasize the occupationally specific portion of the Perkins' definition. Generally, curricula are developed to provide program completers with a more advanced level of skills than those provided to secondary-level program completers. However, both postsecondary and secondary levels tend to cluster their vocational courses in the following seven occupational program areas: agriculture; business and office; marketing and distribution; health; home economics (family and consumer science); technical; and trade and industry. Because postsecondary vocational education is provided by a variety of institutions, the National Center for Education Statistics (NCES, 1996) has clustered them into the following six categories for comparison purposes: public 4-year; private, nonprofit 4-year; public 2- to 3-year; public vocational-technical institutes; private, nonprofit less-than-4-year; and private proprietary. Even with this clustering, however, the NCES points out that it is extremely difficult to gather accurate data on postsecondary vocational enrollments because of the nature of the students served. Some choose to sample single courses in multiple program areas, some enroll in one or two courses in a single program area to develop specific skills without intending to earn a certificate or degree, and still others declare a major with the intention of earning a certificate or degree. Because most of the data on postsecondary participation are based on attainment of a certificate or degree as a result of program completion, the NCES cautions that the current numbers do not present a total picture. Nevertheless, the data on participation are striking.

According to the NCES (1996), data from the National Assessment of Vocational Education indicate that during the 1989-90 academic year, 5.8 million students were enrolled in postsecondary vocational education; that represents approximately 35 percent of all undergraduate postsecondary enrollments, and approximately 50 percent of the nonbaccalaureate undergraduate population. The largest segment of these students, 60 percent, was being served by public 2- to 3-year institutions, primarily community colleges, followed by private proprietary institutions with 22 percent, public 4-year with 7 percent, public vocational-technical with 4 percent, private nonprofit 4-year with 4 percent, and private nonprofit less-than-4-year institutions with 3 percent. Thus, 4-year institutions were only serving 11 percent of the total number of postsecondary vocational students.

Business programs, with approximately 17 percent of all nonbaccalaureate majors, were the most popular postsecondary offerings during this period, followed in order by technical at 12 percent; health at 11 percent; trade and industry at 8 percent; occupational home economics at 2 percent; marketing and distribution at 1 percent; and agriculture at less than 1 percent. The data also indicate that enrollment patterns vary by the type of institution as well. Business majors were more prevalent at private nonprofit 4-year, private proprietary, and public 2- to 3-year than at public 4-year institutions, while trade and industry majors were more likely to be found at public vocational-technical institutes and private proprietary schools than at all of the other types of postsecondary institutions.

The NCES data also contains information on participation in nonbaccalaureate postsecondary education by members of the targeted populations identified in the Perkins Act. Females comprised 57 percent of the 1989-90 student population, and they were the majority at all but one of the six types of postsecondary institutions. At public vocational-technical institutes participation rate for males and females was approximately equal. Females also represented 54 percent of the total number of students enrolled in vocational majors, with public 4-year institutions being the only category within which male enrollments exceeded female enrollments.

Although the majority of nonbaccalaureate postsecondary students included in the NCES data were white (74 percent), the racial and ethnic percentages tended to vary by the type of institution. At public and private 4-year institutions, public 2- to 3-year schools, and public vocational-technical institutes, approximately 75 percent of students were white. At private proprietary institutions, approximately 40 percent of the students were from a minority group. Almost 66 percent of nonbaccalaureate black students were enrolled as vocational majors, while approximately half of all students were enrolled in vocational programs.

Additional analysis of the nonbaccalaureate postsecondary student data from the 1989-90 academic year by NCES revealed that (1) students from lower-socioeconomic-level families were more likely to report majoring in a vocational program than those from higher-level families; (2) unmarried students with dependents were more likely to report majoring in a vocational program than any other group; (3) academically disadvantaged students were no more likely to report majoring in a vocational program than were non-educationally-disadvantaged students; and (4) disabled students were no more likely to report majoring in a vocational program than were nondisabled students.

In terms of employment, approximately one-half of all the vocational education graduates between the ages of 18 and 34 held jobs in a field related to their technical or occupational training. Moreover, vocational graduates who were employed in a field related to their training were more likely to earn more than $2,000 a month than those vocational graduates who were not employed in their field, based on a survey of income and program participation.

CURRENT AND FUTURE ISSUES

The issue at the forefront of the agenda for both political and economic forums is workforce development. However, if postsecondary vocational education programs are to capitalize on this convergence of interest, three primary issues must be addressed: partnerships, remediation, and transferability.

Partnerships

Articulation, 2 + 2, and advanced credit agreements all exemplify existing partnerships between secondary and postsecondary programs. Unfortunately, most are simply paper exercises that provide few real benefits for enrolled students in terms of shortening the time or credits needed to complete a program of study, providing an integrated curriculum, or presenting opportunities for further study/degrees. Since our society has so successfully promoted the idea that postsecondary degrees are the only way to achieve career success, parents and students now seek career paths rather than closed-ended job preparation. Thus, these limited partnerships are a major liability for postsecondary vocational programs; one that must be rectified since the majority of present and future jobs are in the skilled-labor areas of the workforce—not the professional ones.

Tech prep programs were created to address this liability. They require secondary-level study that consists of rigorous academic and technology courses that are seamlessly linked to career preparation in a postsecondary program of study. While many of these programs tout themselves as successful, closer inspection suggests that of a functional integrated curriculum between secondary and postsecondary institutions remains a major problem. One strategy for addressing this problem calls for reformulating the existing secondary/postsecondary partnerships using national skill standards as the focal point. This approach is being implemented through a pilot project currently underway in Pennsylvania that uses the standards and levels of certification developed by the National Institute for Metalworking Skills (NIMS) Inc. Since metalworking certification is awarded on successful completion of both written and performance tests, the need for standardization and integration of curriculum issues is eliminated. Likewise, the levels of skill development associated with levels of certification provide distinct demarcations in time, content, and facility requirements, thus eliminating the issue of distinguishing between the content of secondary and postsecondary programs.

Postsecondary vocational programs also must reinvigorate their partnerships with business and industry. The traditional practices of begging for resources and inviting representatives to serve on ineffective advisory groups has only served to alienate business and industry. It has also reinforced the perception that educators are unwilling to provide programs that meet the needs of the workforce.

Institutions in Pennsylvania are finding that adopting the NIMS standards has additional benefits. First, use of the standards clearly demonstrates a commitment to preparing individuals for workforce requirements—particularly when NIMS representatives must approve the facility and equipment through on-site evaluation. Second, determination of a student's success or failure on performance tests must be made by a panel of industry representatives, based on tolerances established by NIMS rather than by the instructor or the institution.

Partnership with business and industry can also provide customized instruction. Responding to a need from a local employer, Broome Community College created a certificate program in Applied Technology that consists of six courses designed to enhance employees' job performance. It also provides a base from which they can enter one of the Associate in Technology degree programs offered by the college (Habel, 1996).

Apprenticeship training programs are another type of partnership that secondary programs must consider. A desire to enhance its apprenticeship training programs led the United Brotherhood of Carpenters (UBC) and Joiners to create such a partnership with Pennsylvania State University. As a result, a three-level certification program, combining customized courses and work experience, was created for UBC's apprenticeship trainers. After completing the third-level certification, instructors can continue toward an associate degree and/or a baccalaureate degree.

Like all segments of the educational community, postsecondary programs must defend current funding while trying to secure sorely needed additional funding. Thus, they must build partnerships with federal, state, and local governments to insure that officials at all levels understand the role that vocational programs play in economic development plans. Community colleges must continue to work more with corporate partners to better meet the needs of stakeholders in respective service areas. Currently, partnerships have been identified between the following colleges and businesses:

- Central Piedmont Community College (in North Carolina) and Okuma America
- Cuyahoga Community College (in Ohio) and Ford Motor Company
- Dallas Community College District (in Texas), and the National Corporate Supplier Training Network
- Delta College (in Michigan) and General Motors Corporation
- Foothills-DeAnza Community College District (in California) and Hewlett-Packard
- Humber College (in Toronto) and the Canadian Plastics Training Centre
- Johnson County Community College (in Kansas) and Burlington Northern Railroad
- Kirkwood Community College (in Iowa) and AEGON USA
- Lane Community College (in Oregon) and Symantec Corporation
- Monroe Community College (in New York) and Eastman Kodak Company
- Moraine Valley Community College (in Illinois) and Autodesk, Inc.
- South Seattle Community College (in Washington) and the Boeing Company
- Sinclair Community College (in Ohio) and the Reynolds & Reynolds Company
- St. Louis Community College (in Missouri) and McDonnell Douglas Corporation

Remediation

The remediation of basic skills for high school graduates has become an increasingly large problem for postsecondary institutions, particularly those that practice an "open-door" admissions policy. Jacobson (1993) cites a Center for the Study of Community Colleges report that indicates that about 30 percent of all English courses offered by two-year institutions are remedial. According to statistics from the U.S. Department of Education, there are approximately 612,000 first-time freshmen in remedial courses throughout the higher education system; 63 percent are at public two-year institutions. At these postsecondary institutions, 41 percent of first-time freshmen are enrolled in some kind of remedial course (Lazarick, 1997).

The editors of *USA Today* call for national standards to reduce the crisis that exists in remedial education and some states have taken action. An editorial in the newspaper notes that California has passed legislation to phase out most remedial courses at state colleges and universities by 2007. Florida now requires college students who fail remedial courses once to pay when repeating the classes. In Montana and West Virginia, state legislators want high school districts fined if their graduates can't produce college-level work (*USA Today*, 1997). Remedial and/or developmental education will undoubtedly provoke controversy during the next decade. Postsecondary technical institutions, especially community colleges are in the best position to restore lost academic skills and provide skills that students never obtained.

However, we must also consider other forms of remediation. Employed workers who need to retrain or upgrade their skills and displaced workers represent two additional categories of clientele who need access to vocational programs. For example, Jamestown Community College joined forces with Everywoman Opportunity Center, the Cattaraugus County Employment Training Program, and the Olean

BOCES Center to create a program to prepare displaced homemakers for careers in machining. The community college provided remedial education in math and reading skills, the opportunity center provided support services, the BOCES provided machining training, and the employment and training office provided screening and testing (Crawford, 1993).

Ashley and Kurth (1988) reviewed the available research on displaced worker assistance and concluded that the jobs created by new knowledge and technology will require workers to possess a better mastery of basic skills and higher-order thinking skills. Therefore, they concluded that community college programs should center on providing skills that will make workers less vulnerable to displacement and more prepared to secure good jobs. This can be accomplished, in part, by identifying employment opportunities and the requisite skills and then designing education and training programs flexible enough to serve the clientele.

However, if postsecondary institutions are to succeed in preparing individuals for careers, they must reverse the trends reported by Hoyt and Lester (1995). Their recent survey of 1,046 adults included the findings that (1) the career needs of 18- to 25-year old adults are not being met; (2) only 30 percent had discussed career plans with a counselor; (3) only 36 percent reported making a conscious career choice or plan; and (4) 47 percent reported that their primary sources of career information were television, magazines, and newspapers. Postsecondary institutions need to have resourceful counselors who can help adults understand the new workplace, the relationship between family and work, androgogy, diversity of customers and co-workers (in terms of age, nontraditional attributes, ethnicity, and race), and career assessment tools (Kerka, 1995).

Transferability

Each year an increasing number of two-year postsecondary education students from both technical and college-transfer programs transfer to four-year institutions within their respective service areas. These nontraditional students (average age: 29) frequently balance part-time academic enrollment with part-time employment in pursuit of an associate degree. A *transfer student* according to Cohen (1993), is one who begins his or her college work at a two-year postsecondary education institution, earns a minimum of 12 semester credits within four years, and then transfers to a baccalaureate institution within an additional four years.

Technical and college transfer students usually succeed following their move to four-year institutions. However, they often do not follow a prescribed time frame or plan of study. Nevertheless, they are well prepared for the workplace and preparation is a key objective of these nontraditional students (Cross, 1982; Shearon, Brownlee, & Johnson, 1990).

CONCLUSION

Postsecondary vocational education institutions, both public and proprietary, have been a vital force in ferreting out, responding to, and serving the diverse needs of stakeholders in their service areas. Many of these institutions bridge urban and rural interests; develop partnerships with business and industry; link secondary education, apprenticeship training, and four-year colleges; provide remediation; and upgrade technical skills of incumbent workers to allow them to stay abreast of a highly technical and global workplace.

However, if postsecondary vocational education institutions are to remain viable, they must ensure that program completers are equipped with skills and information that are transferable in two primary ways: (1) through allowing entrance into degree programs that are aligned with a career path and (2) through addressing the requirement of the workplace regardless of where in the nation that workplace is located.

Most high school students indicate that they intend to pursue a college degree to secure a good job. Vocational programs cannot ignore the societal pressure that is shaping the vision held by these students. Therefore, faculty, admissions personnel, and counselors must be able to present their programs as open-ended career paths that give students opportunities to successfully transfer into advanced certificate or degree programs.

References

Ashley, W. L., & Kurth, P. K. (1988). *Displaced worker assistance programs: A review of the research*. Columbus, OH: The National Center for Research in Vocational Education, Ohio State University. (ERIC Document Reproduction Service No. ED 303 593)

Beckman, B. M., & Doucette, D. (1992). Community college workforce training programs: Expanding the mission to meet critical needs [On-line]. Mission Viejo, CA: League for Innovation in the Community College. Available: www.league.org.

Brint, S., & Karabel, J. (1989). *The diverted dream: Community colleges and the promise of educational opportunity in America 1900-1985*. New York: Oxford University Press.

Carl D. Perkins Vocational and Applied Technology Education Act Amendments of 1990. Public Law 101-392, Sec, 521(41).

Cohen, A. M. (1993). *Celebrating transfer: A report of the Annual Transfer Assembly*. Los Angeles: Center for the Study of Community Colleges. (ERIC Document Reproduction Service No. ED 358 877).

Crawford, T. F. (1993). Campus bands together with community organizations to train displaced homemakers to become machinists. [On-line]. Mission Viejo, CA: League for Innovation in the Community College. Available: www.league.org.

Cross, K.P. (1982). *Adults as learners*. San Francisco: Jossey-Bass.

Gose, B. (1997, July 11) Community college in Virginia attracts Ph.D.'s— As students. *The Chronicle of Higher Education*, p. A33.

Habel, K. P. (1996). College industry partnership. [On-line]. Mission Viejo, CA: League for Innovation in the Community College. Available: www.league.org.

Hoyt, K. B., & Lester, J. N. (1995). *Learning to work*. Alexandria, VA: National Career Development Association.

Jacobson, R. L. (1993, July 21). Challenges for community colleges. *The Chronicle of Higher Education*, p. A14.

Kerka, S. (1995). *Adult career counseling in a new age*. Columbus: Clearinghouse on Adult, Career, and Vocational Education. (ERIC Digest EDO-CE-95167)

Lazarick, L. (1997). Back to the basics: Remedial education. *Community College Journal*, 68 (2), 11-15.

Lazarick, L. (1998). Managing the computer invasion. *Community College Journal*, 68 (5), 26-29.

Lee, J. B., & Merisotis, J. P. (1990). *Proprietary schools: Programs, policies, and prospects*. Washington, D.C.: Association for the Study of Higher Education. (ERIC Digest ED 331 338)

Lerner, M. J. (1987). *Articulation between for-profit private occupational schools and secondary vocational programs/colleges and universities*. Information Series No. 315. Columbus, OH: National Center for Research in Vocational Education, Ohio State University, 1987. (ERIC Document Reproduction Services No. ED 284 063)

Myers, L. W. (1993, August 11) The mission of community colleges [Letter to the editor]. *The Chronicle of Higher Education*, p. B4.

National Center for Education Statistics. (1996). *Vocational education in the United States: The early 1990s*. (GPO No. 0-16-048429-4). Washington, DC: U.S. Government Printing Office.

Pennsylvania Council on Vocational Education. (1995). Report to the Pennsylvania Department of Education Bureau of Vocational Education. Harrisburg, PA: Author.

Shearon, R. W., Brownlee, I. A., & Johnson, D. N. (1990). *Student diversity and the emerging workforce: The changing profile of students in North Carolina Community Colleges*. Raleigh, NC: Department of Adult and Community College Education.

USA Today. (1997, November 24).

Vaughn, G. B. (1995). *The community college story: A tale of American innovation*. Washington, DC: American Association of Community Colleges.

Venn, G. (1964). *Man education and work: Postsecondary vocational and technical education*. Washington, DC: American Council on Education.

Richard A. Walter *is currently an assistant professor of education, Workforce Education & Development, Pennsylvania State University, and director of the Pennsylvania Center for Vocational-Technical Education Professional Personnel. In addition, he is the editor of the Occupational Education Forum (OEF), a professional refereed journal in vocational education. His professional career began as a vocational teacher and cooperative education coordinator at the Sun Area Vocational Technical School in New Berlin, Pennsylvania.* ***Edgar I. Farmer*** *is professor-in-charge, Workforce Education & Development, Pennsylvania State University. He has served as director of graduate programs in the Department of Adult & Community College Education and coordinator of Industrial & Technical Education at North Carolina State University. He has worked extensively with school districts, government agencies. and other universities as a consultant in vocational education programs. He has served on the program improvement panel (PIP) for the National Center for Research.*

RECLAIMING A LOST LEGACY: INTEGRATION OF ACADEMIC AND VOCATIONAL EDUCATION

*By Debra D. Bragg**

Recognizing that all students could benefit from a curriculum that emphasizes challenging academic and vocational content, this chapter provides a historical perspective on academic and vocational integration and then explores contemporary factors that have coalesced to make integration a priority of the 1990s. Various definitions and approaches used to implement academic and vocational integration in high schools and community colleges are presented. Though little research has been conducted, the chapter considers what is known about the impact of integration. It concludes with a discussion of current and future issues destined to influence policy and practice.

A HISTORICAL PERSPECTIVE ON INTEGRATION

Around the year 2000, we find ourselves posing questions similar to those posed nearly 100 years ago. Questions regarding how best to prepare young people for fulfilling futures are timeless. In spite of new terminology, many features of the argument remain the same. At the turn of the twentieth century, as now, educators looked forward to remarkable technological advancements and a strengthening global economy. They also faced an increasingly diverse citizenry; growing concerns about youth employment, crime, and safety; and rising disparity in the workforce preparedness of the general populace (Wirth, 1992). Then, as now, the nation debated ways to structure public schools to address the complex issues facing society. As today, many people wanted most of all to enhance the quality of teaching and learning for all students.

Controversy continues to swirl around turn-of-the-twentieth-century decisions about education, and particularly about the call to separate academic from vocational education. Though philosopher John Dewey pleaded for "education *through* occupation" rather than "education for occupation" (Grubb, 1995b, p. 13), the opposing view prevailed in the Smith-Hughes Act of 1917. Following a German model, Smith-Hughes advocated the separation of aca-

**The author would like to acknowledge Darcy McGrath, Sandy Dunkel, and other colleagues on the Illinois Task Force for Integration who assisted in formulating many of the best ideas presented in this chapter. She also acknowledges the insights and inspiration provided by W. Norton Grubb and Norena Badway, two pioneers in the integration of academic and vocational education.*

demic from vocational education, while also asserting a uniquely American perspective. Rather than disconnecting academic and vocational education entirely, Smith-Hughes supported situating both within the comprehensive high school, believing that the growing diversity of the American student population (along with the increasing complexity of American industry) would be best served by having high schools offer both tracks (Wirth, 1992). Early federal legislation (and its successors into the 1980s) therefore played an important role in distinguishing academic from vocational education, creating a tension that has intensified over the years. Distinctions between academic and vocational education were made even clearer during recent debates over educational reform. In the early 1980s, *A Nation at Risk* (U.S. Commission on Excellence in Education, 1983) heightened awareness about the failures of public education, warning that the nation's social and economic security were threatened by a weakening public school curriculum. To address the problems, the report's authors advocated strengthening academics through a "back to the basics" approach that neglected vocational education almost totally. Countering the report's recommendations, the U.S. Department of Education issued *The Unfinished Agenda* (National Commission on Secondary Vocational Education (NCSVE), 1984), which acknowledged problems with America's schools, but pointed to a different solution:

> We should give all students a balanced mix of academic and vocational experience in their high school curriculum. . . . What is really required today are programs and experiences that bridge the gap between the so-called "academic" and "vocational" courses. The theoretical and empirical bases as well as the practical and applicative aspects of academic courses and vocational courses must be made explicit and meaningful. (NCSVE, 1984, pp. 12-14)

For more than a decade, experts have pleaded for a serious re-examination of academic and vocational tracking (see, for example, Oakes, 1991, and Plihal, Johnson, Bentley, Morgaine, & Liang, 1992). Roegge, Wentling, and Bragg (1996) asserted that "the 'vocational' and 'academic' or 'college preparatory' educational tracks have been separated by an ever-widening intellectual, philosophical, and perceptual chasm" (p. 37). Set apart from academic curricula, vocational education can narrow in its focus on immediate job preparation, limiting students' chances of obtaining stable employment associated with participation in postsecondary education. Academic education can also narrow when separated from vocational education, losing its relevance and applicability to current problems and issues that concern students. Though the detrimental effects of tracking are noted widely, particularly for poor and minority students, its positive influence on preparing students for the college prep curriculum by emphasizing rigorous academics for selected students gives it tremendous staying power.

With little change evident in practice, contemporary federal legislation has attempted to bring about a new philosophy concerning academic and vocational education. The Carl D. Perkins Vocational and Applied Technology Act Amendments of 1990 are clear about the importance of integrating vocational and academic education. In large measure, the law primarily intends to raise academic standards for more students. According to Stasz and Grubb (1991),

> The [Perkins II] Amendments require that every program supported by federal funds integrate academic and vocational education in such programs through coherent sequences of courses so that students achieve both academic and occupational competencies (Section 235). Federal legislation therefore provides both the resources for integration and the pressure to do so. (p. 4)

Commenting on the significance of the 1990 vocational amendments, Rosenstock noted that the new legislation "is unlikely to grab the attention of regular educators. But it should. The act is an important step in redirecting vocational education and, ultimately, in restructuring our high schools for the twenty-first century" (1991, p. 434). Wirth concurred: "The curricular structure that characterized vocational education for the past 75 years no longer fits. [New] vocational and academic education should be broadly integrated; vocational education should move from narrow, occupationally specified, skill-based training to instruction in 'all aspects of an industry'; [and] vocational education should forge strong links with economic development efforts in a community" (1992, p. 168). Wirth not only supports the notion of integrating academic and vocational fields, but he suggests other changes needed to make vocational education more meaningful and effective in modern times, including broadening its focus beyond specific jobs and linking it to community needs. Another important feature of the 1990 amendments is the endorsement of academic and vocational integration at both secondary and postsecondary levels, including making it a central feature of new curricular models that build deliberate linkages between high schools and community colleges, called *technical preparation* (*tech prep*). These changes were welcomed by community-college constituencies that advocate a more prominent role for postsecondary education (see, for example, Parnell, 1985). Demonstrating a predisposition for academic and vocational integration, the Commission on the Future of Community Colleges (1988) endorsed stronger linkages between academic and vocational education even before passage of the 1990 amendments, saying, "Only by placing emphasis on *both* can all students help in the building of community" (p. 20).

THE MANDATE TO INTEGRATE

The reasons for integrating academic and vocational education are complex and varied. They are economic, educational, and societal in nature. Set apart, no single rationale can produce a change this far reaching. Brought together, however, disparate factors create a potent package, one forceful enough to challenge long-standing assumptions about curriculum and pedagogy.

A prominent argument for integration lies in its linkage to workforce preparation and economic prosperity. Continuous change—seen as vital to keeping America's economy productive and healthy—puts demands on individual workers and the educational institutions that prepare them. Several national task forces and commissions have raised these concerns, including the Secretary's Commission on Achieving Necessary Skills (SCANS, 1991). The SCANS commission recommended that all students learn work-related competencies, including in their academic courses. Bailey (1995) notes parallels between the tenets of academic and vocational integration and high-performance workplaces, where workers must function in increasingly complex environments. He emphasizes how integrated academic and vocational education can focus on problem solving and cross-functional teamwork. For students to succeed in high-performance workplaces, they need to experience integrated curricula designed to enhance their higher-order thinking and problem-solving abilities (Schell & Wicklein, 1993).

A persuasive argument can be made for academic and vocational integration on economic grounds, but the concept represents more. Many educators (academic and vocational alike) believe that schooling is fundamentally about enabling students to better understand and develop themselves and the world around them as neighbors, family members, workers, consumers, and citizens. For them, seeing academic and vocational integration from only an economic perspective is unduly limiting. Paralleling ideas of John Dewey, integration can become a liberating force, leading to multiple educational goals for all learners (Grubb, 1995a; Wirth, 1992). Recognizing the importance of integrating academic and vocational education to enhance all aspects of education, Badway and Grubb (1997, p. 12) suggested ways of broadening vocational education and strengthening its connection to civic goals by focusing on "citizenship issues such as the role work plays in society, the causes and effects of technological developments, the evolution of American work ethic concepts, the role of individual workers within an organization, the history of occupations and labor movements, or public policies toward technology and employment."

Providing additional momentum to the movement, curriculum integration is occurring on a wider scale. In fact, the need to reintegrate curriculum is not limited to academic and vocational subjects. Starting with the elementary and middle grades and extending into higher education, examples of integration can be found at all levels of the educational system and involve nearly all disciplines. Jacobs reminds us that "the starting point for all discussion about the nature of knowledge in our schools should be a thorough understanding of the disciplines" (1989, p. 7). Each discipline takes a particular perspective and poses unique questions, making learning logical and efficient. In aiming for efficiency, schools may have lost some of their ability to make education relevant. No doubt the disciplines are essential, but they may not sufficiently engage all students in sustained and progressive learning. Integrated curriculum can bring education to life by associating abstract ideas with real-world problems. Research from cognitive science supports this supposition, showing how more relevant, active, and contextualized pedagogy can produce more effective learning for diverse student populations (Raizen, 1989; Resnick, 1987).

Instructional innovations can operate hand in hand with integration activities. Changing philosophies about how faculty and students should interact with one another reinforces a shifting paradigm from teaching to learning (Barr & Tagg, 1995; Boggs, 1995). By borrowing from the strengths of teaching traditions in both academic and vocational arenas, faculty can develop a richer and deeper array of instructional strategies (Rosenstock, 1991). Faculty can therefore better address the wide variety of learning styles and preferences that students bring to the classroom, helping them to become more engaged in learning. New technologies can expand the idea of academic and vocational integration even further by giving faculty and students the opportunity to go beyond the physical boundaries of a classroom and the confines of a calendar (Illinois Task Force on Integration, 1997). The Internet provides a global perspective, linking ideas and information in ways heretofore thought impossible. Virtual reality offers an unlimited arena for integration as it places new experiences at the user's fingertips. Moreover, new technologies can link classroom- and work-based learning. A 1995 report by the U.S. Congress entitled *Learning to Work* points to the importance of creating an adequate telecommunications infrastructure to stimulate the development of computer-simulated work-based learning. In locales separated by distance, time, or other immutable circumstances, technology offers an important way to integrate curricula and connect people with ideas.

Finally, and possibly of greatest importance, curriculum integration can build a sense of community within schools and colleges, although Fullan (1992) reminds us of how difficult it can be to change school culture. Implementing a more collegial and collaborative environment is not likely to happen quickly, but it is a laudable goal of any curriculum integration effort. Where high schools and community colleges work to integrate curriculum, a more supportive atmosphere develops that allows faculty to work together more productively. Thus, curriculum integration helps to bridge the distinct islands that occur in nearly all educational institutions. Through curriculum integration, faculty and students become active participants, motivating them to learn and grow together.

DEFINING ACADEMIC AND VOCATIONAL INTEGRATION

Integration of academic and vocational education has many definitions. *Contextual learning*, *applied academics*, *applications-based instruction*, *interdisciplinary studies*, and *career majors* or *career clusters* are but a few of the most popular names. Refusing to assign academic and vocational integration one particular label, Roegge (1991) argued that

> it is a broad concept which entails the blending together of concepts, principles, and content from 'academic' disciplines (e.g., English, mathematics, science) with context, applications, and/or skills from 'vocational' areas (i.e., industrial technology; agriculture; home economics; business, marketing and management; health occupations). (p. 1)

Bolt & Swartz (1997) think of the integration of academic and vocational education similarly but they use the term *contextual learning,* which they define as

> learning that occurs in the most effective and natural manner, associating classroom theory with real-world application. Learning occurs most effectively when information is acquired in the context of its natural use. . . . Contextual learning seeks to reconnect work and education, curriculum and instruction, different disciplines, and students of various levels and talents. In short, contextual learning is the conduit to applied knowledge. (p. 81)

Applied academics are a specific example of contextual learning. According to Pedrotti and Parks (1991), applied academics are characterized by "the presentation of subject matter in a way that integrates a particular academic discipline (such as mathematics, science, or English) with personal workforce applications (hands-on laboratories dealing with practical equipment and devices)" (p.70). Off-the-shelf or homegrown courses in applied math, physics, and communications such as technical writing, environmental science, or Principles of Technology fit this description (Hull, 1993, pp. 58-59). Courses like these have existed for many years, but their recent adoption has been encouraged by the 1990 vocational amendments, particularly Title IIIE, The Tech Prep Education Act. The implementation of tech prep and applied academics is so consistent, it is nearly impossible to distinguish between the two in some schools (Bragg et al., 1997). Similar to applied academics, applications-based *instruction* uses "knowledge from the academic disciplines to solve concrete problems that workers might encounter" (Pauly, Kopp, & Haimson, 1995, p. 12), often in vocational classrooms or workplace settings. Of course, it is important to point out that these and the previously discussed applied approaches are not only concerned with content, but also pedagogy. Gray and Herr (1995) described applied learning modalities as those that are "active, not passive" and that emphasize "problem solving, knowledge, and skills that are needed by problem solvers" (p. 158). Hands-on or experiential teaching and learning approaches are central to contextual learning and applied academics. In fact, they are essential to nearly any approach chosen to integrate academic and vocational education.

Another way of conceptualizing integrated curriculum comes from the long-standing notion of *interdisciplinary studies,* which are approaches associated with all levels of education. Jacobs (1989) explains that interdisciplinary studies take "a knowledge view and curriculum approach that consciously applies methodology and language from more than one discipline to examine a central theme, issue, problem, topic, or experience" (p. 8). Klein and Newell (1997) extend this perspective by pointing out that "in interdisciplinary courses, faculty interact in designing a course, bringing to light and examining underlying assumptions and modifying their perspectives in the process. They also make a concerted effort to work with students in crafting an integrated synthesis of the separate parts that provides a larger, more holistic understanding of the question, problem, or issue at hand" (p. 404). The interdisciplinary approach therefore offers a broader and deeper approach to curriculum integration.

Finally, *career majors* or *career clusters* go beyond the confines of a course by restructuring a sequence of courses (i.e., curriculum) for a particular group of students, as with tech prep or other school-to-work transition programs (Bragg et al., 1997), or an entire student population (Grubb, 1995b). Career majors/clusters are considered a *systemic* approach to integrating academic and vocational education. They bring the vocational purpose of schooling to the forefront and restructure both academic and vocational education to support it. This approach—so foreign to high schools—predominates in higher education. Consequently, by identifying career majors/clusters in high school, there is a focus for academic and vocational integration that extends to the postsecondary level. At first, career majors/clusters provide the basis for integration using different venues, which range from career academies to magnet schools. Then, at the postsecondary level, learning communities can be developed, using career majors/clusters as the centerpiece of curriculum redesign where students take a series of academic and vocational courses structured to meet degree requirements and to qualify them for full-time employment.

Considering the various aspects of academic and vocational integration, it is also important to point out what integration is not. Quite simply, academic and vocational integration is not intended to be less rigorous or challenging than standard curricula. Creating watered-down courses misses the point. Rather, academic and vocational integration should increase standards by using the context of work, family, and community life (i.e., all aspects of modern life) as the vehicle for engaging students in learning the most central, essential aspects of the academic disciplines. No doubt the future will demand more advanced academics, not less. So, to knowingly weaken academic content would be a serious mistake. Ensuring that all curriculum—both academic and vocational—is highly rigorous and relevant is vitally important to all students.

IMPLEMENTATION OF ACADEMIC AND VOCATIONAL INTEGRATION

The scope and impact of academic and vocational integration varies widely. Some integration efforts require minimal alterations to existing curriculum and methods while others demand extensive restructuring. Recognizing this range of approaches, Stasz and Grubb (1991) referred to academic and vocational integration as a "fuzzy" reform (p. 1), one laden with contradictory goals and ambiguous outcomes. They point out how integration "can result in changing the content of a single course or restructure the way students learn in all courses" (p. 4). Armstrong (1980) offers a schema for classifying curriculum integration, identifying four levels based largely on the degree of faculty and student responsibility for integration. At one end of the spectrum are approaches limited to a particular course. At the other are models affecting nearly all aspects of the curriculum, which more closely parallels the progressive ideas put forth by John Dewey nearly a century ago.

At the first level, students take a selection of courses from different disciplines, but none of the information in them is linked except for the connections the students make themselves. Whatever curriculum integration goes on, it occurs only within courses, creating *within-course integration.* At the second level, courses remain independent, but they are organized to facilitate student learning through a culminating experience offered via a course, project, or work-based learning experience. This second level is labeled *capstone integration.* At the third level, faculty become more involved in the integration process, jointly creating linked courses and programs of study that combine subject matter from different disciplines, sometimes involving team teaching. At this level, we begin to see *cross-curricular integration.* At the fourth level, various fields of knowledge are combined into a new, intellectually coherent entity, referred to as *transdisciplinary integration.* Finally, although not mentioned by Armstrong, another level of academic and vocational integration is possible: *cross-setting integration.* This level encourages integration from high school to college, school to work, or school to community.

Within-Course Integration

In its most limited form, *within-course integration* requires students to select academic courses from a cafeteria-style list to meet graduation requirements. The secondary level includes some vocational offerings, but they are usually elective. By comparison, at the postsecondary level, selection of a major dictates both academic and vocational course selection, but the courses can be sequenced haphazardly, more at the convenience of the student than the logic of the curriculum (Grubb, 1996). Imposing a deliberate sequence of related academic and vocational courses can build curricular coherence, helping both faculty and students to see the underlying logic of the integration strategy. However, within-course integration leaves a great deal to chance since neither faculty nor students may grasp the underpinnings of the curriculum. This limitation need not be confined to traditional courses. Applied academics and interdisciplinary courses can be affected similarly when they are not systemically linked to the overall curriculum.

Applied academics. The method of adding new academic content to vocational courses or supplying vocational content to academic courses is called *infusion* (Grubb, Badway, Bell, & Kraskouskas, 1996). Infusion is used to create applied academics courses involving math, science, and communications/English, presumably because these disciplines have priority under the 1990 vocational amendments. Either purchased from a vendor or developed locally, applied academics are used widely to integrate academic and vocational content. Because of their accessibility, ready-made or off-the-shelf applied academics courses have the advantage of encouraging a quick start-up, but they may do little to restructure the overall curriculum. On the other hand, locally developed applied academics courses can spread the ownership for integration across the curriculum, enhancing the ability of teachers to link different subject matter. Often, however, local curriculum development falters because neither academic nor vocational faculty know enough about each others' subject matter. They also lack a thorough understanding of the fundamental principles of curriculum design, particularly in a collaborative mode.

Though applied academics courses have become quite common, little empirical research has been done to determine their impact on learners. In reviewing the literature on applied academics for the National Assessment of Vocational Education (NAVE), Stasz, Kaganoff, & Eden (1992) found anecdotal evidence in support of applied academics, but few studies having substantial methodological rigor to yield conclusive results. Of the 10 studies reviewed, 4 presented positive opinions from teachers and students concerning applied academics courses; 3 showed improved test scores for students enrolled in applied math or communications, although no comparison groups were used; and 3 showed similar or slightly better student performance using control groups and pre- and post-tests for applied math or Principles of Technology. Cautioning against generalizing these preliminary results, the NAVE study concluded that some evidence exists to support the effectiveness of the Principles of Technology course and, to a lesser extent, applied math, but too little is known about other applied academic courses to draw firm conclusions (Boesel, Rahn, & Deich, 1994).

In addition to the NAVE summary, three recent studies show that students completing Applied Mathematics 1 and 2 over a two-year period performed similarly to students who completed Algebra 1 over a one-year period (Center for Occupational Research and Development, 1994; Keif & Stewart, 1996; Tanner & Chism, 1996). The results suggest applied math can be as effective as traditional mathematics, providing a vehicle for teaching mathematics to students who are unlikely to take algebra without the applied math option. Still, these findings raise concerns about the rigor of the mathematics curriculum, and it is not surprising that a concern with applied academics is whether they will be accepted for college credit and transfer from two-year to four-year college (Hull, 1993, p. 23-24). Though some progress has been made (Boesel, Rahn, & Deich, 1994), the perception that these courses are less than college level hampers their widespread adoption.

Interdisciplinary courses are distinguished from applied academics because they tend to focus less on skill enhancement and to concentrate more on knowledge acquisition and critical thinking. By combining the humanities and liberal arts and sciences with technologies, interdisciplinary courses are created under such titles as History of Technology; Technology and Civilization; Technology and Human Values; Connecting Technology and Our Lives; Science, Technology, and Social Change; The Future of Technology and Work; and The Worker in America (Badway & Grubb, 1997; Bragg, Reger, & Thomas, 1997; Grubb, Badway, Bell, & Kraskouskas, 1996). These courses can be considered a more advanced form of within-course integration because deliberate planning time is required of faculty for collaboration during the course-design process. Team teaching often accompanies interdisciplinary courses, although it is not universal. Administrative concerns also arise, such as the granting and transference of credits since these courses sometimes quality for college credit or transfer (Grubb, Badway, Bell, & Kraskouskas, 1996).

Compared with applied academics courses, interdisciplinary courses appear far less common. High schools and community colleges offering tech prep are more than twice as likely to offer applied academics courses than interdisciplinary courses, although more interdisciplinary courses are being offered each year (Bragg et al., 1997). After evaluating the Mid-American Multidisciplinary Project, a high school interdisciplinary demonstration project involving mathematics, science, and technology education, Schell and Wicklein (1993) reported that students held a strong perception that the project helped them to better understand math, science, and technology subjects. Student enthusiasm related positively to their perceptions of their own ability to think, work in teams, and transfer learning. Despite these encouraging exploratory results, no other studies were found concerning the impact of interdisciplinary courses on student achievement.

Capstone Integration

The approach known as *capstone integration* can strengthen the connections between academic and vocational content by requiring that students combine their learning from various courses and demonstrate mastery through a culminating course, project, or work-based experience. At the secondary level, students often fulfill a capstone experience through a senior project that "consists of a written report, a physical representative of some kind—requiring the use of vocational shops in most cases—and an oral presentation" (Grubb, 1995b, p. 73). Sometimes, in-school learning experiences are supplemented with or replaced by an out-of-school learning experience where students participate in work-based learning. The senior projects at Thomas Jefferson High School for Science and Technology (TJHSST) typify this approach. Students at TJHSST conduct independent research and participate in "internships where classroom theories and concepts are tested in real-life conditions" provided by the school's business partners (Tsuzuki, 1995, p. 138).

Capstone integration also appears at the postsecondary level where occupational certification or licensure can be contingent on end-of-program performance. At community colleges in Columbus and Dayton, Ohio, advanced students complete capstone projects in several technical fields, including the business, computer, manufacturing, and construction arenas (Grubb et al., 1996). At Sinclair Community College in Dayton, students design manufacturing plants, including designing plant layout and materials handling procedures. At Columbus State Community College, students design microcomputer operations for small businesses, which includes designing forms, data entry and retrieval, and hardware and software assessments. Also at Columbus State, students in the construction trades follow a local building project from beginning to completion, enhancing students' understanding of all aspects of the construction industry.

Though evidence of the effectiveness of capstone integration is limited, Tsuzuki (1995) reported positive findings for students engaged in capstone projects in high schools in Delaware and Oregon. Self-report data provided by students showed increased time spent on homework and class work, improved written and oral communications, and improved time management and organizational skills. Tsuzuki also reported positive benefits for teachers, including improved attitudes toward academic and vocational integration and collaborative curriculum development activities. Capstone integration has the added benefit of providing multiple methods of learner assessment, a strategy advocated by educational reforms such as the Coalition of Essential Schools.

Cross-Curricular Integration

Cross-curricular integration is much less prevalent than the previous two levels, partly because it is more deliberate and time consuming to execute. Even so, the degree of interaction can vary, depending on how closely faculty relate their subject matter and coordinate their instructional strategies. Without a concerted effort to plan during joint meeting times, link instruction through coordinated classroom projects, and facilitate learning using related academic and social events, cross-curricular integration can fail. Writing across the curriculum, linked courses, career academies (primarily secondary), and learning communities (primarily postsecondary) are prominent approaches to cross-curricular integration. They demonstrate the range of restructuring possible with cross-curricular integration.

Writing Across the Curriculum (WAC) is an example of cross-curricular integration in which both academic and vocational instructors throughout an educational institution work to incorporate writing in their courses. Successful cross-curricular integration efforts do not happen without serious effort. Teachers implementing WAC must be shown how to incorporate writing exercises in their courses. "The best WAC efforts, therefore, provide instructors some resources to modify their course content, as well as the rationale and peer support to do so" (Grubb, Badway, Bell, & Kraskouskas, 1996, pp. 5-6). Countering the accolades that WAC has received for improving student writing competencies and revitalizing faculty enthusiasm, McGrath and Spear (1991) argue against its practices in community colleges. Claiming that WAC weakens and distorts the disciplines, McGrath and Spear claim, "thinking of writing as a generic learning tool implicitly detaches it from particular intellectual methods, traditions, and disciplines" (p. 123). This criticism illustrates that, as curriculum integration spreads and deepens, the disciplines are bound to be affected, possibly in both positive and negative ways.

Other cross-curricular efforts are evident at both the secondary and postsecondary levels, including Communication Across the Curriculum and Humanities Across the Technologies. Consistent with the broader conception, Illinois Valley Community College (IVCC) infuses integrated modules across the curriculum in the following areas: chemistry in auto tech and agriculture, reading in child care, art in plastics and computer-aided drafting, and computer applications in humanities courses. Special thematic projects allow students from different curriculum areas to examine particular issues and concerns surrounding recycling and rivers (Bragg, Reger, & Thomas, 1997).

Linked courses involve the deliberate connecting of two courses, most often one academic and one vocational. The two courses can be scheduled back to back or simultaneously through a block-scheduling arrangement. Often, however, the courses remain separate, but academic and vocational faculty plan jointly to establish viable relationships between the subjects. Some academic and vocational courses are natural partners, such as health occupations and science, early childhood education and psychology, law enforcement and sociology, and business and math. When the subjects are merged into a new subject such as health sciences or child psychology, this approach is known *as fused integration* (Plihal, Johnson, Bentley, Morgaine, & Liang, 1992). At the postsecondary level, such pairings can provide transfer credit, enhancing the integration of transfer-oriented and vocational courses. A few examples of linked courses at the postsecondary level are the pairings of physical science and engineering materials at Southwestern Community College in Iowa, medical terminology and anatomy/physiology at the Community College of Allegheny County in Pennsylvania (Grubb, Badway, Bell, & Kraskouskas, 1996), and speech and business at the College of DuPage in Illinois (Bragg, Reger, & Thomas, 1997).

Career academies are most evident at the secondary level. They offer an alternative curricular arrangement to the academic, vocational, and general tracks that appear in most high schools. According to Stern, Raby, and Dayton (1992), approximately 150 career academies were offered in the United States by the early 1990s, mostly in California and New York City. However, the 1990 vocational amendments and tech prep and the subsequent School-To-Work Opportunities Act of 1994 (STWOA) have all advocated academic and vocational integration, so more career academics are likely to have developed in recent years. Recognizing some variability in approach, Raby (1995) recommends the following key components for career academies: (a) a core academic program consisting of English, math, science, and/or social studies; (b) technical and workplace skills development through courses that parallel occupations prominent in the local community; (c) a school-within-a-school environment that encourages integration of the core academics and technical courses; (d) a sustained relationship between a cohort of teachers and students over multiple years; (e) strong career development including career guidance, job placement, and assistance with college applications; (f) work-based learning facilitated through effective school/business partnerships; and (g) linkages to other compatible educational reforms, such as tech prep. Nearly 40 percent of tech prep consortia in the United States report that they offer a career academy as a part of their local tech prep curricula (Bragg et al., 1997).

Like other integration models, the research on career academies is limited, but evidence of their impact is positive, especially for students at risk of dropping out of high school. Career academies in California that are designed for at-risk students have shown reduced dropout rates and increased enrollments in postsecondary education (Stern, Dayton, Paik, & Weisberg, 1989). In a review of several evaluations of career academies, Stasz, Kaganoff, and Eden (1992) criticized the research designs and methodology used to study most career academies but still concluded: "Academy programs generally improve student attendance, credits taken, and grade point averages, and decrease number of courses failed and instances of dropping out. These effects are uneven across sites, however. Strongest effects appear in year one, decline by year two, and then disappear by year three" (p. 54). Although, Boesel, Rahn, & Deich (1994) pointed out, "Reduced dropout rates are a cumulative effect of the academies. They are one of the benefits that are not lost even though academy 'effects' fade from year one to year three. This means that although seniors in academies are no less likely to drop out than seniors in control settings, the cohort of academy seniors includes students who probably would have dropped out earlier if they had attended other schools" (p. 96). Hence, career academies have had a net social benefit because of their ability to keep students in school and enhance their later education and employment opportunities.

Learning communities have strong parallels to career academies, but they usually occur at the postsecondary level. They have experienced enormous growth over the past two decades, though their roots extend back to early twentieth century American higher education (Matthews, Smith, MacGregor, & Gabelnick, 1997). Yet, in many community colleges, learning communities have emerged only recently, offering clusters of programs or coordinated courses designed to produce a common core of student outcomes. Grubb, Badway, Bell, and Kraskouskas (1996) argue that

> the most important aspects of self-conscious learning communities are the emphasis on multi- [or inter-] disciplinary study; the de-

> velopment of institutional structures... that overcome the fragmentation of conventional educational institutions; the integration of skills from various disciplines and content areas; and the development of more active approaches to teaching, with seminars, discussion groups, and projects more common than conventional lectures (p. 12).

Students participating in learning communities move through clusters of courses as a cohort (group), and faculty work (and usually teach) as a team to offer courses and programs that combine academic and vocational curricula, with coordinated and unified themes. More complex forms of learning communities *are federated learning communities* where thematically linked courses are taken by a cohort of students and a master learner (usually a faculty member); *coordinated studies* occur when students are taught in an intensive block mode using a central theme and a variety of teaching methods (Schaad, 1997). Learning communities such as these could be used to model workplace realities in an academic setting, although few such learning communities are known to exist.

Learning communities at LaGuardia Community College in Long Island City, New York, are some of the earliest documented in any community college setting. LaGuardia offers a cluster of academic and vocational courses to student cohorts, along with a one-credit integrating seminar to encourage integration across the various courses. Each of the several different clusters operating at LaGuardia adopts a theme such as the one on "Work, Labor, and Business in American Life" (Matthews, Smith, MacGregor, & Gabelnick, 1997, p. 460). Whereas planning occurs throughout the semester, the classes are not usually team taught. Also at LaGuardia, learning communities provide the structure for educational programs offered to welfare recipients (Grubb et al., 1996, p. 13).

Several learning communities appeared in a recent study of academic and vocational integration in the Illinois community college system (Bragg, Reger, & Thomas, 1997). As part of its tech prep initiative, McHenry County Community College pioneered a learning community in an office systems technology (OST) program, the Academy for High Performance. The curricular framework for the Academy provides for cross-curricular integration, work-based learning, college/business partnerships, and up-to-date standards and high expectations linked to industry-based competencies. At another Illinois community college, the College of DuPage, the faculty uses a cluster model in the business program to link seven business and marketing courses to create a flow-of-work simulation. Similarly, Illinois Valley Community College offers the MIMIC (Making Industry Meaningful in College) project where students in business, engineering design, accounting, manufacturing, and electronics form teams to produce, market, and sell a product. A newly developed MIMIC project replicates this approach for students in child care services.

Finally, Black Hawk College in Illinois has experimented with a learning community designed for a small cohort of freshman developmental students, engaging them in a core curriculum along with a one-hour-per-week discussion group. A career decision-making course accompanies four other academic courses to encourage students to focus on their career goals. Faculty act as instructors, planners, and co-learners in most aspects of the program. Research shows positive results for this model, including the heightening of students' abilities to set career goals since most students declared career goals by the end of the semester (Schaad, 1997). Retention was high for students in the program too. Only one of the initial group of nine left college during the freshman year.

Transdisciplinary Integration

Such a level of curriculum integration is achieved only rarely. According to Armstrong (1980), "it demands understanding the epistemologies and methodologies of other fields and, in a team effort, requires building common vocabulary and assumptions" (pp. 53-54).

Jacobs (1989) suggests that transdisciplinary integration goes *beyond* the disciplines. It starts with a problem, and ultimately new knowledge is created to help solve it. This level of integration comes closest to what Mourad (1997) describes as *interdisciplinarity*, or the combining of various disciplines to create new disciplines useful in solving real-world problems.

In a recent issue of *The Review of Higher Education*, Mourad criticized the fragmentation and rigidity of the academic disciplines, challenging faculty to consider the benefits of interdisciplinarity as a new way to create knowledge more applicable to practical problems. If this idea moves from the margins to the center of academic debate, it could impact how teaching and learning occurs throughout the entire educational system. However, little evidence exists to suggest that the integration of academic and vocational education comes anywhere close to reaching this level of innovativeness. Transdisciplinary integration is likely to occur only when faculty and students engage collaboratively in problem solving using new combinations of academic subjects applied to emerging occupational fields. This might involve integrating math and science with new career fields associated with business, engineering, computer science, or health.

Cross-Setting Integration

Thus far, the focus of academic and vocational integration has been within a particular setting, mostly a high school or community college. The emphasis has been on *horizontal integration* (i.e., integration across the curriculum at one level of the educational system), rather than linking various levels, which is referred to as *vertical integration*. With the introduction of tech prep and school-to-work programs came a mandate to sequence a program of study from secondary to postsecondary education and from school to work, extending the possibilities for academic and vocational integration beyond the traditional high school setting.

Though not all tech prep initiatives offer a sequential, integrated academic and vocational curriculum extending from high school through community college, all should and many do (Bragg et al., 1997; Silverberg, 1996). Tech prep therefore provides the mandate, resources, and conceptual format for local educational regions to implement academic and vocational integration. With serious implementation, tech prep can reach a sizable proportion of the student population, using a combination of various curriculum integration approaches. Applied academics courses are a mainstay of tech prep; however, other integration models are also used quite often, especially ones involving the design of new curricula around career majors/clusters. Career academies and interdisciplinary courses are used less often, but their use is growing. To link secondary and postsecondary education vertically, formal articulation agreements are common for vocational curricula, but less so for academic courses. Because of its focus on programs of study rather than particular courses, advanced curriculum articulation has the best chance of creating vertically integrated academic and vocational curricula. Fortunately, more advanced curriculum articulation is reported as high schools and community colleges become more experienced with tech prep (Bragg et al., 1997).

Increasingly tech prep is becoming a vehicle for work-based learning, broadening the idea of tech prep from primarily a school-based reform to one consistent with the STWOA and giving students the opportunity to integrate and apply academic and vocational content in real-world settings. Job shadowing, mentoring, internships, cooperative education, professional-clinical experiences, youth or adult apprenticeships, and school-sponsored enterprises are vehicles for work-based learning that can encourage academic and vocational integration in work settings. According to Bragg and Hamm (1996), "work-based learning offers a means to bridge the gap between theory and practice that exists in many traditional school settings, a gap that diminishes student motivation to learn" (p. 1).

In a national study of work-based learning in community colleges, Bragg and Hamm (1996) identified seven factors that contribute to the success of school-to-work transition programs. Two of the factors involve the integration of academic and vocational education. The first is the importance of having an effective school-based learning component that builds on strong faculty relationships within and across a high school and community college, also optimizing the linkages between student services and curricular activities. "Multiple teaching, learning, and support strategies are very evident in exemplary [school-to-work-transition] programs. Their presence helps to support the notion that teaching and learning associated with work-based learning is indeed practical, realistic, and applied, while also being academically challenging" (p. viii).

The second factor contributing to a successful school-to-work program is the ability to capitalize on innovative teaching and learning strategies by using capstone integration, individualized career plans (ICPs), workplace and in-school mentoring, articulation agreements that enhance vertical integration, and multiple methods of work-based learning, such as co-op along with school-sponsored enterprises or structured internships combined with apprenticeships. Bragg and Hamm (1996) provide persuasive evidence that positive change does not occur because of one intervention alone, but through the use of multiple strategies blended and fine tuned to perform in concert with one another.

CONCLUSION

As in developments that took place a century ago, public education is now trusted with making a positive difference in the lives of youth. However, turn-of-the-twentieth-century political decisions about the structure of the high-school curriculum have produced questionable results, encouraging widespread calls for reform to ensure that the needs of all students are met. The Carl D. Perkins Vocational and Applied Technology Act Amendments of 1990; Title IIIE, The Tech Prep Education Act; and later the School-to-Work Opportunities Act of 1994 are three recent federal responses to the educational reform mandate that have attempted to strengthen all of education—but particularly vocational education—through academic and vocational integration.

Without a precise legislative recipe for academic and vocational integration, many definitions, models, and approaches have evolved, at both the secondary and postsecondary levels. The wide variation of approaches to curriculum integration emerges for numerous reasons, but mostly to address the issues and problems associated with local communities, economics, educational systems, and demographic needs. Thus far, in many locations academic and vocational integration is confined to particular courses, usually applied academics courses. In a few communities, however, curriculum integration has evolved to encompass broader interdisciplinary, cross-curricular, or cross-setting strategies. Using career majors/clusters, career academies, learning communities, tech prep, or school-to-work as vehicles for curriculum restructuring, some high schools and community colleges are beginning to tackle the larger issue of separate and unequal tracking that plagues so many of America's schools. Although the examples are limited, additional time and persistence may produce far-reaching changes. Therefore, public policies that support approaches to academic and vocational integration proven to enhance students' educational and economic outcomes are most desirable.

At the local level, academic and vocational integration cannot be effective without strong, sustained administrative support. This holds particularly true for more advanced integration models that encourage complex curricular designs involving many teachers and students, multiple disciplines, various levels of the educational system, and alternative school and work settings. To develop successful practices often requires changes in schedules, internal and external curriculum review, and new accountability and outcomes measures. Meaningful and lasting change always requires a commitment of resources, dedicated faculty planning time, and active and collaborative professional development. Again, public policy must continue to provide the support needed to make academic and vocational integration successful.

Considering developments throughout the twentieth century, it is no wonder that Grubb (1995a) referred to academic and vocational integration as a "historical legacy" (p.21). Though that idea has appeal, it may vastly overstate the role academic and vocational integration (especially vocational education) has played in public education. If integration is indeed a historical legacy, it seems to be one that has been neglected or at least obscured by misunderstood and misdirected policy and practice. Yet, the 1990s have produced new legislation and different ways of thinking. New approaches to teaching and learning may indeed be emerging, heightening the opportunity to reclaim a lost legacy.

References

Armstrong, R. (1980). Faculty development through interdisciplinarity. *Journal of General Education, 32(*1), 53-63.

Badway, N., & Grubb, N. W. (1997). *Curriculum integration and the multiple domains of career preparation. A sourcebook for reshaping the community college.* Berkeley, CA: National Center for Research in Vocational Education, University of California at Berkeley.

Bailey, T. (1995). The integration of work and school. In W. N. Grubb (Ed.), *Education through occupations in American high schools: Vol. I* (pp. 26-38). New York: Teachers College Press.

Barr, R. B., & Tagg, J. (1995, November/December). From teaching and learning: A new paradigm for undergraduate education. *Change, 27*(6), 13-25.

Boesel, D., Rahn, M., & Deich, S. (1994, July). *National Assessment of Vocational Education, Final report to Congress: Vol. II, Program improvement: Education reform.* Washington, DC: U.S. Department of Education, Office of Educational Research and Improvement.

Boggs, G. R. (1995, December/January). The learning paradigm. *Community College Journal,* 66(3), 24-27.

Bolt, L., & Swartz, N. (1997). Contextual curriculum: Getting more meaning from education. In E. Farmer & C. Key (Eds.), School-to-work systems: The role of community colleges in preparing students and facilitating transitions (pp. 81-88), *New Directions for Community Colleges,* 97. San Francisco, CA: Jossey-Bass, Inc.

Bragg, D., & Hamm, R. (1996, April). *Linking college and work: Exemplary policies and programs of two-year-college work-based learning programs* (MDS-795). Berkeley, CA: National Center for Research in Vocational Education, University of California at Berkeley.

Bragg, D., Puckett, P., Reger, W., Thomas, H. S., Ortman, J., & Dornsife, C. (1997, December). *Tech prep/school-to-work partnerships: More trends and challenges* (MDS-1078). Berkeley, CA: National Center for Research in Vocational Education, University of California at Berkeley.

Bragg, D., Reger, W., & Thomas, S. (1997, October). *The integration of academic and vocational education by Illinois community colleges.* Paper presented at the annual conference of the National Center for Occupational Education, San Antonio, Texas.

Center for Occupational Research and Development. (1994). *A report on the attainment of algebra 1 skills by completers of mathematics I and 2.* Waco, TX: Author.

Commission on the Future of the Community College. (1988). *Building communities:* A *vision for a new century.* Washington, DC: American Association of Community and Junior Colleges.

Fullan, M. (1992). *Successful school improvement.* Bury St. Edmunds: St. Edmundsbury Press.

Gabelnick, F., MacGregor, J., Matthews, R., & Smith, B. (1990). Learning communities: Creating connections among students, faculty, and disciplines. *New Directions for Teaching and Learning,* 41. San Francisco, CA: Jossey-Bass, Inc.

Gray, K. C., & Herr, E. L. (1995). *Other ways to win: Creating alternatives for high school graduates.* Thousand Oaks, CA: Corwin Press.

Grubb, W. N. (1995a). The cunning hand, the cultured mind: Sources of support for curriculum integration. In W. N. Grubb (Ed.), *Education through occupations in American high schools. Approaches to integrating academic and vocational education: Vol. 1* (pp. 11-25). New York: Teachers College Press.

Grubb, W. N. (1995b). A continuum of approaches to curriculum integration. In W. N. Grubb (Ed.), *Education through occupations in American high schools: Approaches to integrating academic and vocational education. Volume I* (pp. 59-81). New York: Teachers College Press.

Grubb, W. N. (1996). *Working in the middle: Strengthening education and training for the mid-skilled labor force.* San Francisco: Jossey-Bass.

Grubb, W. N., Badway, N., Bell, D., & Kraskouskas, E. (1996). *Community college innovations in workforce preparation: Curriculum integration and tech-prep.* Mission Viejo, CA: A joint publication of the League for Innovation in the Community College, National Center for Research in Vocational Education, and National Council for Vocational Education.

Grubb, W. N. (1997). Not there yet: Prospects and problems for "education through occupations". *Journal of Vocational Education Research, 22*(2), 77-94.

Hull, D. (1993). *Opening minds, opening doors: The rebirth of American education.* Waco, TX: Center for Occupational Research and Development.

Illinois Task Force on Integration. (1997). *Academic and occupational integration at the community college.* Springfield, IL: Illinois Community College Board.

Jacobs, H. H. (Ed.). (1989). *Interdisciplinary curriculum: Design and implementation.* Alexandria, VA: Association for Supervision and Curriculum Development.

Keif, M. G., & Stewart, B. R. (1996). A study of instruction in applied mathematics: Student performance and perception. *Journal of Vocational Education Research, 21*(3), 31-48.

Klein, J. T., & Newell, W. H. (1997). Advancing interdisciplinary studies. In J. G. Gaff, J. L. Ratcliff, and Associates (Eds.), *Handbook of the undergraduate curriculum* (pp. 393-415). San Francisco, CA: Jossey-Bass, Inc.

Matthews, R. S., Smith, B. L., MacGregor, J., & Gagelnick, F. (1997). Creating learning communities. In J. G. Gaff, J. L. Ratcliff, and Associates (Eds.), *Handbook of the undergraduate curriculum* (pp. 457-475). San Francisco, CA: Jossey-Bass.

McGrath, D., & Spear, M. B. (1991). *The academic crisis of the community college.* Albany, NY: State University of New York.

Mourad, R. P. (1997, Winter). Postmodern interdisciplinarity. *The Review of Higher Education, 20*(2), 113-140.

National Commission on Secondary Vocational Education. (1984). *The unfinished agenda.* Columbus, OH: National Center for Research in Vocational Education, Ohio State University.

Oakes, J. (1991, November). *Blurring academic and vocational boundaries: Barriers in the cultures of large high schools.* Paper presented at the meeting of the Southern Regional Education Board, Atlanta, GA.

Pauly, E., Kopp, H., & Haimson, J. (1995). *Homegrown lessons: Innovative programs linking school and work.* San Francisco: Jossey-Bass.

Parnell, D. (1985). *The neglected majority.* Washington DC: Community College Press.

Pedrotti, L., & Parks, D. (l991). A solid foundation: The role of applied academics. In D. Hull & D. Parnell (Eds.), *Tech prep associate degree: A win/win experience* (pp. 63-86). Waco, TX: Center for Occupational Research and Development.

Plihal, J., Johnson, M. A., Bentley, C., Morgaine, C., & Liang, T. (1992, July). *Integration of vocational and academic education. Theory and practice* (MDS-065). Berkeley: National Center for Research in Vocational Education, University of California at Berkeley.

Raby, M. (1995). The career academies. In W. N. Grubb (Ed.), *Education through occupations in American high schools: Approaches to integrating academic and vocational education. Vol. 1* (pp. 82-96). New York: Teachers College Press.

Raizen, S. A. (1989). *Reforming education for work. A cognitive science perspective* (MDS-024. Berkeley: National Center for Research in Vocational Education, University of California at Berkeley.

Resnick, L. B. (1987). Learning in school and out. *Educational Research, 16,* 13-20.

Roegge, C. (1991, July). *Setting the stage. A practitioner's guide to integrating vocational and academic education.* Springfield, IL: Illinois State Board of Education.

Roegge, C., Wentling, T., & Bragg, D. (1996, Fall). Using tech prep principles to improve teacher education. *Journal of Vocational and Technical Education, 13(1),* 30-41.

Rosenstock, L. (1991, February). The walls come down: The overdue reunification of vocational and academic education. *Phi Delta Kappan, 72*(6), 434-435.

Secretary's Commission on Achieving Necessary Skills (SCANS). (1991). *What work requires of schools: A SCANS report for America 2000.* Washington, DC: U.S. Department of Labor.

Schaad, D. (1997). *The social and academic integration of community college students participating in a freshman learning community.* Unpublished doctoral dissertation, University of Illinois at Urbana-Champaign.

Schell, J. W., & Wicklein, R. C. (1993). Integration of mathematics, science, and technology education: A basis for thinking and problem solving. *Journal of Vocational Education Research, 18*(3), 49-76.

Silverberg, M. (1996). *The continuing development of local tech-prep initiatives.* Washington, DC: U.S. Department of Education.

Stasz, C., & Grubb, W. N. (1991, November). *Integrating academic and vocational education: Guidelines for assessing a fuzzy reform* (MDS-375). Berkeley: National Center for Research in Vocational Education, University of California at Berkeley.

Stasz, C., Kaganoff, T., & Eden, R. (1992). *Integrating academic and vocational education.* Santa Monica, CA: Rand Corporation.

Stern, D., Dayton, C., Paik, I., & Weisberg, A. (1989). Benefits and costs of dropout prevention in a high school program combining academic and vocational education: Third-year results from replications of the California Peninsula Academies. *Educational Evaluation and Policy Analysis, 11*(4),405-416.

Stern, D., Raby, M., & Dayton, C. (1992). *Career academies: Partnerships for reconstructing American high schools.* San Francisco: Jossey-Bass.

Tanner, C. K., & Chism, P. J. (1996). A comparison of student achievement in applied mathematics for tech prep and algebra 1. In R. Joyner (Ed.), *Proceedings of the Vocational Special Interest Group, American Education Research Association 1996 Annual Meeting* (pp. 95-107). Greenville, NC: East Carolina University.

Tsuzuki, M. (1995). Senior projects: Flexible opportunities for integration. In W. N. Grubb (Ed.), *Education through occupations in American high schools: Approaches to integrating academic and vocational education: Volume I* (pp. 134-147). New York: Teachers College Press.

U.S. Commission on Excellence in Education. (1983). *A nation at risk.* Washington D.C.: U.S. Government Printing Office.

U.S. Congress, Office of Technology Assessment. (1995, September). *Learning to work. Making the transition from school to work* (OTA-HER-637). Washington, DC: U.S. Government Printing Office.

Wirth, A. (1992). *Education and work for the year 2000.* San Francisco: Jossey-Bass.

Debra D. Bragg is an associate professor in the College of Education at the University of Illinois at Urbana-Champaign. She holds a joint appointment in the Department of Human Resource Education and the Department of Educational Organization and Leadership. Dr. Bragg is currently a site director and principal investigator of a national study of tech prep policy and implementation for the National Center for Research in Vocational Education, University of California at Berkeley.

PART IV: SPECIAL TOPICS

Work is love made visible.—Kahlil Gibran

15

VOCATIONAL TEACHER EDUCATION

By Curtis R. Finch

OVERVIEW

In a comprehensive review of research in vocational technical teacher education, Jerome Moss, Jr. (1967) noted that "[a]t present, we are still operating [vocational teacher education] programs primarily on the basis of tradition, 'conventional' wisdom, and personal experience" (p. 26). Thirty years later, it was noted in an ERIC Clearinghouse paper focusing on vocational teacher education reform (Naylor, 1997) that the debate over what to change and how to pursue reform in vocational teacher education still existed. It appears that the task of moving vocational teacher education from a traditional field largely grounded in the past to one that can recreate itself to meet current and future teacher, student, and workplace needs still needs to be completed.

In this chapter, vocational teacher education is examined and critiqued from several different perspectives: what the field has been, where it is today, and how it may prepare for the future. Discussion begins with a brief glimpse of both vocational education's and vocational teacher education's evolution from the early years to the present day and the impact educational reform has had, and will continue to have, on this evolution. Next, progress made in describing what vocational teacher education can be is highlighted. And finally, several teacher preparation and development issues and concerns that should be addressed in the future are presented.

EVOLUTION AND REVOLUTION

Although vocational teacher preparation has a long and rich history, its transformation from an informal process of conscious imitation to formal bachelor's and graduate degree programs continues to evolve. Recent legislation and mandated educational reform have hastened that evolution, especially in areas impacting directly on teacher preparation and development. These changes are considered by some people to be more revolution than evolution. However, others believe reform offers tremendous opportunities to reinvent vocational teacher education for the twenty-first century.

A Rich History

Vocational teaching and teacher preparation have existed in one form or another for thousands of years. As early as 2100 B.C., apprenticeship served as a principal means of preparing to become a master in a trade or craft. Typically the apprentice would live in a master's home and be taught a trade or craft over a two- to seven-year period. Masters were typically obligated to provide the apprentice with the same religious, moral, and civic instruction that they gave their own children (Bennett, 1926).

In this context, the master served as a teacher-leader-worker and as such "had responsibility for developing the whole individual; one who was competent in a trade or craft and would be a contributing member of society" (Finch & McGough, 1991, p. 4). As different employers began to require completion of some formal education as a prerequisite to employment, increased workforce education requirements eventually led to the establishment of higher education institutions. These also included teacher preparation instutions that were initially called *normal schools*.

During the late 1800s and early 1900s, several manual-training normal schools were established that offered formal programs for the preparation of vocational teachers. However, these programs were more the exception than the rule, with most vocational teacher preparation being at its least, nonexistent, and at its best, of mixed quality. A net result was great inconsistency in the quality of vocational teachers (Finch & Crunkilton, 1993, p.6).

By 1900, a rather strong national public sentiment for federal aid to vocational education had developed. As the need for skilled workers increased, industrialists and labor leaders believed that a new national policy could be the starting point to improve quality in preparing persons for skilled positions in the workplace. These feelings were formally presented to the federal government through national organizations. Groups such as the National Society for the Promotion of Industrial Education and the Association of Agricultural Colleges and Experiment Stations led the battle to obtain federal aid for vocational education (Finch, 1991a).

However, the movement to secure federal support was not without controversy. Pressure to institute vocational education legislation in the United States stimulated a debate between those who believed public schools were places where only liberal studies should be taught and those who believed vocational education should be incorporated into the public school curriculum. The choice at that time was "whether schools are to become servants of technocratic efficiency needs, or whether they can act to help [persons] humanize life under technology" (Wirth, 1972, p. 1).

Charles Prosser, a nationally recognized vocational education leader, strongly supported the idea of social efficiency, which contends that American schools should be reformed to meet the needs of a technocratic society. Philosopher John Dewey believed that the industrial education movement of the day had some positive potential but felt it should prepare the way for a humane technological society, "a place where science, technology, and democracy would complement each other" (Wirth, 1972, p. 3). Dewey closely monitored the movement, examined the proposed legislation, and spoke out against certain of its aspects. For example, he strongly opposed dualism, which was, in effect, the separation of academic and vocational education programs.

Eventually, legislators supported federal legislation that would provide each state with financial assistance in the establishment of vocational education offerings. The result of this effort was passage of the Smith-Hughes Act in 1917, the first less-than-university-level vocational education legislation in the United States. This landmark vocational education legislation provided federal funding in support of agriculture, trade and industrial, and home economics programs. Unfortunately for Dewey, it was his adversary, Prosser, who ultimately became the primary author of the Smith-Hughes Act (Finch, 1997b). Prosser's involvement in the legislation insured that it included some funding in support of vocational teaching and administrative activities, thus initiating the formal separation of vocational and academic teaching and teacher education.

The Prosser philosophy became firmly imbedded in the Smith-Hughes Act, and for almost 50 years, related legislation remained virtually unchanged. Even though a number of different vocational education laws followed the Smith-Hughes Act, the Vocational Education Act of 1963 was the first to reflect a significant philosophical shift from the 1917 legislation. Essentially, the 1963 Act stipulated a more comprehensive approach to vocational education and demonstrated for the first time a total federal commitment to funding vocational education. Subsequent legislation further demonstrated the strong federal commitment to support vocational education and to maintain it as a system that was to a great degree separate from academic education (Finch & McGough, 1991)

A World Turned Upside Down

Formal federal recognition of the need for national emphasis on school-to-work transition originated with the Carl D. Perkins Vocational and Applied Technology Education Act of 1990 (Perkins II). This legislation, which is grounded in the notion that the United States is falling behind other nations in its ability to compete in the global marketplace, reflects the evolution of federal support for vocational education. Among its various provisions, the Perkins II legislation offered the 50 states financial incentives to create and operate education programs that have as their goal producing workers who function more effectively, thus increasing United States competitiveness in the current and future international workplace.

The Perkins II legislation ushered in a new era of preparing students to enter and succeed in the workplace. For example, the law shifted emphasis from reactive and rigid vocational education curriculum and instructional models to those emphasizing innovation, flexibility, and collaboration. In contrast with earlier laws that contributed to a wide separation between academic and vocational education, the Perkins II legislation supported the integration of academic and vocational studies. Also included in the Act were provisions for using tech prep to formally link high school and post-high school technical studies in creative ways. Since the legislation enabled educators to become more proactive and less reactive in the design and implementation of vocational education programming, it has provided them with many implementation challenges (Finch, 1997b, p. 72).

From the vantage point of teacher education reform, the Perkins II legislation is most significant. For the first time in over 70 years, a major philosophical shift in vocational education legislation had occurred. A review of the Perkins II Act reveals that Prosser's philosophical beliefs, such as social efficiency and educational dualism, have given way to Dewey's philosophical views, including the creation of a more humane technological society and providing schooling that focuses on collaboration in meeting students' technological and humanistic needs.

As Jennings (1991) noted, the Perkins II legislation was designed to assist vocational education in playing a leadership role through "channeling federal money to programs that integrate academic and vocational education, targeting money more carefully toward programs that produce results, emphasizing programs that serve poor and otherwise disadvantaged people, and easing state regulatory burdens by pushing authority down to the local level" (p. 18).

From a more pragmatic point of view, the legislation has stimulated all educators to rethink what they have been doing for so many years, discover new ways to design more relevant curricula, and provide more meaningful integrated and articulated instruction (Finch, 1997a). This legislative shift has likewise provided vocational teacher educators with opportunities to reconsider ways that vocational teacher education might change to meet the current and future needs of vocational teachers and their students.

As expected, the rethinking process has been very traumatic, and reaction has been varied. Some vocational education administrators have considered retrofitting mandates so they would align with existing programs. Some vocational teachers have wondered how they might avoid getting involved in collaborative curriculum and instruction efforts with teachers of academic subjects. And some vocational teacher educators have begun wishing for the good old days when it appeared that teacher preparation was not so complex.

For all these groups, a fundamental problem with Perkins II legislation has been that, to paraphrase a famous British tune, it turned the world upside down. Some people believe the educational reform described in Perkins II has thrown out over 70 years of traditional vocational education. However, others have viewed this legislation as a tremendous opportunity to change from an outdated system to one that will better serve students who are preparing to enter the world-class workplace.

SEVERAL STEPS FORWARD

During the past decade, both the need and the opportunities have existed to reform vocational teacher education. In some locations, educators have accepted the challenge to change and the effect has been positive. In other locations, educators have not embraced change and results have been disappointing. In light of major concern about change, several developments that reflect change in vocational teacher education are highlighted. They include the impact of educational reform, vocational teacher education program focus, the delivery of vocational teacher education, and vocational teacher supply and demand.

Educational Reform

Legislation in the 1990s has provided educators with a useful starting point from which to reform education. Among changes supported by Perkins II and/or the School-to-Work Opportunities Act are tech prep; the integration of academic and vocational education; linking school- and work-based learning in meaningful ways; school-to-work transition; and building strong alliances between schools, the workplace, and the community.

How have educators in general and teachers in particular coped with these reforms? Results of the most recent National Assessment of Vocational Education (Office of Research, 1994) revealed that four years after passage of the Perkins II legislation, much resistance still existed to the implementation of both tech prep and integration. In addition, most secondary vocational education programs were still quite traditional in both focus and operation, and educators were trying to fit reforms to their existing curricula.

These results come as no great surprise considering that teachers had never been prepared to work with educational reform extending beyond involvement on an individual basis. Since Perkins II and the School-to-Work Opportunities Act both called for reform that actively engages teachers in both horizontal collaboration (across teacher content areas as well as across schools, workplaces, and communities) and vertical collaboration (across education levels including high schools, community and technical colleges, and universities), it is clear that vocational teachers engaged in these reforms must develop new capabilities. When legislation was first enacted, questions were raised about what these new teacher capabilities were and how they might be developed.

Fortunately, research conducted over the past several years has identified a set of new capabilities all teachers (both vocational and academic) will need and how these needs may be met. A study focusing on teachers' roles in the integration of vocational and academic education documented experiences of vocational and academic teachers, principals, other administrators, and counselors who had successfully implemented integration in their schools (Schmidt, Finch, & Faulkner, 1992). Based on this research, professional development approaches that educators can use to facilitate the integration of vocational and academic education were described (Finch, Schmidt, & Faulkner, 1992). These approaches can assist educators in learning to function as members of professional teams, including teams operating within and across institutions.

Case studies that build on the integration

research were prepared to aid educators in developing problem-solving, decision-making, and team-building skills as they implement integration in their schools (Schmidt, Finch, Faulkner, and Kandies, 1995). The cases are organized into four functional themes: (1) Cooperative Efforts, (2) Curriculum Strategies, (3) Instructional Strategies, and (4) Administrative Practices and Procedures. The 46 cases have been field-tested with more than 12 different instructors and more than 400 participants.

Teacher involvement and contributions to school-to-work transition was the focus of a more recent study (Schmidt, Finch, & Moore, 1997). It was posited in the research that teachers engaged in school-to-work transition activities would have a wide range of new and different responsibilities. In the study, teacher activities were identified that contribute to school-to-work success as well as characteristics teachers must have to conduct successful school-to-work programs. Results based on interviews with almost 200 educators and business, industry, and community representatives have numerous implications for the field.

A companion report details strategies that may be employed to meet teachers' professional development needs as they implement school-to-work transition (Finch, Schmidt, & Moore, 1997). Thirteen areas of professional development practice were identified and described in the words of teachers who participated in them and others who were aware of teachers who engaged in different practices. Collectively, these reports offer new ways of conceptualizing how professional development links with educational reform and provide examples and cases that may be used to assist both academic and vocational teachers as they prepare to work in reform contexts.

Program Focus

In response to economic developments, changing legislation, learning research, and other findings and concerns, vocational teacher educators have begun to rethink what the focus of vocational teacher preparation should be. Some of this rethinking has been based on research and some shaped through writing and discussions. Several examples of ways vocational teacher education programs may be reconfigured are offered. Each example has a somewhat different focus; however, collectively they capture the range of potential possibilities available to vocational teacher educators who want their programs to be focused in more meaningful and productive ways.

Principles Underlying Vocational Teacher Education. Principles that can serve as a foundation or framework for vocational teacher education have been examined and debated for some time and much progress has been made. The most comprehensive effort in this area has been conducted by Richard Lynch. Over a period of several years, relevant materials were examined and University Council for Vocational Education representatives met and discussed draft statements. The result was formulation of 10 principles that can serve as a new foundation for vocational teacher education (Lynch, 1996,1997). The principles are as follows:

1. Faculty are committed to their students and to students' professional development as lifelong learners.

2. Faculty use curriculum and instructional techniques to integrate theory with practice, academic and workforce education, professional education and subject matter, and learning theory and workforce preparation.

3. Faculty understand the philosophy, contemporary concepts, research, effective practice, and methods of inquiry related to workforce preparation and development.

4. Faculty use dynamic pedagogy, based on learning theory and practices appropriate for youth and adults.

5. Faculty are partners in learning communities through which they model collaboration and democratic processes for their students.

6. Programs are dynamic and change oriented.

7. Programs are grounded in academic education, workplace subject matter, workplace

processes, technology, professional education and pedagogy, and clinical experiences.

8. Programs reflect cultural diversity.

9. Colleges and universities (and their inherent administrative structures) that offer programs to prepare vocational and technical teachers are committed to such preparation and provide adequate resources to sustain them at high quality levels.

10. Colleges and universities provide a clearly identified group of academic and clinical faculty for whom vocational and technical teacher education is a top priority (Lynch, 1996, p. 77-87).

These principles provide meaningful directions for all aspects of vocational teacher education, extending from curricula to assessment. Hopefully, they will be seriously considered for adoption by all universities that prepare vocational teachers.

Linking Vocational Teacher Education to Workplace Changes. Major consideration for technological changes in the workplace has typically been omitted from vocational teacher education program planning. As Brown and Davison (1991) commented, "society is experiencing rapid changes that are impacting both educational institutions and businesses. Teacher educators must improve their awareness and understanding of these changes to [prepare] vocational teachers who can function more effectively" (p. 285). They then described areas that need to be addressed by educators who intend to reform vocational teacher education programs so they are more closely linked with technological changes in the workplace. Examples of these areas include the following:

• Programs must be more closely aligned with changes in the workplace and workers' job opportunities and needs.

• Vocational teachers should become skilled as "change agents" to help students develop knowledge, skills, and attitudes needed by a diverse workforce that will be functioning within an increasingly competitive, global economy.

• Teachers and students must adapt quickly and effectively to changes in their immediate and global environments. Research is needed to identify these skills and the methods to teach them to teachers.

• Vocational educators must be trained and encouraged to use instructional methods that strengthen the work skills of a wider array of students (Brown & Davison, 1991, p. 292).

A key implication from these statements is that vocational teacher educators must prepare teachers who are sensitive to workplace changes and who can rapidly include these changes in their vocational education curricula. Unfortunately, the extent to which this is done in existing vocational teacher education programs is largely unknown. Thus, as a starting point, it might be useful to see whether each graduating vocational teacher can pass a test covering all the SCANS (Secretary's Commission on Achieving Necessary Skills) skills associated with his or her particular teaching area. If prospective teachers cannot pass such a test, it means educators may want to reconsider how well prospective teachers are prepared for their teaching responsibilities.

Professional Development of Beginning Teachers. Even though teacher educators often discuss the professional development of beginning teachers, few have tested the assumptions that underlie this process. Based on three years of quantitative and qualitative research focusing on beginning vocational teachers (Heath-Camp, Camp, Adams-Casmus, Talbert, & Barber, 1992), a program focusing directly on the systematic professional development of beginning vocational teachers was created and tested (Heath-Camp & Camp, 1992). This teacher induction program offers an adaptable and flexible way for beginning vocational teachers to transition successfully into their new careers and to grow as professional educators. The program's 11 components include: a professional development center, a local professional development coordinator, detailed orientation, structured mentoring, a beginning teacher handbook, a beginning teacher peer-support group, systematic administrator support, ongoing inservice training workshops, certification courses, coaching on reflective teaching, and a professional development plan. Although the program can be quite time consuming to establish and operate, and may cost more to administer that traditional beginning teacher programs, the investment has great potential to pay off in the long term. With its focus on sound teacher-development principles and holistic development processes, the program should be considered for adoption or adaptation by universities and local education agencies who together want to insure that their graduates/beginning teachers receive the best opportunities to be successful in the teaching profession.

International Developments in Vocational Teacher Education. The exploration of program focus in vocational teacher education has in many respects been limited to what is occurring in the United States. Obviously, travel costs, communication problems, and lack of good cross-national linkages restrict what can be accomplished in this area by vocational teacher educators in the United States. Recent developments in Europe have potentially removed some of these restrictions, particularly in the area of access to information. Recently, a major European research and development project titled "New Forms of Education of Professionals for Vocational Education and Training" has been sponsored by the European Commission's LEONARDO program. The project has as its purpose conducting transnational research focusing on the identification of new occupational profiles for vocational education and training professionals as well as establishing new curricula and programs for these professionals. One of the publications prepared by the project's transnational research team includes a chapter titled "Pressures for Change in the Education of Vocational Education and Training Professionals" that was prepared by Graham Attwell (1997). Interestingly, the pressures for change documented in Attwell's chapter are for the most part in close alignment with what vocational teacher educators and others in the United States are saying about the field. Chapter sections focusing on new roles for vocational education and training and human resource development professionals, the reflective practitioner, future-oriented vocational education and training, and a new structure for the education of vocational education and training professionals each offer a wealth of information that has not yet been included in U.S. publications.

As the world-class workplace continues to gain prominence, it will become of greater and greater importance for educators in the U. S. to connect with research and development activities conducted in other countries and identify vocational teacher preparation models and practices that may have potential for implementation in the United States. An additional benefit would be exposure to different ways of thinking about vocational teacher preparation that could ultimately lead to meaningful improvements in how teachers are prepared.

Delivery

For many years, the delivery of vocational teacher education has remained largely unchanged. Basically, the university program served as a catalyst for vocational teacher preparation and development, with faculty members offering their students face-to-face instruction focusing on relevant course content. The impact of educational reform has, however, effected changes to this otherwise traditional process. With its emphasis on teacher team building and collaboration across teaching areas, educational reform has pointed the way to move beyond a traditional vocational teacher education agenda. Although numerous examples exist, the following reflect potentially new areas of emphasis for teacher education delivery:

• Based on a review of 29 different proposals for reforming teacher education, Cruickshank and his associates (1996) identified six promising approaches to improving teacher education that have been often overlooked in teacher education programs. They can offer students opportunities to apply knowledge in realistic situations and allow greater personal reflection than didactic coursework. The approaches include case studies, microteaching, minicourses, protocol materials, reflective teaching, and simulations.

• A study of whole school reform as reflected in Virginia high schools that joined the Southern Regional Educational Board High Schools that Work Consortium revealed teachers had a wide range of different concerns about the change process (Aneke and Finch, 1997). Although some teachers were very advanced and sophisticated in terms of change, others were novices in their thinking about educational reform. It was recommended that professional development activities be fine tuned to better accommodate the wide range of concerns teachers have as they become involved with whole school reform.

• In their comprehensive survey of contemporary approaches to teaching and learning, Biggs, Hinton, and Duncan (1996, p. 135) noted that educational reform has implications for the ways vocational teacher education programs should be changed. They recommended that vocational teacher educators understand lifelong learning and model lifelong learning concepts, focus on their own continuous learning, be as familiar with the workplace as they are with the school setting, and provide learning experiences for prospective teachers that reflect the context of the workplace.

• Based on the evolving nature of professional development, Finch, Schmidt, and Moore (1997) described a paradigm where development assumes a new character that includes greater emphasis on school-based instead of university-based programs, teachers teaching teachers, team teacher development, and continuous development activities. Support for this paradigm may be found in a number of research reports and essays.

These examples reflect the range of creative ways that are available to deliver teacher preparation and development. If vocational teacher education expects to keep pace with the rest of the profession, various new approaches to meet teachers' needs must be examined and tested. Those having the greatest potential to benefit teachers should be implemented.

Teacher Supply and Demand

Determining how many vocational teachers are available to teach and what vocational teaching positions need to be filled has been and continues to be an elusive goal. Some information related to teacher supply and demand is available. Supply and demand surveys conducted over the years by organizations, magazines, and individuals reveal that a continuing need exists for teachers in a wide range of vocational teaching areas (Finch, 1991b).

Unfortunately, some surveys have used a variety of different information sources ranging from university teacher education program representatives to state officials and extant data bases. These and other inconsistencies in survey procedures have contributed to problems with the interpretation and use of results.

First, data gathered by individual vocational teaching areas (e.g., agriculture, business, marketing, trade and industrial) may not be aggregated with data from other vocational teaching areas. A second difficulty is the variation in teacher certification requirements that exist across states. For example, one state might require that a child-care teacher have at least three years of relevant work experience, while a second state may require a bachelor's degree, and a third state may require both a degree and work experience. The net result is that supply and demand data often do not extend beyond individual states.

A parallel difficulty exists regarding secondary versus postsecondary teacher supply and demand. In some states, all secondary vocational teachers must have degrees but postsecondary and/or adult vocational teachers do not need to meet this requirement. Finally, in a number of states, emergency clauses in certification regulations enable vocational teachers to be hired by localities without first meeting basic certification requirements.

In summary, there have been and continue to be a number of interesting vocational teacher supply-and-demand studies completed. Some provide useful information and others do not.

Before this information can be more universally accepted and used to help make informed decisions, agreement must be reached about what actually constitutes vocational teacher supply and demand both within and among states.

CONTINUING ISSUES AND CONCERNS

Although a number of valuable lessons have been learned about how vocational teachers should be educated, broadly based educational reform in the schools as well as evolving teacher preparation structures and teacher development needs will provide vocational teacher educators with continuing challenges.

Vocational Teacher Preparation

Legislation, educational reform, and new conceptions of how teachers should be prepared have had direct impact on the vocational teacher education community. Historically, vocational teacher preparation has been the responsibility of university-based vocational teacher educators. These faculty members, who have typically been white males with doctoral degrees and tenure (Lynch, 1990), tend to have education and experience that aligns most closely with Prosser's philosophy of education. With legislation shifting focus from education where students' vocational and academic studies are separated to education integrating the two areas, current trends fly in the face of what many teacher educators have believed and practiced during much of their professional careers.

As reflected in recent legislation, educational reform and thus change should keep vocational education professionals busy for some time. Research has indicated that teachers take on new and more complex responsibilities in these educational reform settings. Research has also demonstrated that many strategies are available to assist teachers as they prepare to work in settings where educational reform such as integration and school-to-work transition exist.

Unfortunately, there is little evidence that vocational teacher educators have made major structural changes to their programs. Several informal and formal searches for innovative, cutting-edge, vocational teacher education programs have identified only a few programs that are incorporating needed instruction such as the development of horizontal and vertical teacher collaboration skills into their courses.

What implications does this situation have for vocational teacher education? Essentially, vocational teacher educators must embrace contemporary educational and workplace philosophies and practice if they intend to prepare vocational teachers for the next century. Even though this task may require many teacher educators to undergo large-scale professional development, it is central to the survival and growth of vocational teacher education programs in the United States.

The Continuing Development of Vocational Teachers

Since new teachers enter the vocational education teaching profession at the rate of 5 to 8 percent a year, this leaves a high percentage of practicing teachers nationwide who must receive inservice continuing professional development. But in what areas should these people develop?

Research indicates dozens of activities that all teachers can use to help students with their school-to-work transition. Examples include involving students in organized workplace experiences, linking with employers and the community, and including workplace representatives in school curriculum and instruction activities. If teachers want to be more successful at organizing and conducting school-to-work programs they must learn new skills that extend beyond their current capabilities. Examples of these skills include being willing to change with technological advances, understanding the many needs of employers and the community, and having a knowledge of school-based learning that goes beyond specific teaching areas (Schmidt et al., 1997).

How can teachers be developed most effectively and how can vocational teacher educators be of assistance? Little (1993, p. 129) noted that the dominant teacher development model that focuses on broadening the individual teacher's expertise in teaching is not adequate to meet teachers' needs in the current reform climate. Vocational teacher educators are thus faced with the task of testing and selecting different development models or even creating a hybrid model that best suits the vocational education field. However, creating a new model that focuses only on vocational teacher development is at odds with what many educational reforms are attempting to do—turn the educational environment into a place where all teachers work together to better meet students' educational needs.

Answers to the professional development issues that have been raised depend on how eager teacher educators are to personally develop the professional and technological skills needed by teachers in exemplary high schools and community and technical colleges where educational reforms such as integration, tech prep, and school-to-work systems have been implemented. After teacher educators master the applied level of expertise needed to be successful in educational reform, they should be quite capable of organizing and operating a professional model or models to improve the ways teachers teach.

FOOD FOR THOUGHT

Why has change in vocational teacher education lagged so far behind educational reform in the public schools, and what can be done about it? How can vocational teacher educators provide more meaningful professional development experiences for teachers in the schools? Which teacher education delivery models and strategies have the greatest potential to assist aspiring and practicing vocational teachers? Some of these questions have been addressed and all of them certainly must be answered. However, in order to make change happen, vocational teacher educators must recognize their new roles in educational reform, develop their own talents in this area, and provide the necessary leadership to recreate vocational teacher preparation and development for the twenty-first century.

References

Aneke, N. O., & Finch, C. R. (1997). Teachers' stages of concern about a schoolwide reform. *Journal of Vocational Education Research, 22* (1), 55-70.

Attwell, G. (1997). Pressures for change in the education of vocational education and training professionals. In A. Brown (Ed.), *Promoting vocational education and training: European perspectives* (pp. 107-122). Tampere, Finland: University of Tampere.

Bennett, C. A. (1926). *History of manual and industrial education up to 1870.* Peoria, IL: Author.

Biggs, B. T., Hinton, B. E., & Duncan, S. L. S. (1996). Contemporary approaches to teaching and learning. In N. Hartley & T. Wentling (Eds.), *Beyond tradition: Preparing the teachers of tomorrow's workforce* (pp. 113-146). Columbia, MO: University Council for Vocational Education.

Brown, J. M., & Davison, L. J. (1991). Adapting vocational education teacher training programs to work place changes. *Journal of Studies in Technical Careers, 8* (3), 285-295.

Cruickshank, D. R., & Associates. (1996). *Preparing America's teachers.* Bloomington, IN: Phi Delta Kappa Educational Foundation.

Finch, C. R. (1991a). *Foundations of vocational education in the United States.* Paper presented at the Vocational Teacher Education College, Hameenlinna, Finland.

Finch, C. R. (1991b). *Teacher preparation, qualifications, and demand.* Paper prepared for the National Assessment of Vocational Design Conference, Washington, DC.

Finch, C. R. (1997a). *Research on implementing education and training policies in the United States.* Paper presented at the Seminar on International Vocational Education and Training Policies sponsored by the Institute for Educational Research, University of Jyvaskyla, Finland.

Finch, C. R. (1997b). School-to-work transition in the United States. *International Journal of Vocational Education and Training, 5* (1), 69-84.

Finch, C. R., & Crunkilton, J. R. (1993). *Curriculum development in vocational and technical education* (4th ed.). Needham Heights, MA: Allyn & Bacon.

Finch, C. R., & McGough, R. L. (1991). *Administering and supervising occupational education.* Prospect Heights, IL: Waveland.

Finch, C. R., Schmidt, B. J., & Faulkner, S. L. (1992). *Using professional development to facilitate vocational and academic education integration: A practitioner's guide.* Berkeley, CA: National Center for Research in Vocational Education, University of California, Berkeley.

Finch, C. R., Schmidt, B. J., & Moore, M. (1997). *Meeting teachers' professional development needs for school-to-work transition: Strategies for success.* Berkeley, CA: National Center for Research in Vocational Education, University of California, Ber-

keley.
Heath-Camp, B., & Camp, W. G. (1992). *Professional development of beginning vocational teachers: Implementation system.* Berkeley, CA: National Center for Research in Vocational Education, University of California, Berkeley.
Heath-Camp, B., Camp, W. G., Adams-Casmus, E., Talbert, B. A., & Barber, D. (1992). *On becoming a teacher: An examination of the induction of beginning vocational teachers in American public schools.* Berkeley, CA: National Center for Research in Vocational Education, University of California, Berkeley.
Jennings, J. F. (1991). Congressional intent. *Vocational Education Journal, 66* (2), 18-19.
Little, J. W. (1993). Teachers' professional development in a climate of educational reform. *Educational Evaluation and Policy Analysis, 15* (2),129-151.
Lynch, R. A. (1990). *A national data base for teacher education.* Berkeley, CA: National Center for Research in Vocational Education, University of California, Berkeley.
Lynch, R. A. (1996). Principles of vocational and technical teacher education. In N. K. Hartley & T. L. Wentling (Eds.), *Beyond tradition: Preparing the teachers of tomorrow's workforce* (pp. 73-89). Columbia, MO: University Council for Vocational Education.
Lynch, R. A. (1997). *Designing vocational and technical teacher education for the 21st century: Implications from the reform literature.* Information Series No. 368. Columbus, OH: Clearinghouse on Adult, Career, and Vocational Education.
Moss, J., Jr. (1967). *Review of research in vocational technical teacher education.* Minneapolis, MN: Minnesota Research Coordination Unit in Occupational Education, University of Minnesota.
Naylor, M. (1997). *Vocational teacher education reform.* Digest 180. Columbus, OH: ERIC Clearinghouse on Adult, Career, and Vocational Education.
Office of Research. (1994). *National assessment of vocational education: Final report to Congress.* Washington, DC: Office of Educational Research and Improvement, U. S. Department of Education.
Schmidt, B. J., Finch, C. R., & Faulkner, S. L. (1992). *Teachers' roles in the integration of vocational and academic education.* Berkeley, CA: National Center for Research in Vocational Education, University of California, Berkeley.
Schmidt, B. J., Finch, C. R., Faulkner, S. L., & Kandies, J. (1995). *Preparing teachers to successfully integrate vocational and academic education: A case study approach.* Berkeley, CA: National Center for Research in Vocational Education, University of California, Berkeley.
Schmidt, B. J., Finch, C. R., & and Moore, M. (1997). *Facilitating school-to-work transition: Teacher involvement and contributions.* Berkeley, CA: National Center for Research in Vocational Education, University of California, Berkeley.
Wirth, A. (1972). *Education in a technological society.* Scranton, PA: International Textbook Company.

Curtis Finch is a professor of Vocational and Technical Education at Virginia Polytechnic Institute and State University. A graduate of General Motors Institute, in Michigan; Pittsburg State University, in Kansas; and Pennsylvania State University, he has been employed as an automotive technician, technical instructor, technical training administrator, vocational teacher educator, researcher, research manager, international studies director, and graduate program chair. His international assignments include serving as a senior Fulbright scholar and technical education consultant in the Republic of Cyprus, technical education specialist with an education sector assessment of Egypt, visiting researcher at the University of Jyvaskyla (Finland), visiting scholar in Scandinavian countries, visiting lecturer in New Zealand, and others. He has written or co-written more than 200 publications and consults internationally in vocational education curriculum, leadership, and human resource development.

16

CURRICULUM ISSUES

By David J. Pucel

This chapter is organized into two major sections. The first is the changing context, expectations, and views about curriculum practices in vocational education. The second presents major curriculum issues that arise as vocational educators attempt to address these changes.

THE NEW CONTEXT OF VOCATIONAL EDUCATION CURRICULUM

Expectations

Frost suggests that the role of education in society has been and continues to be essentially the same. "Basically education in all societies aims at orienting the individual to his [or her] social and physical environment." (Frost, 1966, p. 8) Consistent with this view of the role of education, vocational education and its practices have always mirrored the society of the times. Given recent changes in society, the expectations for vocational education and vocational education curriculum have changed dramatically during the past decade. These changes are probably more dramatic than any since the beginning of the twentieth century. During the early 1900s, expectations for how individuals should be prepared for life and work changed as a result of society moving to the industrial age. Eventually vocational education was included as part of the high school curriculum in response to the need for students to be prepared for industrial-age society and work. Federal legislation, such as the Smith-Hughes Act of 1917, helped promote changes in schools by providing financial incentives to schools which incorporated vocational programs.

Now vocational education is again feeling the impact of changes in society as society has moved from the industrial age to the information age. It is increasingly clear that what students need in order to be adequately prepared for life and work today is far different from that needed in the past. Educators, policy makers, and the public are calling for educational reform, and vocational education is a major part of that reform. This reform raises many issues and calls for major changes in the vocational education curriculum.

The role of vocational education in the high schools has increasingly become to provide students with educational experiences which will allow them to develop an understanding of technology associated with career clusters as they explore their interests and occupational goals, while providing relevance for academic education. There is also an increasing concern that high school vocational programs be articulated with postsecondary programs designed to help students develop occupationally specific competencies aimed at employment. The hope is that students will not have to repeat instruction they already have had in high school when they enter a postsecondary institution. In order to provide incentives for schools to implement change, Federal legislation such as the Perkins Act and the School-To-Work Opportunities Act have again been put in place to subsidize change. Funding has been focused on specific programmatic adoptions such as tech prep and school-to-work (STW).

Secondary schools are being asked to focus their attention on pre-occupational education through programs such as tech-prep (Brustein, 1993). The tech prep initiatives have experienced rapid growth and close to one-half of all secondary school districts included in the National Assessment of Vocational Education (5,441 out of 11,527) reported having tech prep agreements with postsecondary institutions in 1993 (National Assessment of Vocational Education, 1994). Many more have implemented tech prep programs since. The following is a brief summary of the seven major elements required of federally funded tech prep programs. (Brustein, 1993):

- An articulation agreement. (An arrangement between secondary and postsecondary institutions to develop a seamless tech prep program focused on an occupational cluster.)
- Appropriate curriculum design. (Two years of secondary and two years of postsecondary non-duplicative education as part of a program containing vocational and applied academic courses.)
- Curriculum development. (Funds to support efforts to adapt the curriculum.)
- Inservice teacher education. (Inservice for vocational and academic teachers to implement the curriculum.)
- Counselor training. (In-service for counselors to recruit and help students in tech prep programs.)
- Equal access for special populations. (Provisions for special populations to have equal access to tech prep programs.)
- Preparatory services. (Services provided to those not yet enrolled in a tech prep program.)

These new programs recognize the need for those wishing to prepare for specific occupations requiring less than a baccalaureate degree to have an adequate background in basic education such as science, math, language arts and social studies. They also recognize that there is a wide range of occupations from which students can choose and that students should be exposed to a range of occupations. Therefore, the occupational component of tech prep programs is not focused on preparing students for specific occupations such as a carpenter, secretary, or agricultural technician, but on clusters of occupations such as a manufacturing, heath, technical, or business cluster.

In addition to modifying the school-based components of vocational education, there is also a major school-to-work movement which promotes extending the educational environment beyond the classroom. (Brustein, 1994) STW programs typically have overlapping goals with tech prep. Their unique feature is that they promote student experiences beyond those found in the typical classroom. Sample student goals are to:

- Develop and maintain a lifework plan.
- Identify a career web or pathway.
- Have contextual learning experiences and demonstrate authentic performance.
- Have work-based learning experiences.
- Have easy access to articulated education experiences.
- Have nonschool education/training experiences that are documented and made part of their academic record.
- Have access to, and interaction with, individuals who assist them in transition from education to employment.

An example of such goals for Minnesota with a more detailed description are available on the web site: *http://children.state.mn.us/stw/info/whatis/learner.html*.

Given the changing expectations and funding to support them, vocational education at all levels has been developing programs aimed at re-alignment with the needs of society. The old Smith-Hughes view of vocational education, which has been severely criticized, is being replaced with something new.

Academic education is also being criticized as not meeting the needs of most students as they prepare for their future lives and work. The major criticism is that academic education is often abstract and has little relevance to the average student. Academic teachers are being asked to teach in an applied fashion which shows students how what they are learning is relevant to society. An increasing number of academic educators are advocating that their programs be re-designed to make them more functionally related to society. They still believe there is a need to concentrate on academic basics, but suggest a need to teach those basics in a more functional manner around real-life applications. Such changes have been supported by major academic subject groups such as the National Council of Teachers of Mathematics (Kurtz et.al., 1990), and the National Center for Improving Science Education (National Center for Improving Science Education, 1989). Support for making all school curricula more functionally related to life and work has also come from the national movement advocating that all educational programs be outcome-based, which requires the specification of the outcomes students will be expected to attain upon completing the programs (Spady & Marshall, 1991). As the academic programs become more applied, how academic subjects and vocational education can work together has become a major focus of curriculum revision. Most believe that academic and vocational educators should work together to provide skills needed for career preparation and for academic preparation. Table 16.1 contrasts some of the changing ideas about the role of high school vocational education curricula within this new reform environment.

As the vision of the role of high school vocational education has changed from preparing students for direct entry into the world of work in a specific occupation to providing students with experiences related to a career cluster, the need for occupationally specific education has increasingly been assumed by technical and community colleges. However, even at the postsecondary level, vocational education has been changing. The need for a broad base of academic skills as well as technical skills required to function in the world of work has led most technical and community colleges to require general studies components as part of their vocational programs. Many have developed associate degree programs which have a liberal education component transferable to four year colleges.

In recognition of the fact that some students at the secondary level will desire and benefit from specific occupational education, many states have adopted some version of a postsecondary options program. These programs allow students who are in high school to take specialized courses at community or technical colleges as part of their high school programs. This provides students with options to develop specific occupational skills, but allows high schools to staff and build facilities around the new expectations.

Evolving Curriculum Concepts

In order to create high school vocational courses which meet the new expectations for vocational education, major curriculum concepts which impact curriculum design have been evolving. Among them are integration, articulation, career majors or pathways, and project-based instruction. Although these concepts have existed in some form in the past, they are being redefined and clarified and their implications for curriculum design are becoming more apparent.

Integration is the process of different subject matter fields cooperating with one another to develop a unified instructional program that provides instruction in each of the subject matter areas on a need-to-know basis as students complete real-world activities related to life and work. For example, language arts, sci-

Table 16.1—Contrast of Old and New Concepts Underlying Quality High School Vocational Education	
Old	**New**
High school vocational programs should be stand-alone programs which teach limited related academics (e.g., business math, carpentry math) as well as highly specific occupational preparation.	Vocational programs should be part of a total instructional program to prepare students for careers, and for continued learning in their careers. Therefore, vocational instructor is part of an instructional team. All students should receive a quality academic education in addition to participating in vocational education.
Students should be prepared to enter specific occupations such as carpenter, secretary, or data entry technician.	Vocational programs should focus on career majors which include sets of vocational courses and academic courses related to clusters of occupations
Vocational program' s success should be judged based on the number of people who go into occupations or additional education directly related to their training directly after high school.	Vocational program success should be judged based on the number of students who find the programs *helpful* in preparing for occupations in a career major during and after high school.
Vocational programs are only for students planning to directly enter the world of work.	Quality vocational programs should be the center core of the program of studies for many students. They should provide a focal point for learning which makes schooling relevant to students' lives.
Vocational courses should focus on the technical skills associated with occupations.	In addition to learning sample technical skills, all students should be expected to master SCANS generalizable work skills, and to participate in exploratory experiences outside of school related to their future goals.

ence, math, social studies, and vocational instructors could develop an instructional program around the need for hot water for hygiene in an African country. The solution might be a solar water-heating device. The science instructor could teach concepts such as heat absorption, focusing light, and the effect of color on heat absorption. The math instructor could teach mathematical concepts around calculating the shape of a reflector that will focus light to generate the amount of heat that will need to be captured to efficiently heat the water. The vocational instructor could teach the metalworking, finishing, and assembly required. The social studies instructor could teach about the cultural values of the people regarding hygiene and its implications for the economy. The language arts instructor could teach research techniques and writing around the searching out of required information and the writing of a final project report. Although this example indicates how multiple subject-matter areas might cooperate, integration also often occurs with only two subject matter areas cooperating.

Articulation "... is a process for coordinating different levels and/or systems of education. The purpose of educational articulation is to enable the learner to make a smooth transition from one level/system to another without experiencing delays, duplication of effort, or loss of credit" (McCormick, 1980, p. 9). For

Table 16.2—Sample Vocational Curriculum

Sample specific careers	Sample vocational major courses	
Electrician Draftsperson Auto mechanic Welder Machinist Electrical inspector Electrical engineer Architect	9th grade Wood technology Basic drafting Metal technology Power mechanics	10th grade Computer appl. Keyboarding Metal technology
	11th grade Architectural drftg. Auto mechanics Electrical power Digital electronics	12th grade Machine drawing Building construction Auto mechanics II Welding

example, a high school might have a manufacturing program providing experiences related to a cluster of manufacturing occupations, such as machinist, production control assistant, welder, and automated systems technician. In designing the courses the high school staff would meet with the postsecondary staff of the local community/technical college which provides occupational-specific education in these areas to determine how courses might be developed to allow those completing the high school program to enter the postsecondary programs and receive credit for what they did in high school.

A career major or pathway is a series of quality vocational and academic courses which reinforce one another and provide a student with the academic and vocational competencies required to focus high school instruction around a career goal. For example, the following might be a set of vocational major courses for a broad technical cluster adopted by a small comprehensive high school. The courses would be designed with the sample technical careers in mind. (See Table 16.2.)

In addition, an appropriate sample of academic courses would be selected to complement the vocational courses to satisfy local graduation requirements. (See Table 16.3.)

Project-based instruction is a methodology for implementing applied learning around authentic real-world career experiences. Although vocational educators have had a long history of teaching around projects, the new view of projects does not treat the end product of the project as the major focal point of instruction, but treats the project as a vehicle around which instruction from all subject matter areas can be anchored. The major goal of the project is to focus learning and not to produce a product. One could consider the development of the solar heating device in the discussion of integration presented above as an example of project-based instruction.

Table 16.3 Sample Academic Complement
English - 4 yrs. (composition, literature & speech)
Math - 3 yrs. (2 yrs. algebra, 1 year geometry)
Science - 3 yrs. (1 yr. biology, 1 yr. physical science with labs)
Social Science - 3 yrs. (1 yr. geography, 1 yr. Canadian history)
Electives - 3 yrs.

As part of the new view of project-based instruction, the steps in completing a project no longer focus only on the steps a skilled person would complete in order to complete the project. Supplemental learning activities are embedded in the project to achieve additional goals besides completing the project.

For example, the following types of activities might be included as students complete projects: Ask for a demonstration on how to do something; consult with an instructor or other students about alternatives; visit actual work sites to observe and talk with people on the job; work as part of a team to determine the most effective way to approach the project; attend a presentation by an industry representative; review the instruction manual; present your findings to the class; research alternative ways of completing the activity; write a report detailing how you completed the project; select a career you would like to explore further; interview a person to determine what they like or dislike about their job.

Changes in Curriculum Practices

Curriculum practices are changing to meet the new needs. Some major areas of change are: how course goals should be developed and what they should include; how content should be identified and who should identify it; how and who should deliver instruction; and how course achievement should be evaluated. In most cases, the need for change on each of these dimensions is equally applicable to secondary and postsecondary education.

Course goals have been expanded to include many dimensions not formally addressed by vocational education in the past, when those developing vocational courses would have been expected to teach students the technical skills and knowledge required to perform in an occupation. These were often determined through an occupational (task) analysis to identify what people actually do on the job. Since most work prepared for through vocational education during the industrial age tended to involve psychomotor skill, what a person does with their hands, that became the primary focus of instructional methodology. Charles Allen (1919), one of the first people who wrote about instructional methodology for vocational education, advocated teaching only essential manipulative skills necessary to perform a current job, and that view persisted as a basic concept underlying vocational education.

Today the goal of teaching students the technical skills and knowledge of occupations is only one dimension of what is expected of vocational courses. Other typical goals are that students will: experience authentic career activities representative of the career major(s); master academic and SCANS (Secretary of Labor's Commission for Achieving Necessary Skills) employability competencies associated with career activities; complete their work to workplace-quality standards; adopt safe practices and safety consciousness; solve workplace problems during the completion of projects which provide experiences with typical career activities; research a career of personal interest to which course content applies and maintain a lifework plan; have work-based learning experiences; have easy access to articulated education experiences; have nonschool education/training experiences that are documented and made part of their academic record; have access to, and interaction with, individuals who assist them in transition from education to employment. Often these goals are no longer being established solely at the local level; but also as national and statewide initiatives (e.g, tech prep, STW).

Course content is obtained from a variety of sources to accomplish this wide variety of goals. Although the sources of course content and types of content presented below are equally applicable to secondary and postsecondary vocational education, the way in which that content is addressed at each of these levels has changed. In the past both secondary and postsecondary vocational programs were expected to prepare students for direct employment. Therefore, they both focused on specific occupational skills needed for direct employment.

If secondary vocational education is to concentrate on broad career majors and postsecondary vocational education is to focus on specific occupational preparation, then the occupational breadth of these two types of programs should be different. When developing a secondary vocational program around a business cluster, one would want to find occupational content applicable to many different business occupations (e.g., data processing, accounting, word processing, entrepreneur). At the postsecondary level, a particular program might focus just on data processing or accounting. In other words, although the types of skills to be addressed in secondary and postsecondary programs might be the same, the occupational specificity of the skills to be taught would be different.

Typical occupational analyses are still being conducted to determine the technical skills to be included in a course, but they now need to be expanded to include cognitive and affective skills, not only traditional psychomotor skills which focus on procedures requiring the physical manipulation of things. Cognitive skills (focused on decision making) and affective skills (focused on interpersonal relations and how a person treats data and things) are also viewed as important.

To ensure this broader view of required skills, national skills standards are being established to provide benchmarks for the types of skills needed in various occupations. The National Skill Standards Board (NSSB) was created by the Goals 2000 Educate America Act of 1994. The standards are being established by groups representing each occupation to provide guidelines for certifying that individuals meet industry skill standards. Those developing skill standards are available at the web site *http://www.nssb.org*. In addition to skills standards, vocational education is being asked to help students develop employability skills, which are referred to as the SCANS skills and can be found at the web site *http://pueblo.pc.maricopa.edu/MariMVSE/SCANS/SCANS.html*.

They were identified by the Secretary of Labor's Commission for Achieving Necessary Skills. The SCANS skills include a three-part foundation consisting of basic reading, writing, arithmetic, listening, and speaking skills; thinking skills; and personal qualities, such as displaying responsibility, self-esteem, and honesty. They also include five competencies relating to resources, interpersonal skills, information, systems, and technology.

Soon O*NET (Occupational Information Network) will be available as a replacement for the old *Dictionary of Occupational Titles*. The new structure of O*NET is currently available on the web site *http://www.doleta.gov/programs/onet/*.

All of these national efforts at identifying skills people will need to succeed in the workplace are gradually replacing the notion that local job analyses should determine the content to be taught in vocational programs. Just as academic subject matter areas have had national standards which are used to judge the content requirements of academic courses, the national goal is to have vocational programs aimed at career preparation standards.

How and who should deliver vocational education is changing as well. The belief that the vocational instructor should provide the technical as well as the related academic instruction for those in vocational programs is no longer viewed as appropriate. Often students were taught "related academics" by the vocational instructors, which was a subset of the academic fields needed to perform in an occupation (e.g., business math, carpentry math, business communications). Emphasis is now being placed on integrated instruction where the vocational instructors and the academic instructors work as a team to provide technical skills related to an occupational cluster and quality academic skills.

Also, in the past vocational education was delivered primarily within the classrooms and laboratories of schools. Instruction was delivered by the instructor through mainly lecture and demonstration, and students were expected to apply what they learned by doing what they were demonstrated and answering questions. This type of instruction often led to "monkey-see, monkey-do" instructional techniques. Students did what the instructors showed them and repeated back information instructors taught them. Although this instructional technique worked well when it was expected that students would be treated the same way when they entered the workplace (employers would show employees what to do and they were to do it, and if they needed to do something different employers would again show them what to do), this technique does not fit with the new employment expectations of the information age.

Employees in the modern workplace are expected to solve problems, think for themselves, adapt to new situations, upgrade their own skills when needed, work in teams, be responsible for their own activities, etc. For students to be prepared to do these things, instructional practices must change.

Instruction must be delivered in ways that will allow students to problem-solve, work in teams, search out information, explain what they are doing and why, and apply academic skills within their career area. This requires the instructors to change their role from one of presenting all of the information students need and solving all of the problems to one of presenting students with situations requiring them to search out information and coming up with their own problem solutions, as individuals or in teams.

How course achievement should be evaluated has also changed. Typical achievement at the vocational course level in the past concentrated on the extent to which students mastered occupational skills and knowledge. Although these are still important, they currently are not the only foci of student evaluation. Given the broader goals, such as teaching students how to problem solve, to develop generalizable employability skills, and to learn how to learn, all vocational courses must also include instruction and evaluation focused on these skills as well. In addition, evaluation techniques to provide feedback on the extent to which students have accomplished educational goals through work and community-based activities must also be developed and implemented.

At the program evaluation level it is important to recognize that the criterion for judging the success of a vocational program has changed. There is much less emphasis on how many people went directly into a related occupation or additional occupationally related education directly after completing the program. Although this is still a reasonable goal at the postsecondary level, it is no longer the sole goal of secondary programs.

Other criteria must now be applied to evaluating vocational programs, such as how many students were helped to make an occupational choice, how many students found academic instruction related to their vocational major more satisfying than the typical abstract academic instruction, how many students remained in schools because they found their education functionally related to their futures, and how many students established contacts as part of their vocational programs which facilitated their transition from school to the real world.

MAJOR CURRICULUM ISSUES

As the changes in expectations for vocational education and their implications for curriculum presented above continue to permeate the schools, a number of major issues are being debated. How they are resolved will have a profound impact on the future of vocational education.

Failure to change will lead to a removal of vocational education programs from the schools because they will no longer be viewed as relevant to the needs of current society. Changing in ways that give up the unique nature and contributions of vocational education will also lead to its demise. The following issues seem to be those most hotly debated within vocational education and between vocational educators and others.

If the role of secondary vocational education is not to prepare students for particular occupations, why not have the academic programs in the high school adopt applied learning methods and do away with secondary vocational education?

At times principals, superintendents, and academic instructors view vocational education as an alternative methodology for teaching academic skills. This view suggests if vocational education at the high school level is no longer focused on specific employment, then its primary function is to provide opportunities for students to apply what they have learned in other classes. Given this view, vocational education has no substance of its own.

This view has recently been presented by the National Association of Secondary School Principals (NASSP) in its publication, *Breaking Ranks: Changing an American Institution*, a document which promises to change the American high school. NASSP recommends: more focus on applied learning; a focus on academics without recognition of the value of technical competencies needed for work; and a focus on using vocational education as a vehicle for applied learning, without recognizing the value of the development of competencies for work (National Association of Secondary School Principals, 1996).

In contrast, a national group assembled by the U.S. Department of Education to establish criteria for judging the quality New American High School has affirmed the need for high school vocational education and its unique substance. Many of the criteria specified relate directly to the new role for vocational education in the high school.

The criteria established by the group were to: help students achieve high levels of academic and *technical skills*; teach students in the context of a *career major* or other special interest; *offer hands-on learning*—in classrooms, workplaces, or community service; access a wide range of *career* and college information; prepare students for college and *careers*; work with teachers in small school-within-schools; win the support of a caring community; receive extra support from adult mentors; benefit from *strong links with postsecondary institutions*; and use technology to enhance instruction and learning (American Vocational Association, 1996).

The debate over whether vocational education has substance or is essentially a vehicle for teaching other subject matter is probably the most important issue currently facing vocational education. How that issue is resolved will form the basis for most other decisions regarding secondary vocational education.

Should there be a difference in the roles of secondary and postsecondary vocational education?

Some believe that there should be no difference in intent or methodology of secondary and postsecondary vocational programs but only in the types of occupations for which people are prepared. They believe that secondary programs should prepare students for less technically demanding occupations and postsecondary should prepare students for occupations requiring high levels of skills.

Another group believes that attempts at preparing students for specific occupations at the high school level can only lead them to being prepared for low-level jobs, and that taking so much time to prepare students for a specific occupation will short-change their academic education, which they will need in order to be flexible in the workplace of the future. They also believe that given the changes in society, the public is demanding a refocusing of high school vocational education. This group believes high school vocational programs should focus on clusters of occupations which allow students to explore and to develop some basic employability and technical skills related to a career area and that specific occupational preparation should be delayed and accomplished at the postsecondary level.

How should student achievement expectations be established?

Many vocational educators have adopted what might be considered a "special needs education" view of what students should accomplish in a vocational course. This view is that each student should be kept occupied in the classroom by activities she/he finds interesting and relevant to the content of the course, and should be judged based on the effort they make toward completing those activities. They argue that this is the best way to meet the needs of the individuals.

The opposing group believes that, just as

with math or science, there should be clear instructional goals for each vocational course which all students should achieve, and that students should be judged based on a mastery standard. They argue that vocational courses should be rigorous and that students should feel a personal sense of quality accomplishments upon completing a course. They argue that one of the reasons that large portions of able students do not participate in vocational courses is that they feel they are a waste of time. Broadening the goals of vocational courses and holding instructors and students accountable for attaining those goals is viewed as necessary for vocational education to maintain credibility within the schools and with the public.

What is the difference between applied academics and vocational education?

Some believe they are the same. This group believes vocational education is no more than a vehicle for teaching applied academics. The major curriculum premise from which this group develops curriculum is to identify the academic content to be taught and then to find occupational examples which demonstrate how the academic content is applied. This is the technique used by the Center for Occupational Research and Development (CORD) in its Principles of Technology program.

Although this technique is excellent for developing applied academics and showing its relevance, another group believes such programs are not a replacement for vocational courses. They believe this approach relegates vocational education to a methodology and does not recognize the unique aspects and benefits of vocational education content.

The latter group believes the vocational curriculum should focus on providing students with a meaningful subset of the technical skills and employability skills associated with occupations. They believe this has value in accomplishing many of the goals of the ideal American high school. They would start the process with determining the occupational foci of a course and then sample skills associated with those occupations. They would then develop authentic instructional experiences to either prepare a student for direct entry into the occupation or to allow the student to explore and develop a set of skills relevant to an occupational cluster.

The key difference between these two views is based on their perspectives of whether the development of skills and experiences related to an occupation or occupational cluster have value. The first group minimizes the need for a systematic presentation of content related to an occupation or occupational cluster. They see the need to do so related with math, science, social studies, and language arts, but not vocational education. The second group believes there is a unique substance to vocational courses that requires the same type of rigorous planning and delivery of vocational courses as those used with academic courses.

Is the development of the SCANS general employability skills all that students need to be prepared for work?

The way one resolves this issue also has a profound impact on how one views vocational education at the high school level. If one believes that the SCANS general employability skills are all that are needed to be prepared for work, there is no need for vocational education related to specific occupations or clusters of occupations. Many are currently concerned that during the implementation of STW programs the focus on generalizable employability skills will lead to a reduced recognition of the unique contributions of vocational education. The group that views vocational education goals and the SCANS goals as the same would move to abolish vocational education and to incorporate STW activities within all courses in the schools. They believe that it is not important which occupation a person is considering as a career or that there are specific technical skills associated with those careers. They believe that the nature of the types of experiences a person has in any setting can develop the SCANS skills.

The other group believes that the SCANS skills are important as students pursue meaningful experiences with technical skills associated with an occupation or occupational cluster. However, they believe that vocational programs should provide students with skills related to their career majors and that the learning of problem solving, SCANS skills, and other major emphases in preparation for work can be most meaningfully done within the context of a career. This group also believes that when students have a career in mind, even if they change it later, they can have a more meaningful anchor for all of their academic education.

SUMMARY

Throughout this chapter there has been a constant emphasis on the relationship between future vocational education and the needs of society. Also, the issues that have been highlighted have dealt mainly with issues of perspective and philosophy regarding the role and value of vocational education to society. That is because of a belief that the future of vocational education will be determined not through refining its current delivery system, but in determining what it should deliver and why and adjusting its delivery system accordingly. Vocational education must be reformed into a readily identified and valued program in order to survive.

Vocational education must adapt the curriculum to include: relevant occupational competencies that will allow a person to develop expertise in a career major; technological problem solving; planning, organizing, and working the completion skills; teamwork and interpersonal skills; the belief that preparation of people for work is valued in our society; reinforcement and development of SCAN skills; and reinforcement and development of academic skills.

If vocational education is to survive, issues such as how it differs from academic education, what unique student goals can be accomplished by having vocational education in the curriculum, whether vocational education is a methodology or a content area, and how quality vocational education programs should be judged, must be addressed. Vocational education will never go back to what it was during its glory days of the industrial revolution and the industrial age, but it can have a glorious future if it changes to meet the new needs of society.

References

Allen, C. R. (1919). *The instructor, the man, and the job.* Philadelphia: J. B. Lippincott.

American Vocational Association. (1996). President Clinton honors 266 Blue Ribbon schools at White House. *Vocational Education Weekly, 9* (10), 5.

Brustein, M. (1993). *AVA guide to federal funding for tech prep.* Alexandria, VA: American Vocational Association.

Brustein, M. (1994). *The School-To-Work Opportunities Act: Overview.* Alexandria, VA: American Vocational Association.

Frost, S. E., Jr. (1966). *Historical and philosophical foundations of western education.* Columbus, Ohio: Charles E. Merrill.

Kurtz, V. R., et al. (1990). Special issue. *School Science and Mathematics, 90* (6), 451-574.

McCormick, F. (1980). *An overview of articulation efforts in vocational education: Implications for state planning.* St. Paul, MN: Education Operations Concepts. (ERIC Document Reproduction Service No. ED 199 558)

National Assessment of Vocational Education. (1994). *Final report to Congress.* Washington: U.S. Department of Education.

National Association of Secondary School Principals. (1996). *Breaking ranks: Changing an American institution.* Reston, VA: National Association of Secondary School Principals.

National Center for Improving Science Education. (1989). *Science and technology education for the elementary years: Framework for curriculum and instruction.* Andover, MA: The Network.

Spady, W. G., & Marshall, K. J. (1991). Beyond traditional outcome-based education. *Educational Leadership, 49* (2), 67-72.

***David J. Pucel** is a professor in the Department of Work, Community, and Family Education at the University of Minnesota, St. Paul. Holding a bachelor's degree from the University of Wisconsin (Stout), a master's degree from the University of Illinois, and a Ph.D. in vocational technical education and educational psychology from the University of Minnesota, Dr. Pucel specializes in developing instructional and evaluation systems for secondary and postsecondary education and human resources development for business and industry. He has written three books* *on curriculum systems, is writing a fourth on revitalizing secondary vocational education, has published numerous articles in professional journals, and has given many presentations at local, state, national, and international meetings. He has worked very closely with SREB (Southern Regional Education Board) High Schools that Work in revitalizing high school vocational education. He has also been responsible for teacher education programs in industrial, technology, business, and marketing education.*

GENDER EQUITY IN WORKFORCE EDUCATION

By Susan J. Olson

This chapter provides an overview of trends and issues in women's workforce participation, trends in their educational attainment, gender equity legislation for education, enrollment trends of females in workforce education programs, female career education and development, current research on nontraditional female enrollment in workforce education, and recommendations for the future. The emphasis on gender equity for females arises from the economic disadvantages created for this group due to inequities in education and in the workforce.

Changes in the family have greatly altered how we prepare our youth and adults for work and family responsibilities. The American family has undergone many changes in this century due to adaptations to evolving technologies, economics conditions, and social trends. Three major trends continue to impact the family: the decline of the traditional family due to divorce and widowhood (aging) and delayed marriage; the tendency of women to have fewer children and to have some later in life; and shifting economic roles within the family, including participation in the labor force. These family changes have impacted women's participation in the labor force.

WOMEN'S WORKFORCE PARTICIPATION TRENDS

"In the decade before World War II, only 24.4 percent of women worked for pay. Today . . . 99 percent of women in America will work for pay some time during their lives" (U.S. Department of Labor, 1994, p.10). Currently one in every six families is maintained by a woman, and more families than ever are relying on women's earnings (Aurdene & Neisbett, 1992; U.S. Department of Labor, 1996). For this reason, raising women's status in the labor market has been called the family issue of the new millennium.

Although approximately half of the American workforce is made up of females, most women still enter traditionally female jobs (Spain, 1997; U.S. Department of Labor, 1997a). Traditionally female occupations are those that employ 75 percent or more females. For example, in 1990, 60 percent of professional women worked in nursing and teaching (U.S. Department of Labor, 1997a) and only 2 percent of the skilled trades were represented by women (Spain, 1997). Although women are rapidly moving into "male" occupations, their numbers are still small. An increasing number of men also are taking up traditionally female occupations, but those who do so earn more than women in the same jobs (Center on Education and Training for Employment, 1992).

Women make up 45 percent of the workforce, but 57 percent of people who live in poverty (Spain, 1997). More adult women than men live below the poverty level (U.S. Department of Commerce, 1994). The feminization of poverty continues in today's workforce. More than 20 percent of women of color, that have some college education, live in poverty, while only 3 percent of men with the same educational background live in poverty (Nettles, 1991). Thirty-four percent of all female-headed households are poor, with 51 percent of African-American and 53 percent of Hispanics being poor (Kates, 1991). Families most in jeopardy of poverty are those headed by women, particularly women of color (Burbridge, 1992).

By the year 2050, 47 percent of the total United States population will be Asians, Hispanics, blacks, and other persons of color ("A Spicier Stew," 1992). By the year 2000, 50 percent of workers will be aged 50 and over (Johnson & Packer, 1987). In 1970, 40.3 percent of U.S. households were comprised of married couples with children under 18; in 1992, only 25.5 percent were (U.S. Bureau of the Census, 1994). The labor force is growing older, female, more culturally diverse, and less likely to be married with children.

Women's labor force participation rates vary by race and ethnicity. Labor force participation for black women rose between 1986 and 1996—from 56.9 percent to 60.4 percent. Historically, black women have had much higher rates than white or Hispanic women (U.S. Department of Labor, 1997b). In 1996, black women participated at a rate of 60.4 percent; white women participated at a rate of 59.1 percent. By the year 2005, it is projected that black women's participation rate will be slightly less than white women—58.8 percent versus 62.6 percent—with Hispanic women having the lowest participation rate. Black women are more likely to work full-time than white women. Black female teenagers are four times more likely to be unemployed than black women between ages 35 and 44.

According to a recent Census Bureau report, 55 percent of new mothers returned to work within a year of giving birth in 1995 (as cited in "Mother Is Working," 1997). This is up from 31 percent in 1976. The older and more educated the mother, the more likely she is to return to work before her baby turns one year old, with 77 percent of college-educated mothers aged 30 to 44 in this group. Women are working outside the home in greater numbers than ever before.

Occupational Segregation

"Women have worked in nearly every trade at some time, in some culture. What was considered appropriate work for women varied from culture to culture throughout time, and often according to class. What was considered 'men's work' in one time or place was 'women's work' elsewhere. . . . [However] women's wages have always been lower than men's" (Gray, 1994, p. 1).

Numerous research studies indicate the existence of a wage gap between female and male workers due to occupational segregation by gender (Tavakolian, 1994; Vella, 1993; Wood, 1993). Between 1900 and 1970, little has changed in the gender segregation of occupations. Women tend to enter occupations that are lower-paying occupations than men, work fewer hours, and have less job experience and fewer skills that are valued (Nasal, 1992).

Nearly all women (80 percent) work in traditional areas of employment (Faludi, 1991) with most working in low-paying occupations such as clerical, child care, or service occupations. In general, careers dominated by men pay higher salaries and are considered higher-status than those traditionally held by women (Bernstein, Reilly, & Cote-Bonanno, 1992).

Relatively few women are in blue-collar occupations, with under 3 percent of mechanics and 2 percent of construction workers (Women's Action Coalition, 1993). Even within these occupations women are concentrated in certain fields, such as machine operators, rather than craft workers or transportation workers. Women represent only 9 percent of the second highest-paying occupational group (craft, precision metal, and specialized repair (Herr & Gray, 1995). On the other hand, these traditional male-intensive craft and operative jobs are growing more slowly, while traditional female occupations in food preparation and health services are more plentiful. Unfortunately, studies have shown that women trained in traditionally male jobs are less likely to be employed and earn lower wages than men receiving the same training (Hargrove, Frazier, & Thomas, 1983; Streker-Seeborg, Seeborg, & Zegeye,1984).

No matter how we measure it, women's earnings are below those received by men (U.S. Department of Labor, 1993). Several factors influence the earnings gap between women and men. Women tend to have less job seniority, greater job turnover, less education, less experience, and fewer of the needed skills. With women receiving more education and employers providing child-care benefits, flextime, and family-leave policies, women are having greater opportunities to meet family responsibilities with few work interruptions.

Research has found that wages of working women did not increase relative to those of working men between 1920 and 1980 because the skill (as measured by education and experience) of working women did not increase relative to working men over this period (Smith & Ward, 1984). These researchers also concluded that women's real wages between 1950 and 1980 account for almost 60 percent in the growth of women's labor force during the period. Females are likely to earn less than their male counterparts (Center on Education and Training for Employment, 1992), and they are also more likely to experience slower advancement and more unemployment than males (Stipp, 1992).

There are persistent earnings differences between males and females with the same educational attainment (National Center for Education Statistics, 1996a). Among full-time, year-round workers, males at each educational level earned more than females. The size of the gap in constant dollars has declined since 1970. Between 1960 and 1994, male recent high school graduates not enrolled in college and recent high school dropouts were more likely than female counterparts to be employed.

According to the United States Department of Labor (1997a), of the 20 leading occupations for employed women in 1996, four required a college education. The top five with the greatest percentage employed were secretaries (98.6 percent), registered nurses (93.3 percent), receptionist (92.9 percent), bookkeepers (91.9 percent), and nurse's aides (88.9 percent).

The leading occupations for employed black women in 1996 were all in service occupations (in this order, from most to least): nursing aides, cashiers, secretaries, supervisors, retail sales, janitors, cooks, maids, registered nurses, elementary school teachers, and social workers. Note that, of these occupations, only three require college education (U.S. Department of Labor, 1997b). None of these occupations are nontraditional. Six out of 10 black female service workers were employed as nurse's aides, orderlies, janitors, cooks, and maids. Less than a million black women work in trade occupations, farming, forestry, and fishing. However, 45 percent of all black-owned businesses are owned by women.

LEGISLATIVE BACKGROUND

Provisions have been written into numerous pieces of legislation over the years to include females in training and employment opportunities. Generally, minimal—or no—appropriations of funds were provided to carry out these provisions (Schraeder, as cited in Burbridge, 1992).

The first critical piece of legislation written, funded, and enforced for the education of females of all ages was Title IX. Other pieces of legislation include the Women's Educational Equity Act (WEEA) of 1974 (Public Law 101-39205); the Carl Perkins Vocational and Applied Technology Act of 1990, Title IIB and Title IIIC; the Jobs Training Partnership Act (JTPA);

the JTPA NEW (Nontraditional Employment for Women) Act (PL 102-235); the JTPA 1992 Reform Amendments (PL 97-300); the Women in Apprenticeship and Nontraditional Occupations (WANTO) Act; and JOBS programs offered through the Department of Social Services specific to the education of girls and women.

National affirmative action guidelines opened the building trades to women in 1978. That same year President Carter provided Executive Order 11246 of the Office of Federal Contract Compliance Programs to set national job goals for women using federal funding (Eisenberg, 1992). Title 29 of the Apprenticeship Regulations of 1978 stipulated that slots were to be filled by women equal to their representation in the workforce. Today, however, women account for 7 percent of total U.S. apprenticeships (Herr & Gray, 1995).

The Perkins legislation has provided funding for states to have gender-equity coordinators since 1976. This funding came as a result of Congress learning that vocational classes were still segregated by gender. In 1984, another amendment to the Perkins Act established a set-aside that funds programs that help address gender-equity issues and help single parents and displaced homemakers. Goals of the Perkins Act seek to foster enrollment of students in vocational programs that are "nontraditional" for their gender (e.g., auto mechanics for female students and nursing for male students).

School-to-work (STW) legislation requires programs to show how their plans will increase opportunities for women (and other groups) in careers that are not traditional for their gender. In 1993, Wider Opportunities for Women conducted an investigation of how STW demonstration sites were serving young women (Milgram & Watkins, 1994). Findings showed that new and supposedly "state of the art" training continues to perpetuate gender bias and gender stereotyping that can result in continued wage disparities between men and women. These researchers did note that young women can succeed in nontraditional programs. A model program in Flint, Michigan, in Manufacturing Technology, shows promise in recruiting and retaining young women in automotive technology.

Tech prep. Some efforts have reportedly been made to promote participation in tech prep among females, minority students, and economically disadvantaged students, but the success of these efforts is not yet clear. The National Assessment of Vocational Education (Office of Educational Research and Improvement, 1994) does not address gender enrollments in tech prep or school-to-work initiatives.

Women in Apprenticeship and Nontraditional Occupations (WANTO) is providing federal grants to improve opportunities for good jobs for women by providing technical assistance to employers and labor organizations. These grants provide access to training, opportunity, and advancement (U.S. Department of Labor, 1997b).

Title IX. According to the Girls Count Gender Equity Assessment (as cited in Vote, 1995), Title IX is not fulfilled. Educational institutions are rarely in compliance. Females are choosing or channeled into occupational areas that are traditionally female and low-pay. The WEEA program supports the development of model projects designed to ensure educational equity for girls and women (U.S. Department of Education, 1997). Many of these projects address nontraditional occupational choice for girls and women (Wolfe, 1991).

JTPA works on major competency areas training youth in pre-employment skills, basic educational skills, and job-specific skills. To qualify, youth need to be 16 years of age and older and meet low-income or economically disadvantaged guidelines.

NEW serves low-income or economically disadvantaged females (JTPA eligible) with a focus on single parents/disadvantaged homemakers and pregnant single women. These programs focus on those who are academically able to enter and succeed in vocational skills training (Vote, 1995).

JOBS. As of 1992, the social service JOBS

program was available to new or existing JOBS participants. The participants must demonstrate academic ability to enter and not be enrolled in vocational skills training or postsecondary education.

TRENDS IN EDUCATIONAL ATTAINMENT

Females have increased their levels of education and are exceeding males in the levels of education received. The more education one has, the higher the probability that person will be in the labor force. (U.S. Department of Labor, 1997a). This is true for all persons, regardless of gender or race and is more evident among black women than white or Hispanic women.

As educational attainment increases, unemployment rates decrease. Black women with less than a high school diploma experience a six times higher rate of unemployment as compared with high school graduates—14.2 percent compared with 2.6 percent.

In 1995, women were more likely than men to have completed high school. Ninety-one percent of female labor force participants held a minimum of a high school diploma, compared to 88 percent for men (U.S. Department of Labor, 1996). More women are completing high school. Although the rate of teenage pregnancy more than doubled since 1980, from 1 percent to 2.5 percent, dropout rates have declined 30 percent at the same time graduation requirements have increased (U.S. Department of Education, 1997).

In 1993, 28 percent of men and 26 percent of women held a degree above the high school level (Bruno, 1993). Women were less likely than men to have an advanced degree, but more likely to have an associate degree or vocational degree. By 1995, the education gap between men and women narrowed (U.S. Department of Commerce, 1997). Eighty-two percent of men and women over age 25 held a high school diploma, whereas 46 percent of women and 50 percent of men had completed some college or more.

According to the National Center for Education Statistics (NCES) (as cited in Herr and Gray, 1995), only 8.4 percent of males and 3.7 percent of females expected to work as technicians and even fewer expected to work in the skilled trades. According to Herr and Gray, for the class of 1992, 85.2 percent of young women expected to go to college as compared with only 68.8 percent 10 years earlier.

Women now equal men in freshmen enrollments in higher education, but many will be scrambling for the few jobs that require college degrees (Herr & Gray, 1995). The U.S. Department of Labor predicts that 1 in 3 college graduates will not find college-level employment (Herr & Gray, 1995).

The percentage of high school graduates aged 16 to 24 enrolled in college the following October after graduation has increased for males and females since 1973. In 1973, 50 percent of males and 43 percent of females were attending college; in 1983, about half of the males (52 percent) and half the females (53 percent) were in college. By 1994, more females (63 percent) than males (61 percent) were enrolled in college (NCES, 1996a). However, at the two-year college level, males still out-enroll females. In 1972, 15 percent of males and 15 percent of females were enrolled in two-year colleges, but by 1994, 23 percent of males and 19 percent of females were enrolled in two-year colleges (U.S. Department of Education, 1997).

Among white, black, and Hispanic recipients of associate degrees in 1991, females were more likely than males to complete a degree in business or health, while males were more likely to complete a degree in technology fields (e.g., computer and information sciences, engineering and science technologies) (NCES, 1996a). Males were much more likely than females to have taken courses in physical sciences, mathematics, computer science, engineering, and economics. Females were also more likely than males to have taken life sciences, psychology, and sociology.

In 1971, only 18 percent of women, compared to 26 percent of men, had completed four or more years of college. Between 1960 and 1989 women attending college doubled (NCES,

1996b). Women now make up half of all college students, and half the degrees awarded through the master's degree are to women. Women in the United States now have greater access to higher education than do women in Great Britain, Germany, and Japan (Meece & Eccles, 1993). Between 1976 and 1986 there was a 29 percent increase in the number of women earning bachelor's degrees in science and engineering (National Science Foundation, 1990).

Workforce Education Enrollment Trends

"The term *equity* describes a concept whereby students make career choices based on inherent talents and abilities rather than on stereotypes or biased expectations. Equitable education is a vehicle that allows students equal access to the curriculum in order to encourage a broader range of career choices" (Foldesy & Foldesy, 1993, p. 69).

The National Center for Research in Vocational Education (NCRVE) (1996) finds that vocational education continues to show stereotyped program enrollment patterns, with about half of school districts not offering provisions to reduce gender bias and those that did offering programs with highly varied quality. The American Association of University Women (AAUW) (Wellesley College Center for Research on Women, 1992) finds that vocational education continues to keep females from rewarding careers. This report finds that seven of the eight vocational program areas are predominantly one gender or the other, with the only exception being marketing education. These findings are consistent with other reports on enrollment patterns in vocational education (Center on Education and Training for Employment, 1992; Wolfe, 1991).

According to the National Assessment of Vocational Education (Office of Educational Research and Improvement, 1994), economic outcomes for women with vocational training surpass those for men. Women are more likely than men to improve their wages and earnings with vocational training, to find a match between training and employment, and to benefit from completing a degree.

When examining trends in gender participation in vocational-technical programs, one must also look at the economic context of this behavior. There continues to be a tremendous expansion of job opportunities in office, clerical, and service occupations that are traditionally female and declines in job opportunities in trade and industry that are traditionally male. Therefore, it is not surprising to find that females have benefited from their training better than males. Studies have found that women are more likely to find jobs in occupations for which they have been trained than are men (Campbell, Basinger, Dauner & Parks, 1986).

Trends in Secondary Vocational Education

Enrollment in vocational education coursetaking has declined over the past decade. The drop for both general labor-market preparation and consumer and homemaking education was particularly large (NCES, 1996b). Boys earn slightly more vocational credits than girls, but because girls earn more of their vocational credits in consumer and home economics, boys earn notably more occupationally related credits. Girls do not prepare for labor-market work to the same extent as boys. This can be partly explained by girls' slightly greater enrollment in college-prep track courses (Office of Educational Research and Improvement, 1994). Vocational majors were somewhat more likely than their academic counterparts to be male and to be from a racial-ethnic minority. They are also older and were more likely to be economically independent from their parents (Office of Educational Research and Improvement, 1994).

Most vocational program areas have gender-stereotyped enrollments (Office of Educational Research and Improvement, 1994). Agriculture, trade and industry, and to a lesser extent, technical communications have predominantly male enrollments. Business, health, and occupational home economics have predominantly female enrollments. Only marketing has a balanced enrollment.

Gender stereotyping is greater among students who concentrate in an area (and are thus more likely to be preparing for jobs in that area) than it is among all students taking courses in an area. For example, 78 percent of the students who earned any trade-and-industry credits in 1990 were male, but fully 91 percent of those who concentrated in this area are male. Similarly, while 66 percent of the students who earned credits in health were female, 87 percent of health concentrators were female. In almost every area, vocational enrollments in general show less change in gender distribution over time than do enrollments of vocational concentrations. For example, agriculture in general has changed from 71 percent to 72 percent male, but concentrators changed from 88 percent to 77 percent male.

Only three of the six labor-market areas with gender-stereotyped enrollment show any reductions in gender bias from 1982 to 1990 (Office of Educational Research and Improvement, 1994). Women have increased their representation in agriculture and technical/communication, but not in the trades, while men have increased their representation in business. Female graduates were significantly more likely than male graduates to concentrate in business. In contrast, male, Native-American, and economically and academically disadvantaged graduates were more likely than their counterparts to concentrate in trade and industry.

Between 1982 and 1994, enrollment in consumer and homemaking education rose for males, from 0.3 credits to 2.9 credits and doubled for females, from 1.0 credits to 2.2 credits. Occupational specific coursework fell for both groups from 3.3 to 1.7 credits for males and from 2.5 to 1.3 credits for females. Both groups increased their academic credit earned, with females earning more academic credits (NCES, 1994).

Postsecondary Enrollments in Vocational Enrollments

Since 1970, the enrollment pattern of women has reversed that of men. In 1990, women outnumbered men in postsecondary education. Some (Office of Educational Research and Improvement, 1994) associate this increase with the increase in the number of women who completed high school. Women's college enrollment increased from 49 percent in 1970 to 67 percent in 1991.

More vocational than academic majors are highly gender-segregated. For example in 1989, 10 of 21 vocational majors enrolled at least three-quarters of students of one gender, compared to only 4 of 19 academic majors. The most predominantly male vocational majors are found in the traditional trades (engineering, transportation, precision production, mechanics, and construction), while among academic programs, they include the physical sciences and philosophy. The most predominantly female majors include vocational majors in health, business support, consumer services, and home economics, and academic majors in legal assisting, education, and public affairs. Since 1986, predominantly females fields are now enrolling more male students, but predominantly male fields are not increasing their enrollments of females.

Workforce Education Faculty

There are few role models for women and minorities outside of a narrow range of occupational fields. Within secondary vocational programs, women teachers are concentrated in health (83 percent), occupational home economics (92 percent), office occupations (64 percent), and consumer and homemaking (96 percent); they have low representation in fields such as agriculture (6 percent), technical occupations (12 percent), trade and industry (9 percent), office occupations (12 percent), and technology education (4 percent). Minority teachers are concentrated in home economics (15 percent), office occupations (12 percent), and technology education (12 percent) (National Center for Education Statistics, 1994). Darling and Sorg (1993) found individual teachers perpetuate gender-role stereotypes in vocational education, with many claiming that improving gender equity is a low or nonexistent priority for most vocational educators. Almost all the teachers in agriculture (93 percent), technical education (96 percent), and trade and industrial education (91 percent) are male (Office of Educational Research and Improvement, 1994).

The trade and industrial area offers the greatest opportunity for economics gain, yet we continue to require a minimal level of education. Trade and industry as well as technical teachers were more likely than other vocational teachers to have earned less than a bachelor's degree, and, along with health teachers, were older when they first began to teach (National Center for Education Statistics, 1994).

Erekson and Trautman (1995) found that 90.4 percent of the industrial teacher education faculty were white and 95.5 percent were male. Despite some recent efforts in the profession to attach females to the field of industrial-technical teacher education, few minorities and women are found.

FEMALE CAREER EDUCATION AND DEVELOPMENT

Parental education and in particular family income influence career development of girls. (Mortimer, 1992). Families with limited incomes are more likely to invest in and encourage a son's education than a daughter's. Also, the value system of working-class or lower-income parents place girls in homemaker roles; thus, less emphasis is placed on occupational preparation and career development. Overall, mothers have been found to be a big influence to attend college (Herr & Gray, 1995). "Parents as daily models provide cultural standards, attitudes, and expectations and, in many ways, determine the eventual adequacy of self-acceptance and confidence, of social skills and of [gender] roles. The attitudes and behavior of parents while working or discussing their work is what the children respond to and learn" (DeRidder, 1990, p. 3).

Family influences will vary with the culture. For example, girls from Korean-American families are expected to choose careers that are less stressful and less demanding, with flexible schedules so they can take care of their families (Kim as cited in Lankard, 1995). Cultural values, stereotypical feminine role perceptions, role conflict, fear of career impact on family life, and low self-esteem affect women's participation in the world of work (Nowark & Ward, 1989). Sex-role socialization may lead to restricted career exploration and choice by women, as females are expected to be mothers, and males are expected to be workers (Harding & Beyard-Tyler, 1984).

The status associated with career opportunities is transmitted to children at an early age. Classifications of occupations as "male" or "female" by students can be measured as early as kindergarten (Teglasi, 1981; Weisnar & Welson-Mitchell, 1990). When asked to select the "best" jobs, the choices of elementary students corresponded more closely to masculine than to feminine stereotypes (Teglasi, 1981).

Bernstein, Reilly and Cote-Bonanno (1992) found that knowledge about nontraditional careers was significantly related to age, type of school, parental status, marital status, and race, as well as to the mother's and father's occupation. A strong relationship has been found between knowledge of nontraditional careers and attitudes toward them. Students who were most knowledgeable were most likely to be nontraditional in their attitudes.

Robbin (1992) conducted a study of a school in New England with a working-class community. The school was made up of 1,088 males and 601 females, with only 41 students enrolled in nontraditional training programs. This study found few students felt their junior high school guidance counselor provided any breadth of career choices. These same students had only 18 percent of their parents working in nontraditional careers, but 47 percent of the females and 17 percent of the males were interested in nontraditional careers. Most (64 percent) of these students felt that females worked for the same reason as males. These students also showed an awareness of occupational segregation by their knowledge of pay inequities. It was interesting to note that 24 percent of the males and 56 percent of the females thought that more men should enter nursing, child care, and clerical jobs.

Although programs to change attitudes and behavior toward nontraditional careers have not always been successful, the Achieving Sex Equity Through Students (ASSETS) training intervention has provided significant changes in attitudes of high school students toward women in nontraditional careers (Cote-Bonanno, 1994; Mitchell, 1994).

Access to Technology

Some are calling access to information "the civil rights and economic rights issue of the twenty-first century" (Stuart, as cited by Kerka, 1995, p.1). Some argue that early conditioning and emphasis on gender equity in computer use could lead to children having the informational skills essential for developing needed career skills.

Gamboa (1997) sites a Girl Tech executive stating, "Girls need to be literate and have these information technology skills or it will affect their future career choices. It will limit their opportunities" (p. A1). Conservative estimates find that 80 percent of the entertainment and learning software is purchased by boys or for boys. "The whole area of invention and science and mathematics should be open to them [girls] as it is to boys. But we should encourage them [girls] in different ways" (Swanson as cited by Gamboa, 1997, p. A1). Studies show that girls and boys interact with technology differently. Boys want to duel with the machine, while girls want to use it as a tool (p. A1).

RESEARCH ON NONTRADITIONAL PROGRAMMING EFFORTS

"Once presented with the opportunity to participate in career-oriented programs featuring nontraditional fields (e.g., science, manufacturing, and technology) and provided with equal opportunity to learn, female students perform at equal or better levels than their male counterparts and develop similar aspirations" (National Center for Research in Vocational Education, 1996, p. 7). Often females who enter nontraditional vocational programs must deal with gender-related problems before they can begin to learn (Lakes, 1991; Rainey & Borders, 1997; Read, 1994). The problem they must deal with is the behavior of the other students, future coworkers, faculty, staff, and administrators. Wider Opportunities for Women (1990) identified such barriers as sexual harassment, unsupportive family and friends, gender-role stereotypes, lack of support services, lack of nontraditional role models, and isolation in the classroom. Yuen (1983) identified other barriers that inhibit enrollment in nontraditional courses, including low self-esteem, external locus of control, fear of failure, fear of success, and lack of role models. The elimination of these barriers requires faculty and administration that are willing to go against the current social order (Keohane, 1990).

The NCRVE (1996) reports three primary barriers to female enrollment in nontraditional occupations: safety issues, family influence, and program reputations. Safety issues revolve around personal safety rather than general shop safety issues. Family issues revolve around the female students' current family and future family prospects influencing their aspirations. Parents and relatives have crucial influence on female student decisions. Programs that are receptive to the family and enhance their future education and career opportunities were perceived to have good reputations

Sanogo (1996) conducted a study of traditional and nontraditional female enrollees in school-to-work programs in Pennsylvania: "Despite an aggressive marketing campaign and the presence of gender enrolled in programs in most secondary schools, very few females have enrolled in programs that are nontraditional for their gender" (p.18). Eleven percent of enrollees were in metalworking, manufacturing, and engineering, and 0.4 percent were in agriculture. These females reported that they wanted to attend college (68 percent), two-year college (21 percent), and postsecondary vocational training (4.1 percent).

Factors influencing these young women to enroll in nontraditional education included:

money and benefits (93.8 percent), personal reasons, interest, etc. (93.8 percent), favorable working conditions (87.5 percent), and parents (87.5 percent). Traditional enrollees had similar factors that influenced their enrollments, but in different priority order, as follows: personal reasons, interest, etc. (96.5 percent), favorable working conditions (86 percent), and money and benefits derived from the job (80.7 percent).

Of the barriers perceived by these young women in traditional and nontraditional programs, isolation or being the only female in the program (75 percent) was most common. Next to this, nontraditional enrollees identified lack of self-confidence (68.8 percent) and lack of female role models (68.8 percent). Those enrolled in traditional programs identified gender discrimination and sexual harassment by male classmates (61.4 percent) as other barriers to participation. Disapproval of parents also was an identifying barrier for these women, with very few parents supporting nontraditional careers for their daughters, and lack of support from teachers and guidance counselors was also cited. These students felt the hardest part of choosing to enroll in a nontraditional program was peer pressure. The isolation and the general feeling of not being accepted were of concern. Sexual harassment is a factor that can be controlled in student recruitment and retention in nontraditional program process.

Sexual Harassment

Sexual harassment—to exclude, demean, or intimidate—occurs in schools, the workplace, and society at large (Burge & Culver, 1994). According to the *Washington Post* (Jordon, 1993), 85 percent of all girls and 76 percent of all boys said they have been sexually harassed in some way in school.

Kane and Frazee (1978) found that 65 percent of female high school students in nontraditional courses reported harassment by male classmates and by some teachers. Lakes (1991) and others ("Breaking Through," 1992; Spain, 1997; Nichols & Kanter, 1994; Greene & Stitt-Gohdes, 1995) have emphasized the importance of establishing mentor relationships and support groups for non-traditional students to help them handle the stresses they encounter. Close ties with business and industry can also help with this transition.

Stein, Marshall, and Tropp (1993) found in their study that young women are more likely to be sexually harassed than their male classmates, and that, even when they report the harassment, in 45 percent of cases no action is taken. When teachers and other adults do not intervene, they send the message to both girls and boys that this behavior is okay. Some states have developed specific legislation to deal with sexual harassment.

Peers can be a major influence in the educational success or failure of those enrolled in nontraditional programs. To prevent/eliminate sexual harassment, it must be clear that this type of behavior will not be tolerated. Often the dominant gender will rally to intimidate the nondominant gender.

A 1992 Chicago Women in the Trades survey of about 500 tradesmen found that more than half worked in shops where sexual harassment occurred and women were not given proper job training (as cited in Spain, 1997). Between 1991 and 1996, the number of sexual harassment claims rose from 52 percent to 72 percent.

Factors for Successful Workforce Equity Programs

Baldus (1996) found that success factors included attitude, determination, work ethic, and mentor or support groups. These were more critical than traditional barriers such as lack of child care. Culver and Burge (1985) found that females in male-intensive programs had significantly higher self-concepts than females who had entered female-intensified or gender-balanced areas of study.

To create an inclusive workforce educational environment, faculty need to assure that instructional materials and examples are diverse by race, gender, ethnicity, disability, and age. To integrate women into nontraditional occupations, these women need to be assessed for their interest and for their perceived barriers to workforce education, and must be provided with mentoring, role models, and support groups. Early dissemination into high school programs is important for postsecondary programs. Pre-apprenticeship classes and jobs are good exploratory avenues, as are classes associated with a trade or technical field of interest. Challenges to be met include employers not training enough, emphasis on college school-to-work, parents' and societies' attitudes, and harassment. Cunanan and Maddy-Bernstein (1993) provide strategies for recruitment and retention of nontraditional workforce education students (see Tables 17.1 and 17.2).

Lozada (1997) provides an example of how women are contributing to innovative programming for preparing students in the construction industry. In this model program in Miami, Florida, the program's leader is a woman, and the lead carpentry teacher is also female. This teacher shares with her students how she was able to use her skills to earn enough money for college.

One of the major attractions for women to blue-collar jobs such as carpentry, auto mechanics, and plumbing are the higher salaries that are available compared to pink-collar clerical and office jobs. Tradeoffs for the higher salary may include dangerous or unhealthy conditions, seasonal layoffs, and the almost inevitability of sexual harassment or ostracism by male coworkers (Carter, 1994, p. 71).

ISSUES AND RECOMMENDATIONS FOR THE FUTURE

There is a need for additional research that examines the role of education in preparing women for their future economic roles. Women will constitute over half of the future labor force (U.S. Department of Labor, 1997a). A majority of the new female workers will be women of color. More attention needs to be given to the examination of gender and ethnic/racial differences during adolescence (Meece and Eccles, 1993; McWhirter, 1997). Also, more attention should be addressed to the area of peer pressure on students' achievement and motivation. According to Pollard (1993) peers are not seen as a source of positive peer support of achievement for African-American students. Bailey (1993) found that opposite-gender peers actually create a negative peer environment. As compared to boys, girls report a greater fear of harassment that negatively impacts school attendance, participation in class, and study habits. Maccoby (1990) concluded that peers were the main reason for maintaining gender-segregated behaviors and preferences.

Meece and Eccles (1993) are also concerned about the serious lack of attention given to gender and ethnicity/race in teacher preparation programs in this country. By the year 2050, 47 percent of the total U.S. population will be Asians, Hispanics, blacks, and other persons of color ("A Spicier Stew," 1992).

Women's labor-force growth is expected to increase faster than men's—16.6 percent between 1994 and 2005 as compared to 8.5 percent for men. Women will increase their share of the labor force from 46 percent to 48 percent (U.S. Department of Labor, 1997a). According to *Training* magazine (as cited by Spain, 1997), 70 percent of companies offer instruction on sexual harassment. Some see hostility for women in male-dominated industries.

Mends-Cole, a sex-equity coordinator, finds it "imperative that women be made aware of obstacles they may encounter on the job when they work in nontraditional occupations" (as cited by Spain, 1997, p. 18). She goes on to say that "male coworkers are sitting around waiting for them to fail or crack under pressure."

Career education is needed for the girls of today and tomorrow. All teachers need to be prepared in career education from early childhood on up. Teacher education needs to include equity and career education for all of its future and inservice teachers.

As the preceding discussion suggests, the vocational-technical education system has not been very successful in moving girls and women into nontraditional jobs and careers. This is not surprising since few resources have

Table 17.1—Recruitment Strategies

- F Develop summer orientation programs in which males participate in traditionally female programs and females participate in traditionally male trade areas.
- F Advertise in school publications inviting females to call for information about a traditionally male program.
- F Encourage female students who are currently enrolled in nontraditional occupational (NTO) programs to assist recruiters during high school recruitment fairs.
- F Compile a listing of financial aid assistance available to females interested in entering nontraditional programs.
- F Include representations of females in audiovisual, instructional, and orientation materials used during recruitment fairs and career days.
- F Identify and visit female students who are potential students in nontraditional programs prior to their enrollment in high school.
- F During recruitment fairs, address the fear of peer disapproval with females who are potential nontraditional program students.
- F Encourage parents to play a strong role in supporting their daughter's career choice.
- F Arrange job-site visits and experimental work experiences to introduce female students to nontraditional careers.
- F Design curriculum for career classes at the junior level to reflect a variety of occupations.
- F Establish a mentor network for women interested in entering nontraditional occupations.
- F Provide employability skills information through presentations in required high school vocational courses in order to reach all women students in target programs.

Source: Center for Education and Development, as cited in Cunanan, E.S., & Maddy-Bernstein, C. (1993), p. 5.

Table 17.2—Retention Strategies

- Send introductory letters to female students in nontraditional programs to welcome them and apprise them of the support service available.
- Assist students in identifying one person (relative, friend, instructor) who is supportive of their nontraditional occupational (NTO) career path.
- Provide and encourage participation in support groups so that NTO students can meet and can share problems, concerns, and successes.
- Disseminate monthly and quarterly newsletters to all females enrolled in NTO programs.
- Offer shadowing experiences with nontraditional workers in the field.
- Encourage students' participation in related professional seminars and state and national vocational organizations.
- Eliminate any stereotyped instructional materials from the classroom.
- Offer stamina-building and weight-lifting classes to female students in NTO programs.
- Offer tutoring to NTO-program students who may need to "catch up" due to lack of preparation for the subject matter.
- Establish a place which advises students to meet with an advisor before withdrawing from an NTO program.
- Enforce fair and consistent discipline, dress standards, safety regulations, achievement expectations, and grading procedures for all students.
- Provide on-site child care, transportation, and assistance with textbooks and other required educational materials, tools, and uniforms.
- Sensitize teachers to the effects of bias, stereotyping, and discrimination on students.

Source: Center for Education and Development, as cited in Cunanan, E.S., & Maddy-Bernstein, C. (1993), p. 5.

been devoted to gender equity in vocational-technical education (Wirt, Muraskin, Goodwin, & Meyer, 1989). According to the National Assessment of Vocational Education (NAVE) (Office for Educational Research and Improvement, 1994), gender equity grants were distributed to a relatively small number of districts and, even then, they tended to be very small. They also found a certain amount of cynicism among administrators about efforts to achieve gender equity.

Funding for the single parents and displaced homemaker programs went to a few districts, and the amounts received were very small (around $8,000), with money being spent on counseling and ancillary services rather than to upgrade institutions in low-income areas. The National Assessment of Vocational Education (Office of Educational Research and Improvement, 1994) found that disabled and academically disadvantaged girls were more likely to be trained for low-level service jobs than other girls were, although this difference did not appear for disabled and academically disadvantaged boys in vocational education.

"Critical education may help students to see how capitalism, labor, the consumer, and individual workplaces profit from and reproduce patterns of gender, racial, class and other forms of segregation and discrimination. . . . educators can be agents [of change] facilitating students' understanding of injustice and developing alternative methods for transforming society" (Carter, 1994, p.78). Carter (1994) provides numerous classroom activities that could be used by academic and workforce educators alike to crucially examine equity in the workplace. She provides a list of 10 videos to stimulate class discussions (documentaries such as *Women of Steel: The Life and Times of Rosie the Riveter*).

The Supreme Court will not review affirmative action. This may well end preference hiring based on race and gender (Beacon Journal Wire Service, 1997). There has been a great deal of noncompliance with existing federal programs. With movements such as these, will gains be lost? Only time will tell.

Douglass (1987) cites a lack of research in vocational education as a major barrier to the development of effective strategies in dealing with gender equity issues. Klein (1994) examined research on gender equity since 1972 and concluded that a more systematic development of comprehensive research on the promotion, delivery, and achievement of gender equity is needed.

Dougherty and Ellibee (1997), from the National Center for Research in Vocational Education, provide quality standards for school-to-work curriculum that include equity and diversity standards. Vocational education curricula must reflect content which portrays and celebrates the active participation of all individuals in the nation's workforce, communities, and educational institutions. According to the U.S. Department of Education (May, 1996), 29 states at the secondary level and 20 states at the postsecondary level have established standards to assess gender equity in vocational education programs.

More often than not, there is more talk than action. Dale Parnell "summarizes the current stage of educational reform [for equity in workforce education]. . . . Since everyone knows the problem, we need to adopt the Noah principle: No prizes for predicting rain, only prizes for building arks" (as cited in Hoerner and Wehrley, 1995, p. 118). Also: "Teach the whole student, nothing but the student, so help the student" (Dr. W. Leventry, professor of educational psychology, Indiana University of Pennsylvania, 1977).

References

A spicier stew for the melting pot. (1992, December 21). *Business Week*.

American Association of University Women (AAUW). (1993). *Hostile hallways*. Washington, DC: Author.

Aurdene, P., & Neisbett, J. (1992). *Megatrends for women*. New York: Villail Books.

Bailey, S. M. (1993). The current status of gender equity research in American schools. *Education Psychologist, 28* (4), 321-339.

Baldus, L. (1996). Wisconsin Technical College System Board Equity Staff Development Workshops and Services—Phase V. Final Report. Stout,WI: University of Wisconsin, Stout. (ERIC Document Reproduction Service No. ED 395 213)

Beacon Journal Wire Service. (1997, November 4).

Court will not review affirmative action. *The Beacon Journal*, p. Al.

Bernstein, J. D., Reilly, L. B., & Cote-Bonanno, J. F. (1992). *Study to examine student knowledge and attitudes toward nontraditional careers.* Upper Monclair, NJ: Life Skills Center, Montclair State University. (ERIC Document Reproduction Service No. ED 397 143)

Breaking through the glass ceiling: A career guide for women in government. (1992). Washington, DC: National Capital Area Chapter.

Bruno, R. R. (1995, December). *What's it worth? Field training and economic status: 1993*, pp. 70-51. Washington, DC: Current Population Reports, U.S. Bureau of the Census. [On-line]. Available: http://www.census.gov

Burbridge, L. C. (1992). *New economic trends for women's employment: Implications for girls' vocational education.* Wellesley, MA: Wellesley College. (ERIC Document Reproduction Service No. ED 360 492)

Burge, P. L., & Culver, S. M. (1994). Gender equity and empowerment in vocational education. In R. D. Lakes (Ed.), *Critical education for work: Multidisciplinary approaches.* Norwood, NJ: Ablex Publishing Corp.

Campbell, P. B., Basinger, K. S., Dauner, M. B., & Parks, M. A. (1986). *Outcomes of vocational education for women, minorities, the handicapped, and the poor.* Columbus, OH: National Center for Research in Vocational Education, Ohio State University.

Carter, P. A. (1994). Women's workplace equity: A feminist view. In R. D. Lakes (Ed.), *Critical education for work: Multidisciplinary Approaches.* Norwood, NJ: Ablex Publishing Corp.

Center on Education and Training for Employment. (1992). *Vocational equity in Ohio.* Columbus, OH: Center on Education and Training for Employment, Ohio State University.

Cote-Bonanno, J. F. (1994). *The effect of achieving sex equity through students on high school students' attitudes toward women in nontraditional occupations.* Unpublished doctoral dissertation, Seton Hall University, South Orange, NJ.

Culver, S. M., & Burge, P. L. (1985). Self-concept of students in vocational programs nontraditional for their sex. *Journal of Vocational Education Research, 10* (2),1-9.

Cunanan, E. S.. & Maddy-Bernstein, C. (1993). Working together for sex equity: Nontraditional programs make a difference. *TASSP (Technical Assistance for Special Populations Program) Brief, 5* (1), 5.

Darling, C. W., & Sorg, S. E. (1993). A new attitude. *Vocational Education Journal, 68* (30), 18-22.

DeRidder, L. (1990). *The impact of parents and parenting on career development.* Knoxville, TN: Comprehensive Career Development Project. (ERIC Document Reproduction Service No. ED 325 769)

Dougherty, B., & Ellibee, M. (1997). *Curriculum quality standards for school-to-work: A guidebook.* Berkeley, CA: National Center for Research in Vocational Education. (ERIC Document Reproduction Service No. ED 402 219)

Douglass, R. S. (1987). *Access to quality vocational education: A sex equity perspective. Design papers for the national assessment of vocational education,* II-32. Eisenberg, S. (1992, August). Vocational education in the school reform movement. *Women's Educational Equity Act Publishing Center Digest,* pp. 6, 8.

Erekson, T. L., & Trautman, D. K. (1995). Diversity or conformity? *Journal of Industrial Teacher Education, 32* (4), 92-94.

Faludi, S. (1991). *Backlash: The undeclared war against American women.* New York: Crown.

Foldesy, G., & Foldesy, E. M. (1993, November/December). Occupational education: Equity issues. *The Clearing House, 67* (2), 69-70.

Gamboa, G. (1997, November 2). Girls are missing in action on technology's front lines. *The Beacon Journal,* pp. A1, 10.

Gray, M. C. (1994). *A history of women in the trades for integration with the gender equity in education and the workplace curriculum.* Fairfield, ME: Vocational Curriculum Resources Center of Maine. (ERIC Document Reproduction Service No. ED 396 124)

Greene, C. K, & Stitt-Gohdes, W. L. (1995, April). Factors that influence women's choice to work in the trades. In R. L. Joynor (Ed.), *AERA vocational education special interest group proceedings.* American Educational Research Association annual meeting. (ERIC Document Reproduction Service No. ED 383 883)

Hargrove, L. A., Frazier, W., & Thomas, T. (1983). *Comprehensive analysis of follow-up data for students enrolled in traditional and nontraditional vocational and technical programs.* Oklahoma City, OK: Oklahoma State Department of Vocational and Technical Education.

Haring, M., & Beyard-Tyler, K. C. (1984). Counseling with women: The challenge of nontraditional careers. *School Counselor, 31* (4), 301-309.

Herr, E. L., & Gray, K. C. (1995). *Other ways to win: Creating alternatives for high school graduates.* Thousand Oakes, CA: Corwin Press.

Hoerner, J. L., & and Wehrley, J. B. (1995). *Work-based learning: The key to school-to-work transition.* New York: Glencoe/McGraw Hill.

Johnson, W. B., & Parker, A. E. (1987). *Workforce 2000: Work and workers for the 21st century.* Indianapolis, IN: Hudson Institute.

Jordon, M. (1993, June 2). Sexual harassment complaints starting in grade school: Taunts, intolerance on theists, survey finds. *The Washington Post,* p. A1.

Kane, R. D., & Frazee, P. E. (1978). *Women in nontraditional vocational education in secondary schools.* Arlington, VA: RJ Associates.

Kates, E. (1991). Transforming rhetoric into choice: Access to higher education for low-income women. In L. R. Wolfe (Ed.), *Women, work, and school: Occupational segregation and the role of education* (pp.181-197). San Francisco: CA: Westview.

Keohane, N. O. (1990). Educating women students

for the future. In J. Authur & S. K. Bilken (Eds.), *Changing education* (pp. 3-13). Albany, NY: State University of New York Press.

Kerka, S. (1995). *Trends and issues: Access to information: To have and have not* . Columbus, OH: ERIC Clearinghouse on Adult, Career, and Vocational Education.

Klein, S. S. (1994, November). Continuing the journey toward gender equity. *Educational Researcher, 23,* 13-21.

Lakes, R. D. (1991). In the male domain: Females in nontraditional vocational education. *Occupational Education Forum, 19* (2), 17-23.

Lankard, B. A. (1995). *Family role in career development, ERIC Digest No. 164.* Clearinghouse on Adult, Career, and Vocational Education. Columbus, OH: Ohio State University.

Lozada, M. (1997, March). A constructive education. *Techniques, 72* (3),12-18.

Maccoby, E. E. (1990). Gender and relationships: A developmental account. *American Psychologist, 45,* 513-520.

McWhirter, E. H. (1997). Perceived barriers to education and career: Ethnic and gender differences. *Journal of Vocational Behavior, 50,* 124-140.

Meece, J. L., & Eccles, J. S. (1993). Introduction: Recent trends in research on gender and education. *Educational Psychologist, 28* (4), 313-319.

Milgram, D., & Watkins, K. (1994, March). *Ensuring quality school-to-work opportunities for young women.* Washington, DC: Wider Opportunities for Women and American Youth Policy Forum.

Mitchell, P. A. (1994). *Sex role attitude change as a result of a two-day human relations training workshop for high school students.* Unpublished doctoral dissertation, Columbia Pacific University.

Mortimer , J., et al. (1992). *Influences on adolescents' vocational development*. Berkeley, CA: National Center for Research in Vocational Education. (ERIC Document Reproduction Service No. ED 352 555)

Mother is working before baby is walking. (1997, November 26). *The Beacon Journal*, p. A1.

Nasal, S. (1992, October 19). Women's progress stalled? Just not so. *The New York Times,* pp. 1, 10.

National Center for Education Statistics. (1994). *Sex and racial/ethnic characteristics of full-time vocational education instructional staff* (Publication No. NCES 82-207B). Washington, DC: U. S. Department of Education.

National Center for Education Statistics. (1996a). *The condition of education 1996* (Publication No. 96-304). Washington, DC: Office of Educational Research and Improvement.

National Center for Education Statistics. (1996b). *Findings from vocational education in the United States: The early 1990's.* Washington, DC: Office of Educational Research and Improvement. Available on-line: http://www.ed.gov/NCES/pubs/voced/95024.html

National Center for Research in Vocational Education. (1996, Fall). *Voices of Diversity. Brief No.6.* Berkeley, CA: The University of California at Berkeley. Available on-line: http://www.ncrve.berkeley.edu

National Science Foundation. (1990). *Women and minorities in science and engineering.* Washington, D.C.: Author.

Nettles, S. M. (1991). Higher education vs. a route to self-sufficiency for low-income women and women on welfare. In L. R. Wolfe (Ed.), *Women, work, and school: Occupational segregation and the role of education* (pp.155-167). San Francisco, CA: Westview.

Nichols, N. A., & Kanter, R. M. (1994). *Reach for the top.* Boston, MA: President and Fellows of Harvard College.

Nowark, M. L., and Ward, S. (1989). Determinants of women's career aspirations. *Equal Opportunities International, 8* (6), 1-6.

Office of Educational Research and Improvement. (1994). *National Assessment of Vocational Education: Interim report to Congress.* Washington, DC: U. S. Department of Education.

Pollard, D. S. (1993). Gender, achievement, and African-American students' perceptions of their school experiences. *Educational Psychologist, 28,* 341-456.

Rainey, L. M., & Borders, L. D. (1997). Influential factors in career orientation and career aspiration of early adolescent girls. *Journal of Counseling Psychology, 44* (2),160-172.

Read, B. K. (1994). Motivational factors in technical college women's selection on nontraditional careers. *Journal of Career Development, 20,* 239-258.

Robbin, D. J. (1992, August). Gender equity in vocational education. *Women's Educational Equity Act Publishing Center Digest*, pp. 1-2, 5.

Sanogo, C. C. (1996, Spring). Facilitators and barriers to female participation in school-to-work: Tradition versus nontraditional programs. *Occupational Educational Forum, 23* (1), 16-24.

Smith, J. P., & Ward, M. P. (1984). *Women's wages and work in the twentieth century.* Los Angeles, CA: RAND Corporation.

Spain, V. (1997, April). No easy path for women in non-traditional careers. *Techniques, 72* (4), 17-21.

Stein, N., Marshall, N. L., & Tropp, L.R. (1993). *Secrets in public: Sexual harassment in our schools, a report on the results of a Seventeen magazine survey.* Wellesley, MA: NOW Legal Defense and Education Fund and Wellesley College Center for Research on Women.

Stipp, D. (1992, September 11). The gender gap. *The Wall Street Journal,* p. B8.

Streker-Seeborg, I., Seeborg, M. C., and Zegeye, A. (1984). The impact of nontraditional training on the occupational attainment of women. *The Journal of Human Resources, 19,* 452-471.

Strong employment gains spur inflation worries. (1994, May 17). *Washington Post*, pp. A-l, A-9.

Tavakolian, H. R. (1994). Gender bias in the 1990's. *Equal Opportunities International, 13* (1/2), 18-27.

Teglasi, H. (1981). Children's choices and value judgements about sex-typed toys and occupations. *Journal of Vocational Behavior, 18,* 184-195.

U. S. Bureau of the Census. (1994). *Statistical Ab-*

stract of the U.S. (114th Ed.). Washington, DC: U.S. Government Printing Office.

U. S. Department of Commerce. (1994). *Income, Poverty, and Validation of Noncash Benefits:1994.* Washington, DC: Bureau of Census. Available on-line: http://www.census.gov

U. S. Department of Commerce. (1997, March). *How we're changing demographics: State of the nation 1997* , p. 23. Washington, D.C.: Bureau of the Census, Economic and Statistics Administration. Available on-line: http://www.census.gov

U. S. Department of Education. (1996, May). *Accountability systems in vocational education: Performance standards and core measures.* Available on-line: http:www.doe.gov

U. S. Department Education. (1997, June). *Title IX: 25 Years of Progress.* Washington, DC: Author. Available on-line: http://www.education.edu

U. S. Department of Labor. (1993, December). *Facts on working women: Earnings differences between women and men.* Washington, DC: Women's Bureau. Available on-line: http://www.dol.gov/dol/wb

U. S. Department of Labor. (1994). *Working women count: A report to the nation.* Washington, DC: Women's Bureau.

U. S. Department of Labor. (1996). *Facts on Working Women: 20 facts on women workers.* Washington, DC: Women's Bureau. Available on-line: http://www.dol.gov/dol/wb

U. S. Department of Labor. (1997a). *Women's jobs 1964-1996: More than 30 years of progress.* Washington, DC: Women's Bureau. Available on-line: http://www.dol.gov/dol/wb

U. S. Department of Labor. (1997b). Facts on working women: Black women in the labor force. Washington, D.C..: Women's Bureau. Available on-line: http://www.dol.gov/dol/wb

Vella, F. (1993). Gender roles, occupational choice, and gender wage differential. *The Economic Record, 69* (207), 382-392.

Vote, C. J. (1995). *Guidance and counseling curricula and programs which prepare adolescent females for the world of work: Recommendations for the school-to-work initiative. Review of literature.* Denver, CO: Colorado State Community College and Occupational Education. (ERIC Document Reproduction Service No. ED 382 875)

Wellesley College Center for Research on Women. (1992). *How schools shortchange girls: A study of major findings on girls and education.* Washington, DC: American Association of University Women Educational Foundation.

Weisnar, T. S., & Welson-Mitchell, J. E. (1990). Nonconventional family life styles and sex stereotyping in six year olds. *Child Development, 61,* 1915-1933.

Wider opportunities for women. (1990). *Program and policy agenda 1989-91.* Washington, DC: Author.

Wirt, J. G., Muraskin, L. D., Goodwin, D. A., & Meyer, R. H. (1989). *Summary of findings and recommendations: National assessment of vocational education.* Washington, DC: U.S. Department of Education.

Wolfe, L. R. (Ed.). (1991). *Women, work, and school: Occupational segregation and the role of education.* San Francisco: Westview.

Women's Action Coalition. (1993). *Women's Action Coalition statistics: The facts about women.* New York: The New Press.

Wood, R. G. (1993). Pay differences among the highly paid: The male-female earnings gap in lawyers' salaries. *Journal of Labor Economics, 11* (3), 417-441.

Yuen, C. Y. (1983). Internal barriers for women entering nontraditional occupations: A review of literature. *Occupational Education Forum, 12* (2), 1-14.

***Susan J. Olson** is an associate professor and coordinator of the technical education program in the College of Education at The University of Akron, Ohio. She holds a bachelor of science degree and a master's degree in education from the Indiana University of Pennsylvania and a Ph.D. from the Pennsylvania State University. Her other publications focus on postsecondary technical instructor preparation, distance learning, and women's career development. She serves as a referee for the* Journal of Industrial Teacher Education *and the* Journal of Workforce Education *(formerly the* Occupational Education Forum*).*

18

A CANADIAN PERSPECTIVE ON VOCATIONAL EDUCATION AND TRAINING

By John Gradwell

Canada's system of vocational education and training (VET) is complex, diverse, and changes frequently. Each province and territory has jurisdiction over its own curriculum, standards, program delivery, graduation requirements, and finances. This chapter discusses issues common to all provinces and territories.

Historically, Canada has not developed national goals and standards for its workforce. The provinces have tended to perceive such efforts as usurping their authority. Also, coordination and sharing of information between the provinces has been minimal and their strategies have changed over time.

> There has been a recurring cyclical swing from regarding VET and other "general" forms of education, as totally separate entities to attempting to merge them into a comprehensive system, and then a few years later to divide them once again, with VET being isolated in specialized centers. (Gradwell, 1997a)

Provincial jurisdiction, due to the British North American Act of 1867, which gave control of education to the provinces, results in regional differences. In some areas, comprehensive secondary schools provide many options for students. In others, specialized vocational centers bring a critical mass of students to one central location. Some schools concentrate on generic skills common to a cluster of occupations, while others prepare students for specific entry-level job skills. Because of its regional diversity, Canada's labor market needs must be understood at both regional and local levels.

Lamoureux, Gradwell, and Rusnell, in their report to the Prosperity Secretariat (June 1992, p. 2), pointed to the result of lack of consensus and stability at the top level: "In the ever-changing environment of federal-provincial relations and the array of provincial training initiatives sponsored and withdrawn in response to federal funding strategies, vocational training at the secondary school level has not had a stable environment."

Recent VET program initiatives have generally emphasized short-term training with short-term income support and inflexible funding requirements. This emphasis on trying to fulfill immediate needs comes partly from an inability to match training with job opportunities due to a lack of reliable forecasts for training supply and demand.

Finally, business and industry have seen little involvement compared with their counterparts in some other countries.

This chapter attempts to address common Canadian VET issues related to:

1. Nonuniversity-oriented courses offered in secondary schools that have programs related to skilled trades, technical studies, business studies, and other applied subjects.

2. The approximately 70 percent of the school population that goes to work without proceeding first to postsecondary education.

3. The need of all elementary and secondary students for involvement in experiences that provide understanding of the technological world.

In particular, it addresses the following question. What are the critical issues for all provinces and territories if Canada is to compete economically with nations that have national goals, understand the value of lifelong learning, promote excellence in their bid to compete internationally, and have developed an efficient system of training programs that closely links education to the world economy?

TEN CRITICAL ISSUES

Working with two colleagues, I defined 10 critical issues in the Prosperity Secretariat Learning report. Many of these issues do not solely "belong" to VET, but relate equally to all facets of education. The remainder of this chapter will discuss them at some length.

1. Facilitating lifelong learning—*The use of all appropriate means of formal and informal learning to update and upgrade a person's knowledge by moving frequently between work and learning institutions throughout life.* With achievement of the goal of lifelong learning, the traditional distinction between "schooling" and "work" will be obsolete. Education must be seen as an on-going part of life, not as mere preparation. With it comes a certain independence in that an individual decides what must be learned and selects from the entire range of community resources available. Students must understand the need to return to school and to acquire more skills. Because of international competition, there is no place for low-skill workers in Canada. Currently, school and work are still treated separately, when they should be seen as parts of a seamless whole. We tend to ceaselessly debate whether we should promote "academic" education or "vocational education" rather than concentrate on transitions, connections, and generic skills that fulfill the needs of both types of education.

As I stated earlier (Gradwell, 1997a, p. 9), "Without system building, innovative programs run the risk of simply remaining disjointed components with no overall vision. By contrast if each component is viewed as a building block which forms a unified whole, including education and industry partners, students and staff can work together to achieve the target they designed together."

The extent to which programs meet this challenge can be judged by their ability to provide guidance and career advising, allow for transfer from one field to another, and ensure availability to a broad range of stakeholders. If educators and the public view VET as providing limited opportunities, we must make major changes to become a respected part of lifelong learning.

2. Making school relevant—*Facilitating a coherence between what students learn in school and what they experience in life so as to increase their interest, attendance, and motivation to learn.* Work is a part of life for the vast majority of adults. Adolescents also value work, as can be seen in the high percentage who work part time while studying. However, most teachers do not address the centrality of work in everyday life.

Educators tend to say that the best preparation for work is a sound general education. On the other hand, they also promote vocational programs to a limited group of students. Both approaches are predicated on the premise that education and work are separate entities.

> Canada's educational system marches to an "academic drummer" whose beat is out-of-step with the need of students and the economy. Secondary schools are focused on the 15 percent of students who are university bound; the remaining 85 percent are destined to "lesser" pursuits. Vocational education is viewed as part of the "failure" path—a place where at-risk and

> low-potential students can be occupied without disrupting the 'important' business of schools. (Lamoureux, Gradwell, & Rusnell, 1992, p.2)
>
> Almost every policy discussion of secondary education in the last 50 years has commented on the need to move schools away from their focus on academic courses aimed at preparation for university. After decades of advocacy all over the country, we must recognize that programs aimed at preparation for work continue to be peripheral to secondary schools in Canada. There are few, if any, general secondary schools in which courses or programs related to preparation for work are as important as the traditional academic subjects. (Levin, April 1995, p. 4)

If, as Levin suggests, there is consensus on the need for schools to move away from their exclusive focus on academic courses aimed at university entrance and there is reason to believe that preparation for work is the main reason many students go to school, how can change come about?

Much of the debate concerning what should be taught at the secondary school level assumes an either/or base. That is, career preparation and so-called "basic" subjects are mutually exclusive. On the contrary, one may support the other. Academics are often best learned in real-life context. VET can provide the context to relate theory to practice. When properly taught, all career programs include abilities in communication, mathematics, and science. By relating one subject to another school becomes relevant.

In considering the value of work to education and the varied ways to incorporate work into the classroom, we should consider the following:

- Relating class activities to skills that students acquire through part-time jobs.
- Selecting from a broad range of work experiences. These could range from one-day job shadowing to "apprenticing" to a craftsperson for a portion of every week for a year or more.
- Providing work experience in the local community for teachers. Many teachers have only known life in academia. Arranging a broad experience in business or industry would give teachers a different view on life.
- Giving recognition for students' competencies in situations other than a formal school setting.

As I noted earlier (Gradwell, 1997b), "The mind works by linking what is known with what one needs to know. To function at the highest level, where real thinking takes place, students need to make connections between the new material and what they already know. . . . [S]tudents comprehend only to the extent that knowledge fits into their experience and the way they have organized past information."

Learning is best retained if it is taught in a real-life context, or at least related to one. Therefore, ideal VET programs would include a substantial field component, giving students experience with up-to-date equipment and an understanding of the culture of work.

3. Achieving a parity of esteem—*Ensuring that careers with practical components are as valued as so-called white-collar jobs by reversing the image of vocational education as a second-class alternative.* John Dewey, one of the most respected educators of the twentieth century, believed that vocational and academic education should not be taught separately. Furthermore, he felt that combining the two could "revitalize school learning and eventually aid in social transformation." (Wirth, 1991, p. 62)

Almost every policy discussion of secondary education in the last 50 years has commented on the need to move schools away from their focus on academic courses aimed at preparation for university. Yet, programs aimed at preparation for work continue to be peripheral to secondary schools in Canada. Benjamin Levin noted that "neglected calls for reform have been repeated all over the country with the result that there are very few, if any, general secondary schools in which courses or programs related to preparation for work are as important as the traditional academic subjects. Work-oriented programs tend to exist for students seen as nonacademic, as options subject to displacement, as credits that cannot be applied to postsecondary studies in related fields." (Levin, 1995, p. 29)

As I wrote (1997a),

> Most students will not enter and succeed in university, unfortunately; however, we have not been able to articulate an alternative strategy that can convince the majority of school personnel or the general public to realize the value of VET at the secondary school level. While we are convinced that "learning for life" should include "learning for work," the two have often been treated separately by the educational community, despite the fact that learning is increasingly an on-going part of work throughout one's lifetime. . . . The skills required for a job and those needed to continue to college or university are not that different. Rather than creating separate routes we need to foster a rapprochement that will result in what Europeans call a 'parity of esteem' between applied learning and abstract learning according each one an equal value" (pp. 5 & 6)

As stated by Mark Holmes (1989), education can broadly be seen to serve six general purposes: intellectual, cultural, social, expressive, vocational/economic, and moral/spiritual. Most of these purposes are automatically accepted as features of a broad general education. Only the vocational purpose has to continually fight for approval.

When VET is separated and looked on as an alternative to the favored path, it attracts less-able students, less-qualified teachers, and fewer resources. Viewing it as the place to channel "problem" students results in a poor image even with excellent curriculum and teachers. However, poor image must be addressed on several fronts, including: type of student; currentness of equipment; staff qualifications; linkages to higher and continuing education; and availability of counselors who value VET and have full knowledge of its program and career opportunities.

Some provinces try to give greater esteem to VET programs by mandating a "back to the basics" approach up to and including grade 11, believing that by admitting into VET students who have completed or nearly completed regular high school, the standards will be raised. The problem with this is that, first, VET becomes an option "selected" by only a few students, not a program available to all throughout high school. It becomes the less-favored alternative and continues to attract only those students who perceive themselves as lacking the ability to aim for university. Second, due to the delay in availability of VET, the dropout rate from high school increases.

Some public awareness campaigns aim to change the perception of VET as relying almost completely on manual skills. Another way to increase its status is to emphasize programs such as robotics, computer-aided design, and computer programming, placing the focus on high technology careers and emphasizing the the link between science and technology. Also, the Skills Olympics can raise VET's visibility through local, national, and international competitions in a variety of occupations.

The real debate about VET versus academic education stems from a view that vocational education is based on teaching a narrow set of skills that could be classified as training rather than education. Such skills are specific to a narrowly defined job that contains no transferable skills. The best response does not focus on the advanced technology skills inherent in some careers. While "high technology" jobs often receive the most publicity, they account for a very small percentage of the labor force. We must draw the public's attention to the more demanding requirements of the workplace. The question of esteem, should be based on the concept of lifelong learning and transferable skills, and particularly on the acquisition of scientific and technological concepts that are increasingly a part of all but the lowest service jobs.

4. Establishing partnerships—*Improving communication and mutual understanding among all stakeholders to better utilize available resources and stimulate new ways to provide appropriate learning opportunities.* Most people would not say that schools should take on all responsibility for educating youth. However, the schools have adopted roles that once belonged to the family, the church, or community groups. What schools must do now is form partnerships with other organizations such as employers, labor unions, and other educational institutions. Having available a variety of places for learning gives people the option of a flexible and unique program. Needless to say, connecting all pieces together to form a "seamless garment" for an individual student is a major challenge for schools in Canada and elsewhere. Partnerships can only be effectively formed when goals and priorities are clearly established and corporate priorities are understood.

In spite of their many potential benefits, few schools form diverse partnerships. Partnerships take time and energy. However, "these real environments can help schools remain current with new technologies, provide realistic experiences, and keep in touch with employers concerning current worker requirements. In some cases partnerships will match training to local job needs so people can stay and work in their own community" (Gradwell, 1997a).

The Economic Council of Canada (1992) lists the following ways that employers can partner with schools: (1) career days, at which local employers host students; (2) provision of awards; (3) sponsorship of summer science camps; (4) work experience for teachers; (5) adopt-a-school programs; (6) co-op work experience for students; (7) supplying of employees to teach special courses in the schools; (8) involvement in curriculum planning; (9) provision of guest lecturers; (10) assistance with graduate certification; and (11) provision of equipment and facilities.

Three types of work experience that involve industry can aid in specific skills acquisition:

• *Apprenticeship,* which some view as the best way to acquire in-depth career knowledge and others view as ill-suited to address the speed of changes in the workplace today.

• *Cooperative education*, which usually involves equal amounts of work and education experience during a school year.

• *Short-term experience* (sometimes called *work-study*), in which students spend two or three weeks in industry or business, normally at the end of their program, as a capstone to in-class experience.

Apprenticeship has a long and honorable history and has been one of Canada's chief sources of skilled labor. However, it has recently been criticized in the face of increasing technological change. The Canadian Red Seal program has improved the mobility of workers through the establishment of national standards. Changes are also needed to curriculum content, sequencing, streamlining of training time, and indentured time. Sweeping changes and cooperation between governments aimed at educational and curriculum reform, union participation, and employer agreement are needed to ensure common standards that will provide a pool of skilled trades persons.

The Canadian Vocational Association's (1987) *Review of Apprenticeship* (1987, pp. 27-29) listed common concerns:

• The need to integrate women into the apprenticeship system.

• The need to overhaul the Interprovincial Standards Program (Red Seal) and to introduce its levels of education nationally.

• The barriers to mobility caused by apprenticeship's certification procedures, union quotas, and hiring practices.

• The need to mesh apprenticeship with federal job creation strategies.

• The need to upgrade apprenticeship programs, create core programs, and develop competency-based, rather than time-based, programs.

• The need to expand the system from one that is based largely in the manufacturing and construction trades.

5. Establishing technology foundation courses—*Ensuring technological literacy for all secondary school students, including the role of technology in their daily lives in general as well as technology in the world of work in particular.* Literacy in modern society involves both the traditional ability to read and write and the increasingly important technological literacy.

Both should be addressed throughout the years of formal education.

Yet little has been done to address the challenge of designing educational programs that will promote technological literacy for Canada's youth. All students should be able to solve problems in a creative, innovative way or select appropriate physical and human resources and produce a product that responds to a stated need. Students and teachers alike must know how to retrieve information from on-line data bases, CD-ROMs, and information networks. Students need practice in searching for information, making sense of it by confirming and reformulating it and using it to answer a defined question. However, as I wrote earlier (1996) "professional leadership still attempts to grapple with the task of forming a subject that will not be defined as preparing a student to enter the world of work, but one that will retain a practical component while ensuring general appeal to most, if not all, students" (p. 247).

A case can be made that schools are reactive, not pro-active, in terms of the latest technologies. Also, schools have never considered the positive effects of students starting their first work experience. More than two-thirds of secondary school students work part time and experience the technologies in daily use in the workplace.

Core skills to establish a foundation in technology that would promote adaptability, transferability, and flexibility include:

- Career education that gives students information and experience related to work.
- Entrepreneurship qualities, including autonomy, creativity, and self-confidence.
- Enabling technologies, including practical skills with opportunities to conceive, model, and visualize ideas in concrete forms. Enabling technologies, at the forefront of technological change, include advanced manufacturing, advanced materials, biotechnology, and information technologies. Their economic and social potential changes the way we live.

High schools cannot focus on every career, but they can form career clusters to allow for career exploration. Careers can be grouped in many ways. One example is:

- *Arts and communications*. Includes careers in photography, public relations, radio, journalism, visual arts, virtual reality, interactive multimedia, television, film and live performance.
- *Health, recreation, human, and public services.* Includes careers in education, counseling, health care, child care, dental care, hotel, government, law, consumer affairs, research, sports.
- *Engineering, industrial, and scientific technology*. Includes careers in architecture, electronics, engineering, automotive manufacturing, building trades, horticulture, transportation, construction, physical science.
- *Business and marketing*. Includes careers in sales, public relations, finance, advertising, telecommunications, hotel and restaurant, network systems, travel and tourism, insurance, foreign service.

6. Defining the new basics—*Revising and updating the set of basic knowledge, skills, and attitudes that all students must posses regardless of their chosen career.* The debate over whether a general academic-focused education is better than vocational education often blurs when we speak of generic skills. Are abilities such as punctuality or creativity work-related skills or life skills? Does viewing schooling as strictly "academic" and focusing on a curriculum that has intellectual value exclude development of analytical abilities or the ability to be a critical consumer?

The world of work has changed. Just-in-time delivery, flexible manufacturing systems, and zero defects are three concepts that illustrate a dedication to innovation, creativity, quick response, and reliability. But are these part of the schools' "new basics" or are schools wedded to a "back to old basics" movement? Is the traditional set of academic skills as essential for success in formal education as we have assumed? Common sense, backed up by research, suggests that a much narrower subset is necessary for success in a specific occupation and these subsets differ according to occupation. Several reports in Western countries have attempted to move academics in the direction of generic skills that can transfer from one occupation to another. Generic skills should aim to produce articulate thinkers who search, analyze, manipulate, and apply information in new and innovative ways.

The so-called "employability skills" designed by the Conference Board of Canada are generic intellectual and social skills that are organized not in a fragmented way, as usually happens in schools, but in a way that calls for precise

Table 18.1—Employability Skills Profile
The Critical Skills Required of the Canadian Workforce

Academic Skills	Personal Mgmt. Skills	Teamwork Skills
Those skills which provide the basic foundation to get, keep and progress on a job and to achieve the best results	The combination of skills, attitudes and behaviors required to get, keep and progress on a job and to achieve the best results.	Those skills needed to work with others on a job and to achieve the best results
Canadian employers need a person who can:	Canadian employers need a person who can demonstrate:	Canadian employers need a person who can:
Communicate · Understand and speak the languages in which business is conducted · Listen to understand and learn · Read, comprehend and use written materials, including graphs, charts and displays · Write effectively in the languages business is conducted **Think** · Think critically and act logically to evaluate sitiations, solve problems and make decisions · Understand and solve problems involving mathematics and use the results · Use technology, instruments, tools and information systems effectively · Access and apply specialized knowledge from various fields (e.g., skilled trades, technology, physical sciences, arts and social sciences) **Learn** · Continue to learn for life	**Positive Attitudes and Behaviors** · Self-esteem and confidence · Honesty, integrity and personal ethics · A positive attitude toward learning, growth and personal health · Initiative, energy and persistence to get the job done **Responsibility** · The ability to set goals and priorities in work and personal life · The ability to plan and manage time, money and other resources to achieve goals · Accountability for actions taken **Adaptability** · A positive attitude towards change · Recognition of and respect for people's diversity and individual differences · The ability to identify and suggest new ideas to get the job done—creativity	**Work with Others** · Understand and contribute to the organization' s goals · Understand and work within the culture of the group · Plan and make decisions with others and support the outcomes · Respect the thoughts and opinions of others in the group · Exercise "give and take" to achieve group results · Seek a team approach as appropriate · Lead when appropriate, mobilizing the group for higher performance

plans and goals, and for a combination of self-discipline and teamwork. (See Table 18.1.)

Many of the competencies in the Conference Board of Canada's list, except for literacy and numeracy, do not necessarily involve curriculum content. Forty years ago our secondary schools helped us develop the competencies needed in the labor market by ensuring that we followed dress codes, completed work on time, were punished for tardiness, were checked for honesty, and could listen to and follow instructions. But today workers must respond immediately to the need for goods and services. Graduates should know how to make decisions, develop work plans, and take calculated risks.

7. Enhancing leadership—*Developing leaders and public figures who can develop effective programs and convey a positive image of VET to the general public.* Human resource development is vital to Canada's future as a world leader but development will only succeed through leadership foresight, skill, and expertise. Vocational educators are known more for strong knowledge of their career fields than for organizational knowledge. Leadership often arises more from years of dedicated service to an organization than from true potential for leadership.

A leader ensures a free flow of information up and down the organization to promote cooperation and understanding, rather than creating hierarchical structures. The essence of leadership should be on getting everyone to participate, encouraging teamwork.

Leaders view people as the most valuable assets. They propose but do not impose. They try to build a consensus among their followers. They try to reduce disparities among various groups, such as by increasing opportunities for women. They realize that with new technologies growing increasingly more accessible, the decisive factor in the future will be human resources. Leaders must provide vision and follow up with structure, programs, and resources.

Colleges frequently include both general and vocational programs under the same roof, such as the *Colleges d'enseignement generales et professionels* (CEGEP) in Quebec. Leadership there first went to those with a "classical" background, which can set up a bias in resource allocation. To succeed and compete, vocational administrators must gain expertise in management.

8. Ensuring educational quality—*Enhancing the image and reputation of VET by developing a shared vision, ensuring quality progress, and producing competent graduates who are self-motivated.* Quality control is essential for any operation—especially one that promotes professional skills. The quality of VET instructors, curriculum, learning activities, teaching materials, and other resources must be first rate. Program entrance and completion requirements must match the highest standards of industry and business.

Lack of respect for quality in VET programs may partially result from Canada's historical image as a "drawer of water and hewer of wood" that depends on low-tech industries. That simplistic view does not take into account industrial changes over the past 40 years, nor various Acts dealing with training limitations that responded to immediate rather than long-range needs. These include:

- The 1960 Technical and Vocational Training Assistance Act, which promoted cost-sharing agreements for provincial expansion of comprehensive and vocational schools.
- The 1967 Adult Occupational Training Act, which replaced these agreements and allowed the federal government to purchase training for targeted groups such as women, native, or disabled peoples, as well as for high-skill areas.
- The 1985 Canadian Job Strategy, which emphasized training in the private sector as opposed to public institutions.
- The 1989 Labour Force Development Strategy, which further encouraged businesses to increase their involvement in labor force development.

As stated in The Prosperity Secretariat Learning report which recognized the perceived lack of quality in VET programs:

> Enrollment in vocational courses is viewed by many school administrators, teachers, counselors, students and parents as a poor choice, and one which restricts opportunities for most secondary school students. Course standards are considered to be low and credits often may not be acceptable for entry into further study in postsecondary institutions. Access to, and availability of, vocational courses has been reduced in secondary schools. Mandatory graduation requirements of increased academic credits and additional compulsory courses have decreased opportunities for career exploration in optional courses. (Lamoureux, Gradwell, & Rusnell, 1992, p.1)

The question of ensuring quality may be partly resolved when vocational educators take time from their work stations and establish a shared vision of the contribution they can make for Canada's future prosperity.

An international study by the government of Canada (1990) found seven key themes in education/training in eight nations (USA, Australia, Germany, France, United Kingdom, Sweden, New Zealand, and Japan) that help to ensure educational quality:

1. National goals and objectives.
2. Lifelong learning.
3. Gearing up for international competition.
4. Excellence/effectiveness in education and training.
5. Close links between education and the economy.
6. Promotion of social equality and cohesion.
7. Encouraging efficiency in the system.

Quality in education must also take into account recent industrial quality control practices, such as *quality control circles* and *zero defects* requirements. The trend in occupational preparation programs toward competency-based vocational education (CBVE) also reflects a search for quality and accountability, as it aims to ensure effective and efficient program delivery. Competency-based programs include course objectives related to a detailed analysis of the occupation, evaluation methods, and certified student achievement based on mastery of course objectives. It focuses on clearly defined outcomes that are assessed in terms of student behaviors. One technical center offers a "warranty of skills" for its graduates, which allows employers to send students back for remedial work. In addition, a "training bonus voucher system" allows graduates access to 30 additional hours of training without charge for up to two years after they leave school.

9. Rethinking the structure of VET—*Integrating the separate components or programs of VET into a coherent whole that can be easily understood and accessed.* The organization and operation of VET in Canada is not simple. Various governing authorities, public and private schools and institutions, and provincial and federal policies and initiatives all have a role to play. Articulation, collaboration, and integration between programs and services has been poor.

In restructuring, we must design a system that students, parents and employers can easily understand. Relationships between organizations and different training paths should be clearly stated.

The VET's structure is also influenced by the structure of the high school. Many provinces set up comprehensive high schools in the 1960s and 1970s. These were founded on the premise of offering a full range of academic and applied courses. Some schools even achieved the aim of full integration of academic and applied courses. In many, this direction has been reversed. Schools reached a pinnacle of enrollment and then started to decrease in size. At the same time, equipment installed in the 1960s and 1970s became outdated. Unable to afford the cost of new equipment and with the potential number of clients reduced, VET courses suffered a period of benign neglect and were gradually dropped by many schools.

In restructuring, we might ask whether VET should be privatized. Many other nations fund VET through corporate levies that generally amount to 0.5 percent to 1.0 percent of payroll. Companies that provide training for their employees have their levies returned. However, even if this direction were desirable, statistics show that 75 percent of private sector Canadian companies have no worker training. In addition, schools have limitations in staffing, teacher training, and physical plants.

The New Urban High School Network (http://www.bpic.org) has considered restructuring and developed a good set of design principles for an urban high school that combines academics with school-to-work programming for all students. They recommend that schools:

- Incorporate work-based and community-service learning into a school-wide curriculum.
- Enable students to perceive a clearer connection between school experiences and future careers.
- Integrate vocational and academic teaching and learning.
- Teach through hands-on projects that address student interest and encourage critical thinking.
- Have teachers serve primarily as resources, advisors, and guides.
- Create flexible schedules that accommodate teacher teamwork, teacher planning time, work-based learning, and project-based learning.
- Directly involve families in children's education.
- Deeply imbed the school itself in the community.
- Eliminate distinctions between college bound and vocational education.
- Allow for smaller, personalized learning communities.
- Give all students equal access to a core set of experiences.
- Hold all students to a high standard while offering them the support to be successful.

The Canadian Restructured School Plan (CRSP) model (Canadian Vocational Association, 1992, pp. 9-12) offers more restructuring guidelines:

- Shift from a system where students are admitted to school on an annual or semiannual basis to flexible entry and exit.
- Shift from a rigid time-bound credit structure to a flexible competency-based curriculum.
- Shift from the lock-step graded structure to a nongraded, continuous progress, individualized approach.
- Shift from teacher-centered instructional mode to one that is learner-centered and teacher directed/assisted/managed.
- Shift from an evaluation system that reports student progress in percentages or letter grades to one that reports on competencies mastered and mastery level reached.
- Shift from a structure that compares student achievement with others in the group, to achievement based on the individual's own progress.
- Shift from a physical structure in which most institutional areas are of uniform size to one that facilitates large group and small group instruction, as well as independent study.
- Shift from a student counseling system that depends on one or two professional guidance counselors, to one in which "homeroom" teachers assume a major advisory role.
- Shift from an industrial model with a bureaucratic top-down structure to a professionally oriented collegial one in which teachers are encouraged to function as decision makers.

The CRSP Model includes guided independent study, small and large group instruction, variable intake and exit points, use of technology in the delivery and management of institutions, student evaluation based on clearly defined performance criteria, student self-evaluation, continuous program, advanced placement based on performance assessment, elements of mastery learning, and close consultation with stakeholders (e.g., teachers, parents, employers, postsecondary institutions).

The CRSP model also has similarities to recommendations made for changing apprenticeship. Tom Watson (1986) suggested ways to modernize apprenticeship that include competency-based training, multiple entry/exit classroom instruction, computer-assisted or individually prescribed instruction, improved on-the-job experiences, self-paced instruction manuals, and simulated training experiences.

10. Encouraging students to complete schooling.—*Using a combination of prevention strategies, intervention strategies, and school-to-work transition strategies to encourage students to make rational decisions concerning their futures.* Canada has a relatively high percentage of students who do not complete secondary school. The average for those who drop out is around 30 percent. Educational systems need to provide ways to increase the rate of retention in secondary schools.

It is undisputed that secondary schools promote university entrance as their primary goal. It is equally established that two-thirds of students will not go directly to postsecondary education, yet little emphasis goes to strengthening the relationships between schooling and employment. This includes a failure to provide students with mentors—a need acknowledged by the Canadian Vocational Association (1992, p. 5).

Work has changed dramatically since the 1950s, but many school programs have changed little. To secure employment in the next decade young people will have to be both well educated and diversely skilled. However, most students, particularly the dropouts, leave school without aspirations, skills, or prospects. Staying in school often depends on whether students have a vision of their future, and that depends on whether a student identifies with the options available. Ensuring an interface between secondary and nonuniversity postsecondary institutions is helpful. As I have noted earlier (1997a), "Joint planning between two educational levels ensures that the technical core can be studied in the last few years of secondary school, and the technical specialty courses follow at the college level. Horizontal articulation within the secondary school plus vertical articulation to the CEGEP or community college level fosters a partnership not only between academic and vocational educators but between one level of education and the next in order to promote applied academics as a primary means of teaching" (p.7).

CONCLUSION

Over the past quarter of a century, the workplace has experienced a profound transformation due to economic, technological, and demographic changes. The impact of international trade agreements, the increased education and skill requirements and the changing demographics of employees have forced Canadians to reexamine how VET can adequately respond to an increasingly complex and ever-changing workplace.

Within a context of lifelong learning, the productive capacity of the nation cannot be separated from educational establishments. Education and training must be effectively connected to eliminate barriers to mobility and continuance. In particular, the barrier between academic and vocational education, long since outdated, must fall for good. At the same time, VET's manner of delivery should change to ensure that new knowledge and skills can be conveniently acquired. When employees can select how to upgrade or retrain, they will be in charge of managing their own performance. Knowledge is now the key commodity. Both industry and education must be transformed into learning organizations if we are to lead in the twenty-first century.

References

Canadian Vocational Association. (1987). *Review of apprenticeship in Canada*. Ottawa: Canadian Vocational Association.

Canadian Vocational Association. (1992). Canadian Restructured School Plan—First Progress Report. (Progress Report CRSP). Ottawa: Canadian Vocational Association.

Conference Board of Canada. (1992). *Dropping out: The cost to Canada*. Ottawa: Conference Board of Canada.

Economic Council of Canada. (1992). *The new face of poverty: Income security needs of Canadian families*. Ottawa: Minister of Supply and Services.

Economic Council of Canada. (1992). *Education and training in Canada*. Ottawa: Minister of Supply and Services.

Government of Canada. (1990). *An international perspective*. Ottawa: Department of Secretary of State.

Gradwell, J. B. (1996). Philosophical and practical differences in approaches taken to technology education in England, France, and the United

States. *International Journal of Technology and Design Education 6* (3), 239-262.

Gradwell, J. B. (1997a). Why do we exist? Forming a model for vocational education. *Canadian Vocational Journal 32* (3), 5-9.

Gradwell, J. B. (1997b). Educational reform: A cerebral exercise? *P.A.P.T. Sentinal 13* (1), 23-24.

Holmes, M. (1989). The character and quality of Canadian education: Some contemporary issues. In *Forum: To Be Our Best—Learning for the Future*. Montreal: Corporate Higher Education Forum.

Lamoreux, M., Gradwell, J., & Rusnell, D. (June 1992). Prosperity secretariat learning: Building a foundation for prosperity. West Vancouver: Spectrum Vocational Testing Ltd.

Levin, B. (1995, January). Educational implications of a changing labor market. Paper presented to the National Consultation on Career Development, Ottawa.

Levin, B. (1995, April). How schools respond to changes in work. Paper presented at the Canadian Vocational Association Research Colloquium, Moncton, New Brunswick.

Watson, T. (1986, May) Apprenticeship: Time served or time-saving? *Canadian Vocational Journal 22*, 1.

Wirth, A. G. (1991). Issues in the vocational-liberal studies controversy (1900-1917): John Dewey vs. the social efficiency philosophers. In D. Carson (Ed.), *Education for work: Background to policy and curriculum*, pp. 55-64. Philadelphia: Open University Press.

John Gradwell is associate dean, McGill University, Montreal, Canada. Educated in England and the United States, he has an international perspective on vocational education and training. He has written extensively in the field of technical education in both English and French. His books include Techno 200: An Introduction to Teaching and Shaping our World.

19

TRENDS AND ISSUES IN WORKFORCE EDUCATION FOR SPECIAL POPULATIONS

By Lynda L. West and Arden Boyer-Stephens

INTRODUCTION

Trends in workforce education continue to reflect issues that merit serious consideration by caring and concerned educators who believe that special populations have a major role in workforce development. Special attention now goes to various diverse, targeted populations through legislation, public policies, and federal initiatives. Recent welfare reform exemplifies the fact that society has set a priority for a disenfranchised population to gain occupational training to become productive, contributing members of society. Previous legislation related to employment and training, vocational education, special education, and vocational rehabilitation identified and defined special populations that should receive special consideration and support services that would help them acquire job skills.

This theme continues today, though it has taken a different direction. No longer are there special "set-aside" funds in vocational/technical education specifically designed for special populations, such as the disadvantaged and the disabled. However, the effort to "include" special populations and the desire for training them is still advancing. For example, when reviewing legislation, such as the School to Work Opportunities Act (STWOA), the Welfare Reform Act, and the 1997 Amendments to the Individuals with Disabilities Education Act (IDEA), we can see clearly that society and the federal government recognize the need for special populations—for *all* students, including those with disabilities—to have access to work-based learning, school-to-work transition services, and vocational/technical training, if they are to play roles as productive, contributing members of society.

Changing demographics of American schools, cultural diversity, and the continued increase in special education numbers have raised a flag that says "caution" to educators. Walker (1991) said, "Every student is at risk for some reason. We cannot wait until a student is labeled as such to intervene; rather, we must plan for the success of *all* students" (p. 112). With the increasing recognition that all students have special needs, and the trend toward including all in various programs, society has signaled that educators must promote a healthy learning environment and design appropriate educational programs.

Special populations have been defined in a variety of ways and wear many different labels, such as *economically* or *academically dis-*

advantaged, dropouts, pushouts, underachievers, slow learners, disabled, special needs. The process of attaching labels to different students is still a controversial practice. However, federal legislation continues to use labels to describe students with certain characteristics. The single label most frequently used in education circles is *at-risk*.

Manning and Baruth (1995) believe that the education world has concluded that countless numbers of children and adolescents are at risk of dropping out of school and have no hope of future gainful employment. They are likely to become parents at a young age, to suffer from sexually transmitted diseases, to become addicted to drugs or alcohol, to be low achievers at all educational levels, and to live in unending poverty. The list is endless. Therefore, Manning and Baruth contend that educators must: (1) understand at-risk students, (2) know at-risk conditions and the consequences, and (3) know established and proven at-risk programs designed to meet individual learner needs (p. 4). Regardless of the at-risk condition, educators who prepare students in the new century must be professionally prepared and competent to direct the educational experiences of special populations. This philosophy is consistent with the concept of special education, the understanding that each student is an individual who requires an individualized education plan, and that "a one size fits all" curriculum does not work. Greater vision and a more thoughtful approach to designing curricula and programs for students from special populations require partnerships and collaboration among various professionals in education and the community at large.

There are various movements leading us into the new century that accentuate the focus and efforts of workforce development for special populations. Each aims to direct special populations in a positive, productive way. Brief descriptions of these movements follow:

Systems change: An effort to change large systems (such as health, mental health, education, and so forth) to better respond to the needs of their clients and consumers, cut red tape, mesh eligibility requirements, reduce paperwork, and create a seamless system of support services that is responsive to the clientele.

School reform: An effort to restructure the traditional form of schools, education, teaching, and learning, with the goals of enhancing student learning, increasing teacher and administrator accountability for student progress, and making schools more responsive to *all* learners.

Welfare reform: An effort to provide employment and training experiences for those in poverty and without job skills, to help them acquire the technical and social skills they need for employment.

School-to-work: An effort to tie curricula and appropriate learning activities (such as work-based learning) to work for *all* students and to provide employers with a skilled labor force that can meet the demands of the new century and global competition.

School-to-work transition: An effort to tie curricula, skill development, and support services into a meaningful transition plan for students with disabilities to better prepare them to exit the school system with a workable plan of resources, options, and next steps for the future.

Self-determination: An effort to train students with disabilities in decision making, self-advocacy, and social skills so that they can better represent themselves, their strengths, and their potential for employment, as well as take advantage of various residential living options in the future.

Inclusion: An effort to include students with disabilities in general academic settings with nondisabled peers in the least restrictive environment that is in the students' best interest and compatible with necessary available support services.

These movements are sometimes confusing to administrators and teachers, who at times view them as conflicting initiatives. They need not be. If a systematic, well-planned professional development sequence is in place, the similarities, mission, philosophy, goal, and objectives of various movements frequently coincide and support each other. The primary goal should be to shape the educational opportunities of all students, including those in special populations, to meet their individualized needs, regardless of the label they do or do not carry, so that all will have successful futures and improved quality of life.

PARTNERSHIPS

Vocational/technical training for special populations emphasizes partnerships. Partnerships bring various stakeholders together to achieve educational opportunities for special populations that would not otherwise be available. Partnerships frequently bring divergent philosophies, expertise, opinions, frames of reference, and emotions into the same room to struggle with two questions: (1) What are students' needs and the educational experiences that will assist them in transitioning from school to work/careers/life and, (2) who is responsible and what role do they play in insuring that student needs are met? The term *collaboration* is frequently heard as the answer. However, no one person has responsibility for delivery of instruction and support services needed to assist students with special needs transition. Effective teams are critical. There are legislative requirements that collaboration take place, and there are various strategies, considered to be best practices, for achieving successful transition for students with special needs. Teams of educators, parents, students, and community representatives together make important decisions with far-reaching consequences for students.

COLLABORATION

Collaboration has been the buzzword during the past decade. Federal, state, and local agencies struggle to find strategies to work together for the benefit of their clientele. This urge to work together is not totally altruistic, but instead often arises primarily from funding constraints faced by all agencies. Many federal- and state-level grants were awarded during the early 1990s to encourage state and local agencies to "plan" toward collaborative efforts. Planning efforts were designed to identify barriers to working together and produce the necessary actions needed to remove the barriers. These efforts laid the foundation for multimillion dollar federal grants awarded to states for *system change*. Ventures in system change require looking at the "big picture" and changing structures, operating procedures, policies, and rules (Kerka, 1997). The result should be a seamless system of services directed toward those who need them.

Two recent pieces of legislation requiring systems change significantly impact special needs populations. *Transition system change grants* support states' efforts to improve adult outcomes for students with disabilities. The grants mandate that states that receive federal funds collaborate with state vocational rehabilitation agencies. The grants also strongly recommend including the Department of Labor (Employment Security, Economic Development) and local agencies. The *School to Work Opportunities Act* (STWOA) require strong collaborative efforts between education and labor. The STWOA focuses on three concepts: school-based learning, work-based learning, and connecting activities. The STWOA involves all students, while transition grants concentrate on students with disabilities. Both require system change, both support productive adult roles for students, and both compel education and labor to work closely together.

Under the transition system change grants for students with disabilities, special education and vocational education are mandated to examine environments that students with disabilities will enter as adults and make the curriculum and program changes necessary to foster success in those future environments. Vocational instructors must provide appropriate accommodations for individual students with disabilities to successfully complete course work. These accommodations may include oral testing, extended time for tests and assignments, use of a calculator, taped textbooks, and the use of a variety of teaching strategies. If curriculum outcomes require significant modification, pass/fail grading systems are frequently used. For example, a student with a disability might need to master fewer competencies than other students in a particular course.

Vocational education also shares the responsibility for the transition to work or further education of students with disabilities. Funding of vocational education rests partly on students obtaining employment related to the course work taken. For students with disabilities who take vocational education, transition services become more important because they are mandated in federal legislation and transition system change grants. Vocational education advisory committees can prove useful in securing job placements for all students, including those with disabilities. A vocational instructor can describe a students' skills and advisory committee members can survey community employers to determine the best placement match for the student. Advisory committees can also inform vocational instructors of employer needs so they can make the curriculum more relevant.

Vocational instructors know about further education opportunities in their fields. Relationships with apprenticeship organizations and articulation agreements with higher education institutions provide the most important transition bridges—in addition to an active advisory committee—that vocational instructors can build. Many students with disabilities can succeed in technical schools and colleges if those institutions offer appropriate accommodations and support services. Under the Americans with Disabilities Act (ADA), employers, too, must provide appropriate accommodations in the workplace for individuals with disabilities.

The STWOA requires inclusion of students with disabilities in programs and services developed locally or statewide. Transition services neatly fit into the STW ideals. All students can benefit from exposure to workplaces, internships, and paid employment during their high school years. Employer mentoring programs help students determine their career interests, strengths, and weaknesses. The placement of students with disabilities in *appropriate* internships and employment is essential. Students with disabilities should be able to explain their disability and describe accommodations they need in a particular workplace. A release of information must be signed before an instructor can discuss a student's disabilities with an employer. It is better for the student to express his or her needs directly to the employer.

A vocational instructor can help by conducting mock interviews with students before their employer interviews and a special education teacher can review self-advocacy skills. This enables students to practice talking about their strengths and necessary accommodations for job performance. The instructor must thoroughly understand job requirements and employer expectations. The special education teacher must make sure the student is comfortable discussing strengths and disabilities from a positive perspective. Currently, this occurs through student-led individual education plan (IEP) training or a futures planning process, though not all districts use such strategies. Both the student-led IEP and the futures planning process are gaining popularity in special education practice.

Special education and vocational education have employed *work-based learning* for more than 25 years. Special education has designed the *work-study* program for students who need on-the-job training techniques. This program offers students credit for paid employment. While the students involved can perform in the workplace, they may not pass academic performance standards for graduation. Should these students receive a regular diploma for graduation? School systems' major challenge is to prepare students for independent, productive lives. Yet the debate over academic standards, the diploma, and certification of attendance for students with disabilities is still unresolved. States are trying various solutions, but we have not achieved national consensus regarding this matter.

The *cooperative occupational education* program (COE) has been a part of vocational education for many years. This program offers students credit for paid employment in areas related to their course work. Both the work-study program and COE require an individualized training plan that outlines competencies students will learn on the job. Students enrolled in both work-study and COE also take a related class (i.e., school-based learning) for at least one period a day.

Vocational instructors may need to ask about STW programs in their district, as well as available transition programs and services. The vocational school director may be aware of these programs, especially the STW program. The special education director can provide information about transition services and programs. Instructors should make every effort to become knowledgeable about these programs and involve their students with the services offered. No one instructor can do it all—collaboration with other programs, services, and community employers can greatly help and benefit all students.

TRANSITION PLANNING

Transition planning for students in special education requires successful partnerships and the use of a wide variety of successful strategies known as *best practices*. Kohler (1993) identified the following best practices in transition: vocational training; parent involvement; interagency collaboration and service delivery; social skills training; paid work experience; individual plans/planning; interdisciplinary transition teams; follow-up employment services; employer input; integration/least-restrictive environment/mainstreaming; community-based instruction; vocational assessment; community-referenced curricula; vocational, social and residential outcomes; daily-living skills training; IEPs reflecting transition goals; career education curricula; employability skills training; formal interagency agreements; early transition planning; and integrated academic skill training. Educators engaged in the process of transition planning for students with disabilities have proven these practices significant. They are an excellent checklist to use when preparing for transition planning for the individualized education plan.

Individualized Education Plans

Individualized education plans came into existence in 1975. The quality and significance of IEPs has long been debated, yet they remain a required part of the rights of students with disabilities. Transition planning is a mandated part of the IEP. During the reauthorization of the 1997 Amendments of the Individuals with Disabilities Education Act, transition is defined and mandated as early as age 14:

> Section 602. Definitions
>
> (30) TRANSITION SERVICES—The term *transition services* means a coordinated set of activities for a student with a disability that
> (A) is designed within an outcome-oriented process, which promotes movement from school to post-school activities, including postsecondary education, vocational training, integrated employment (including supported employment), continuing and adult education, adult services, independent living, or community participation;
> (B) is based upon the individual student's needs, taking into account the student's preferences and interests; and
> (C) includes instruction, related services, community experiences, the development of employment and other post-school adult living objectives, and, when appropriate, acquisition of daily living skills and functional vocational evaluation.
>
> Section 614 (d) (1). Individualized Education Programs
> (vii)(I) beginning at age 14, and updated annually, a statement of the transition service needs of the child under the applicable components of the child's IEP that focused on the child's courses of study (such as participation in advanced-placement courses or a vocational education program);
> (II) beginning at age 16 (or younger, if determined appropriate by the IEP Team), a statement of needed transition services for the child, including, when appropriate, a statement of the

interagency responsibilities or any needed linkages; and

(III) beginning at least one year before the child reaches the age of majority under State law, a statement that the child has been informed of his or her rights under this title, if any, that will transfer to the child on reaching the age of majority under section 615 (m); and Section 614 (d). Individualized Education Programs.

(5) FAILURE TO MEET TRANSITION OBJECTIVES—If a participating agency, other than the local education agency fails to provide the transition services described in the IEP in accordance with paragraph (1) (A) (vii), the local education agency shall reconvene the IEP Team to identify alternative strategies to meet the transition objectives for the child set out in that program.

The IEP can have transition infused into a document as specific goals and objectives (as in some states and some districts) or attached in a separate document, referred to as the *individualized transition plan* (ITP). Regardless of the format, it is an integral and critical part of the educational plan for the student with disabilities, as he or she prepares to exit the school system and enter the world of work. Many consider this not only the "school to work" part of their education, but also their "school to life" plan. States, districts, and teachers have their own understanding of the term. Consequently, a variety of strategies are used to respond to this legal mandate for students with disabilities. Some districts use vocational assessment to determine a student's direction, some use a futures planning process, others use the self-directed-IEP process, and still others use career portfolios or career pathways to insure that students have their transition plan in place. The strategies can be generally described as follows:

• *Vocational evaluation/assessment:* A comprehensive process (including formal and informal strategies) conducted over a period of time and involving a multidisciplinary team, to identify individual preferences, aptitudes, interests, and education and training needs to aid in planning an individual's transition from school to work.

• *Futures planning:* A process constructed to guide students to think carefully about their futures, strengths, interests, and goals, and to determine the path necessary to achieve their goals.

• *Self-directed IEP:* A process through which a student with disabilities takes the lead role in facilitating his or her own IEP planning, meeting, and/or facilitation after careful and explicit training by the special education teacher.

• *Career portfolios:* A purposeful collection of student work that exhibits the student's efforts to present a carefully crafted portrait of what he or she knows and can do (Sarkees-Wircenski & Scott, 1995).

• *Career pathways:* Area clusters of occupations/careers grouped together because many of the people in them share similar interests and strengths. All pathways include a variety of occupations that require different levels of education and training. Students select a career pathway to explore career, jobs, and skills. (Texas Education Agency, 1997)

ISSUES FOR THE FUTURE

The issues facing general education and vocational education have, as yet, few solutions. It is important however, to be aware of the issues and their impact on special populations.

Academic Standards

No one would disagree that children need to receive education to become independent, productive adults. The disagreement is *how* this should occur and exactly *what* children need to know. The academic standards movement has addressed academic core courses (math, English, science, and social studies). Standards can be considered on at least three different levels: (1) *content standards* are essentially what teachers are supposed to teach; (2) *performance standards* define levels of mastery; and (3) *opportunity-to-learn standards* relate to the availability of resources, programs, and staff in quantities that truly give children the opportunity to attain high standards (Noddings, 1997). Questions arise around special populations regarding the level of attainment that students with special needs can realistically reach. Should content and performance standards be the same for children of all ability levels? What performance quality level must a student achieve to meet requirements for graduation from high school? Might future career goals help to determine various content and performance levels? How should the education system *fairly* go about determining content and performance levels for all children? None of these issues has been resolved, although some states have tried. New York has established two ninth-grade earth science courses, a two-semester course and a three-semester course. Course expectations are the same and students take the same examinations; only the time given to learn the material differs. Kentucky allows students with severe disabilities exemption from meeting the state's performance standards (Improving America's Schools Act, 1996). Advocates for students with special needs are concerned about these "exemptions." Proposals to include *all* students generally offer one set of standards. However, student performance will vary immensely, whether a student has special needs or not. This performance issue is the crux of the challenge for implementing standards that apply to all students.

Vocational/technical education areas can more easily issue standards. Competencies taught come directly from industry and curricula developed around industry needs. However, if students lack basic academic skills (reading, writing, and mathematics), vocational educators must incorporate those skills into their curricula

National Skills Standards

Vocational education has been a forerunner in establishing content and performance standards. Most vocational courses have tasks defined by business and industry and levels of performance associated with each task. However, tasks have usually been established on a local or state level. The National Skills Standard Boards were established to define competencies (tasks) for various industries. All states would recognize these competencies. Because vocational education content and performance are grounded in business/industry needs, little disagreement evolves around the standards. However, the inclusion of students with special needs has generated discussion about performance levels. Due to their close association with the world of work and their knowledge of its needs, vocational educators are more open to students with special needs. The workplace has and will always require people with diverse abilities. Vocational curricula can be designed to allow each individual to reach maximum potential and gain skills for some level of employment. For example, students in automotive technology go on to further education after high school or they can be prepared for entry-level employment in oil lubrication shops, muffler shops, and so forth, immediately after graduation.

The National Skills Standards will enable vocational educators to refine their current competencies to include identified national competencies in business and industry. These changes will increase students' geographic mobility as the skills they acquire will cross local and state boundaries.

Curriculum/Instruction

Academic classrooms have taken on a new look in the last few years. The value of interdisciplinary units, thematic units, and block classes is accepted at all levels of education. English and social studies teachers at the middle and high school levels team teach around core themes, integrating language arts, literature, and history. Math and science teachers have created similar integrated units. Secondary education is learning from elementary education that relationships and *connections* among various subjects enhance the social and intellectual growth of students. Methods involving smaller class sizes, schools within a school, career-related magnet schools, career academies, project-based learning, teachers as academic advisors to small groups of students, and core teacher teams that work with a group of students over two or more years are being used to encourage connections as students get older. Educators have begun to apply cognitive research to their teaching. The recognition of learning styles and multiple intelligence has been the basis for applied academics at the secondary level. Some students learn abstract concepts when allowed to use the concepts in real-world applications. This approach helps students build problem-solving abilities and social skills by working in teams. Vocational education has always used these applied learning concepts in curriculum and instruction. So it is no surprise that most students in vocational programs succeed, even though they may have difficulty with traditional academic course work. The incorporation of academic skills into technical education is fairly easy, because students in this context can easily recognize the importance of math, reading, or writing. They realize that they apply these skills to achieve their career goal.

Some academic teachers have embraced *applied academics*; which uses real-life applications of academic learning. For example, a physics teacher has students build bridges, explain how and why an internal combustion engine works, or build a musical instrument to learn physics, math, research, and writing skills (Vo, 1997). Many districts encourage collaboration between vocational and academic teachers to enhance instruction both academically and vocationally.

With the passage of the School to Work Opportunities Act, curriculum reform took on a broader perspective, including the needs of students in the workplace. *Work-based learning*, as defined in the Act, is familiar to all educators. Few schools have truly implemented this concept for *all* students. Hamilton and Hamilton (1997) have defined various levels of work-based learning: (1) field trips and job shadowing, (2) service learning and unpaid internships, and (3) employment. However, not all employment is work-based learning. Programs defined as true work-based learning are paid internships, apprenticeships, cooperative education (offered through both vocational education and special education), and subsidized employment training. Schools are trying to connect with business to increase work-based learning opportunities. During the first half of 1996, 200,000 students participated in job shadowing or mentoring, 110,000 participated in paid or unpaid internships, and 12,000 took part in multiyear apprenticeships (Hess, 1997).

The school-to-work (STW) movement in education offers many benefits to students with special needs. Many of these students learn through tactile and kinesthetic means, remember concepts better when they can see them in operation (applied), and behave more appropriately in the work world than they might in school. Also, the opportunity to engage in real work assists them with realistic career decisions and fosters the ability to self-evaluate strengths and weaknesses. Vocational education teachers, through their community linkages, partnerships, and advisory committees, can easily arrange for appropriate work-based learning opportunities for all their students, including those with special needs.

Technology

Our schools are undergoing a technological revolution. Teachers are searching for quality instructional uses for digital portfolios, graphing calculators, multimedia, access to the Web, and other available technological advances. In one study that involved 150 elementary and secondary teachers, 60 percent rated themselves as beginners with computers (Ham, 1997). These teachers wanted to be more involved in planning for technology use, and to have more access to computers, more technical support, and substantially more professional development in instructional technologies. Public schools spend more on technology but reduce money spent on training teachers to use it (Miller, 1997). Recent studies indicate that when technology is used to support instruction, students improve their achievement, attitude, self-concept, and relationships with teachers (Fawcett & Snyder, 1997). The use of the World Wide Web, e-mail, and interactive computer lessons lets students learn more and better prepare for the challenges of the twenty-first century. In vocational education, the need for continual upgrading is even more crucial. The technology in business and industry changes constantly and vocational education must keep up with both equipment and techniques. As vocational education and the workplace become more technologically advanced, job requirements also increase. Future environments will demand students' ability to use technology efficiently. This necessity impacts the education and transition of students with special needs.

As the workplace becomes more technologically advanced and job demands increase, vocational instruction becomes more technologically oriented. Students enrolled in vocational courses need basic skills in reading, writing, and math, as well as problem-solving skills and the ability to work with others. An integrated curriculum teaches or reinforces these skills through the acquisition of advanced technological skills. Students with disabilities and other special needs can take advantage of the new technologies available to them that will help them gain the skills they need for the workplace. Multimedia and interactive computer programs allow learning for students with visual, tactile, and kinesthetic styles. Application of concepts to real-life problems encourages problem-solving skills. The use of speech synthesizers and scanning equipment permits students with reading disabilities to access the printed word. Calculators, talking calculators, and graphing calculators can help students with math deficiencies. Various types of adaptive equipment and assistive devices can also be used in the workplace.

Vocational instructors know and understand the equipment and technological capabilities needed in their fields. Their knowledge forms the base for the creative design of appropriate accommodations that will allow and encourage students with disabilities to gain competencies in the program. With the help of special education teachers, adaptive technology specialists, and vocational resource educators, instructors can devise accommodations that enhance access and promote success for students with disabilities in their program areas.

Professional Development

Vocational educators can take advantage of professional development activities offered by their school district. Professional development increases the knowledge base and familiarity with instructional strategies, such as cooperative learning and peer-assisted learning, which apply to all students—and especially to those with special needs. For example, cooperative learning requires assigning roles to students. Role assignment can play to the strengths of a student with special needs. For example, a student who can speak well can serve as the reporter for a group. One who draws well might develop a poster on the content of a unit. Districts often offer inservice programs related to special education or unique strategies for students with disabilities. Vocational educators can take advantage of these opportunities, which allow them both to get better acquainted with special educators and to increase their repertoire of classroom instructional strategies. The recent reauthorization amendments for special education legislation require the presence of a "general educator" at IEP meetings. A vocational instructor may be requested to attend. A basic knowledge of special education acquired from district inservice can help the vocational educator understand and contribute to the student's future goals.

Vocational educators also attend conferences and workshops related to their specific fields. Here, instructors should ask about strategies to teach the content to special populations. The presenter or the audience may have ideas to take back to the classroom and implement. Such dialog proves useful for finding ways to improve instruction. The school-to-work movement has begun to give educators opportunities through internships to visit employers and bring back to the classroom and curriculum relevant concepts and vocabulary for students. The growth of these professional development opportunities is then valuable to teachers and students alike.

CONCLUSION

Regardless of the label or terminology educators use to refer to students with special needs, at-risk or otherwise, their goal is to prepare *all* students for the high-skill jobs of the future that will keep America competitive in the global marketplace. (Note that this will also have the effect of reducing the growing gender/ethnic-based gap between the "haves" and "have nots.") We need to seriously prepare students for the future workforce through a coherent curriculum and experiences. Students must graduate with real skills, a career focus, and a road map to further training or education (California Institute on Human Services, 1997, pp. 4-5).

Transition planning and school-to-work efforts are forcing an agenda to include special populations in workforce development practices for the twenty-first century. Regardless of this, the new vocationalism has greater sustainability because business, education, civic, and governmental leaders are focusing on standards and assessments for needed skills in the workplace. Employers want to improve the skills of their labor force. Public education is identifying more closely with the workplace, with particular attention paid to those noncollege-bound students who will assume positions in postindustrial workplaces. These individuals need reading, writing, computation, and communication skills as a foundation.

Satisfying and sustained employment is a critical aspect of adult life. The ability to obtain and hold a job indicates a capacity to participate fully in our society. To individuals in special populations, employment brings status, respect, and financial independence. Years of education are of little value unless students can become vocationally productive and self-sufficient (Sarkees-Wircenski & Scott, 1995, p. 692). Vocational educators have the skills and knowledge to make vital contributions to the lives of *all* the students they serve.

References

California Institute on Human Services. (1997). *School-to-work: All students as participants.* Rohnert Park, CA: Author.

Fawcett, G., & Synder, S. (1997, October). An upgrade for learning. *Techniques, 72* (7), 30-33.

Ham, V. (1997, November). Teachers speak up about managing technology. *Educational Leadership, 55* (3), 67-68.

Hamilton, S. F. & Hamilton, M. A. (1997, May). When is learning work-based? *Phi Delta Kappan, 78* (9), 677- 681.

Hess, M. A. (1997, Fall). Linking learning to livelihoods. *Curriculum Update.* Alexandria, VA: Association for Supervision and Curriculum Development.

Kerka, S. (1997). *Developing collaborative relationships* (Practice Application Brief). Columbus, OH: Center on Education and Training for Employment.

Kohler, P. (1993, Fall). Best practices in transition: Substantiated or implied? *Career Development for Exceptional Individuals, 16* (2), 107-123.

Manning, M. L., & Baruth, L. G. (1995). *Students at-risk.* Needham, MA: Allyn and Bacon.

Miller, J. A. (1997, October). Online, off-track. *Techniques, 72* (7), 13-15.

Noddings, N. (1997, November). Thinking about standards. *Phi Delta Kappan, 79* (3), 184-189.

Sarkees-Wircenski, M., & Scott, J. L. (1995). *Vocational special needs.* Homewood, IL: American Technical Publishers.

Standards: What are they? (1996, Spring). *Improving America's school: A newsletter on issues in school reform.* [On-line]. Available at: http://www.ed.gov/pubs/IASA/newsletters/standards/ptl.html

Texas Education Agency. (1997). *Career pathways tool book.* Austin, TX: Texas Education Agency.

Vo, Chuong-Dai. (1997, May). Toying with physics. *Techniques, 72* (5), 14-17.

Lynda L. West *is a professor of special education in the Graduate School of Education and Human Development at The George Washington University. She earned her Ph.D. in education at the University of Missouri-Columbia. Dr. West has held leadership positions in several professional associations. She served as director of Missouri LINC, a statewide resource center that provided technical assistance and interdisciplinary training to state and local educational agencies. Missouri LINC was jointly funded by Missouri Department of Education, Divisions of Vocational Education, Special Education, and Vocational Rehabilitation. She held a joint appointment in special education and vocational education at the University of Mis-*

souri. She also served as a board member of a rehabilitation facility in Missouri. Dr. West is a published author, public speaker, national consultant, and teacher trainer. Her expertise is in the areas of inclusion, career education, functional curriculum, community-based instruction, vocational-technical education, and transition from school to work. She was previously a teacher of at-risk students in Kansas City Missouri Public Schools. **Arden Boyer-Stephens** *is the coordinator of student services at the Columbia Career Center in Columbia, Missouri. The career center is a secondary vocational-technical school and is a part of the Columbia Public School District. Dr. Boyer-Stephens works primarily with students who have disabilities and at-risk students enrolled in technical programs. She works collaboratively with instructors to develop and adapt curriculum and assessments for this population. Earlier, she served as assistant director and then director of Missouri LINC. Dr. Boyer-Stephens has also worked for private, not-for-profit rehabilitation agencies, as a rehabilitation counselor, program director, and vocational evaluator. As an adjunct professor, Dr. Boyer-Stephens has taught courses for the Departments of Vocational Education, Special Education, and Educational and Counseling Psychology for the University of Missouri-Columbia. She has served in leadership roles in many state and national organizations and has published in the areas of vocational special needs, vocational assessment, career education, and transition.*

PART V: FUTURE PERSPECTIVES

Work is the meat of life, pleasure the dessert.—
Bertie Charles Forbes

RESEARCH PRIORITIES AND NEEDS IN VOCATIONAL EDUCATION

By Martin B. Parks and Ross E. Moreton

As vocational educators reflect on possible directions for research in their field, little is clear or absolute. What is emerging, however, is that "responsive" research in vocational education will likely be faced with the same demands for accountability and relevancy now faced by instructional designers and teachers. Traditional, discipline-based research, as adopted by most university programs in education, has too long driven the research agendas and funding priorities of vocational education research.

There are emerging alternatives and innovations, however, to complement the traditions of vocational education research. In addition to reviewing the changing role of research in vocational education and findings of federally funded research in vocational education over the last decade, this chapter will explore the promise of applied, action research practices for both classroom teachers and graduate students in the field. The chapter concludes with a discussion of potential research topics for vocational educators.

THE CHANGING ROLE OF RESEARCH IN VOCATIONAL EDUCATION

As the nature of today's workplace differs from that of the past, so should the nature of related research. Today's workplace is characterized (Lankard, 1996) by global competition, cultural and ethnic diversity, rapidly evolving technologies, and less hierarchical management processes that require workers to employ skills in areas not traditionally thought of as "vocational" (e.g., critical thinking, problem-solving, and communication skills). These characteristics lead us to the following observations about the role of research in the emergent workplace: (a) the purposes for research are changing (including the conditions of work itself), (b) the types of research routinely generated is no longer sufficient, and (c) a greater pool of active researchers in vocational education must be established.

Purposes for Research in Vocational Education

Like most research in social sciences, research in vocational education continues to reflect the dual purposes of discipline-based theoretical testing and systematic problem-solving. Vocational educators wishing to explore theory, and to develop theoretical lines of inquiry, traditionally work in "research" universities or in institutions studying the evolution and creation of social policy. Such institutions, however, are often influenced by political and economic realities that may redirect the purposes of the research. Rather than support research for the value of the inquiry involved, research productivity and support in these institutions is too often related to levels of funding, grants awarded, or articles published in journals read almost exclusively by colleagues at other research universities and institutions (Frantz, 1991).

Increasingly, demands both inside and outside the traditional system call on researchers in vocational education to expand their inquiry from a discipline base to something more akin to a systems base. Senge (1990) calls systems thinking the "fifth discipline" because it integrates or fuses the disciplines of personal mastery, mental models, shared visioning, and team learning into a cohesive body of theory and practice. Senge drives home the importance of systems thinking as follows:

> . . . systems thinking makes understandable the subtlest aspect of the learning organization—the new way individuals perceive themselves and their world. At the heart of a learning organization is the shift of mind—from seeing ourselves as separate from the world to connected to the world. . . . (p.12)

Demands for systems thinking are predicated on the belief that the purposes served and the needs addressed by research in vocational education have changed. The very processes and outcomes of research in vocational education are affected by the changes occurring in the modern workplace. As the workplace positions itself for global competition, clear identification of the unique characteristics that will sustain a competitive advantage has become essential to the continued growth and development of the workforce. The successful, competitive modern workplace will (a) incorporate applied research designs and processes that accommodate and celebrate the diversity of its employees and consumers; (b) embrace emerging technologies and experiment actively in the design and delivery of products and services to accommodate a global marketplace; and (c) participate internally and externally in efforts to develop vocationally complementary skills in problem-solving, communications, critical thinking, and team building. An alternative systems-based approach must be established to include such innovations as interdisciplinary, collaborative research and partnerships between research producers and consumers in the workplace and the educational system.

Imbedded in the "systems" approach is the commitment to communicate with even broader sectors of the public, such as consumers and policy makers. Research in vocational education cannot continue to be conducted by and reported to educators only. Potential collaborators in a systems approach might include providers of and participants in entrepreneurial/proprietary education, publishers of educational materials, developers and purveyors of educational technology, nonprofit environmental and consumer organizations, and representatives of governmental agencies. A systems-based rationale for expanding the circle of research collaborators includes the goal of raising the quality and relevance of the knowledge generated to help insure implementation of innovations suggested by the research.

Types of Research Important to Vocational Education

In a call to insure that research in vocational education continues to influence the field's policy and practice, Johnson (1995) recommends that vocational education researchers focus on research that involves (among other outcomes) collaboration, qualitative methodologies, and "practical" dissemination strategies. This is clearly a shift away from the multiple quantitative strategies that have dominated the field for so long. Though vocational educators at the university level conduct multiple forms of inquiry and publish their results in recognized, scholarly journals, vocational teachers and trainers in business and industry face the challenge of interpreting the findings and applying them to their diverse settings and learners.

Vocational education research should continue its emphasis on traditional approaches as the primary vehicle for developing new knowledge in specific areas of content expertise, yet traditional educational research is not infrequently challenged regarding its perceived lack of relevance to the teaching and learning process in the schools and in business and industry. A systems-based collaborative approach could help address this concern. Vocational education research designs that incorporate multiple "researchers" (including university faculty, classroom teachers, learners, and business/industry participants) can help address the challenge.

The perceived value of qualitative research methods (e.g., historical research, ethnographic studies, case studies, and interviews) to vocational education continues to grow. Custer (1996) submits that "while quantitative methodologies have, among other things, the advantages of objectivity and generalizability, there are levels of understanding that simply cannot be attained apart from intensive involvement with people, institutions, and situations " (p. 4). Qualitative methods of inquiry provide as well for the incorporation of context. Custer concludes that vocational educators "would benefit from research embedded in a rich understanding of the complexities of the various contexts with which we interact" (p. 4).

Action research is a specific type of qualitative research that holds promise for vocational education. Action research suggests that educators use the results of their own inquiries to change and improve their classroom practices. It has been described as an informal, qualitative, formative, subjective, interpretive, reflective, and experiential model of inquiry (Hopkins, 1993), in which all individuals involved in the research study are knowing and contributing participants.

Creating New Researchers in Vocational Education Research

According to Stephen Kemmis (1982), *action research* is a form of collective self-reflective inquiry undertaken by participants in social situations to (a) improve their own social or education practices, (b) improve the situations and environments in which they work, and (c) understand the practices they are using and the methods through which they carry them out. According to Kemmis and McTaggart (1988), the approach to action research must be collaborative and the group must engage itself in a critical examination of the action of individual group members. Action research allows for a spread of involvement and commitment to the curriculum and the ways in which we deliver it. Action research can encourage teachers, students, and educational professionals—in other words, educational professionals from different spheres of education—to work together more closely.

McNiff (1993) contends that "educational research was split into its contributory disciplines of philosophy, psychology, sociology, and history. Research in this tradition tended to be done on other people, rather than in a collaborative inquiry with them. Teachers' hopes of coming to grips with their everyday practical class problems were being deceived by the current insistence on this being the only acceptable view of research" (p. xvi).

Action research represents a growing field of educational research whose chief identifying characteristic is the recognition of the pragmatic requirements of educational practitioners for organized reflective inquiry into classroom instruction. Action research is a process designed to empower all participants in the educational process (students, instructors and other parties) with the means to improve education practices (Hopkins, 1993).

Today's graduating or beginning vocational teachers will spend most of their teaching lives in the twenty-first century (Harrison, 1987). Vocational teachers in today's classrooms have multiple responsibilities that continually require more knowledge and experience than educators needed in earlier years. According to Milanovich (1986), being an effective vocational teacher today means having knowledge and/or experience in four areas: (a) a specific skill area; (b) instructional planning, implementation, and evaluation; (c) classroom and laboratory management; (d) and occupational experience. Tomorrow's vocational teachers will need to have competency in all of these areas, and they will need to develop skills in examining their own practice.

Deshler and Ewert (1995) trace the origins of action research in schools to the work of Buckingham (1926), who questioned the assumption that if traditional educational researchers reported their findings to practitioners, the practitioners will modify their methods to make them conform to the newly discovered research findings. He claimed evidence to discount the effectiveness of transferring research findings to practical applications. The primary principle that supports action research is that educators will likely make better decisions and engage in more effective practices if they participate in their own research activities. Action research has been used mainly in school-based curriculum development, teacher inservice education or professional development, and projects to improve a school or school systems (Deshler & Ewert, 1995, p. 4). Kemmis (1982) credits Dewey (1929) with advocating that teachers should control the educational research agenda and participate in conducting inquiries to test the worth of educational knowledge.

Deshler and Ewert (1995) identify the following underlying assumptions of action research: (a) action research will improve practice through scientific problem solving; (b) teachers and other educational practitioners are central to the research process; (c) the research follows a flexible and inductive process; (d) theory and practice can be linked through action research; (e) the process requires a link between reflection and action; (f) the research is focused on a single unique situation; and (g) methods are eclectic and innovative to specific situations (p. 5). In short, action research is intended to be a workable technique for practicing vocational classroom teachers.

Essential design elements of action research are as follows:

- A problem is identified.
- An intervention strategy is drafted and reviewed.
- The intervention is carried out.
- The intervention is monitored and observations are collected in various forms.
- Revised or alternative intervention strategies are drafted and reviewed.
- The revised or alternative intervention strategies are implemented.
- The cyclic process repeats until a sufficient understanding or successful solution of the problem is achieved.

As noted, the process is cyclical in nature and aims to provide a deeper understanding of a given situation, starting with conceptualizing and specifying a problem and moving through several interventions and evaluations.

In research conducted by Northfield and Mitchell (1995), teachers indicated that research by other teachers offers significant advantages in identifying and analyzing classroom incidents—teacher researchers frame their own theory and find the generalizations of others an effective vehicle for clarifying their own experiences. Personal rewards for involvement in research include increased respect for professionalism, greater job satisfaction, greater public esteem, stimulation of new ideas, and improved classroom environments.

McClean (1995) regards action research as a particularly strong component of effective school reform, as it encourages collaborative learning by doing, improves shared practices, and encourages teachers to work together as a group. The implications for developing context-specific strategies to integrate academic with vocational education are clear.

CRITICAL FINDINGS OF RECENT FEDERAL RESEARCH IN VOCATIONAL EDUCATION

Though vocational researchers continue to investigate issues and problems beyond the scope of federal mandates (Carl D. Perkins Vocational and Applied Technology Act, Tech Prep Education Act, School-to-Work Opportunities Act), the findings summarized below reflect the emphasis provided by federal legislation and policy toward educational reform (integrating academic and vocational education, tech prep, school-to-work, workplace literacy, and performance standards and measures).

Integrating Vocational and Academic Education

The Carl D. Perkins Vocational and Applied Technology Act of 1990 mandated that state and local agencies integrate vocational and academic education to help students achieve both academic and vocational competencies. Grubb, Davis, Lum, Plihal, and Morgaine (1991) identified what have become the "eight models of integration," with brief descriptions, as follows:

1. *Incorporating more academic content in vocational courses.* This model encourages vocational teachers to incorporate more academic materials and outcomes in their vocational courses of study. Generally, vocational teachers will explore the occupational demands in terms of communication and computational skills and will design learning activities in the vocational courses to meet these occupationally related requirements.

2. *Curricular alignment through the modification of both vocational and academic courses.* This model takes a more "systems-based" approach to integrating academic and vocational education. Instead of, or in addition to, modifying individual courses, curricular alignment seeks to revise entire curricula in both scope and sequence to achieve greater academic and vocational competencies. This model involves a system-wide commitment and involvement of both academic and vocational faculty.

3. *The academy model.* This approach to integration requires a restructuring of the secondary school vocational experience. Sometimes referred to as a school-within-a-school, the academy involves a small group of academic and vocational faculty working as a team within the greater context of the secondary school. Selected groups of students work with the team for instruction in science, mathematics, English, and the vocational subject over a two- to three-year period. Students take other subjects in high school, but without benefit of the academy model.

4. *Combining vocational and academic teachers to enhance academic competencies in vocational programs.* Accomplished through some variation of teaming, this approach to integration involves vocational and academic faculty working together to design and, in some cases, deliver both academic and vocational course elements. As practiced most frequently, academic faculty work closely with vocational colleagues to provide materials and approaches to infuse academic components into the vocational curriculum.

5. *Occupational high schools and magnet schools.* This strategy for integration involves the designation of certain campuses for students interested in particular occupational programs or clusters of programs. As conceived, this approach aims to attract academic and vocational faculty who want to collaborate with each other, with potential employers, and with students to achieve both vocational and academic competencies.

6. *The senior project.* The senior project is promoted as a culminating experience (or series of experiences) wherein students are given the opportunity to demonstrate both vocational and academic achievement through a single "capstone" project or through a series of projects. A holistic approach to integration, this model involves both academic and vocational faculty in determining competency achievement through jointly inspired and evaluated projects.

7. *Occupational clusters and career paths.* Another restructuring strategy for integration, the development and designation of occupational clusters can occur in either secondary vocational-technical schools or in comprehensive high schools (providing the comprehensive high school supports a substantial variety of vocational offerings). In this model, teachers are assigned to occupational clusters rather than to more traditional departments, which leads to greater opportunities for collaboration among faculty. Career paths are developed in

consultation with both academic and vocational faculty to result in employment or postsecondary programs that will build on skills already achieved.

8. *Making academic courses more vocationally relevant.* Still another teaming strategy, this model involves vocational teachers working with academic faculty to infuse career and vocational concepts in traditionally academic courses. Standard academic outcomes in reading, writing, and mathematics come, in part, through use of occupationally relevant materials.

Bodilly, Ramsey, Stasz, and Eden (1992) investigated the integration of academic and vocational education in eight schools in five states (California, Kentucky, Ohio, Oregon, and Virginia). Strategies for integration identified by the research included teaming of academic and vocational teachers, joint time together for teams, and new organizational structures that empowered teachers. Conclusions drawn about integration activities included the following: they could apply to all types of high schools; they are best approached as school improvement efforts; they often take years to implement successfully; they flourish in an environment that has supporting rules and regulations already in place; they require substantial investment; and they promote rethinking of conventional approaches to educational delivery.

Tech Prep

Bragg (1994) cites Parnell (1985) as providing the conceptual framework underlying what has become known as the *tech prep initiative*. Parnell conceived of a 2 + 2 tech prep associate degree model intended to provide an articulated career pathway for secondary-to-postsecondary success in vocational-technical study. By definition, tech prep (Brustein, 1993, p. 14): (a) leads to an associate degree or two-year certificate; (b) provides technical preparation in at least one of the following fields: engineering technology, applied science, mechanical, industrial, or practical art or trade, agriculture, health, or business; (c) builds student competence in mathematics, science, and communications through a sequential course of study; and (d) leads to employment placement.

Among the main emerging tech prep models are the following (Bragg, 1994): (a) *pre-tech prep*, which includes four years of secondary plus two years of postsecondary tech prep; (b) *adult tech prep*, which is intended for postsecondary adult students with academic or vocational skill deficiencies; (c) *integrated tech prep*, which incorporates academic and vocational outcomes through career clusters; (d) *work-based tech prep*, which employs the workplace as a primary component of the instructional delivery system; and, (e) the *tech prep bachelor's degree*, which is built on a postsecondary 2 + 2 model only.

In a more recent study, Bragg (1997) attempted to use concept mapping to identify, classify, and rank order student outcomes for use in developing evaluation strategies for tech prep programs. Critical findings indicated that educators, students, and employers considered the following learning outcomes (in priority order) to be most critical for tech prep programs: (a) personal attributes, attitudes, and employability skills; (b) school-to-work transitions; (c) technology and quality management; (d) information use and decision making; (e) work and interpersonal relationships; (f) educational attainment; (g) communication skills; (h) mathematics and science knowledge; and (j) democratic and participatory strategies.

School-to-Work

A primary purpose of the School-to-Work Opportunities Act is to provide transition programs to prepare noncollege-bound youth for initial full-time employment and for rapidly escalating workplace demands for such characteristics as critical thinking, effective communication, and problem-solving skills. Strategies employed to achieve these transitions include integrating academic and vocational outcomes, providing work-based as well as school-based experiences, and articulating secondary-to-postsecondary education and training opportunities.

Stern, Finklestein, Stone, Latting, and Dornsife (1994) classify school-to-work programs as either (a) *school-and-work* programs, in which students work and attend school during the same time period or (b) *school-for-work* programs, in which students receive instruction intended to prepare them for work.

Schmidt, Finch, and Moore (1997) explored effective teacher activities and characteristics that contribute to school-to-work success. The researchers interviewed 199 teachers, administrators, counselors, employers, and community representatives at 11 community sites throughout the United States to identify best school-to-work practices. They identified the following 10 activities (teacher activity themes) as contributing to school-to-work success: (a) involving students in organized workplace experiences, (b) helping students to understand the workplace, (c) involving workplace representatives in school curriculum and instruction, (c) providing workplace experiences for students through school activities, (d) including a workplace focus in school instruction, (e) learning about the workplace in ways that contribute to better teaching, (f) working in the workplace, (g) initiating and maintaining contact with employers and the community, (h) designing classroom experiences around workplace expectations, and (i) following up on current and former students. As to what teacher characteristics were found to be most conducive to successful school-to-work programs, the researchers found the following:

1. Understand and meet students' needs, which includes accepting and valuing students, as well as developing students as individuals and establishing working relationships with them.
2. Establish and maintain relationships with the workplace.
3. Know the workplace.
4. Communicate effectively about school-to-work programs.
5. Be adaptable and open to change.
6. Demonstrate positive attitudes toward work.
7. Be professional in appearance and conduct.
8. Apply school learning to the workplace.
9. Know schools and schooling.
10. Be knowledgeable and competent in teaching area.
11. Use creative and innovative teaching methods.
12. Be committed to teaching.

Schmidt, Finch, and Moore (1997) contend that effective school-to-work faculty must not only be skilled at teaching but should also have the ability to forge and maintain linkages between the school and the workplace. These and the other characteristics and activities enumerated above can serve as the framework for professional development strategies for teachers, administrators, and employers who want to succeed at school-to-work transitions.

Workplace Literacy

"Whether or not schools are to blame for adult illiteracy, the stakes are now viewed as being too high for the U.S. government to neglect" (Lewis, 1995, p. 60). The government has tried to address adult illiteracy through such federal legislation as the National Literacy Act of 1991 and by funding the National Workplace Literacy Program. Defined as literacy tied to workplace knowledge, *workplace literacy* includes not only basic academic skills, but such emerging competencies as effective communication skills, critical thinking, learning attack skills, and team-building.

Lewis (1995) used a multiple-case research design to investigate three vocational institutions to determine what practices best define workplace literacy in those institutions.

Significant findings included the following: (a) vocational institutions can offer workplace literacy interventions effectively, including collaboration with employers and organized labor to assess needs, evaluate materials, test skill levels, develop relevant curricula, and provide culturally and ethnically diverse workplace settings; (b) vocational institutions tend to succeed in workplace literacy efforts when they can offer customized, "brokerage" services designed to meet not only the needs of learners but of the corporate partners as well; and (c) vocational institutions' historical strengths in such interventions as open-entry, open-exit education programs; just-in-time training; collaboration with employers and organized labor; and individualized instruction formats designed to address the variance in learner initial abilities encourage participant commitment and program completion.

In a recent study completed for the National Center on Adult Literacy, Mikulecky and Lloyd (1996) sought to evaluate the effectiveness of 10 groups of learners in workplace literacy programs at six companies. Their findings indicated that the programs that most effectively improved learners' literacy performance, literacy strategies and processes, and learners' beliefs and plans were related to literacy. Further, the researchers suggest that substantial learner gains in literacy can be linked to an environment saturated with workplace reading and writing materials, opportunities for regular discussion and feedback regarding learner progress, changing beliefs about personal literacy effectiveness, and future educational plans.

Performance Standards and Measures

For secondary schools, the educational reform movement of the 1980s arose from perceived demands for more rigorous standards for high school graduation and heightened requirements for entrance to college. To address these demands, high schools began a series of self-reflection and evaluation efforts that resulted in legislation—School to Work Opportunities Act, Goals 2000: Educate America Act, Improving America's Schools Act—aimed at reforming and revitalizing the secondary school experience in the United States. In response to legislative mandates, vocational institutions have undertaken both programmatic and schoolwide efforts to establish new forms of organization leading to more effective teaching and learning.

Added to these thrusts is the corporate sector's growing demand to push for reforms to equip students with skills needed for a "high performance," decentralized workplace where workers must take on greater responsibility, collaborate effectively, and involve themselves in decision making. Several national reports in recent years underscore industry's demand for employees with competencies in these areas (Commission on the Skills of the American Workforce, 1990; Secretary's Commission on Achieving Necessary Skills, 1991).

The Carl D. Perkins Vocational and Applied Technology Education Act of 1990 not only advanced the concept of such reforms as integrated academic and vocational competencies, but required vocational education programs to develop and implement a system of performance standards, assessment measures, and services that provide "strong experience in and understanding of all aspects of the industry students are preparing to enter, including planning, finance, management, technical and production skills, underlying principles of technology, community issues, labor issues, and health, safety and environment" (Carl D. Perkins Vocational and Applied Technology Act Amendments of 1990). Criteria for the design of states' systems of performance measures and standards include the following: the measures should have clear, precise definitions; outcomes should be easily measured; the accountability system should include a manageable number of outcome measures; standards must be justified in terms of success in either the workplace or further education; and the information generated by the accountability system must be routinely accessible.

New approaches identified by Inger (1995) for assessing programs may include the following: (a) *total quality management* (TQM), which focuses on evaluation that aims to improve both educational processes and learning outcomes; (b) the *student success model*, which encourages students to set high standards, document their goals and intended outcomes, and monitor their outcomes; (c) *value-added assessment,* which involves gathering baseline information about entry-level academic and vocational competencies and to compare with exit-level performance competencies, including competencies of personal growth and development; (d) *concept mapping,* an approach that enables diverse groups or teams of practitioners to describe how their programs work and then to use that shared understanding to influence outcomes; and (e) *performance assessment,* an umbrella term that describes a variety of techniques designed to assess knowledge, skills, and attitudes in ways other than or in addition to standard paper and pencil tests.

Ananda, Rabinowitz, Carlos, and Yamashiro (1995) recommend an approach to standards development through coalition building. These authors encourage the following considerations when integrating industry standards with educational reform efforts:

1. Build on existing data. Data is mounting in most states regarding the development of industry standards and educational reform efforts. A thorough review of existing literature and technical reports should provide the framework for drafting appropriate standards.

2. Involve as many stakeholders as possible in the standards drafting process. Representatives from government, industry, labor, education, parents, and students should take part in the standards drafting process.

3. Plan for extensive validation of the standards developed through external review, surveys, and focus groups. These strategies offer additional opportunities to involve other stakeholders not originally part of the drafting process. Professional organizations, labor organizations, college educators, workers, and supervisors could all provide input, clarification, credibility, and acceptance of the results.

Though addressed in the Perkins Act, strategies and directions for implementing successful measures and standards remained unclear. Stecher, Hanser, Rahn, Levesque, Klein, and Emmanuel (1995) recommend the following changes in the legislation to help establish the framers' intention regarding performance measures and standards: (a) add a coordinating function to help assure integration and collaboration among the separate components of the legislation; (b) require that a system of performance measures and standards be incorporated in reform strategies as a tool for program improvement; (c) clarify the requirements for measures and standards; and (d) increase the amount of technical assistance to local systems to support systemic change.

LEADING POTENTIAL RESEARCH TOPICS FOR VOCATIONAL EDUCATORS

This chapter has attempted to review the changing role of research in vocational education to include purposes, types of research important to vocational education, introduction of a specific strategy (action research) that holds promise for teacher-led research in vocational education, and a summary of critical findings of recent federal research in vocational education reform efforts (i.e., the integration of vocational and academic education, tech prep, school to work, workplace literacy, and performance standards and measures). The discussion surrounding each of these components has resulted in the identification of the following "top 10" research topics for vocational educators: (a) higher-order versus basic skills, (b) integration of academic and vocational education, (c) transition from school to work and family life, (d) vocational education's role as a change agent, (e) curriculum content collaboration models, (f) the nature of work, (g) vocational education and the economy, (h) vocational education delivery systems, (i) the teaching and learning process in vocational education, and (j) assessing student learning/outcomes.

Higher Order versus Basic Skills

Examining how teaching and learning occur in basic and technical skills has long been the mainstay of vocational education. Yet with increasing demands for "higher-order" skills in such diverse areas as critical thinking, decision-making, problem-solving, and interpersonal relationships (team building, collaboration, participation) to meet the workforce expectations of the future, we must conduct focused research on the interaction among these skills and effectiveness in the workplace.

Questions such as the following may help direct researchers who hope to address this issue: (a) What are the necessary basic skills for the workplace of the future? (b) What are the higher order skills for each employment setting? (c) Are many of the same skills required in a variety of settings? (d) How can each best be learned or acquired?

Integration of Academic and Vocational Education

It is clear from much of the current research in education reform that future successful completers of vocational education programs must show evidence of knowledge and abilities in areas of study traditionally defined as academic. To that end, much current research has focused on the kinds and types of academic preparation needed to provide a competitive advantage for vocational education students. Continued focus in this arena is critical. However, in addition to a focus on the kinds of knowledge and skill outcomes required of future vocational education participants, a commitment between academic and vocational faculty must be established to allow collaboration on research that examines the role of vocational and career education for learners not traditionally considered "vocational." Research emphasis to this point has focused almost solely on the integration of academic components in vocational courses of study. More research is needed as well in the integration of vocational and career components in traditionally academic courses of study. This research might address such questions as: How can we apply existing models of integration to our specific situation? If we define knowledge/learning by specifying the outcomes we want, how might this enhance integration efforts? What are the true barriers to the integration process? How might we overcome any barriers? Collaborative teacher-led research in context (i.e., in comprehensive high schools, postsecondary institutions, and vocational skills centers) may help to achieve this goal.

TRANSITION FROM SCHOOL TO WORK TO FAMILY

The primary arenas of modern life include learning, work, and family. While these arenas clearly overlap and each affects the other, it is also clear that vocational education research must investigate these linkages more directly and with innovative approaches. Quantitative research is limited to investigating known variables. Qualitative strategies may help to identify variables for further investigation and to identify relationships among the arenas of learning, work, and family that are worthy of research in the broader social context.

Vocational education's role as change agent. If vocational education is to fulfill its promise, it must begin to articulate its role as an agent of social and educational change. From a historical position of being acted "upon," vocational education must assume leadership toward a future educational milieu that helps to define work and the workplace rather than simply serving market demands. Vocational research can clearly provide new understanding and direction not only for the development of the field, but for the development of successful global citizens.

Curriculum content collaboration models. The promise of collaboration among and between educators sorely needs successful models. Research leading to model identification, testing, and dissemination is vital. Such research might ask: What models exist? Are they successful and why? If not, what conditions or factors must we consider and modify? In addition, research into alternative forms of collaboration leading to more effective vocational curricula that involve stakeholders from government, organized labor, business, industry, and social services could help to establish viable standards for curriculum quality.

The nature of work. Vocational education must actively participate in the global conversation regarding the nature of work itself. As the character of work evolves, so must vocational education. The promise of vocational education will likely be realized only through a thorough understanding and participation in the global socio-political context. Potential questions include: What will future work "look" like? If work takes place at home, or in isolated settings, how will psychological, social, and other human relations needs be met? If work becomes more collaborative, what combination of skills, attitudes, and work ethics will allow maximum effectiveness?

Vocational education and the economy. Vocational education has been supported traditionally because it has been viewed as a viable source of skilled workers and because it affects the economic development potential of the larger community. The specific impact of vocational education on the economic development of its participants, employers, and the larger society remains unclear. Anecdotal reports of microeconomic effects and speculation regarding macroeconomic potential are not sufficient. Collaborative research between vocational educators and economists should address—among other related topics—such vital areas as human capital investment strategies, the impact of entrepreneurial activity, the role of technology in workforce development and economic growth/viability, and the interactive effects of a global economy and vocational education.

Vocational education delivery systems. Work-based versus school-based vocational education has captured the imagination of vocational educators as it incorporates the basic tenant of task learning and performance in a setting that truly represents the workplace of intention. Further, work-based vocational programs promise to provide opportunities for learners to (a) discard "differed learning" for "just-in-time" applications of newly learned knowledge and skills, (b) apply higher-order skills to problems occurring in "real time" and with authentic personnel, and (c) apply practical and abstract skills in a meaningful context. Research as to the efficacy of alternative delivery systems must be built into the design of such systems before their piloting or adoption. Research is also needed to determine the impact of such alternatives, including results related to significant differences in learning outcomes and employment success.

The teaching and learning process. At the very heart of the educational enterprise is teaching and learning. Effective teaching begins with the effective preparation of teachers. This holds true for vocational education as well as for other disciplines. Vocational education teachers must prepare not only in their vocational content areas, but in related academics and teaching strategies that lead to higher-order intellectual skills and emotional understanding. We need to conduct research on evaluation and assessment of linkages between teacher professional development approaches and vocational student learning outcomes. Results of existing and future research linking educational reform strategies to teaching and learning in vocational education should serve to strengthen vocational education's role in preparing the global workforce.

Assessing student learning outcomes. While all indicators of program success (job placement, earnings, access for underrepresented populations) are valuable topics for continuing research, a research agenda that focuses on learning outcomes, may provide the most assistance to vocational educators in the future. To this point, competency testing designed to assess acquisition of appropriate skills and knowledge is the most common method used to assess learning outcomes. Yet using competency testing as the sole measure of achievement of learning outcomes may not make sense. We need to conduct research into the extent to which the following variables may account for variance in learning outcomes assessments: economic and social factors, test-taking abilities and phobias, virtual performance (as measured by a standard competency assessment) versus actual performance evaluation in the workplace, and as yet unspecified or standardized assessments for emerging workforce expectations in such related areas as higher-order thinking skills, decision-making abilities, and collaboration.

References

Ananda, S., Rabinowitz, S., Carlos, L., & Yamashiro,

K. (1995, December). *Skills for tomorrow's workforce —WestEd policy brief #22* [On-line]. Available: www.wested.org/policy/pb_skill.htm

Bodilly, S., Ramsey, K, Stasz, C. & Eden, R. (1992). *Integrating academic and vocational education: Lessons from eight early innovators*. Berkeley, CA: National Center for Research in Vocational Education. (ERIC Document Reproduction Service No. ED 353 407)

Bragg, D. (1994). *Emerging tech prep models: Promising approaches to educational reform*. Berkeley, CA: National Center for Research in Vocational Education. (ERIC Document Reproduction Service No. ED 371 142)

Bragg, D. (1997). *Educator, student, and employer priorities for tech prep student outcomes*. Berkeley, CA: National Center for Research in Vocational Education. (ERIC Document Reproduction Service No. ED 404 474)

Brustein, M. (1993). *AVA guide to federal funding for tech prep*. Alexandria, VA: American Vocational Association.

Buckingham, B. (1926). *Research for teachers*. New York: Burdett & Co.

Carl D. Perkins Vocational and Applied Technology Act Amendments of 1990.

Commission on the Skills of the American Workforce. (1990, June). *America's choice: High skills or low wages!* Rochester, NY: National Center on Education and the Economy.

Custer, R. (1996). Qualitative research methodologies. *Journal of Industrial Teacher Education, 34*(2), 3-6.

Deshler, J., & Ewert, M. (1995). *Participatory action research: Traditions and major assumptions* [On-line]. Available: http://tgd.uoguelph.ca/~pi/pdrc/articles/article.1

Dewey, J. (1929). *The sources of a science of education*. New York: Liverright Publishing Co.

Frantz, N., Jr. (1991). Practice-oriented research or research-oriented practice. *The Journal of Vocational Education Research, 16*(4), 35-43.

Grubb, W., Davis, G., Lum, J., Plihal, P. & Morgaine, C. (1991). *The cunning hand, the cultured mind: Models for integrating vocational and academic education*. Berkeley, CA: National Center for Research in Vocational Education. (ERIC Document Reproduction Service No. ED 334 421)

Harrison, C. (1987). Education for tomorrow's vocational teachers. *ERIC Digest, 67*. (ERIC Document Reproduction Service No. ED 289 998)

Hopkins, D. (1993). *A teacher's guide to classroom research*. Philadelphia: Open University Press.

Inger, M. (1995). *Alternative approaches to outcomes assessment for postsecondary vocational education*. Berkeley, CA: National Center for Research in Vocational Education. (ERIC Document Reproduction Service No. ED 389 849)

Johnson, S. (1995). Will our research hold up under scrutiny? *Journal of Industrial Teacher Education, 32*(3), 3-6.

Kemmis, S. (1982). Action research in retrospect and prospect. In S. Kemmis & R. McTaggart (Eds.). *The action research planner*. Victoria, Australia: Deakin University.

Kemmis, S., & McTaggart, R. (1988). *The action research planner*. Victoria, Australia: Deakin University.

Lankard, B. (1996). Job training versus career development: What is voc ed's role? *ERIC Digest*. (ERIC Document Reproduction Service No. ED 395 217)

Lewis, T. (1995). Inside three workplace literacy initiatives: Possibilities and limits of vocational institutions. *Journal of Industrial Teacher Education, 33*(1), 60-82.

McNiff, J. (1993). *Teaching as learning: An action research approach*. London: Routledge.

McClean, J. (1995). *Improving education through action research: A guide for administrators and teachers*. Thousand Oaks, CA: Corwin Press.

Mikulecky, L. & Lloyd, P. (1996). *Evaluation of workplace literacy programs: A profile of effective instructional practices*. Philadelphia, PA: National Center on Adult Literacy. (ERIC Document Reproduction Service No. ED 393 013)

Milanovich, N. (1986). Vocational-Technical teacher certification—Where are we? And where are we going? In A. Robertson (Ed.), *Achieving excellence in vocational teacher education*. New York: Institute for Research and Development in Occupational Education.

Northfield, J., & Mitchell, I. (1995, April). *Bringing a research focus into the teaching role*. Paper presented at the annual meeting of the American Educational Research Association, San Francisco, CA.

Parnell, D. (1985). *The neglected majority*. Washington, DC: Community College Press.

Schmidt, B., Finch, C. & Moore, M. (1997). *Facilitating school-to-work transition: Teacher involvement and contributions* [On-line]. Available: ncrve.berkeley.edu/MDS-938

School-to-Work Opportunities Act, P.L. 103-239.

Secretary's Commission on Achieving Necessary Skills (1991). *What work requires of schools: A SCANS report for America 2000*. Washington, DC: U.S. Department of Labor.

Senge, P. (1990). *The fifth discipline: The art and practice of the learning organization*. New York: Doubleday/Currency.

Stecher, B., Hanser, L, Rahn, M., Levesque, K., Klein, S., & Emmanuel, D. (1995). *Improving performance measures and standards for workforce education*. Berkeley, CA: National Center for Research in Vocational Education. (ERIC Document Reproduction Service No. ED 382 802)

Stern, D., Finklestein, N., Stone, J., Latting, J., & Dornsife, C. (1994). *Research on school-to-work transition programs in the United States*. Berkeley, CA: National Center for Research in Vocational Education. (ERIC Document Reproduction Service No. ED 369 923)

__Martin B. Parks__ is program professor of vocational, technical, and occupational education and associate dean for research with the Programs for Higher Education at Nova Southeastern University in Fort Lauderdale, Florida. He holds a Ph.D. in comprehensive vocational education from Ohio State University and pursues a research agenda in the areas of workforce training and development, alternative delivery systems for vocational education, vocational education research priorities, and vocational education futures. __Ross E. Moreton__ is dean of the Programs for Higher Education at Nova Southeastern University in Fort Lauderdale, Florida. He earned a B.S. from Carson-Newman College, an M.A. from East Tennessee State University, and an Ed.D. from the University of Mississippi. He has held leadership positions in and remains an active member of the American Vocational Association, the National Association of Industrial and Technical Teacher Educators, and the American Technical Education Association.

21

FUTURE PERSPECTIVES IN VOCATIONAL EDUCATION

By William Blank

Anyone contemplating the future of any field—including vocational education—should perhaps consider multiple perspectives. One perspective involves looking at the past to determine how the present evolved. A second perspective involves taking a critical look at the major forces in place or emerging in the present. Finally, we can anticipate what the future might hold for society at large and what impact these societal changes might have on the particular field. I have considered these perspectives in writing this chapter.

Trying to anticipate our future is speculative at best and highly inaccurate at worst. No doubt, you recall futurists from times past who predicted that by now we would all fly to work in personal helicopters, work only three or four days a week (yeah, right!), and have robots at home to perform menial tasks. These and many other predictions for the future have failed to materialize. I hope that the future of vocational education outlined in this chapter will seem less laughable to those looking back on it 20 or 30 years from now.

Two very different approaches could be taken in presenting future perspectives in vocational education. The first might dwell more on the "most likely" future while the second would focus on the "desired" future. Emphasizing the former might result in pessimism and conservatism. Keeping a more hopeful view of the future allows more freedom to explore, to challenge, and to even dream. In this chapter, I choose the more hopeful outlook. Finally, I will focus primarily on the major, fundamental shifts in the mission, purpose, structure, and image of our field.

WHAT WE MIGHT CALL OUR FIELD

The terminology used to describe our profession has undergone many changes. Terms used routinely just a few years ago including *vocational education, technical education,* and *occupational education* are becoming used rarely or with added modifiers (or even apologies). In a recent survey of members of the American Vocational Association (AVA), almost 60 percent of respondents favored changing the name of the association. Even within the larger field of vocational education, some program areas have undergone name changes to present a more contemporary image. Home economics is now *family and consumer sciences*, industrial arts has become *technology education*, and vocational agriculture is now called *agriculture and natural resources education.* Even if the profession resists pressure from without to change its image and its label, there will continue to be forces from within that will shape our profession's future name.

Two trends seem to contribute to this shift in terminology. First is the conscious effort by vocational educators at all levels to depart from the past and put a fresh face on our enterprise. Among the reasons for doing so is an attempt to distance ourselves from long-held perceptions (and misperceptions) about the field. The label *vocational education* has triggered less-than-flattering images in the minds of many people—including policy makers, potential students, parents, and academic educators. These images sometimes include the notions of a dumping ground, a place of last resort for troubled youth, lack of rigor, or narrow training and preparation for low-wage/ obsolete jobs. While these negative images are most often ill deserved and in no way characterize the many high-quality, progressive vocational education programs in existence, such negative stereotypes are, unfortunately, all too prevalent.

Another trend giving impetus to terminology change is the gradual broadening of the purpose and mission of vocational-technical education beyond preparation for specific jobs to preparation for broad careers. In our field today, many of programs, departments, and schools include one of the following titles rather than "vocational": *workforce education, workforce development, career preparation, workplace education, technological education, applied technology,* or *technical preparation.*

Eric Ries (1997) reports

> At the state office in Minnesota it's known as "lifework development." In Arizona it's "school-to-work education." It's the focus of "career and technology centers" in Rhode Island, "applied technology" and "technical" institutes in Florida, "workforce development centers" in Wyoming. In Maine, you'll find Biddeford Regional Center of Technology; in Ohio, Great Oaks Institute of Technology and Career Development. (p 32)

What will the future hold regarding the terminology that describes our field? This is very hard to predict, given the rapid changes we see in attitudes toward vocational education and considering the lasting impact of major school reform efforts underway and those likely to emerge in the future. We can probably assume, however, that whatever label people use 10, 20, or 30 years from now to describe the field historically known as "vocational education" it will probably include terms that convey the following concepts:

- The holistic career development of the individual
- Successful transition from one level or setting to the next along a lifelong continuum of education and training
- Emphasis on education rather than training
- An image of preparation for a highly technical, demanding workplace

Whether we rediscover the term *occupational education* or use terms like *technological education* or *workforce education,* we can probably be assured that the term *vocational education* will continue to slip into disuse. Consider the results of a survey conducted recently by AVA. In 26 of the 40 states responding to the survey, the term "vocational education" did not even appear in the title of the division or office administering vocational education programs in that state.

CAREER PREPARATION: ONE OF THE PRIMARY PURPOSES OF K-12 EDUCATION

One of the most hopeful developments now emerging that would significantly impact the field of vocational education (under whatever future name it may have) is for schools and school districts across this country to formally adopt a new dual mission for schooling in America: preparation for further education and preparation for economic self-sufficiency. This would represent a major departure from the predominant one-dimensional mission of K-12 education in the U.S. today. Very few would argue—if we examine where emphasis, rewards, and resources go—that the primary goal of schooling in America is to do well on tests and get admitted to a four-year university.

Such a limited mission of education only serves the needs of a small percentage of students who can successfully traverse the following maze: (1) graduate from high school, (2) gain admission to a university, (3) actually complete a university degree, and (4) ultimately secure stable employment in a career for which a college degree is required. The percentage of beginning high school students who successfully make it past all four of these hurdles is much smaller than most people realize. While reliable numbers are hard to determine, the total probably involves less than 15 percent of beginning ninth graders. The anachronistic mission of schooling poorly serves the needs of the huge number (perhaps 80 to 85 percent) of students who do not ultimately secure a university degree and commensurate remuneration. This is particularly true for the large number of high school graduates who "endure" a university prep curriculum, then enter a four-year university but exit with only a student loan to pay off, shame and embarrassment for dropping out, and few options for beginning a career with a future.

In the future, the new dual mission of K-12 education will be to prepare all learners for postsecondary education (community college, technical center, or university) and for entering a career field that pays a living wage and that has opportunities for advancement. We can envision the formal mission statement affixed to the wall in the lobby of the high school of the future including a phrase like "... our primary mission is to provide each student with opportunities to lay the foundation for achieving long-term economic self-sufficiency by successfully preparing for the next major steps in their lives, whether further education, further career preparation or immediate entry into the workforce." Such a mission—if taken seriously—would dictate dramatic changes in philosophy, purpose, and curriculum. It would also thrust occupationally related educational experiences into a co-equal role with the academic disciplines, which, unfortunately will probably continue to dominate our K-12 curriculum well into the future.

Such a mission statement would make the current approach of providing a university preparatory curriculum for virtually all high school students obsolete indeed. It would dictate that serious attention go to helping every learner—college bound or career bound—prepare for the immediate future whether in the classroom, factory, or office. It would thrust vocational education directly to the forefront of education for all students. Although the school-to-career movement currently underway represents a good start down this path, it has hardly resulted in the wholesale adoption of career preparation of all students as a central goal of schooling. In the not-too-distant future school-to-career transition for all learners will no longer be viewed as a separate, externally funded, vocationally driven "program", but, rather, as an integral, institutionalized component of the American educational system. Educators, parents, and students will all recognize that preparation for self-sufficiency is just as important as preparation for higher education and the transmission of culture.

The recently adopted national standards of the American School Counselor Association represent evidence that such a change is already taking place. One of the three major strands of standards is *career development*. Specific standards under that strand focus on (a) acquiring the skills to investigate the world of work and knowledge of self, (b) using strategies to achieve future career success and satisfaction, and (c) understanding the relationship between personal qualities, education and training, and the world of work. The career counseling role of guidance counselors is beginning to take on the very same importance as their academic counseling role.

Imagine seeing on one page of a high school graduation program from the 2010s a list of the colleges and universities graduates have been accepted to and on the facing page a list of the companies other graduates have accepted employment with! We can also imagine high schools in the future having as many high-tech/high-wage occupation career events as they do college events! We can even envision, in the distant future, high schools having not only an international baccalaureate (IB) program for the academically gifted but also an international workforce education (IWE) program for the highly motivated student who pursues rigorous studies leading to workplace preparation of world-class quality!

A BROADER ROLE AND MISSION

One of the striking shifts that I hope will occur in vocational education is a broadening of its role and mission even beyond that which we have seen during the past 10 years. Historically, the public has seen the primary mission of vocational education as that of preparing youth and adults for gainful employment in specific occupations through participation in formal programs of study at less than baccalaureate level. This has been reflected in federal and state legislation and in funding. However, the decade of the 1990s saw this traditional mission expand to not only pre-employment preparation but also to provide learners with a firm grounding in all aspects of an occupation or career field. Recently, people have begun to recognize occupational education as invaluable preparation for sustained self-sufficiency—not just preparation for an immediate job.

A look at a contemporary definition of our profession offered by Gray and Herr (1998) shows how much the mission of vocational education has changed during the past quarter century.

> Workforce education is that form of pedagogy that is provided at the prebaccalaureate level by educational institutions, by private business and industry, or by government-sponsored, community-based organizations where the objective is to increase individual opportunity in the labor market or to solve human performance problems in the workplace.(p.4)

Many previous definitions of vocational education focused on programs—their level, length, purpose, type, and so forth. Gray and Herr's more contemporary definition focuses more on the career development of the individual and enhancing global competitiveness of the workforce. They add that

> The definition suggests that workforce education has two missions. One is to promote individual opportunity by making students more competitive in the labor force, thus allowing them to pursue personal career goals. The other mission is to make a nation economically strong and firms internationally competitive by solving human performance problems of incumbent . . . workers. (p. 4)

Perhaps when more legislators and policy makers realize that every young person will enter the workforce and that college is only a two- to five-year temporary detour for those who will complete an associate or bachelor's degree, we will see vocational education experiences become an integral part of every young person's formal school experience before he or she graduates from high school.

Will this come to pass? Know one knows, but some observers see it as a distinct possibility. Wirth (1997) observes:

> A possibility that jumps out of all of this is that by 2000 we may be moving toward the idea of making some form of technical education a part of general education for all American students. I am not sure of just what issues that possibility would pose for vocational/technical educators. (p. 49)

In school systems of the future we may see occupationally related school-based and work-based learning experiences at the K-12 level included as an important part of every learner's school experience. Of course, if every student was required to engage in formal learning experiences aimed at career preparation, the primary goal of such experiences would not necessarily be preparation for immediate employment, but would be broader in scope. Goals for this newer, broader form of vocational education might include the following.

Developing technological competence. Students from kindergarten through postsecondary education may one day enroll in occupationally related learning experiences as often as they take mathematics or English. Policy makers of the future may see that workplace-focused learning can provide a valuable vehicle for acquiring literacy and competence in a host of technology applications, devices, systems, and skills found in the workplace. Technology in the future may become so expensive, so complex, and so fast changing that the only way to expose younger learners to it is through learning experiences coordinated with the workplace. Gaining technological competence may become just as basic as reading, writing, and mathematics. Vocational education's role in helping learners achieve technological competence may thrust the profession into the forefront of educational reform in the future.

Work ethic development. Another rationale future educators might use to justify including broad vocationally related experiences for all learners will involve facilitating the development of positive work attitudes and values. Perhaps by early in the 2000s, employers will have succeeded in convincing education policy makers that these concerns are as important as academic skills and knowledge—perhaps even more so. We will have also concluded that one of the most central life roles of adults is that of *worker*. Hopefully, we will understand that being successful in the role of "productive worker" has an enormous impact on success in all the other life roles, such as parent, spouse, home owner, citizen, and leisure-time consumer. Vocational education's role in fostering a strong work ethic and appreciation for all forms of productive human endeavor—yes, including blue collar work—may become one of the central goals of such experiences for students. Such experiences may begin in the early elementary grades and continue through higher education.

Career development. Another likely goal of these broader occupationally related learning experiences will be to facilitate the career development of all learners. Policy makers of the future may finally realize that making life-impacting career decisions is too important a process to leave to chance alone. Schools of the future will expose students from young ages through graduation to a wide array of careers and occupations. Gone will be the days of the occasional career day and guest presentation dominated by speakers who represent only the professions. Tomorrow's students will be continually exposed to jobs and careers at all levels including the crafts, trades, and high tech employment. This exposure will come through frequent visits to work sites, regular visits to schools by incumbent workers on loan from employers, and virtual experiences on the job through technology. Students of tomorrow will be able to spend a day at a wide variety of work sites and observe the work flow, experience the stress, and see how academic skills are actually being used in a host of occupations simply by donning a headset.

BLURRING OF LINES BETWEEN ACADEMIC AND VOCATIONAL EDUCATION

A visitor to the future will no doubt observe that the clear distinctions between vocational education and academic education will continue to blur. School restructuring efforts such as career academies and school-based enterprises will prove successful and will contribute significantly to the merging of these two historically separate disciplines. Gone will be the days of separate academic and vocational departments or buildings on campuses. Even at the technical institute and community college levels, we will see more instructional, programmatic, and administrative integration between the two fields.

We may even see a demand for middle and secondary teachers who not only are certified in one or more academic disciplines but also have broad occupational work experience. Vocational teachers may also be recruited who not only have preparation and work experience in one or more vocational fields but also have expertise in the academic disciplines. The future should bring student learning materials that dramatically integrate academic and work-related concepts and skills. Textbooks, video presentations, and similar curricular materials will blend the lines between abstract, theoretical academic content and its application and use in the contemporary workplace.

POSTSECONDARY TECHNICAL EDUCATION—A HIGH-PRESTIGE OPTION FOR MORE YOUTH

Perhaps one of the most significant changes we will see during the next several decades is the gradual reversal of the "four-year university degree for all" mentality that now pervades our society. This shift should thrust postsecondary technical education into the limelight that it has struggled to find while always being overshadowed by a four-year university education. The future will surely see this trend reversed.

Gray and Herr (1995) describe several parallel trends that have taken place during the past decade or so that most likely cannot continue much longer. Several are contradictory and troubling. Among them are:

• An ever-increasing number of high school youth say they want to go on to a four-year university after high school. The percentage of high school graduates who indicated plans to enter a four-year university increased from 63 percent in the mid 1970s to 84 percent in the mid 1990s. The overwhelming reasons college freshmen report for entering a university is to "get a better job" and "make more money". Among the high school graduates who go on to two-year colleges, the overwhelming percentage enroll in AA university parallel programs rather than in technical programs. Young people continue to believe that a four-year degree is the ticket to a good, high-paying job.

• Most high school graduates aspire to work within the professional ranks—57 percent of males and 74 percent of females—while professional-level jobs remain only about one-fifth of the jobs that exist in the U.S.

• During the past 15 years, the percentage of parents who recommend that their kids go to college increased fastest among those whose kids had the worst academic track record. Sixty percent of the students in the lowest quartile of high school achievement reported that their parents wanted them to go on to a four-year university. Well over half of the high school students in the lowest quartile in performance reported that their teachers recommended that they go to college.

• The cost of going on to higher education—particularly four-year institutions—continues to rise dramatically. During a recent twelve-year period, the average total costs for higher education rose 32 percent while median family income in families with children of college age dropped 2 percent.

• Between 1990 and 1995, the number of student loans doubled. Only about half of those who begin a bachelor's degree program ever finish, and many of those who do not finish default on their student loans.

• Both the demand and salaries for technical workers with one or two years of postsecondary training have increased, while the percentage of high school students interested in or even familiar with such options has declined.

I hope that in the not-too-distant future the nation will awaken from its "four-year university education for all stupor" and realize that trying to push almost everyone into a four-year university education is counterproductive for students, for their parents, for the taxpayers, and for the nation as a whole. I also hope that policy makers, parents, guidance counselors, teachers, and students themselves will come to accept several unmistakable facts:

• A one-year certificate or two-year associate degree from a technical center or community college can lead to an excellent career with a competitive salary, full benefits (including tuition reimbursement for going on to a university later), prestige, and fulfillment. In many states, the average starting salary of graduates from community college associate of science degree programs significantly exceeds the average starting salary of those with bachelor's degrees. Currently, the average salary of workers in the skilled trades in the U.S. exceeds the average salary of those with baccalaureate degrees (excluding those who work in the classical professions of law, medicine, and so forth). This trend is likely to continue or increase.

• Most students who begin a four-year baccalaureate degree program at a university never finish. In addition, many students who drop out default on their students loans.

• A large percentage of graduates from four-year universities have a significant problem finding employment commensurate with their education. Large numbers of college graduates are either unemployed for lengthy periods or are grossly underemployed in jobs for which a college education is not required.

Finally, this nation will awaken to the realization that a university degree is not a guaranteed ticket to the good life. Increasing numbers of high school students, their parents, their teachers, and their guidance counselors will come to realize that we are vastly underutilizing a marvelous system that we already have in place that can help high school graduates prepare for high-wage employment in only a year or two: our national network of technical centers and community colleges.

I hope that in the future, we will believe that transitioning from high school to a technical center or community college is just as acceptable and desirable—and perhaps even more financially rewarding—than going from high school to a four-year university, particularly for students with limited academic background or limited financial resources. This will be seen as especially true for the large number of high school graduates who simply do not know "what they want to be when they grow up." The $50,000 career exploration experience at a major university will be viewed in the future as wasteful in terms of both financial and human capital.

Enrollment in technical institutes and community colleges will most likely grow in the future, particularly in the high-tech/high-wage fields. In comprehensive community colleges, the technical education mission will no longer take a back seat to the university parallel program. Most community colleges will offer an even wider array of technical and career programs on their main campuses, at branches and remote sites, and through distance-learning channels than they do today. Rarely will one hear a high school student say when asked where he or she is going after graduation, "Oh, I'm only going to the community college".

CHANGING PROGRAM STRUCTURE

Although it has served us well during much of the twentieth century, the current organizational structure of vocational education along traditional occupational lines such as business, agriculture, marketing, family and consumer science, industrial, and similar lines will likely shift dramatically with changes in the workplace. We can only imagine what the economy and the workplace of 2010 or 2020 will look like, but we can count on it looking very little like it does today.

It would be hard to imagine a successful worker 30 years into the future not being highly skilled in many aspects of technology and having a broad understanding of how businesses work. With technology that we can only imagine, it is likely that tomorrow's workers will be involved in more and more aspects of the various functions of a business's enterprise. For example, the future salesperson will get heavily involved in marketing and in product design and manufacturing; the future health care worker may perform many of the office-related functions done today by receptionists, data entry clerks, and secretaries by using the latest technology. The future agriculture worker will need even more proficiency in technology, marketing, office systems, and environmental and health concerns.

Some observers believe the very nature of "jobs" themselves will change dramatically. Bridges (1994) writes:

> The modern world is on the verge of another huge leap in creativity and productivity, but the job is not going to be part of tomorrow's economic reality. There still is and will always be enormous amounts of work to do, but it is not going to be contained in the familiar envelopes we call jobs. In fact, many organiza-

> tions are today well along the path toward being "de-jobbed". (p. 64)

Bridges explains that the conditions that created the concept of separate and distinct jobs in the first place—the emergence of the factory with long standardized runs of identical products—is rapidly fading away. The world of production is moving rapidly toward shorter production runs, customized products, work teams, and technology taking over the repetitive tasks. He adds that "[t]oday's organization is rapidly being transformed from a structure built out of jobs into a field of work needing to be done" (p 64).

In other words, the clear distinctions between the duties and competencies of workers in the various traditional vocational fields (agriculture, health, public service, marketing, and so forth) will increasingly blur in the future. We will probably see some combining, renaming, and emerging of new fields of specialization within the broader field of vocational education. We may even see these distinct divisions disappear entirely! Vocational programs of the future may focus more on helping learners acquire broad, transferable workplace competencies, learn a great deal about how business and industry works, and gain skills in the use of a wide array of work-related technology rather than master the specific competencies of any single occupation. Job preparatory programs at the secondary level may continue their decline and may disappear altogether. The role of "vocational" experiences at the high school level may be to prepare graduates to know how to learn well and how to quickly acquire the technical aspects of any occupation.

CONTINUING EVOLUTION OF INSTRUCTIONAL DELIVERY

How occupationally related educational experiences are organized, packaged, and delivered to "clients" will change over the next several decades—largely driven by advances in technology. The current system of textbook-driven, instructor-dominated, classroom-based, fixed-time vocational-technical education programs will undergo dramatic changes. A visitor from the 1990s to a vocational education classroom in the 2010s would see many changes in the way instruction is organized and delivered.

Textbooks will be replaced or augmented by devices that might be described as "books on a chip" with readers that students can wear on their wrists or hold in their hand. The portability of such learning resources will make it easy for people to learn at home, on the job, or in places other than traditional school facilities. Instruction in complex physical skills and technical procedures, now done via videotape and videodisk, may be delivered by portable units worn on a belt and viewed in an eyepiece or headset. Students will practice difficult, dangerous, or expensive operations the first several times using these "virtual performance" devices before ever giving their first real injection, making their first sale, or lighting their first welding torch.

PART OF A COMPREHENSIVE WORKFORCE DEVELOPMENT SYSTEM

A time traveler to the future would see that formal, pre-employment occupationally related education and training delivered to high school and post-high-school clients in this country would be part of a comprehensive, aggressive, national workforce development system. Those in education and those in labor will have finally proved instrumental in forging an overall system to respond to the short- and long-term employment-related education and training needs of youth and adults and to the workforce needs of employers. The needs of both sectors will be fully integrated into a national system. In the future, it will be said that the U.S. is no longer the only major world economy without a comprehensive workforce development system.

The federal government, state governments, organized labor, and the business community will, I hope, have found ways to work closely together to regularly update employment projections (particularly for rapidly emerging occupations), feed this information into a national and state system of vocational education, and then respond rapidly by shifting educational capacity to high-need areas. Such information will be systematically and accurately shared throughout the educational system so that students in the elementary and middle grades (and their parents, counselors and teachers) will continue to receive the most current and accurate career-related information to help them make more informed career decisions.

CHANGES IN TEACHER EDUCATION

I hope that in the future we will have learned important lessons from the crisis of the 1990s regarding the preparation of instructors for vocational education programs. I hope that in the early decades of the twenty-first century, teacher education capacity will be restored in many teacher education institutions around the country. This, most likely, would be accomplished through specially targeted funding so that these, usually small, specialized—but vital—vocational teacher education programs will not experience the same fate of many of those in the latter half of the twentieth century. Many earlier programs did not survive the intense competition for shrinking resources with larger more recognizable teacher education programs such as special education, elementary education, and secondary education.

Another reason that future vocational teacher education programs will be able to reemerge and to thrive is that they will be able to sell themselves as viable units, not just within schools or colleges of education, but as components of a larger economic development infrastructure. Successful programs will have convinced university presidents, provosts, and education deans that such programs don't just prepare vocational teachers, leaders, and support personnel, but they also prepare professionals who, in turn, prepare students to enter the workforce. All will see that an adequately prepared workforce is critical to economic development and a healthy economy. Successful vocational teacher education programs will very likely have been able to secure stable, protected funding by selling themselves as important economic development components.

References

Bridges, W. (1994, September 19). The end of the job. *Fortune,* 62-73.

Gray, K. G., & Herr, E. L. (1995). *Other ways to win—Creating alternatives for high school graduates.* Thousand Oaks, CA: Corwin Press.

Gray, K. G., & Herr, E. L. (1998). *Workforce education—The basics.* Boston: Allyn & Bacon.

Ries, Eric. (1997, December-November). To "V" or not to "V"? *Techniques, 72* (8), 32-37.

Wirth, A. G. (1997). An emerging perspective for policies for American work and education. In A. J. Pautler, Jr., & D. M. Buffamanti (Eds.), *Winning ways* (pp. 44-54). Ann Arbor, MI: Tech Directions Books.

***William Blank** is a professor in the Adult & Vocational Education and Human Resource Development Department, University of South Florida, Tampa. He has taught at the secondary and postsecondary levels and served in industry as a technician, drafter, and engineer. Blank is heavily involved in school reform—particularly high school reform. He works with schools around the country in exploring ways to reinvent the school curriculum and structure to better connect what happens in schools with what happens in the "real world." He has delivered presentations on various aspects of academic and vocational education at national conferences and has provided consulting assistance to educational institutions and companies in South Africa, New Zealand, Zimbabwe, Honduras, Jamaica, Scotland, and Canada. His publications include* Handbook for Developing Competency Based Training Programs *(Prentice-Hall) and* Promising Practices for Connecting School To The Real World-Co-ed. *(USDOE).*

THE TRANSITION FROM SCHOOL TO CAREERS

By Albert J. Pautler, Jr.

In recent years, much attention has been directed to the role of schooling in preparing youth for meaningful careers beyond high school. In many ways, the current concern for school-to-employment transition makes me recall the career education movement of the early 1970s, which was ably directed by Sidney Marland and Kenneth Hoyt.

Education journals such as the *Phi Delta Kappan* and *Educational Leadership* have published many articles on school-to-work transition theory. Many other publications, including *Fortune, Newsweek,* and *Time*, have also published articles related to employment, the global economy, the quality of the American workforce, Japanese education, German apprenticeships, and so forth. Many have discussed their concern for the school-to-work transition of our youth.

In addition, many reports have been prepared and released for public review and consideration. The report of the Grant Foundation (1988) *The Forgotten Half: Non-College Youth in America* focused the attention of interested people on the issues associated with school transition of high school graduates. This was followed by the 1990 report *America's Choice: High Skills and Low Wages* and the SCANS reports *What Work Requires of Schools* and *Learning a Living: A Blueprint for High Performance.*

This chapter includes a section on self-examination of my own transition experiences and that of one of my former students. It then continues with the "flow and pool" concept and school transition experiences. I include the importance of empirical data on former high school graduates as a starting point in data development. Several recent studies of former graduates are mentioned.

TRANSITION EXPERIENCES

Reflect for a few moments on your high school transition experiences. The use of the word "transition" refers to the passage from high school to the individual's next career development phase. Was your experience easy, difficult, or very difficult? Did you transition from school to work, school to school, school to the military, or school to unemployment? From whom did you seek help in making your transition? My personal experiences follow.

I attended Catholic elementary and high schools. My senior class numbered about 30. If it were not for Sister Mary of Good Counsel, my senior-year English teacher, I don't know where I would be today. We did not have guidance or school counselors at our high school in the 1950s. Guidance and direction came from parents and teachers. During fall term, Sister assigned us a major term paper on what we planned to do after high school graduation. It was a big effort for all of us in the class. For some reason, I choose technical teaching as a career goal. I graduated from high school, entered college, graduated from college, obtained a teaching position (industrial arts), taught electronics for 10 years, completed advanced degrees, moved to university teaching at Rutgers University in New Jersey, and then to the University at Buffalo. I had a smooth, though not easy transition, with supportive and loving parents and then wife and four children.

I also want to share with you the experiences of a young man in one of my classes at the University at Buffalo to compare transition experiences. His name is Bruno, and this is a true story.

By the time Bruno entered his junior year in the Buffalo (New York) Public Schools, he had been in the United States just three years. He had started to speak English but could not yet understand the phonology or the syntax of the language. He experienced school as boring and irrelevant to the rest of the world around him. Bruno has told me that he "felt lonely and like a fish out of water."

Bruno decided to drop out of high school. Two days after he left school, he joined the United States Marine Corps and flew to Parris Island (South Carolina) for basic training. (Note that today this would not be possible because most services require high school graduation.) Bruno finished high school in the Marines by attending night school at the Subic Bay Naval Base in the Philippines. After his tour with the Marines, he returned to Buffalo and found part-time work as a laborer. He then entered a Comprehensive Employment and Training Act (CETA) program that lead him to attend a state college in Buffalo. He completed a B.S. in Italian and a B.A. in English. After finishing his undergraduate work he was hired by the Buffalo Board of Education as an elementary foreign language teacher of Italian.

He now teaches in the same district that he left as a high school dropout. He considers himself very lucky and is now doing graduate work and working toward certification as a school administrator.

I consider Bruno's transition a difficult one. He made it to college and then into the workforce and teaching profession. He is a positive role model for all young people, but Bruno might not be allowed to enlist in the Marines today without a high school diploma. What will the Brunos of the future do?

These are but two transition experiences. I consider mine easy as compared with Bruno's. Yet, the end results of both of these example transition experiences strike me as positive. My concern is with the millions of other transition experiences that are not documented at this time. College teachers using this book may want to have their students discuss their own transition experiences or write short essays about them.

NATIONAL LONGITUDINAL STUDIES

Those interested in reviewing national longitudinal studies that deal with school-to-employment transition should see Robert Nichols's (1993) "The National Longitudinal Studies: A Window on the School-to-Employment Transition." Nichols reviewed the four major longitudinal studies spanning the four decades from the 1960s through the 1990s.

These four studies started with Project Talent under the direction of John Flanagan in 1960 (Flanagan, Dailey, Shaycoft, Orr, & Goldberg, 1962). This was followed by the National Longitudinal Study of the High School Class of 1972, which included a sample of 19,000 seniors from some 1,070 schools (Taylor, Stafford, & Place, 1981). The third major study was the High School and Beyond study sponsored by the Center for Educational Statistics (1987) and based on the 1980 sophomore cohort. The fourth major study was the National Education Longitudinal Study of 1988.

THE FLOW AND POOL CONCEPT

You may learn about the *flow and pool concept* through the writings of Grant Venn (1964, 1970) in his *Man, Education, and Work* and *Man, Education, and Manpower* books. This concept has remained very important during the years since Venn's works were published, and it is significant to the school-to-careers effort.

The concept applies to youth graduating from high school. Some youth will graduate and flow into various forms of postsecondary education. Others will flow into various types of employment, including military careers. Still others will flow into the "pool of the unemployed or underemployed."

Venn's works clearly indicated that the flow of people into the pool of the unemployed must be stopped to change the unemployment situation of youth in America. But, as a matter of fact and history, this will not occur. It seems to be a right of passage for some high school graduates to flounder for several years, perhaps to ages 24-27, before they are fully absorbed into the labor market.

We need to examine the school-to-work transition experiences of high school graduates in terms of the flow and pool concept. High school graduates usually exit schooling using one of three routes: school to more schooling, school to employment, or school to unemployment. Venn's flow and pool concept seems to suggest that educators, in fact all of society, must do more to stem the flow of high school graduates into the pool of the unemployed. This is based on the assumption that jobs do exist in the labor market for all high school graduates who seek and desire them. Graduates' skills bases acquired through schooling must be skills needed in today's global workforce. The flow and pool concept that Venn wrote about many years ago is as relevant today as it was in the 1970s.

SCHOOL TRANSITION EXPERIENCES

The control of public school education in the United States is under the control of the states. The policies for elementary and secondary education are made at the state level and implemented in local school districts.

In the United States, we have a very diverse educational delivery system controlled by local school boards. These boards are in urban, suburban, and rural areas. Those familiar with the work of Jonathan Kozol's (1991) *Savage Inequalities: Children in America's Schools* know that funding for education varies from district to district. The educational programs available to students and the services provided therefore vary a great deal. Educational opportunity is not equal in the United States.

Each of the 17,000-plus school districts in the United States really needs to know about the school transition experiences of their graduates. Most districts are very proud of those graduates accepted into college and report data related to them to the community. Seldom reported to the community is data about those not going on to college. The basic purpose of American public school education is to prepare graduates for more education rather than employment after graduation. The one exception may be students who major in vocational education programs.

In the spirit of the career education, school-to-work, and school-to -careers movements, the basic purpose of public education should be to prepare all students for further education and employment. At the present time it appears that most attention goes to those who plan to attend college.

National statistical data indicates that 25 percent of those under age 29 have completed and earned bachelor's degrees. Some 60 to 70 percent of high school graduates may in fact enter college, but nationwide only about 25 percent will graduate from college. This is national data. School districts must have data regarding graduates' transitions. This is the only way to make curriculum and program decisions that will be of value to graduates in making their transition. Does your district have such an empirical database to establish benchmarking data?

LOCAL BOARDS OF EDUCATION

Local boards of education have a responsibility to their communities to be aware of what happens to graduates within their school districts. This does not just mean short-term follow-up data collected on graduation, but both short- and long-term data. Board members should insist on knowing about all high school graduates and their transition experiences, including those going on to higher education, those entering employment, those entering the military, and those flowing into the pool of the unemployed. Data from graduates out of school for four years would also be of interest to school board members in making future policies for their districts.

We read a great deal about total quality management (TQM) and total quality control (TQC) in business and in schools. TQM is concerned with quality control—and what better way to demonstrate that in school than to know what really happens to high school graduates in each school district.

Each school district should have available transition data for every graduating class. Ideally, this database should go out at least four years from the time of graduation. The database would report on the experiences of all graduates, not just those going on to postsecondary education. Such a database should prove helpful in program and curriculum planning within the district.

Ideally, school districts moving in the direction of TQM should concern themselves with developing "benchmark" data for their district and not for comparing results with other districts.

THE CHEEKTOWAGA PROJECT

I approached four school districts in the town of Cheektowaga, New York, and encouraged educators there to involve themselves in a four- or five-year follow-up study of high school graduates. This study was called the Cheektowaga Transition Study. A team from the four districts developed a follow-up instrument for use in contacting former graduates regarding experiences after high school.

In addition, I have worked with several doctoral students who completed research projects on various high school follow-up efforts. One such study was designed to follow up on graduates who planned to attend four-year colleges. Another was concerned with those who went on to community colleges. The third was concerned with those attending an area occupational center and their experiences after high school completion. You may want to find these completed dissertations in dissertation abstracts: (1) Costello, Mary Ann. (1995). "High School Preparation Quality: Students' Perceptions and Experiences in the Transition Process". University at Buffalo; (2) Haberl, May. (1996). "The Graduates of 1989: A Study of Intended and Actual Career Paths and Students' Perceptions of Their High School Years". University at Buffalo; and (3) Ptak, John. (1996). "School to Employment: A Study of Transition Experiences of Recent High School Occupational Education Graduates". University at Buffalo.

School district administrators contacted for the Cheektowaga Transition Study were most cooperative in allowing such studies to take place. Personal research efforts continue and some 18 studies have been conducted in a variety of school districts.

THE STUDENT: THE CUSTOMER

The educational system needs to reaffirm its commitment to the student. (The student is the client, the customer, the reason for the educational system.) Educators must somehow try to encourage students to be more responsible for their own educational program and their future careers. This encouragement must begin in elementary school and really hit its peak during high school.

Educators take credit for the successes of students who do well. Likewise, they must take some responsibility for the failures of other students. This does not imply total credit or total blame for successes or failures. Schooling, as we know, is an extension of the family, home, church, and community. As we hear so often, it takes a whole community to raise the child.

The issue is how educators—especially those working in high schools—can encourage *students* to take more responsibility for their educational program? We must encourage students to actively plan for their transition experiences upon high school graduation. Perhaps we need to revisit some of the literature and projects that were developed during the years of career education practice in the 1970s.

Somehow educators, parents, and other interested parties have to find ways to encourage students to develop a "take charge" attitude when it comes to planning for the transition experience. This take charge attitude must apply to all students: those going on to work after graduation, those entering the military, and those going on to further education. The question remains how this "take charge attitude and desire" can be developed in more students.

WHAT MIGHT WE DO NEXT YEAR?

Waiting 1, 2, 4, or 12 years to make changes in school transition results is much too long. We do not have the time to wait for a long-term solution to a short-term problem. Even a short-term activity may not result in a solution to a short-term problem, but it may help.

Efforts like the Cheektowaga Transition Study take several years to complete and then apply to curriculum modification. Within two years after high school graduation, school districts may have a database on those graduates who have completed a two-year college program. In this same two years, data must be obtained and analyzed that deals with the experiences of those students who directly entered the workforce.

THE HAND-OVER PROCESS

Consider the following: Make sure that each high school graduate is *handed over to some next agency* on finishing high school. Develop some type of *hand-over card* for each graduate to be presented at the same time as the high school graduation diploma. This might be mentioned when students receive their diplomas. For example:

- Graduates accepted by a college or some other form of postsecondary education institution would be handed over to that agency.
- Graduates accepted and entering the military are handed over to that service.
- Graduates seeking and finding full-time employment are handed over to a specific employer.

The process described above may seem simple, but, let me assure you, it is not. It is also not being practiced in school districts as far as the literature reports.

All other graduates (those planning to attend college but not accepted; those seeking employment but not employed; those planning to enter the military but not accepted; etc.) need to be handed over to another agency when they complete high school. By and large, most school districts do not offer counseling services to former graduates on any systematic basis. The basic concern is who will be the hand-over agency? This agency may vary in school districts.

I suggested to an audience in Nashville, Tennessee, that those seeking employment but not employed upon graduation should be turned over to the local office of the state employment service. It may mean sending students by school bus to the local employment office before graduation to let them register for possible employment. This may not be a perfect solution, but at least graduates would know where to go for additional help. A Florida resident in the audience indicated that his community college would be willing to serve as the local hand-over agency for high school graduates. This seems to make sense. You may consider working with your local community college in this way. We have had some success with this approach in Buffalo's school-to-work transition project.

The goal is that each and every high school graduate should be offered the opportunity to be handed over to some next agency or be encouraged to remain in contact with the school district. *Every graduate should know where to turn for counseling services and job placement services the day after high school graduation.* Data is not available to prove that this idea is workable. But it seems worth a try. Please consider it for your district.

How might this work? Who would do it? The idea would have to have the support of the school board and school administrators to implement the process. Most seem to view public school education as preparation for more formal education—specifically, college. What about the 70 percent of the U.S. population that will not graduate from college?

The task (hand over) could best be handled by school counselors assisted by support staff. The effort would take time and cost money—how much would depend on the level of involvement. The point is that each graduate should be handed over to some next agency.

Think of the hand-over card more as a process than an actual paper card. It is the concept and the manner of its application that matters. What now happens to high school graduates who are not accepted into college or the military, or who succeed in finding a full-time job? These young people need our help in making a transition to the next phase of their lives. It is graduates in this group that the Grant Foundation (1988) labeled the *forgotten half* and that may have the most difficult time making a successful transition to their next career goal.

SUMMARY AND CONCLUSIONS

I have tried in this chapter to share some perspectives on learning and earning and the transition experiences of high school graduates. The chapter has explored the transition experiences of two people. I encourage readers to do the same with themselves and others. The Venn concept of the "flow and the pool" was described in some detail. The final section of the chapter discussed the transition experiences and suggested consideration of a hand-over process and some type of hand-over card.

See Appendix A for material from an ERIC document from the Clearinghouse on Adult, Career, and Vocational Education. It provides additional references on issues related to the school-to-work transition.

I recommend that as you move ahead with your plans to develop an STC or STW program you consider three major projects:

- Develop an empirical database on the follow-up experiences of former high school graduates from your school district. Know what happened to former graduates before making changes in the curriculum. You may very well have a system that is working already. Why mess with a good educational system?
- Consider putting in place a hand-over system for your next graduating class. Try a variety of approaches to make sure that *each and every graduate of* your next graduating class is handed over to some next agency.
- Review the empirical database and the hand-over results before making any major curriculum changes in your school district.

References

Center for Educational Statistics. (1987). *High school and beyond 1980 sophomore cohort third follow-up (1986): Data file user's manual.* Washington, DC: U. S. Department of Education.

Flanagan, J. C., Dailey, J. T., Shaycoft, M .F., Orr, D. B., & Goldberg, J. (1962). *Design for a study of American youth.* Boston: Houghton Mifflin.

Grant Foundation. (1988). *The forgotten half: Non-college youth in America.* Washington, DC: Author.

Kozol, J. (1991). *Savage inequalities.* New York: Crown.

National Center for Education and the Economy. (1990). *America's choice: High skills or low wages.* Rochester, NY: Author.

Nichols, R.C. (1993). The national longitudinal studies: A window on the school-to-employment transition. In A. Pautler (Ed.), *High school to employment transition: Contemporary issues.* Ann Arbor, MI: Prakken Publications.

Secretary's Commission on Achieving Necessary Skills. (1991). *What work requires of schools: A SCANS report for America 2000.* Washington: U. S. Department of Labor.

Secretary's Commission on Achieving Necessary Skills. (1992). *Learning a living: A blueprint for high performance.* Washington, DC: U.S. Department of Labor.

Taylor, M. E., Stafford, C. E., & Place, C. (1981). *National longitudinal study of the high school class of 1972 study report update: Review and annotation.* Washington, DC: U. S. Department of Education, National Center for Education Statistics.

Venn, G. (1964). *Man, education, and work.* Washington, DC: American Council on Education.

Venn, G. (1970). *Man, education, and manpower.* Washington, DC: American Association of School Administrators.

***Albert J. Pautler, Jr.**, is a professor of education, Graduate School of Education, University of Buffalo, New York. Earlier, he was a faculty member at Rutgers University, Brunswick, New Jersey, and a high school teacher of electronics in New York. He is the author or editor of several books, including* Vocational Education in the 1990s: Major Issues *(1990),* High School to Employment Transition: Contemporary Issues *(1994), and* Winning Ways: Best Practices in Work-Based Learning *(1997). He has written more than 50 articles on topics dealing with workforce education, curriculum planning, and school-to-work transition. He has also served as a consultant to many organizations including the U.S. Department of Labor, General Motors, DuPont, and the New York State Education Department.*

APPENDIX A—ERIC CLEARINGHOUSE ON ADULT, CAREER, AND VOCATIONAL EDUCATION: SCHOOL-TO-WORK TRANSITION (1995)

The idea for helping youth move from school to the workplace is not new; what is new is the conceptualization of school to work as a cornerstone of schooling. Currently, school to work is envisioned as a "systematic, comprehensive, community-wide effort to help all young people (1) prepare for high-skill and high-wage careers, (2) receive top quality academic instruction, and (3) gain the foundation skills to pursue postsecondary employment and lifelong learning" (Halperin, 1994, p. 4). A number of trends have converged to stimulate the interest in school-to-work transition. These trends, which essentially have to do with economic competitiveness and the changing nature of the workplace, are familiar and can be summed up as follows: the United States is falling behind because it is failing to provide adequate preparation for most new entrants to the workplace, which now demands adaptable and flexible workers with high levels of both academic and technical skills (Brustein & Mahler, 1994; National Governors Association).

The passage of the School-to-Work Opportunities Act of 1994 also spurred interest in the school-to-work transition movement. As a part of its efforts to streamline government, however, the 104th Congress is proposing a major consolidation of employment and training legislation—including school to work—in some form of block grant(s) (D. Stoner, personal communication, January 12, 1995). If these proposed changes are effected, the federal role in school-to-work transition will be sharply reduced. In many states, school-to-work transition programs have gained great momentum and will likely continue without strong federal leadership.

A study of 16 programs (Pauly, Kopp, & Haimson, 1994) drew the following conclusions about contemporary transition efforts:

• School-to-work programs use a variety of program designs (i.e., career academies, occupational-academic cluster programs, restructured vocational education, tech prep, and youth apprenticeship), customized to suit local circumstances.

- Programs are able to serve a broad cross-section of students and to provide access to college and other postsecondary options.
- Extra resources are needed to initiate and implement school-to-work programs.
- Providing large numbers of high school students with intensive work-based learning will require a major effort both to recruit additional employers and expand the commitment of employers currently participating.
- School-to-work programs that start early—by 9 or 10—can reach students before they become disengaged or drop out of school.

A number of issues affiliated with school to work will need to be addressed as states develop their systems. Some critics feel that school to work is just another example of tracking, but one that will screen out poor and disadvantaged youth (Mendel, 1994). Another aspect of this issue is the fear that youth who enter school-to-work programs will be closed out of higher education (Pauly, Kopp, & Haimson, 1994). The following questions reflect other issues surrounding school to work: Does it force youth to make career choices too early? Does it place too much emphasis on preparing youth for occupations and not enough on becoming well-informed and contributing citizens? Do business and industry have the resources to provide the required work-based learning experiences? (Mendel, 1994; NGA, 1994). The following resources can be consulted for further information about school-to-work transition programs.

Print Resources

Brustein, M., & Mahler, M. (1994). *AVA guide to the School-to-Work Opportunities Act.* Alexandria, VA: American Vocational Association.—Following a discussion of the need for the School-to-Work Opportunities Act, this publication presents a detailed discussion and analysis to assist states, educators, employers, and parents in understanding the Act and its requirements.

Council of Chief State School Officers & American Youth Policy Forum. (1994). *Building a system to connect school and employment.* Washington, DC: Authors. (ED 368 938)—This report reflects concerns about the issues related to building a coherent and effective system of youth development and career preparation for young people in the United States.

Halperin, S. (1994). *School to work: A larger vision.* Washington, DC: American Youth Policy Forum.—Halperin challenges educators to construct a total quality system in which each of the parts supports and advances the welfare of all the other parts.

Hamilton, S. F., & Hamilton, M. A. (1994).*Opening career paths for youth: What can be done? Who can do it?* Ithaca, NY: Cornell Youth and Work Program, Cornell University; Washington, DC: American Youth Policy Forum; Cambridge, MA: Jobs for the Future.—Describes an approach for developing a career opportunity system and includes recommendations for components of a system and institutional arrangements and responsibilities.

Jobs for the Future. (1994). *Learning that works: A school-to-work briefing book.* Cambridge, MA: Author.

Katzman, S. (Ed.). (1995). *The role of career education in school-to-work transition. Information Series No. 359.* Columbus, OH: ERIC Clearinghouse on Adult, Career, and Vocational Education, Center on Education and Training for Employment, Ohio State University.—Provides an overview of approaches to career education that complement school-to-work transition, including youth apprenticeship; career academies; career resource centers; career guidance; and elementary, middle school, and high school career education.

Kazis, R., with Barton, P. E. (1993). *Improving the transition from school to work in the United States.* Cambridge, MA: Jobs for the Future. (ED 353 454)—Clarifies and describes aspects of the school-to-work transition problems that need "fixing," discusses trends in program and policy innovation at the local, state, and national levels that might respond to the challenges identified, and proposes policy.

McKay, E. G. (1993). *The forgotten half: Two-thirds—An Hispanic perspective on apprenticeship European style.* Washington, DC: National Council of La Raza. (ED 361 431)—Reports on a Hispanic-based consultation on European-style apprenticeships undertaken to add a Hispanic perspective to the current policy debate about apprenticeships as a school-to-work movement in the United States.

National Governors Association. (1994). *Developing systems of school-to-work transition: A report on state progress. Issue brief.* Washington, DC: Author.—Points out issues, problems, and challenges and includes tables illustrating state school-to-work system elements and school-to-work programs by state.

Ohio Council on Vocational Education. (1995). *Gathering momentum! Transition from school to work.* Westerville, OH: Author.—Describes Ohio's experience in developing a school-to-work system and profiles 23 Ohio programs.

Pauly, E., Kopp, H., & Haimson, J. (1994). *Home-grown lessons: Innovative programs linking work and high school*. New York: Manpower Demonstration Research Corp.—Presents findings and lessons from 16 innovative school-to-work programs in United States' communities on critical concerns of policy makers, educators, and employers.

Pautler, A. J., Jr. (Ed.). *High school to employment transition: Contemporary issues.* Ann Arbor, MI: Prakken Publications.—This discussion of the transition to employment for non-college-bound youth is organized around four major themes: background, reviews of research, analysis of programs, and suggestions for improving the transition process.

Polite, V. C. (1993, April). *If only we knew then what we know now: The school-to-work and school-to-college transitions of African-American males in suburbia*. Paper presented at the Annual Meeting of the American Educational Research Association, Atlanta, GA. (ED 362 601).—Reports on a follow-up study of a cohort of 115 African-American males who attended a predominately African-American suburban school between 1986 and 1989.

Ray, C. A., & Mickelson, R. A. (1993, January). Restructuring students for restructured work: The economy, school reform, and non-college-bound youths. *Sociology of Education 66* (1), 1-20.—Argues that structural changes in the U.S. economy have had a negative impact on student motivation and have shaped the current sense of crisis in U.S. education.

Stern, D., Finkelstein, N., Stone, J. R., III, Latting, J., & Dornsife, C. (1994). *Research on school-to-work transition programs in the United States.* Berkeley, CA: National Center for Research in Vocational Education. (ED 369 923)—Reviews existing research on school-to-work programs classified in two main categories: school-to-work arrangements that allow students to work and attend school and school-for-work programs that provide instruction with the express purpose of preparing students for work.

U.S. Department of Education. *School-to-work: What does the research say about it?* Washington, DC: Office of Research, Office of Educational Research and Improvement, USDOE, 1994. (ED 371 206).—The series of commissioned papers that make up this volume address several questions related to school-to-work transition, including what do we know about non-college-bound youth, what relevant governance issues need to be examined, and where do we go to create a system.

Vocational Education Journal, 69 (3). (1994, March).—Eight articles of this issue focus on the theme of school-to-work transition.

Resource Organizations

American Youth Policy Forum, 1001 Connecticut Ave., NW, Suite 719, Washington, DC 20036-5541 (202.775.9731)

Cornell Youth and Work Program, College of Human Ecology, Cornell University, Ithaca, NY 14853-4401 (607.255.8394)

Jobs for the Future, One Bowdoin Square, 11th Floor, Boston, MA 02114 (617.742.5995)

National Governors Association, 444 N. Capitol St., Washington, DC 20001-1572 (202.638.2144)

S2WTP, an electronic discussion forum on school-to-work transition and tech prep. To subscribe, send a message to <majordomo@cccins.cccneb.edu> with the following command in the body of the message: subscribe s2wtp YOUR INTERNET ADDRESS HERE

(This appendix was developed by Susan Imel with funding from the Office of Educational Research and Improvement (OERI), U.S. Department of Education, under Contract No. RR93002001.)